PATRON SAINTS

PATRON SAINTS

FIVE REBELS

WHO OPENED AMERICA

TO A NEW ART

1928–1943

NICHOLAS FOX WEBER

YALE UNIVERSITY PRESS   NEW HAVEN AND LONDON

For Katharine

CONTENTS

PREFACE

Today we pick up our newspapers and read regularly about another Picasso show, the latest performance of a Balanchine ballet, an exhibition with sculpture by Lachaise or Calder, a new auction record for Brancusi or Balthus. We take it for granted that the New York City Ballet and the Museum of Modern Art are alive and thriving. In the last decade of the twentieth century, these names and institutions are an integral part of our culture.

But what is now generally accepted was, on first presentation, beyond the limits of permissible taste. Sixty years ago, the larger public—rich or poor, with cursory education or doctoral degrees— was horrified by the artistic manifestations of modern thinking. Household appliances, modes of transportation, or medical treatments could be contemporary; paintings and sculpture and the higher forms of entertainment should conjure earlier times. For Picasso and Balanchine and Calder to attain their current stature, and for the City Ballet and MoMA to take root, required the daring and tenacity of their small league of supporters.

A handful of seers paved the way for modernism in America. The activities of some of these individuals are already well known. The pioneers who helped shape our major museums of recent art— Alfred Barr, Hilla Von Rebay, Albert Barnes, and others—have been the subjects of monographs, and the focus of considerable attention. So have many of our most adventurous modern collectors, like John Quinn, Peggy Guggenheim, and Joseph Hirshhorn, as well as other arbiters of modern taste, like Philip Johnson. The main characters in this book—Lincoln Kirstein, Edward M. M. Warburg, Agnes Mongan, A. Everett Austin, Jr., James Thrall Soby, and some of their associates—fall into a different category. While the nature of their contribution is known to insiders and close followers of the art world, many of their interwoven activities of the late 1920s and the 1930s have not previously been considered in depth.

These five individuals were not unique in their involvement with new forms of art. Ever since the Armory Show of 1913, a small number of Americans had supported various expressions of current aesthetic experimentation, most of which had their roots in Europe.

But the new taste was not widespread. Kirstein, Warburg, Mongan, Austin, and Soby all took original and unpopular viewpoints that required courage to defend. While still very young, they were taken or sent to Europe by their parents—France, Italy, and England being, after all, the centers of world culture for most educated Americans of the time. And what they found and brought home was revolutionary.

By championing what few people had dared to consider, these adventurers awakened many of their friends, as well as a segment of the general public. While still college students, Lincoln Kirstein and Edward Warburg—in tandem—gave the public its first look at one startling art form after another: Buckminster Fuller's Dymaxion House, Alexander Calder's Circus, Bauhaus design, and the latest painting, sculpture, and photography. They established a vital precedent for New York's Museum of Modern Art, in which they eventually played an active role. They brought George Balanchine to America. At the same time that they worked feverishly to pay for tutus and studio space and then to bring in the audiences, they helped enable artists as different as Gaston Lachaise and Josef Albers to survive, and gave key support to people ranging from Philip Johnson to Igor Stravinsky. Agnes Mongan fostered an unprecedented appreciation of drawings. By viewing the spontaneous, unplanned sides of artists' work and giving rare vividness to the language of art history, she expanded the appreciation of art. She also changed the notion of what women might do in the male-dominated museum world and academic establishment. A. Everett Austin mounted museum exhibitions of a type America had never seen before. As director of the Wadsworth Atheneum in Hartford, Connecticut, he installed, in the early 1930s, shows of Surrealism and Picasso, where a short time before there had been nothing more adventurous than representational landscape painting. Austin was also the impresario for innovative musical and theatrical performances. James Thrall Soby helped enlarge the American audience for some of the most puzzling aspects of modern art. In the sort of New England suburban household where the expected recreation would have been a bridge game, he ran a Salvador Dali film that only months earlier had caused an uproar in Paris. Through his writing, collecting, and curating, he led people to accept the hitherto alien work of de Chirico, Balthus, and many other painters.

What these five people did was largely behind the scenes, yet it changed the cultural landscape of America. But altruism was by no means their only motive. For each of them, the art they supported helped to establish a much needed sense of self. And because of its free and courageous nature, that art also helped to liberate its champions from repression. It was their means to perceptions and pleasures that might otherwise have been unavailable.

I have not attempted the comprehensive biography that each of my major characters warrants. That would be a very different task. What I have tried to do, rather, has been to convey something of the spirit of these individuals and of the way that they often egged one another on. And I have attempted to illustrate a form of artistic support that, unlike modern government patronage, broke boundaries rather than imposed them.

To varying degrees, Kirstein, Warburg, Mongan, Austin, and Soby all came from a world of privilege. They could have followed timeworn paths. The men could have opted for traditional careers, while Agnes Mongan might have chosen to do no work at all. All might easily have maintained the tastes of their parents, as did most of their contemporaries. Instead, driven by passion, undaunted by constant adversity, and generally eager to amuse as much as to edify, they altered their world.

THE HARVARDITES

I

He was set down as belonging to that odious category of outsiders who hung loosely on the fringes of college life: odd persons going about alone, or in little knots, looking intellectual, or looking dissipated. They were likely to be Jews or radicals or to take drugs; to be musical, theatrical, or religious; sallow or bloated, or imperfectly washed; either too shabby or too well dressed. The tribe of these undesirables was always numerous at Harvard.

—George Santayana, *The Last Puritan*[1]

Boston in 1928 had little use for modern art. The latest developments in painting were deemed immoral and vulgar. People viewed them as anarchistic, an affront to sanity and God. Pictures, sculpture, and building styles should be a buffer against the present, not an exaltation of it. Most people longed for the comforts of tradition, the familiar look of tried-and-true styles. There had been such an uproar after the venerable Boston Art Club showed some Picasso drawings and other contemporary European art that all but one member of its Art Committee had been forced to resign in September. The club issued a public statement that it had "purged itself of modernism."[2] A new and more conservative art committee took the helm. Its chairman, Mr. H. Dudley Murphy, understood the tenor of the times far better than his predecessor had. "We have had an exploitation of modernist art at the club," he told a reporter from the *New York World*. "You know what I mean, that crazy stuff. . . . We believe that people are rather tired of this sort of thing." Murphy gave assurance that people could expect "a definite swing away from extreme modernism to the safer realms of conservatism and 'sanity in art.'"[3]

The first show under the aegis of Murphy's committee opened the new art season that October. The *Evening Transcript* reported that the members had the wisdom to redecorate the galleries with a "mouse-colored velvet" that, unlike the "glaring white barn–like walls" previously in place, made "a background suitable to receive the paintings."[4] Most of those paintings were pleasant if tame exemplars of second-generation American Impressionism. They depicted moonlit pools, bunches of dahlias, and ladies holding parasols. On Joy Street, on Beacon Hill, there was an institution with the promising name of the Twentieth Century Club, but only its name suggested anything streamlined or futuristic. Its exhibitions featured representational canvases of ramshackle New England homesteads, academic sculpture, and maps of Boston alongside sketches of city landmarks. In the commercial galleries one could count on more of the same, or English sporting scenes. Occasionally, a work from the School of Paris might go on view at the Museum of Fine Arts, but John Singer Sargent was considered the master to beat them all. The big shows that November were of Sargent's drawings and of work by the society portraitist Anders Zorn.

Things were not much more advanced on the other side of the Charles River. In Cambridge at Harvard's Fogg Art Museum, one might from time to time see a work on paper or a reproduction of an oil by Cézanne or Van Gogh, even by Picasso, but no such thing would enter the permanent collection. Edward Waldo Forbes, the director of the Fogg, had in 1911 made a decree that was still largely in effect: "The difficulty is, first, that all modern art is not good, and we wish to maintain a high standard. In having exhibitions of the work of living men we may subject ourselves to various embarrassments." [5]

There were, however, three Harvard undergraduates who actually relished such embarrassments. Late in 1928, Lincoln Kirstein, Edward M. M. Warburg, and John Walker III launched an organization "to exhibit to the public works of living contemporary art whose qualities are still frankly debatable." [6] The three college juniors officially founded their Harvard Society for Contemporary Art at a dinner meeting held on December 12 at Shady Hill, the impressive neo-Classical mansion that had belonged to Harvard professor Charles Eliot Norton. Since 1915, Shady Hill had been the residence of Paul Joseph Sachs, who that year had become Edward Forbes's assistant director at the Fogg, and was now his associate director. Sachs had ascended to a full professorship at Harvard in 1927, and the three young men were all under his guidance.

Both Sachs and Forbes liked the idea of the students supplementing the work being done by the Boston Museum of Fine Arts and the Fogg by mounting exhibitions of various aspects of modern art and design. The creation of the new organization helped take the

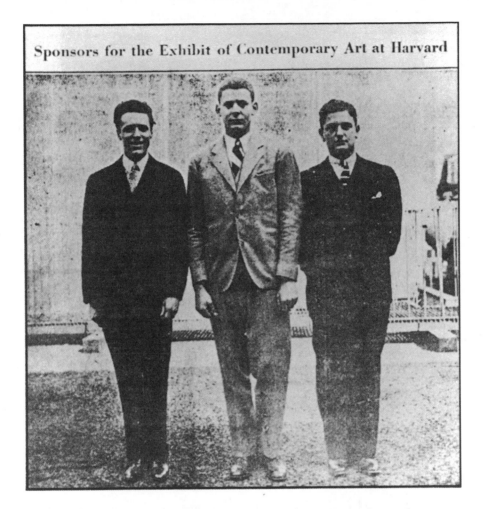

Sponsors for the Exhibit of Contemporary Art at Harvard

John Walker III, Lincoln Kirstein, and Edward M. M. Warburg, the founders of the Harvard Society for Contemporary Art.

pressure off the Fogg's directors to put their necks in the same noose as the management of the Boston Art Club. Sachs and Forbes agreed to serve on the board of the Harvard Society. They volunteered the services of the Fogg staff to help with the more difficult packing and shipping and to defray some of the insurance costs. The Harvard Society for Contemporary Art was the first organization in the country to devote itself to an ongoing program of changing exhibitions of recent art in all its diversity. The latest photography, Bau-

THE HARVARD SOCIETY FOR CONTEMPORARY ART ‧ INC ‧

AT the present moment there is no place either in Boston or Cambridge for the regular exhibition of the various manifestations of modern art and decoration. For practical reasons of policy, the Museums can not hold such exhibitions.

The Harvard Society for Contemporary Art plans to supplement the work being done by the Boston Museum of Fine Arts and by the Fogg Museum of Art.

A gallery will be provided in the Harvard Coöperative Society Building to exhibit to the public works of living contemporary art whose qualities are still frankly debatable. The program for the first year, beginning February 15th, will include Twelve Modern Americans, Contemporary British Art, The Moderns of Mexico, and a showing of the work of Modern Harvard Artists and Architects.

The decorative arts consistent with these national groups will also be seen at the same time in furniture, glass, ceramics and textiles. Along with the paintings exhibited there will be works by the same artists in less expensive mediums, such as drawings, etchings, or lithographs.

¶ The property of The Harvard Society for Contemporary Art is held by a Board of Trustees, which appoint an Executive Committee of Harvard or Radcliffe students, who assume responsibility for the management of the organization for the year. There is also a Consultative Committee of artists and critics who are interested in the Modern Movement in art, and to whom the Executive Committee looks for advice.

¶ The income of the Society is to be derived from the commissions received on sales, and from memberships. There are to be three classes of annual memberships: Sustaining Members who will give fifty dollars or more; Contributing Members who will give ten dollars or more; and Harvard and Radcliffe Members who will pay two dollars annually. Members will receive a discount (five percent) on any purchases, and invitations to a special showing of each exhibition.

¶ This venture, at present in the nature of an experiment, will not only fill an important gap in the cultural life of Harvard University and Radcliffe College, but it will provide the only place in greater Boston where the friends of modern art can see changing exhibitions of the various forms of contemporary artistic endeavour.

We are enclosing a subscription blank in the hope that our undertaking will meet with your approval and have your support.

To THE HARVARD SOCIETY FOR CONTEMPORARY ART ‧ INC ‧

Harvard Coöperative Building
Harvard Square ‧ Cambridge ▸ Massachusetts

I desire to become a { Sustaining / Contributing / Harvard / Radcliffe } member

Enclosed find my check for

_____
                        Signature

Address _____
_____

Statement of Purpose and Membership form of the Harvard Society for Contemporary Art, 1928.

haus design, Mexican realism, and German Expressionism could be seen in bits and pieces elsewhere, but nowhere else was there a conscious effort to present in succession such a range of contemporary expressions. Kirstein, Warburg, and Walker, three privileged college students, managed it all while doing their homework on their laps as they performed guard duty.

Shortly after their dinner meeting at Shady Hill, the trio set out to find space for their organization. They rented two rooms on the second floor of the Harvard Cooperative Building at 1400 Massachusetts Avenue. The main floor housed the Harvard Coop, the local emporium for almost anything students might want to buy. The Coop was directly on Harvard Square. Even in those days Harvard Square was a busy urban intersection with noisy bus and subway stops and taxi stands. Although only a five-minute walk across stately Harvard Yard from the Fogg, the location was a step away from the sanctity of the yard and of the quiet lawns at Shady Hill—and into the ordinary, current, urban world.

Kirstein, Warburg, and Walker wanted the setting to be as stark as possible, a statement of newness and now. There was to be no mousy velvet. The idea was to search in directions where others had not looked before, and to stop imitating the past. They painted the walls white and silvered the ceiling with squares of tea paper. For a table they found a massive block of monel—an alloy of nickel and copper—which they rested on four free-standing marble columns that they had picked up in a defunct ice-cream shop. The chairs were the latest streamlined specimens in tubular steel.

They announced plans to mount an exhibition of recent American art and design in a tradition more native than European. To contemplate such a thing in their industrial-looking space was a radical move. A year earlier, Lewis Mumford, in an article on "American Taste" for *Harper's,* had described the prevalent disdain for any notion of a new or indigenous national style:

> The modern American house can tritely be described as a house that is neither modern nor American. A gallery that today exhibited American taste would be a miscellany of antiquities. The pictures we put on our walls, our cretonnes and brocades and wall papers, our china, our silverware, our furniture, are all copies or close adaptations of things we have found

on their historic sites in Europe and America, or, at one remove, in the museums. Meanwhile the art and workmanship of
our own day remain unappreciated because they have not yet
aged sufficiently to be embraced by the museum.

Mumford asserted that no

> period has ever exhibited so much spurious taste as the present
> one; that is, so much taste derived from hearsay, from imita-
> tion, and from the desire to make it appear that mechanical in-
> dustry has no part in our lives and that we are all blessed with
> heirlooms testifying to a long and prosperous ancestry in the
> Old World. Our taste, to put it brutally, is the taste of par-
> venus.[7]

The Harvard Society for Contemporary Art would prove the excep-
tion.

The founders issued a brochure announcing their plan to show art
not yet tested by time, reiterating their seminal notion of exhibiting
living art of "frankly debatable" value. Their symbol, in the style of
Greek Black Figure vase painting, was a naked, agile, and muscular
man appearing euphoric atop a rearing stallion, with another man
adjusting the horse's bridle and bit. This image of high adventure
would appear on virtually every invitation and exhibition flyer for
the next couple of years. With no explanation or identification beyond the minuscule initials "R.K.," its authorship and symbolism
may have been known to the inner circle, but to the larger audience
were ambiguous. "R.K." stood for Rockwell Kent. Kent, one of
Lincoln Kirstein's favorite designers and book illustrators, had
helped boost the new organization by agreeing to do the logo for a
nominal fee. The precise meaning of his design was hazy, but its
general effect was to suggest action and drama tempered by classic
grace. The implications are clear: that the revival of ancient forms
and established styles is okay, even desirable, so long as the tone is
fresh and the spirit lively.

The brochure included a membership application form. It announced three categories: one for Harvard and Radcliffe students,
with annual dues of $2; "contributing" ("$10 or more"), and "sustaining" ("$50 or more"). Kirstein, Warburg, and Walker were listed

as members of the "Executive Committee." There was also an impressive roster of trustees. Besides Edward Waldo Forbes and Paul J. Sachs this included John Nicholas Brown, a wealthy collector of drawings and scion of an old Providence family; Philip Hofer, a bibliophile and collector; Arthur Pope, a distinguished professor of art history; Arthur Sachs, a financier and Paul's brother; and Felix M. Warburg—Edward's father, and the only trustee who had not been graduated from Harvard.[8] It was a coup for their pioneering undertaking to gain such prominent figures, personally not the least bit inclined toward contemporary art. But here the three students had teamed beautifully. Kirstein was good at formulating ideas, Warburg at communicating them to people who might not have otherwise supported them, Walker at knowing who was who.

The Harvard Society was Kirstein's invention, and he supplied most of the exhibition themes as well as the rationales behind them. "Impetuous . . . knowledgeable . . . overflowing with vitality . . ."[9] is how one of his friends described him. "Brilliant, seductive, violent . . . but isolated and lonely at the same time"[10] is the characterization of another. The tall, broad-shouldered Kirstein was imaginative and articulate, but frequently prickly. With the bearing of a soldier, he generally had a serious and puzzled look on his face. He used his social graces only when the mood suited. He was often cranky and made no effort to mask it. He needed Eddie Warburg and John Walker to deal with the world. The students were promulgating a new gospel, and it took charm to spread it. Eddie Warburg, like Kirstein, also felt great conviction and talked as directly as possible, but he tempered the straight-shooting with a light touch and humor. The dapper, animated Warburg—exotically handsome with his bold features—considered audience response. Kirstein might face his listeners with a misanthropic stare, while Warburg would always come up with a joke. Kirstein had daunting intelligence, but he might ascend a speaker's platform with the glowering look of a voracious, nasty eagle and then proceed to knock down his glass of water; Eddie Warburg had polish, and a deep, broad smile. His connections helped too. The world of philanthropy and patronage is full of tit for tat, and it was hard to turn down one of the banking Warburgs if he asked you to be a trustee or, later on, to lend artworks. Moreover, Eddie or his father could always cover any deficit the new society might incur. And John Walker could help in his special way. Particularly attuned to the Social Register set, looking every bit the well-bred American aristocrat, Walker had the sort of friendships that enabled him to build up the list of sustaining members. Kirstein and Warburg were not really his typical companions; he specialized more in "a number of rich, hard-drinking, bridge-playing friends"[11]—exactly the sort of people one needed to provide funds for a fledgling arts organization.[12] On his own, none of these three young men had what it would take to get a conservative community to consider and support radical art, but as a team they could pull it off.

Lincoln Kirstein had started early as an artistic adventurer. Born in 1906, he was eight when he created "Tea for Three," a dramatics club in which he, his brother George, and their neighbor William Koshland were the members. Even then, he was a systematic organizer. There would be two performances at the Kirsteins' house on Commonwealth Avenue, followed by one at the Koshlands' on nearby Beacon Street; then the pattern would be repeated. For costumes, the boys pulled things out of their parents' closets. Lincoln produced, wrote, and starred in all their plays. They were his obsession; when he and Koshland played baseball at school, and were invariably in the outfield, Lincoln was generally too busy planning the next production to notice when the ball came.

Even before Lincoln Kirstein entered Harvard at the age of twenty, he knew his way around the worlds of art, dance, and literature. When he was fifteen, he published a play—set in Tibet—in the *Phillips Exeter Monthly*. In 1922, when he was sixteen, he made his first art acquisition—an Ashanti moon-fan figure of tulipwood, carved at the Wembley Empire Exhibition. That same year, he and George spent their summer holidays in London in the house their older sister Mina shared with Henrietta Bingham, of the Louisville publishing family. The boys were asleep after a performance of Serge Diaghilev's Ballets Russes when they were roused from their beds and told to put on Mina's orange-and-yellow silk pajamas to dance a pas de trois improvised for them by the brilliant soubrette Lydia Lopokova. Lytton Strachey was among those who viewed the Kirstein brothers' carrying-on. Lopokova was there with her fiancé, Maynard Keynes. A few days later, Keynes took Lincoln to a Gauguin exhibition that Lincoln found unforgettable. He relished these new ways to look at life, and the pioneering styles in which to write, dance, or paint.

Like the setting Lincoln had helped to create for the Harvard Society for Contemporary Art, Mina's London life was a far cry from

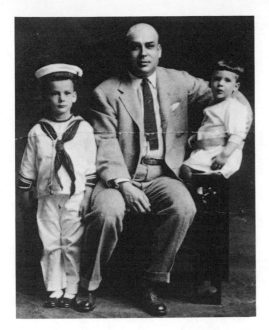

From left to right: Lincoln, Louis, and George Kirstein in 1910.

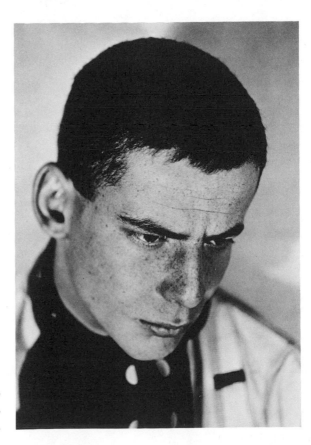

Lincoln Kirstein, photographed by Walker Evans, c. 1927.

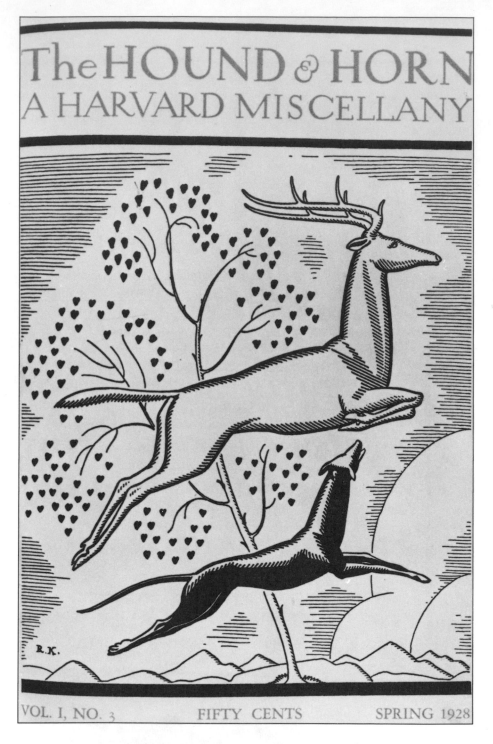

Cover of The Hound & Horn, *Spring 1928.*

the environment in which they had grown up. Their father, Louis Kirstein, was a high-ranking executive—eventually chairman—of Filene's Department Store. The Kirsteins' house was very much the sort of thing Lewis Mumford excoriated in *Harper's*. The foyer was hung in green corded silk. Empire Period torchères, and a marble bust of Louis XIV's finance and culture minister, Colbert, sat on its green marble mantels. The rooms upstairs emulated Isabella Stewart Gardner's Italianate palazzo, Fenway Court. There was a Chinese bedroom completely done with scarlet slipper-satin and black lacquered furniture, niches stuffed with neo-Classical art, and a library decorated with electrotypes of Pompeiian bronzes. A tailor's daughter, Rose Stein Kirstein liked to have as much lace around as possible. The largest painting was a full-size copy of Titian's *Bacchus & Ariadne*. Everything referred to some other place and some time past. This was equally true in the Boston Public Library, of which Louis Kirstein was president. Lincoln regularly visited his father there, crossing inlaid floors under the grand barrel vault with its ornate ceiling reliefs and abundance of marble columns. What Lincoln Kirstein was used to were embellished surfaces and grandiose manifestations of the stages of history.

Lincoln's own tastes went in many directions. When he was twelve his mother had taken him and Mina to Chartres. There he developed such a strong passion for the windows that between high school and college he worked for a year in a stained-glass factory. This fulfilled his father's wish that he learn what an honest day's work meant, and also brought him closer to the craftsmanship that was his heritage, since his paternal grandfather had been a lens grinder in the German city of Jena. Early on his mother had given him two large volumes of masterpieces of world art, and he had been overwhelmed by a Dürer. On summer vacations he looked long and hard at paintings in northern European museums, and made drawings of classical sculpture in the Louvre. At home in Boston he studied decorated books and bought volumes illustrated by Gustave Doré, Aubrey Beardsley, and Arthur Rackham, of whose work the best collection was in the public library. Lincoln also greatly admired the large allegorical murals there: Puvis de Chavannes's *The Muses of Inspiration*, Edwin Austin Abbey's *The Quest and Achievement of the Holy Grail*, and John Singer Sargent's *Judaism and Christianity*. He often met his father in the boardroom, where Sargent's panel of the prophets looked down on them; it moved him greatly.

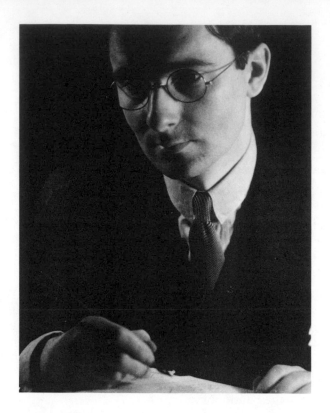

Alfred H. Barr, Jr., photographed by Jay Leyda, New York, 1931–33. Gelatin silver print, 4¾ × 3⅝".

In his first year of college, Lincoln Kirstein went with his mother to the auction of the American collector John Quinn and bought an eight-inch-high statue of a mother and son made in the Belgian Congo. The piece had been found by Paul Guillaume—the Paris-based dealer in African art—and it was Picasso who had advised Guillaume to offer it to Quinn. There was little that Kirstein wouldn't consider so long as it reflected passion and competence. At Harvard he did quite a bit of painting himself, most of it in a rather traditional figurative style. He had heard the painter Leon Kroll say that if a painter had not done a thousand life drawings by the age of twenty, he should forget it. Kirstein did more, in the traditional style one might expect from an artist whose artistic heroes included Antonello da Messina, Antonio Moro, and Anthony Van Dyck. Above all he painted portraits, which by his own description were in the manner of artists ranging from Holbein to Cézanne.

The one rule was that whatever Kirstein cared about, he cared about vehemently. His freshman year at Harvard he and some associates started an undergraduate magazine called *The Hound & Horn,* the first issue of which came out in the fall of 1927. Deeming Harvard's official literary magazine inadequate, this new publication was modeled on the *Criterion,* an English review edited by T. S. Eliot. Like everything Kirstein was to be involved in from that point on, it did not flaunt his name—which appeared only in small type in the list of editors—but the periodical was his idea, and bore the mark of his very strong sense of judgment.

Kirstein selected authors for *The Hound & Horn* who at that time were little known. They were mostly young and unproven. In general their styles were streamlined, their messages candid to a fault. They were bound by no remnants of Victorianism or other old-fashioned forms of acceptability. Independence marked whatever arenas the magazine entered: literature, architecture, painting, photography, music. The first issue had an article called "The Decline of Architecture" by the young architectural historian Henry Russell Hitchcock, along with photographs of recent building design by a young man named Jere Abbott. Abbott was a graduate student at Harvard under Paul Sachs, as was the person with whom he shared an apartment on Brattle Street, Alfred Hamilton Barr, Jr. Both Barr and Abbott were Kirstein's advisers.

Abbott's photos showed the New England Confection Company factory in Cambridge. That Necco building today looks like a straightforward industrial structure, but its inclusion as a triumph of design was startling in 1927. To extol the beauty of unornamented, machined, and coolly functional form was a major step, and a challenge to the usual way of doing things. In advocating this radical aesthetic through *The Hound & Horn,* Kirstein was reflecting Alfred Barr's taste. Besides studying at Harvard, Barr was teaching a course in modern art at Wellesley College. In it, he applauded the Necco factory and assigned his students to visit it. Barr had also written the wall labels for a show of facsimiles of modern paintings at the Fogg. The artists he championed included Gauguin, Matisse, and Picasso. By the standards of the times they were not quite as offbeat and shocking as many of the artists the Harvard Society for Contemporary Art would show, but they evinced Barr's commitment to some fairly adventurous art.

The Hound & Horn issues of the next several years included short stories by Conrad Aiken, Katherine Anne Porter, Kay Boyle, Er-

skine Caldwell, James Joyce, and Gertrude Stein, all of whom were
new writers at the time. There were excerpts from a novel by John
Dos Passos. A story called "Bock Beer and Bermuda Onions" was
by the twenty-year-old Jon [*sic*] Cheever. There were essays by Paul
Valéry, Sergei Eisenstein, and T. S. Eliot, as well as an Eliot bibliography prepared by the Harvard student Varian Fry and an essay
about Eliot by R. P. Blackmur, who contributed frequently. The poetry was by Malcolm Cowley, William Carlos Williams, Conrad
Aiken, e. e. cummings, Horace Gregory, Wallace Stevens, and Ezra
Pound. There was also one poem by Captain Paul Horgan, identified
as a teacher of English at a military school in the Southwest. Roger
Sessions contributed "Notes on Music," and Hyatt Mayor wrote a
piece on Picasso's method. There were occasional reproductions of
paintings—mostly easygoing watercolors—by A. Everett Austin,
the very young Fairfield Porter, and Charles Burchfield. Richly
printed black-and-white photographs were by Charles Sheeler and
Walker Evans. The latter was represented by, among other images,
his striking portrait of a fur-clad black woman on Sixth Avenue in
New York, and *Wash Day,* a shot of laundry hanging on lines.

The back of each issue contained book reviews. When they were
both freshmen, Kirstein had asked John Walker to write some of
these reviews. Kirstein had initially set out to meet Walker after hearing that his room was covered with reproductions of paintings by
Duncan Grant, John Marin, Picasso, and Vlaminck. This must have
made it seem like home territory to Kirstein, since in 1924 Duncan
Grant had done a portrait of Mina; it was also like a sign on the door
saying "interested in modern art and other unusual things." Sensing
that here he would find a soul mate, one day Kirstein had walked in
and introduced himself. Their rapport on *The Hound & Horn* had led
Kirstein to ask Walker to join him in the Harvard Society for Contemporary Art.

John Walker's fondness for art had been the result of a calamity. In
1919, when he was thirteen years old and interested only in football
and skiing, he had been struck with infantile paralysis. His family
lived in Pittsburgh, but his mother took him to New York so that he
could get the best medical treatment. For two years they lived at the
Biltmore Hotel. She would regularly wheel John, who was dressed
in his pajamas, up and down Fifth Avenue in an open barouche.
When his health improved to the extent that he could get into
clothes, she sought places accessible by wheelchair, and the easiest

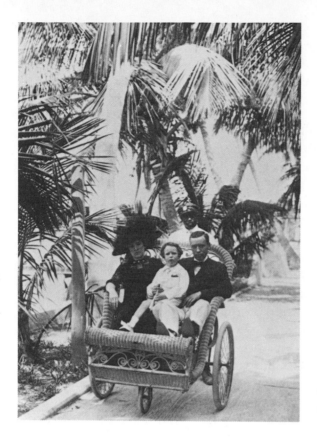

John Walker III and his
parents in Palm Beach,
c. 1912.

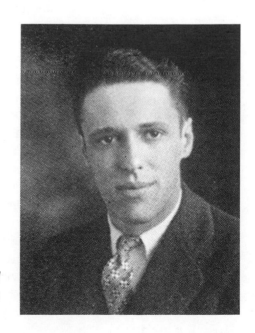

John Walker III, Harvard
College Class Album
photograph, 1930.

was the Metropolitan Museum of Art, with its street-level side entrance, and elevator. At the Met Mrs. Walker saw her son smile with a pleasure she hadn't seen on his face since before he had taken sick. He spent endless hours in the ancient and classical collections, and then discovered the galleries of Dutch and Flemish art of the fifteenth to seventeenth centuries, where he liked to park his wheelchair for prolonged viewings. In little time he knew that he wanted to be a curator.

When Walker and his mother moved back to Pittsburgh, he began to attend the International Exhibitions at the Carnegie Institute. These annual shows were among the few venues in America for modern European art. Walker loathed the pictures his family owned—canvases by chic minor painters like Fritz Thaolow and Aston Knight—but admired much on the contemporary scene. At his country day school he helped form a group of half a dozen boys in which the members took turns reading one another papers on the history of art. When it came time for college Walker chose Harvard because he knew that this was to be his field and people like Sachs and Forbes were there. The family fought hard—everyone else had gone to Princeton or Yale—but he knew what he wanted.

On a visit home during his freshman year, Walker made his first art acquisition—a painting by John Kane called *Old Clinton Furnace*. The asking price at the Carnegie International was fifteen hundred dollars; he offered seventy-five. The saleswoman at the catalog desk laughed in his face, but the next day she telephoned him, chagrined, and said his offer had been accepted. Walker knew Kane slightly; the artist's wife had been his grandmother's cook. He also was well acquainted with the subject of the canvas; it was the blast furnace in central Pittsburgh that his grandfather owned. But to buy a rather primitive rendering of smokestacks and an industrial landscape was a bold move. Walker, however, had long valued what others deemed grim. As much as he enjoyed the galleries at the Met, he had also come to prize the sights of downtown Pittsburgh. As a teenager he spent hours watching work at that blast furnace. He found a bizarre beauty in the flying sparks and workmen sweating away in the hot light. When on one occasion the furnace collapsed and molten iron flowed down a main street of Pittsburgh, he could not take his eyes off this glorious "avenue of glowing pig iron."[13] When Lincoln Kirstein entered Walker's room to tap him for contemporary, experimental ventures that required an original outlook, he had picked the right person.

Not that Walker had had any more exposure to contemporary style at home than Kirstein had. The rooms in which he had spent most of his time as a child—in his maternal grandparents' house in Pittsburgh—resembled an elegant English men's club. They were paneled in mahogany, oak, and walnut. There was chintz everywhere, windows draped in dark brown or dark red velvet, elaborately stuccoed ceilings, massive silver lamps, and leaded glass doors in front of bookcases crammed with leatherbound volumes that had been bought by the yard. Walker's paternal grandparents' house was decorated with William Morris wallpaper and furniture, and Tiffany lamps and chandeliers. Like Kirstein, Walker had grown up in an atmosphere redolent of the widespread American reverence for established traditions. What made a style legitimate was that it had already flourished in Europe for centuries.

Lincoln Kirstein's and Eddie Warburg's families had tried to get the two young men together long before they actually met. Louis Kirstein was a friend of Eddie's brother-in-law, Walter Rothschild. Rothschild was married to the oldest of the five Warburg children—the only girl, Carola. He was sixteen years older than Eddie and one of the top people at Abraham & Straus. A prominent figure in Jewish philanthropy in Boston, Louis Kirstein also admired Eddie's father, who headed many New York charities in keeping with the tradition established by Eddie's maternal grandfather, the wealthy financier Jacob Schiff. From Louis Kirstein's and Walter Rothschild's points of view it made perfect sense for the two students to be friends, because of what they shared both in their backgrounds and in their unusual interest in art. But like most family efforts to create friendships, their initial attempts had backfired. Lincoln and Eddie had carefully avoided each other for almost all of freshman year. By the end of the year, however, the two students discovered that in spite of their families' intentions, and Warburg's being two years younger, they had a lot in common. Well before the time that Kirstein was concocting the Harvard Society for Contemporary Art, they had become fast friends. Warburg had a lot of money and was inclined to be generous with it, which contributed significantly to Kirstein's feeling that he could make the new organization a reality.

Felix Warburg had advised his son to choose distinguished friends who would give sound advice. He warned Eddie against "the money-mad crowd" and mere country clubbers. In spite of his own fondness for "cheerful hours of sport," one had to avoid friends who were good at nothing else. He counseled his son to find "one right companion" instead.[14] For Eddie, Lincoln Kirstein was just the sort of intelligent and inspiring companion his father had in mind, even if he wasn't "right" in the sense that Eddie's older brothers would have considered "right." Although Kirstein had spent a year at Phillips Exeter and two at Berkshire Academy, he had previously gone to public schools and wasn't part of the prep school set. He was the opposite of the easygoing jocks and party boys whom the other three Warburg boys counted as friends. Kirstein cared about books, paintings, and the dance, not about sports and socializing. He could be abrasive in defense of his passions. He was as vituperative as he was imaginative. But he had a sensitivity and awareness that gave Eddie rare ease, and a boundless knowledge and energy that nourished Eddie more deeply than anything on the Harvard curriculum could. Moreover, by recognizing the infectious power of Eddie's wit and kindness, Kirstein enabled the baby of the Warburg household to be effective and useful. To help Kirstein implement his ideas gave Eddie a sense of his own worth.

The art that Eddie Warburg knew best before college was what he could find by walking downstairs in his parents' house. This was a neo–Gothic François Premier–style mansion overlooking the Central Park Reservoir at Fifth Avenue and Ninety-second Street (today it is the Jewish Museum). Designed by C. P. H. Gilbert, the house had painted beam ceilings, elaborately paneled walls covered with tapestries or other collections, ornate wrought-iron lamps and chandeliers lighting the heavy English furniture and the ceremonial silver with which Jacob Schiff had filled his daughter's household to assure proper Sabbath celebrations. Everywhere there were layers over layers, which is what life itself was like. The entrance vestibule had double doors made of glass panels framed with ornate bronze mullions and covered with Belgian lace.

Eddie's father devoted two rooms to a comprehensive collection of early German and Italian woodcuts and Rembrandt etchings that he had built up under the tutelage of William Ivins, a close family friend and a protégé of Paul Sachs; Sachs had recommended Ivins to his position as the curator of prints at the Metropolitan Museum. In the red room Frieda and Felix Warburg kept the paintings they would bring back as souvenirs of trips to Rome, among them four predellas (base panels), attributed to Pesellino, that had originally belonged in a large altarpiece completed by Fra Filippo Lippi after Pesellino's death. In the conservatory adjacent to the red room there

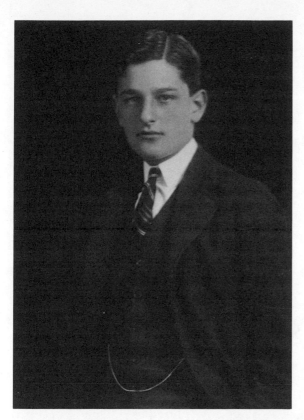

Edward M. M. Warburg,
c. 1927.

The Warburg brothers
in Hamburg, c. 1925.
From the left: Paul, Felix,
Max, Fritz, and Aby,
whose hands are held in a
gesture of supplication to
signify the financial
arrangement with his
brothers.

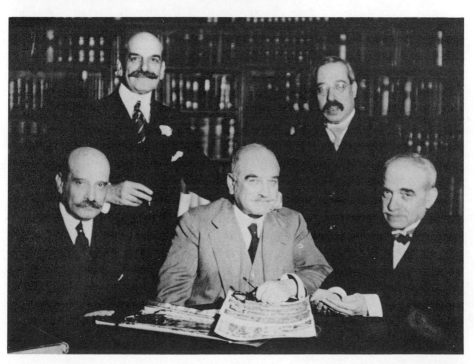

was a so-called Botticelli, in front of which stood on a stand a so-called Wittenberg Bible with a so-called inscription by Martin Luther. In time it would fall upon young Edward to find out the truth about the authenticity of these works. When he was a teenager it was often his task to give visitors the tour of all of these objects when his father had to take a phone call from "downtown"—the offices of the investment banking firm Kuhn, Loeb, where he was a partner—or was off raising money for one of the many charities he supported. Of the five children, Eddie had always been the one to show an interest in art; while his brothers were on the fifth-floor balcony leaning over the elaborate oak balustrade having a spitting contest into the marble amphora in the hall below, he was listening to his father and visiting art historians or other curious onlookers in the two print rooms. As they went through the collection covering the walls, encased in double glass on rotating pedestals (this to allow the viewing of both recto and verso of two-sided images), or stored in black boxes on a billiard table, he carefully noted every scholarly observation as well as all the more prosaic remarks he would store away into his repertoire as a mimic. His parents encouraged his interest in art through a practice then known as "bratting"—akin to tutoring, but less formal—in which an older boy is hired to encourage another in a given field. Eddie's coach was Jo Mielziner, the painter and set designer, who gave him instruction during summer holidays in Aunt Eda Loeb's Seal Harbor home. Eddie also was tutored in music—by Arthur Schwartz, the composer who later wrote "Dancing in the Dark" and other Broadway hits. Schwartz regularly took his young protégé on strolls through Central Park, where he would teach him new tunes.

Felix Warburg's brother Aby had established a precedent in the family for devoting one's life to art. The oldest of the five brothers of whom Felix was the youngest, he was, according to family tradition, entitled to be a senior partner in the Hamburg banking firm M. M. Warburg & Company; like some sort of royal status, such positions were reserved for the oldest two sons. Aby agreed, however, to abdicate—on the condition that his younger siblings would guarantee lifelong support of his research in the field of iconography. Ensconced in his book-filled house in Hamburg, he pursued the consistent use of certain motifs and images in diverse cultures. He opened his library to people like the psychoanalyst Ernst Kris; Erwin Panofsky, whose writings on iconography pioneered the interpretation of symbolism; and E. H. Gombrich, who in time would write

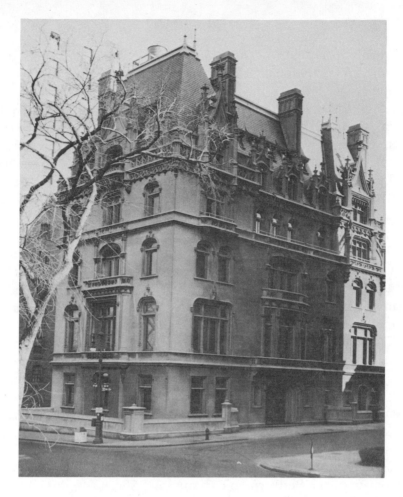

The Warburg house at 1109 Fifth Avenue, c. 1920.

The Story of Art. (Years later, after Nazism forced the removal of Aby
Warburg's library from Hamburg to London in a dramatic nighttime
exodus by boat, Gombrich would head the Warburg Institute at the
University of London and write *Aby Warburg, An Intellectual Biography.*)

But what appealed to young Edward more than the scholarship of
his uncle or the collecting of his parents was the idea of public service. Art was not just something to be studied in libraries or enjoyed
in the privacy of one's home. Consider what happened to the Pesellino predellas. Just at the point when Eddie was getting to know
them well, they were packed up and sent off on loan to the National
Gallery in London. For many years the altarpiece of which they had

originally been part—*The Trinity with Saints*—had been disas-
sembled. The National Gallery had purchased one part of it in 1863,
and received another by bequest and purchased a third in 1917.
Then, in 1929, a fourth panel, formerly in the Royal Collection, had
been presented thanks to Lord Duveen. All that was needed to complete the work was for Felix Warburg to lend the four predellas. A
couple of months after sending them, Felix stopped by to see them
in London. To his shock he found that not only had the altarpiece
been reconstructed, but his panels had been fitted into its base as if
they had always been there. Moreover, the predellas were now attributed to the studio of Fra Filippo Lippi. Naturally Felix was pressed
both to accept the change of authorship and to turn the loan into a
gift. He agreed only after negotiating the terms, which consisted of
an agreement that Parliament change existing laws in order to permit
loans of British-owned paintings outside England, a deregulation
from which the larger world still reaps the benefits.

This concern for public need was typical of Felix Warburg. In 1914
he had become the first treasurer of Jacob Schiff's creation known as
the JDC—the Joint Distribution Committee of American Funds for
the Relief of Jewish War Sufferers—which he then chaired for eighteen years. He also headed the Young Men's Hebrew Association,
organized the Federation of Jewish Charities and became its first
president, and was a leading figure in the American Jewish Committee, the Refugee Economic Corporation, the American Arbitration
Association, the Philharmonic–Symphony Society, and the Hebrew
University in Jerusalem, many of which he had helped to start. Felix
used to liken himself to Heinz's pickles; in his office at Kuhn, Loeb
he had had a special screen built with fifty-seven panels in it, each of
which opened to a file case with material concerning one of the
boards or committees on which he served. By supporting the sort of
art too advanced for museums, Eddie had stepped far from the family orbit, but the Harvard Society for Contemporary Art was also a
new and original form of public service, and as such it was very
much in the family tradition.

I I

Paul Sachs had started out in the German-Jewish banking circle in
New York; he had for a number of years been a partner in his family's

firm, Goldman, Sachs. But as an investment banker, whenever he earned commission money he immediately used it to buy art, which was his true passion. A graduate of Harvard College, Sachs had been asked onto the Visiting Committee of the Fogg in 1911; it was four years later that he realized that art had to be his profession rather than his hobby, moved to Cambridge, and changed careers. But he still had his hand in the closely allied society from which he came. He persuaded Felix Warburg and other old New York friends to take an active role in the Fogg by joining various committees, and to support the museum with generous gifts. By studying with Sachs, Eddie Warburg was playing a part in his father's grand life scheme. Felix Warburg had helped Sachs immeasurably in building up the Fogg. To advise Edward was Sachs's way of repaying the kindness and Felix's way of directly reaping the benefits of his largesse.

For Eddie Warburg, however, Sachs was "a humorless little can-

Faculty of Harvard University Fine Arts Department, Fogg Art Museum courtyard, 1927. Seated in front are Paul Sachs (far left) and Edward Forbes (second from right).

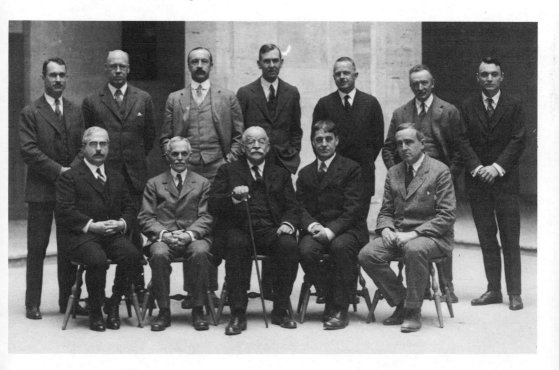

nonball of energy" who flaunted his Phi Beta Kappa key and cried a lot.[15] His rages were frequent, especially toward those who weren't lucky enough to be his social inferior. Sachs was a reverse snob, and found it hard to accept others of his background as serious academics. To be a truly diligent art historian who could recognize authorship and pinpoint iconography, you had to know what it was to work hard to get to where you were. Except for himself, there were to be no gentlemen scholars. It was all right for Sachs to have gone from being an investment banker in the family firm to being an art collector, and from there to being professor and codirector at the Fogg while living in one of the finest houses in the region, but this sort of easy route would not do for anyone else. For that reason Sachs generally treated Kirstein, Warburg, and Walker with the disdain that the rich reserve only for their fellow rich. He resented the three young connoisseurs the way that people who fancy themselves an elite, with exclusive claim to their cultural discoveries and position, resent those who threaten their monopoly on taste and their privileged status as pioneers.

Lincoln Kirstein considers Sachs to have been "a small and nervous man, who hated being a Jew"[16]—and who mainly was very impressed with himself because he lived in Charles Eliot Norton's homestead. From Kirstein's point of view, the extent of Sachs's support of the Harvard Society was that he indulged it; "it was nice if little boys played." He was willing to go that far because the society got him off the hook about the most modern art, a subject with which he was basically uncomfortable. But he was afraid that the new project would get out of hand, and his support was always tentative. As far as John Walker was concerned, Sachs was above all "a stocky, strutting little man" who never could remember who Walker was—"a disheartening experience for a student who had come to Harvard especially to sit at his feet."[17]

The general take on Sachs, however, is that he was a talented navigator in the ways of the world. His "museum course" was the training ground for many of America's future museum directors. Sachs placed scores of people in their jobs; he knew which museum trustee to call in which city. He also kept track of collectors everywhere, thus enabling students to study their holdings, and to secure loans later on when they were working at museums. But much as Kirstein, Warburg, and Walker benefited from Sachs's letters of introduction to get into the collections in Boston, New York, and Washington

where they might see some of the latest art, they often found negotiations with their professor to be torturous.

Edward Waldo Forbes, on the other hand, backed the Harvard
Society completely, whatever the limitations of his understanding of
contemporary art. A grandson of Ralph Waldo Emerson, Forbes was
an easygoing Bostonian gentleman of the old school. He had his
misgivings about modern art at the Fogg, but he sanctioned it at the
Coop. Even Forbes, however, could not keep peace between the
Harvard Society's founders and Paul Sachs. To deal with Sachs—
which was essential if their organization was to take off—the students needed a devoted intermediary. Time and again they brought
on Sachs's ire. Warburg's problem was that he was outspoken and
funny at any cost; Kirstein's that one moment he might be friendly
and gracious, in another he could turn painfully awkward or nasty.
Walker was too smooth and upper-class confident. But in Sachs's
assistant, Agnes Mongan, they had the perfect diplomat to run in-
terference between them and the man to whom they ultimately had
to answer for their new vehicle for modern art. They also had a
fellow believer. Even more than the three young men, Mongan had
come to view artworks as emblems of human life lived deeply and
as gateways to peerless emotional adventure.

At a younger age than any of the founders of the Harvard Society
for Contemporary Art, Mongan had recognized her own passion for
paintings and objects. Born in 1905, she was twelve years old when
her father asked her what she wanted to do when she grew up. Dr.
Mongan—trained as an obstetrician/gynecologist, but now a family
doctor with a general practice—had just come in from his hospital
rounds when he posed the question. He and Agnes were alone at
breakfast in the family house in Somerville, a town that neighbors
Cambridge. The young girl did not know the term "curator" or "art
historian," but she pointed to a Persian rug—of which her parents
had bought a number at auctions—and replied, "I'd like to know
something about that." There was an eighteenth-century reflector on
the wall. It had a convex mirror topped by an eagle, and she adored
it. Directing her finger from the rug to the reflector, she then said,
"I'd like to know something about that, too."

"And that," she added, indicating some silver on the mantelpiece.[18] Her father replied that in that case she should have the best
possible liberal arts education a girl could have, which meant Bryn
Mawr. Having settled the matter, Dr. Mongan started to leave the

room, but he stopped at the door and came back. He told his daughter that her time at Bryn Mawr should be followed by a year in Europe. Dr. Mongan believed that one had to have a taste of the larger world; not only did he never let a day go by without picking up his *New York Times* at a Cambridge newsstand, but he also received the *Manchester Guardian* and *Le Monde* by post. Having himself spent a year abroad after Harvard Medical School, he felt that each of his children should have the same opportunity. Unlike Kirstein's and Warburg's parents, he would not leave his children a fortune. They would need to support themselves. But what he could provide were optimal opportunities for learning.

From the start, the senior Mongans had stressed the acquisition of knowledge for their children. Before her marriage, Agnes's mother, like her many siblings, had been a schoolteacher. She read the classics to her two sons and two daughters for an hour each night, and saw to it that Agnes and her sister Elizabeth learned to play the piano. During successive summer holidays in Maine, the children were taught one year to identify all the local species of wildflowers; the next, mushrooms; and the following, trees. When Agnes's father settled on the idea of her going to Bryn Mawr, he and her mother studied the college catalog. They decided to switch her from Somerville High School to the Cambridge School for Girls so that she could learn Latin, French, and a bit of Italian, and strengthen her background in mythology and literature. It was the sort of discipline from which art historians are made.

As a young girl, Mongan had won a prize for a piece in the *St. Nicholas Magazine*. She liked to write as well as to learn about artworks. At Bryn Mawr she majored jointly in English and history of art. Mongan's main interest was clearly in the latter, however; what her study of English provided above all was a better command of language with which to describe the art objects that held her captive.

At Bryn Mawr there were only three teachers of art history: George Rowley for Oriental art, Edward Stauffer King for northern Renaissance art, and Georgiana Goddard King (no relation to Edward) for everything else. Professor Georgiana King, who had started as a teacher of English, had created the art history department at the college and turned it into one of the best in the country. She had opened the field to women by making Bryn Mawr the first women's college in America to offer a Ph.D. in the subject. On her clearly defined course of becoming a professional art historian,

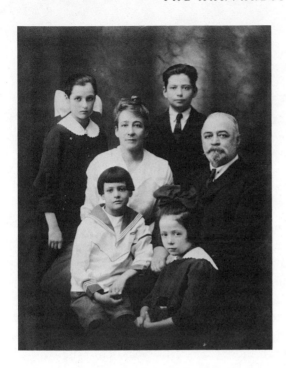

The Mongan family, c. 1915: Agnes and her brother Charles in the background, their parents in the middle, her brother John and sister Betty in the foreground.

Agnes Mongan sitting on running board of Nancy Williams's car, c. 1928.

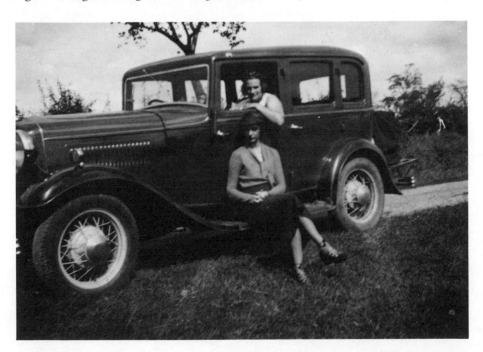

Agnes Mongan could have chosen no better mentor. King was not only immensely knowledgeable, but she was passionate and colorful; everything about her suggested that to follow her way of life would be fulfilling and amusing.

As the head of a department in which men held subordinate positions, King demonstrated that here was a line of work in which a woman might attain the highest stature. In 1914 Bernard Berenson, the renowned connoisseur and scholar, had called King "the best equipped student of Italian art in the United States or in England."[19] Berenson, who had moved to Italy but remained deeply immersed in American collecting and the academic scene, had praised King to the president of Bryn Mawr by saying that only two years after she had founded the art history department there she had created the finest photograph and slide collection anywhere. "B.B." went so far as to ask "G.G."—this is how both were known—to work for him. But, with an institutional loyalty that also became a model for Mongan, G.G. was too attached to the college to leave it. She had attended Bryn Mawr as a student. By the mid-1920s, when Mongan studied with her, she had been there for twenty years, and she would remain for another ten. The venerable institution offered a secure base for a life of adventure and wandering. G.G. went to Europe regularly, often exploring unknown and inaccessible regions of Spain in her search for medieval and earlier artworks. She periodically traveled with Gertrude and Leo Stein, who admired her as a literary critic and a poet; she had struck up a close friendship with Gertrude in 1902 and on visits to Paris became acquainted with many of the artists and writers in Gertrude's life. G.G. was a scholar of Oriental philosophy and of ancient Greek, Latin, and Arabic—in addition to the subjects and languages more directly related to art history. But she always returned to her teaching, enjoying it on her own terms as a campus eccentric. For thirty years G.G. wore the same frayed academic gown as she moved about the Bryn Mawr campus. At dinner she dressed as a Spanish doña, generally in a fitted black suit, often with black lace on her head. The short, stocky woman, with her lively green eyes and her gray hair in its bun, was known for her intolerance of mediocrity and dull people. She was often deliberately contentious. She was so fanatical about grammar and correctness that in her early teaching years she had written *The Bryn Mawr Spelling Book,* more than one hundred pages of words frequently misspelled. In Agnes Mongan, who was one of her best students, she

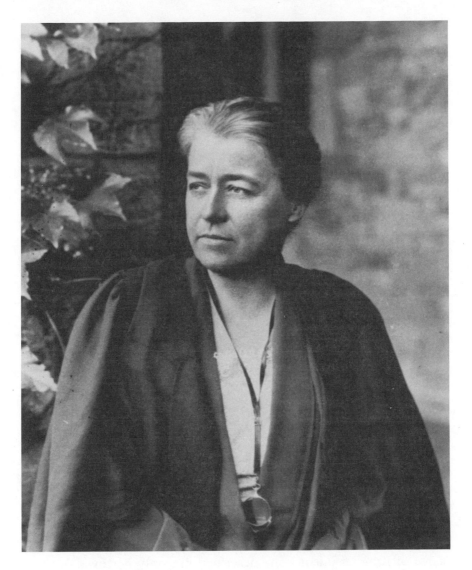

Georgiana Goddard King.

met her match for enthusiasm as well as for accuracy of language. G.G. had also found her equal in tenacity; Mongan was frail and prone to severe bouts of grippe, so much so that at one point King declared her not strong enough to continue in fine arts and sent her home, only to have Mongan promptly return with an opinion from her father that they had underestimated her.

For Mongan, King was a model not only for factual rectitude, but for a belief in art as a spiritual presence. G.G.'s teaching emphasized original observation more than the accumulation of information. In her courses on medieval art, Italian Renaissance painting, and modern art—about which she learned firsthand from the Steins—she lectured spontaneously, rarely glancing at notes. She deliberately eschewed syllabuses or course outlines. The lecture room was totally dark except for the lights of the slide projector, so that students could scarcely take notes. Rather, the young women were to immerse themselves in the visual organization of the paintings and the emotions at play.

Agnes Mongan reveled in what she called "King's capacity to arouse, to electrify, to instruct, and to inspire." On many levels, her teacher became her ideal. She admired King's power to leave her students "inoculated with ideas which leave marks on all their later lives." Here was "a scholar of profound and original research" who went well beyond the realm of scholarship. For Mongan it was impressive that King pursued knowledge and information tenaciously, but what mattered more was that to her other attributes "were added a poet's sensitivity and an unfailing human sympathy. Against this background the work of art was contemplated and judged. Never was it considered as an isolated object remote from life."[20]

Intense aliveness was what Agnes Mongan craved; artworks and their study were vehicles toward it. Not only did Georgiana King recognize the power of paintings and sculpture, but in researching, writing, and teaching about art, she lived richly. King was alert to everything. She charged every moment, not just for herself, but for those who came into her wake. G.G. had the power to heighten experience, and to unveil new extremes of vitality—for which Mongan had enormous appetite. When Mongan characterized the experience of King's students, she described not only her own spiritual adventure, but also her own aspirations for the effect she too would like to have on others:

They know . . . that adventure lurks at every cross-road. . . . For them saints have awakened from stone to living spirit, and sightless eyes have looked beyond the boundaries of this world. The symbol has been made significant. Legend and liturgy have uncovered their riches. They have been moved by the beauty of pure line and stirred by the majesty of form. . . . From the Far

East to Santiago, from the wall paintings of Altamira to Picasso, they know that "it is always the spirit which moves man
to the creation of lasting beauty." [21]

At Bryn Mawr, Mongan came to feel the intoxication with visual
riches that would determine her life's work. She would never lose
her regard for precise knowledge and accurate identification she had
acquired on those summer nature walks in New England, but
the word "magic" also entered her vocabulary and assumed an
importance it never would have for more traditionally Germanic,
iconography-minded art historians. For one of King's courses
Mongan wrote a paper on El Greco in which, in her neat schoolgirl
script on lined paper, she evinced the intense emotional engagement,
both visual and psychological, that would inspire more than sixty
years of work. At the same time she reached—if not with quite the
success that she would later attain—for the writing style that would
seal her success. She also manifested her originality:

> Anyone who has seen an El Greco canvas is not likely to
> forget it. His colors are weird—chalky and often livid. His can-
> vases are packed, even the landscapes are so thickly packed that
> one could not move through their heavy air. But more striking
> than any of these is the look in the eyes of his people. They
> seem, without any of the feline and sinister quality of Mona
> Lisa, to look beyond this world to another.

At that point in her life, Mongan had traveled no farther than the
eastern seaboard of the United States, but this did not prevent her
from grappling nobly with the milieu in which these paintings had
been made. She imbued El Greco's Spain with profound drama,
about which she wrote with an ardent voice that seems intended for
far more than the one-person audience who would be reading this
paper:

> All who really know Spain know her to be a land of violent
> and constant contrasts—and in these contrasts lies her fascina-
> tion. On her plains the dry and scorching heat, which beats
> down with merciless intensity, suddenly gives way to icy winter
> winds which whistle across the same plains just as mercilessly.
> In her people profligate voluptuousness is gone in a night and

in its place there is an opposite extreme of austere ascetism [*sic*]. Passionate devotion to the Virgin exists, with no sense of incongruity, side by side with a love of bull fights. Beauty and ugliness are close and good neighbors, beauty lending the ugliness strangeness, and ugliness lending beauty strength—an arid, barren plain and in its midst a city of fairytale splendor, a cathedral gorgeous with the accumulated treasures of centuries and in their midst a skeleton; the Infanta and her dwarf, Sancho Panza and Don Quixote.

In juxtaposing the simultaneous devotion to Catholicism with more earthbound pleasures, Mongan may have been confronting her own personal dilemmas as well as the background for El Greco. But whatever the conflicts, it was her Romantic vision that won out. She wrote of her subject, "He could paint the human figure with all its rounded contours—but chose to paint the human soul." The conclusion to her paper is, "In El Greco there is positive magic."[22]

After graduation from Bryn Mawr in 1927, it was time for the year in Europe. Dr. Mongan hoped it would be in Oxford or Cambridge and that Agnes would become a writer; her choice was Florence, so that she might study Italian art. She joined a master's degree program organized by Smith College. Led by two professors, Mongan and four other students, all women, spent five months in Florence and the surrounding Tuscan cities. By daylight they viewed art in galleries and churches and private collections. During classes each evening from 5 to 7 and 9 to 11 p.m., they would review everything they had seen. After Florence, the program continued for three months in Paris. On Mondays, when the Louvre was closed, they studied paintings in its galleries through a binocular microscope, from stepladders, and with automobile headlights—while the guards stood around snickering about silly American girls. They went to Berlin, Dresden, Munich, Prague, Vienna, and Venice before returning to Florence, where they had exams in July. Five Italian professors posed the questions in Italian; the women answered in English. There were three hours of oral exams, six hours of written ones. Since a thesis was also required for the Smith M.A., Mongan wrote one on Italian art in the Musée Jacquemart-André in Paris. Rich young men like Kirstein, Walker, and Warburg might be able to pursue their love for art on their own terms; a woman of no great affluence had to go the straight and tough academic route. But whatever the struggles, Mongan thrived. Slight to begin with, she lost twenty-five pounds that year, but considered it all part of a nourishing experience.

She had not done enough by the standards of Smith College, however. When Mongan got back to her parents' house in Somerville and found out that she had passed her exams, she wrote the college to ask that they forward her M.A. Word came back that there were further requirements to fulfill; she needed to take a drawing or painting class. Since she did not want to go to Northampton for this purpose, she signed up at Harvard for Arthur Pope's course in the theory of design. But her troubles were not over. Three weeks into the course, she got word that she should present herself at the registrar's office. There she was asked if she was working toward a Ph.D. To her answer that she only wished to complete her M.A., the registrar pointed to the catalog listing where Pope's course was marked with double daggers. "That means the course has men in it. No woman may take a double-daggered course unless she is working on a Ph.D. President Lowell once discovered a young woman in one of those courses whose serious intent of mind he doubted. He made a rule: No woman may take a double-daggered course unless she is a Ph.D. candidate. Young woman, if you have a quarrel, it is with the president of Harvard University. Good morning." [23]

On her way out of the registrar's office, Mongan ran into the college dean, who came up with a solution. He asked if the same course were offered at Smith, and when she replied that it was, he inquired if the professor there had been trained by Arthur Pope. Again the answer was yes. The dean suggested that Mongan sit in on Pope's classes, but send her papers to Smith to be graded. By this contrivance, a woman who was not a Ph.D. candidate managed to take a double-daggered course at Harvard and thereby complete her M.A. degree.

That same semester, in the fall of 1928, as a Fogg Museum Special Student, Mongan took Paul Sachs's museum course. She also took a course that was routine for Harvard art historians—Edward Waldo Forbes's history of technique, nicknamed "egg and plaster." Mongan, however, was used to doing more than simply studying three subjects. She approached Edward Forbes about part-time employment, but he replied that part-time rarely worked out. She then suggested volunteer work, which he considered equally fruitless. But three weeks after the semester started, she learned that a friend of

hers was giving up her position cataloging the Fogg's drawing collection under Paul Sachs. She went straight to Shady Hill to ask if
she could fill the spot, and Sachs agreed. She ended up as Sachs's
assistant the same semester that the three young men were launching
the Harvard Society. Already a great admirer of *The Hound & the
Horn,* Mongan liked the sound of the Harvard Society for Contemporary Art from the moment she heard about it. Not only were the
exhibition ideas exciting, but the gentlemen proposing them—especially Eddie Warburg—were irresistible.

Kirstein and Warburg, more than Walker, were responsible for the
daily planning of the Harvard Society. Mongan met them almost
daily for lunch at the local Schrafft's as they plotted their course of
action and made plans to exhibit the latest painting and sculpture
from America and abroad. She was in an ideal position not only to
be the Harvard juniors' confidante and friend, but also their aide-de-
camp by occasionally presenting or defending their proposals to
Sachs, or approaching him on other issues. She had great diplomatic
tact. When Frieda Warburg badgered Eddie to find out why, considering all that Felix had done for the Fogg, Harvard had never given
him an honorary degree, it was Mongan to whom Eddie could put
such an awkward point. She could bring up this sort of issue to Sachs
without raising the professor's hackles. In the case of Felix's doctor-
ate the answer was no, but Mongan had managed to ask without
provoking a storm.

Kirstein and Sachs had violent tempers, while Mongan never gave
voice to anger. She knew both how to explain and how to avoid
Sachs's invective. From her employer's point of view, she was easier
than the young men. If Sachs wanted to be the only rich Wall Street
type to make inroads in the art world at Harvard, Mongan offered
no competition. Sachs treated Mongan far more gently than he did
Kirstein or Warburg. A consummate scholar, she provided Sachs a
major service by meticulously researching the Fogg's holdings for
his catalog, and he was grateful to her.

From Mongan's vantage point, not only was Sachs dynamic and
knowledgeable, but he had the added appeal that he prized drawings.
This was not the norm; although a handful of connoisseurs had always esteemed graphic art, most collectors and museum people
cared more for oils. Paintings were easier to display, and made a
strong first impression. For Agnes Mongan, Sachs's elevation of
works on paper to the status of high art led to unimagined pleasures.

Drawings had a unique freshness. For her they offered the honesty and immediacy that bizarre constructions in wire and cardboard, and other expressions of modernism, provided for Kirstein and Warburg. Art that held a charge of emotion could awaken and enliven these three young people with an intensity they had scarcely felt before.

In many ways, Kirstein, Warburg, and Mongan made a likely threesome. In a milieu where reticence was as much a part of the social code as was a firm handshake, they were violently purposeful. Unlike most of her contemporaries, Mongan wished to spend her time looking at art, traveling, and writing—not planning her trousseau; unlike their peers, Kirstein and Warburg preferred to plan startling art exhibitions than toss a football or worry about how to make more money when they got out of college. But it was not just their ardor that made them among Santayana's "outsiders . . . on the fringes of college life." For one thing, there was the matter of background. Ever since primary school, Agnes Mongan had felt the onus of being Catholic and of Irish descent in Boston. One day a classmate in an early grade had precipitately run her fingers over Mongan's forehead; when Mongan asked why, the girl explained that her parents had told her Catholics were all devils, and so she was checking for Mongan's horns.[24] It was still the era when employment ads might say "Irish need not apply." During a vacation from Bryn Mawr when she visited a fashionable classmate in Jamaica Plain, near Boston, she learned that she was the first Catholic and person of Irish descent ever to go up the front stairs of the house; previously they had all used the servants' staircase. Not that this sort of thing shocked her parents when she reported it back home; Mongan's mother's family, the O'Briens, could not be educated in England because they were Catholics, and so had gone to Salamanca.

As Jews, Warburg and Kirstein also felt one step away from the center of things. Even as enlightened a man as Dr. Mongan looked at them askance. Agnes was living back in her parents' house in Somerville where Eddie called with some frequency. When Eddie told Agnes he was wondering whether her father would ask what his intentions were, she replied, "If you have any intentions at all, he won't let you in the door." There were also the clubs that would not consider Jews, the parties at which they would not be welcome.

It was an era when ethnic and religious prejudices were publicly

permissible and widespread. For some people there was, in fact, the
expectation that Jews should come up with a notion like the Harvard
Society for Contemporary Art. Jews were known to be adventurous
art patrons. No one disapproved when the art dealer Valentine Dudensing—one of the main people on whom the Harvard Society
would depend for loans—was quoted to that effect in a 1927 magazine article. Nor did anyone fault the title of the article: "The Jew
and Modernism." Its claim was that

> It is especially to the Jews that we owe the advance in artistic
> appreciation that has been made in the last decade. The Jews are
> forward-looking, they are not afraid of doing things unconven-
> tionally, differently, individually. Intellectually and artistically
> they have made great achievements.[25]

To be viewed a certain way because of one's religion was an inescap-
able reality. Having such clear sense of the boundaries of their existence may have contributed to people like Warburg wanting to
shatter restrictions in the aesthetic realm.

But being Jewish was not the only determining factor for Kirstein
and Warburg. Warburg's three older brothers, after all, were every
bit as Jewish as he was; they simply chose to ignore the fact as best
they could. Wishing to assimilate into American upper-class life,
Fred, Piggy (as Paul was called), and Gerry easily succeeded. Eddie,
on the other hand, had the mixed blessing of being more conscious
of everything: his background, his feeling of being the mama's boy
who wasn't really one of the guys, his relentless sensitivity to his and
other people's feelings. And Lincoln Kirstein had even more of a
nonstop mind and inability to screen. In conversation or writing,
then as now, he touched on everything and masked little. He has
always been blunt about the intensity of both his passions and his
dislikes. His religious obsessions range from sharp awareness of his
Jewish background, to devotion to the mystic Gurdjieff, to Catholicism. He has been keenly aware of his own difference from most
everyone else. This underlies his later depiction of the run-of-the-
mill, easygoing undergraduates who were mostly his opposites but
who fascinated him:

> My school days and college years were gilded by a steady
> succession of enthusiasms for boys and men whose sweaty bril-

liance and appetite for hard liquor during Prohibition seemed to liberate them into a princely criminal ambiance. Dynastic breeding, well-nourished muscle resulted in a general arrest of psychic development. They were, for the most part, uninterested in ideas, presupposed cash, and resembled expensive sleepwalkers in a luxurious dream. No hindrance or tragedy touched them, and I was excited by their assurance of command over their immediate situation, even if it led nowhere but to the countinghouses of State and Wall Streets or big city law firms.[26]

Kirstein may have been enchanted, but it was not his lot in life to follow their course. He and his closer comrades would never entirely fit in with the larger group. They were not good enough athletes. They did not adhere to the same social boundaries. Those who were Jewish were unwilling to try to disguise the fact. To be an outsider was part of their identities.

Kirstein and Warburg were dissimilar in many ways, but both felt apart from the mainstream. One way of coping with their otherness was to cultivate it. If most of their peers regarded them as different, they might as well have a good time and be as outrageous as they wanted. Kirstein and Warburg embraced modernism in part because, knowing that they were out of the mainstream anyway, they elected to foster rather than mitigate their sense of being different.

I I I

The Harvard Society's exhibition of work by living American artists ran from February 19 to March 15, 1929. Although these people's art has since been assembled in countless exhibitions and books, the joint showing in the two rooms above the Coop was one of the first times it was conceived as part of a general movement. A two-page flyer for the show set the tone and announced its purpose. The abundance of clean white space was as striking as the text. A few succinct, no-nonsense paragraphs in bold sans-serif type contained Kirstein's description of the exhibition as "an assertion of the importance of American art. It represents the work of men no longer young who have helped to create a national tradition in emergence, stemming from Europe but nationally independent." The artists for the most part fell into two groups. One consisted of "lyrists" who maintained the "tradition of visual poetry" of Albert Pinkham Ryder. These included Thomas Hart Benton, Arthur B. Davies, Kenneth Hayes Miller, Rockwell Kent, and Maurice Sterne—painters whose work is full of undulating, exotic curves. Their work shares a rough intensity, a look of caring desperately about something. What it distinctly lacks is the "good taste" of pictures by the able but comparatively limp artists whose work was then proliferating in the Boston galleries and arts organizations. The uncouth bravura of the lyrists offered the Harvard Society founders a welcome relief from the excessive politeness that annoyed them in the more fashionable art of the day. Then there were the "realists" akin to Thomas Eakins: George Bellows, Charles Burchfield, Charles Hopkinson, Boardman Robinson, John Sloan, Eugene Speicher, and Edward Hopper. Their canvases in the Harvard show were above all a candid grappling with the realities of contemporary American life. What these paintings depicted were hardly the everyday sights of people like the Kirsteins, Warburgs, and Walkers. Rather, this was the underside of the current national scene—its low-wage earners like Robinson's doleful-eyed window washers and Speicher's *Quarryman* and Miller's *Reapers,* and its everyday sights of ferryboats, dock life, and slums. In his frontal, glamourless depiction of tenement housing, *Williamsburg Bridge,* Hopper encapsulated some of the objectives of these painters, as well as of the students who put them on view: to gloss over nothing, to reveal what was unique to one culture rather than imitative of another, to dwell on the shadows as much as the sunlight.

The exaltation of natural beauty was equally important, however. There was an airy, euphoric watercolor of Mount Chocorua by John Marin, and a Georgia O'Keeffe of a lily. Kirstein's paragraphs explained that Marin and O'Keeffe fell into neither of the major groups and hence proved the "uselessness of all categories." (O'Keeffe's presence also proved the inaccuracy of Kirstein's reference to the artists as "men.") To suggest categories and then debunk that notion was typical of the Harvard Society. Its founders were both ardent and humble. They pointed out that while their selection was a vanguard group with traits in common, these were not the only worthwhile contemporary artists in America.

In addition to oils and watercolors, the opening Harvard Society show also presented sculpture by Gaston Lachaise, Archipenko, and Robert Laurent. From the founders' point of view, Lachaise's robust, unadorned, and uniquely bold bronze woman was the most important single object of the whole show. In addition, there were design objects. These included an "ash and cocktail tray" by Donald Deskey (lent by the artist), plates by Henry Varnum Poor, a vase by Robert Locher, and contemporary glass, textiles, and pewter. The Harvard Society was not unique in linking art and craft, but to show an ashtray next to an oil painting in an "art show"—and to give them equal billing in the catalog—was a brave step. From the start, there seemed to be very little that these three founders would not consider, and no end to the efforts they would take. For this opening show they borrowed works from near and far: from Helen Frick and the Carnegie Institute in Walker's native Pittsburgh; from Duncan Phillips, whose collection Kirstein had gotten to know on visits to Washington; from Samuel Lewisohn, one of Eddie Warburg's New York relatives; and from local sources like Paul Sachs.

The public was happy with the results of their pains. Twenty-five hundred people visited the rooms above the Coop during those first three weeks. A reviewer in the February 20, 1929, *Harvard Crimson* thought the new gallery was off to a good start: "The informal opening yesterday of the first exhibit by the Harvard Society for Contemporary Art showed a restraint which should do much to ensure the success of the new project. By avoiding the sort of sensationalism which shrieks like a spoiled child for attention, those in charge have ensured a tolerant attitude from the more conservative of their patrons without jeopardizing the interest of the more advanced." The Boston papers concurred. They gave extensive space to the show and reproduced some of the paintings—with the largest photos given to the Rockwell Kent.

One of the critics who applauded the American exhibition with the most enthusiasm was Alfred Barr. In the April issue of *Arts* magazine, Barr treated what Kirstein, Warburg, and Walker were doing as a sort of miracle. After discussing the paucity of recent art in the Boston area—and pointing out that "The Museum of Fine Arts has been no more encouraging to the modern than has her sister museum in New York"—he praised the Harvard students and a number of the individual works on view.

Barr also pointed out that not everyone agreed with such an evaluation. The *Boston Evening Transcript*'s Albert Franz Cochrane may not have lacerated the entire exhibition, but of the Hopper he wrote, "By what pretense can such buildings have a claim on art, which, theoretically at least, is synonymous with beauty? Why then dignify them by making them the subject of a painted canvas?" What mat-

THE · HARVARD
SOCIETY · FOR · CON
TEMPORARY · ART
INC · AN · EXHIBITION
OF · THE · SCHOOL
OF · PARIS · 1910
1928 · MARCH · 20
TO · APRIL · 12 · 1929
HARVARD · COOP
ERATIVE · BUILDING
ROOMS · 207-8 · 1400
MASSACHUSETTS
AVE · HARVARD · SQ
CAMBRIDGE · MASS

Cover of the exhibition brochure from "An Exhibition of the School of Paris 1910–1928." The Harvard Society for Contemporary Art, 1929.

tered to Barr was that in spite of such controversy "eleven hundred people visited the gallery during its first week." Here was proof that there was a place in the world for a public exhibition space devoted above all to contemporary art even if it might not be to everyone's liking and had not yet been put to the test of time.

Kirstein was disappointed that the opening exhibition had engendered so little controversy. He had hoped for a scandal, to create a "salon des refusés"—anything but the curse of mainstream acceptance in Boston's conservative newspapers. To get Alfred Barr's approval was one thing, but to be praised in bastions of tradition like the *Boston Herald* and the *Boston Globe*—where the show was applauded—felt like an insult. The effect of the second exhibition, however, was more satisfying. Called "School of Paris 1910–1928," it drew in hordes—some thirty-five hundred people visited during its March 20–April 12 stint—but the critics responded as if they were engaged in a contest in which the goal was to be as degrading as possible.

The artworks that invoked such wrath in the Boston newspapers violated prevailing American standards of restraint and decency. They were too sensuous, and indulged in an unacceptable emphasis on personal pleasure. Consider the paintings lent by the avant-garde collector Frank Crowninshield, editor in chief of *Vanity Fair*. Crowninshield had provided a Braque *Still Life,* nudes by Moise Kisling and Frans Masereel, de Segonzac's *Spring Landscape,* and two pieces of sculpture—Despiau's *Diana* and Maillol's *Standing Nude*. All of these works openly displayed the sort of earthly delights most of their Cambridge visitors either shunned or did not discuss. The Braque still life was probably even more startling than the various nudes. Its dense profusion of ripe quince and pears bulging with life made the simple act of eating fruit almost erotic. The abundance must have seemed like something out of a dream to those accustomed to college dining halls and Harvard's eating clubs. Looking at the rich, lyrical arrangement of exotic forms, viewers could momentarily bask in far greater luxuriance and ease than was their usual ken.

The painting suggested the lushness that France represented for many Americans at the time. Here was a palpable slice of the Paris that had lured A. J. Liebling, Henry Miller, Waverley Root, and others. For those used to Puritan leanness or the well-organized fruit bowls of American Primitive painting, this small canvas offered life on top of more life: pears at implausible angles, a floating goblet set in a sea of fabric patterns and furniture scrollwork. Stabilizing the composition was a thick green bottle of ruby red wine. Still full enough to suggest plenty, but with at least a glassful of wine gone, that bottle wasn't merely an object, but implied present delights. Those who weren't too intimidated to be put off by the new hazy vocabulary of this painting must have had difficulty looking at it and then returning to the dormitory or libraries. One would have longed for the shabbiest Parisian garret instead.

Even more foreign to the Cambridge viewers was de Chirico's *Twin Steeds,* lent by Frederick Clay Bartlett of Chicago. For a population whose idea of horses was of well-groomed creatures kept in neat, English-style wooden barns, here was a plumed white horse in front of the Ionic columns of a Greek portico, with broken temple fragments in the foreground and a rushing sea behind. Both horses' manes blew in the wind so that they resembled flames. To look at such a painting was to be forced to imagine and interpret, either to accept confusion or to consider the incomprehensible and unexpected. That stretch of the mind, of course, was just what Kirstein, Warburg, and Walker were hoping for.

The new art was not just different in style and subject matter. What distinguished it above all was its candor. That candor was about materials, about artistic technique, and about the human psyche. Crowninshield's Despiau bronze sculpture *Diana* was reproduced in *Town & Country* magazine in March 1929, precisely when it was being shown in the exhibition being held in Rooms 207 and 208 of the Harvard Cooperative Society Building. There was a brief text under the illustration. The piece was described as "unaffected and straightforward"—odd values for *Town & Country,* perhaps, but essential to the goals of the three young men at Harvard. The strength of Despiau's bronze was in its stripping away of artifice and getting to the underpinnings of existence without bothering with the periphery. The sculptor was quoted as referring to the need for "building a wall before decorating it" and as having said, "I do not attempt to do well . . . I attempt to do what I wish to do." To give such primacy to personal yearnings rather than outside judgments of quality was a radical and pioneering statement.

These Harvard students knew which private collections and commercial New York galleries to visit to find recent French art. The sources were limited, but offered good pickings. They borrowed major works by, in addition to the artists already cited, Bonnard, Raoul Dufy, Gris, Laurencin, Man Ray, Miró, Modigliani, Pascin, Rouault, Soutine, Vlaminck, and Brancusi. They also arranged an array of objects: Raoul Dufy ceramics and textiles, Lalique ashtrays, leather wallets and cigarette cases bearing the trademarks of Camel and Lucky Strike, a Lenoscier metal vase lent by John Nicholas Brown, and jewelry and silver from Saks. But even though this work was available, its appreciation was not widespread. The Brancusi and Miró elicited reference in the March 28, 1929, *Radcliffe Daily* to "the so-called 'Golden Bird,' an indeterminate brass shape which might have been called anything else just as well" and an "Abstraction Picture" of which the critic said, "You can have the same pleasure from wall paper or children's blocks." The March 22 *Boston Globe* announced that "it is certainly interesting to see what has come out of a movement which was started about 25 years ago in the spirit of a joke by Picasso in Paris," and proceeded to analyze the joke intended by each work. "Take that picture by Pierre Bonnard entitled 'Interior with a Boy.' Now, is that a boy or is it a girl? Perhaps that's the joke in the picture. Of course it may be an androgynous figure. Who knows?" The standards of the *Globe's* critic, A. J. Philpott, were the standards that Kirstein, Walker, and Warburg were up against daily—from their classmates and family members as well as the press. Philpott's sum total of observations on the Modigliani—"All of Amedeo Modigliani's women seem to have exceptionally long necks and noses"—was exactly the sort of crack Eddie Warburg's older brothers would have made less politely.

Constantin Brancusi's "indeterminate brass shape" or "misshapened vase"—as the *Saturday Evening Transcript* called it—was a polished bronze that had resulted from a meticulousness and eye for detail beyond the Boston critics' wildest imaginings. But its language was incomprehensible to the larger audience of 1929. Even worldly Harvard students and knowing professors could scarcely be expected to know what to make of this object. A photograph of *Golden Bird* in *The Hound & Horn* suggests how disturbing and alien a sight it must have been. In unprecedented form, the sculpture exerts ferocious intensity. Adding insult to injury, it is shown directly in front of the disarming Miró, the sculpture's bizarre profile centered against the canvas hanging a few feet behind it. Even to the most sophisticated observers, Miró's painting yields unclear meaning. Its forms relate to stars and spermatozoa—vaguely playful and organic, certainly joyous and high-spirited, but ambiguous. Seen together, the Miró and the Brancusi compound the assault. The Boston and Harvard audience in 1929 was used to frequent cushioning and softening of the edges, to doilies and service plates. Now forthright and startling forms were being shown to them, and in a way that, rather than mitigate their effect, hammered it in. The Miró has only simple wooden strips around it—the equivalent of no frame at all to eyes accustomed to gilded gesso and linen liners. It hangs from two chains. The Brancusi is on a three-part wooden base made of truncated pyramids with a bold sawtooth effect. The "bird" itself is a compact, utterly minimal, undulating ovoid.

But to those who could grasp it, this monumental and confrontational form was supremely gentle. The piece has a dazzling elegance. It represents the ultimate reductionism, a clear statement of how much can be said by how little. Almost thirty-eight inches high, it swells from a base circumference of three and three-quarter inches to one of twenty-one inches about two-thirds of the way up. Even to viewers sixty years later, accustomed to more radically unconventional modern sculpture, it is amazing that everything else rests on, and seems to grow from, that slim bit of tapered bronze underneath the mass. This is, in inert material, the same miracle as birds' legs.

The top of the "bird" is almost as slender as its foot, and there the undulating organic form has been incised, and a right-angled chunk removed. This very simple articulation suggests an open mouth. Either it is chirping rapturously or is about to swallow a worm. The image gains strength because we don't know precisely which of these activities it is. What matters is that the creature is doing something that is emphatically, joyously alive. And while the erect and regal shape does in fact suggest some sort of noble bird, it is of deliberately indeterminate species. Details matter less than essences. *Golden Bird* may refer to an owl or a falcon, but is simple and free-flowing.

Brancusi had photographed this same *Golden Bird* in his Paris studio. In his picture, the piece shines like a beacon or a miniature sun; the photographic light, reflected head-on in the broadest part of the torso, bounces the beams back almost blindingly. Below that light the piece presents a highly distorted reflection of the room. The mirroring—bright, dark, shadowy—is so intense that the overall form

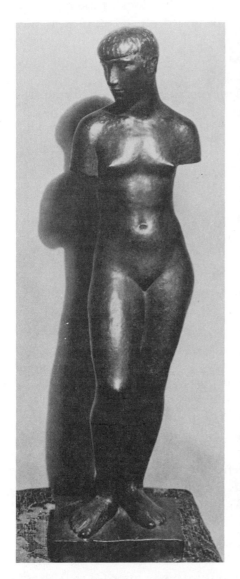 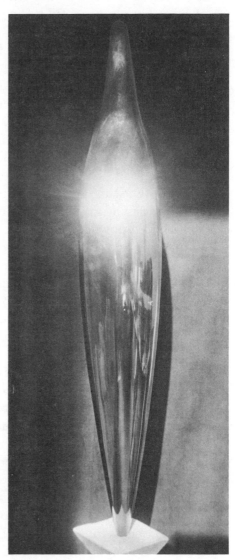

Left: Diana *by Despiau, from* Town & Country *magazine, 1929.*
Right: Brancusi, Golden Bird, *photograph by Brancusi.*

of the sculpture is illegible and becomes secondary to the process of reflection. The result is that *Golden Bird* has the look of the future or of something mythic. By being so simplified yet so complex, it was the essence of the new art and way of thinking. As such it might either instill terror or exhilarate. Kirstein, Walker, and Warburg were exhilarated.

A symbolic viewing of the *Golden Bird* is in keeping with the artist's intentions. Brancusi had been nurtured on the magical golden birds of Romanian folklore—kin to the Russian firebird—bright enough to light fires at midnight and able to cure illness or restore sight to the blind. With their glorious songs, they might even resurrect the dead. The golden bird is, physically and spiritually, a giver of light. To assure that effect, Brancusi had polished his bronze first with a series of gradated files, then with emery paper, and finally with buffing powder and jeweler's rouge—until all traces of his hand disappeared and the sheen took on maximal gloss. This left the bird as weightless and immaterial as it is solid. Rising as if from nothing, the sculpture is not just a guidepost, but a deity. Noble and majestic—yet at the same time able to reflect and hence welcome the surrounding universe—it embodied the healing magic that art might offer.

Lincoln Kirstein does not remember precisely how, as a junior at college, he got the idea of including the Brancusi in the Harvard Society show, but there are a couple of distinct possibilities. For one thing, it had belonged to John Quinn, the New York collector whose auction Kirstein had attended with his mother and who was one of his cultural heroes. Quinn had been a lively patron of both the literature and art of his time: a close friend of the Yeats family, Ezra Pound, T. S. Eliot, James Joyce, André Derain, Henri Matisse, Pablo Picasso, and Brancusi. He owned work by all of them, ranging from the manuscript for *Ulysses* to this and other casts of *Golden Bird*. Quinn had bought the piece directly from Brancusi in 1920, shortly after it had been made. He paid $960. Its buyer after Quinn's death was the Brummer Gallery, a major supporter of Brancusi in New York at that time, who in turn sold it in January 1927 to the Arts Club of Chicago. It was the Arts Club of Chicago that lent it to the Harvard Society. Since this was the only loan of the work from the time of its acquisition until 1934, the piece obviously was not in heavy demand.

It may have been Kirstein's interest in Quinn and his holdings that led him to track the work down. Kirstein had also most likely seen the two plates that reproduced the work in Ezra Pound's essay on Brancusi in the autumn 1921 issue of *The Little Review.* Kirstein, a great Pound enthusiast, included his work in *The Hound & Horn,* and probably read whatever he could find.

Ezra Pound's evaluation of the *Golden Bird* and of Brancusi's related work encompasses many of the abiding concerns, both conscious and unconscious, of the founders of the Harvard Society. For Pound this sculpture exemplified many of the key tenets of contemporary art. He saw it as demonstrating that "Every concept, every emotion presents itself to the vivid consciousness in some primary form." "Vivid consciousness"—a waking up—was central to Kirstein's and Warburg's search, if perhaps less to Walker's. They wanted to see reality and grapple with truth. Aesthetic and emotional frankness, whether in the form of diatribes or of humor, became their cause célèbre. Pound pointed out that "works of art attract by a resembling unlikeness." That break from traditional imitations of reality—and the striving for a new language that might get to the heart of the subject—were among the young men's imperatives.

Pound wrote that

> Brancusi's revolt against the rhetorical and the colossal has carried him into revolt against the monumental, or at least what appears to be, for the instant, a revolt against one sort of solidity.[27]

What Brancusi represented for Pound is on some levels what Brancusi represented for the Harvard Society founders; they too wanted to see notions of monumentality overturned. The *Golden Bird* provided clarification and rightness that offered an antidote to the hierarchies and morass—both visual and psychological—of the world they knew. For centuries sculpture had been statuary—representational whatever the style, and often allegorical. By proving that form alone could be beautiful to the point of being seductive, *Golden Bird* redefined the concept.

Ezra Pound also discussed what it meant to be part of Brancusi's audience:

> . . . the author of this imperfect exposure is compelled to move about in a world full of junk-shops, a world full of more than

idiotic ornamentations, a world where pictures are made for
museums, where no man has a front-door that he can bear to
look at, let alone one he can contemplate with reasonable pleasure, where the average house is each year made more hideous,
and where the sense of form which ought to be as general as
the sense of refreshment after a bath, or the pleasure of liquid
in time of drouth or any other clear animal pleasure, is the rare
possession of an "intellectual" (heaven help us) "aristocracy."

The young Harvard gentlemen were, whether they liked it or not,
members of such an aristocracy—privy to pleasures unavailable to
most people. Yet like Pound they deplored that position as part of an
elite, and hoped that the forms of beauty to which they were fortunate enough to be receptive would, through their exhibitions and the
ensuing reaction, penetrate to the lives of those surrounded by
Pound's "idiotic ornamentations." Whatever the ambience of their
childhoods, they willingly joined this battle against monumentality
in both architecture and language. They too deplored rhetoric. Their
challenge was to everything traditional. They would reconsider not
just aesthetics, but everyday conduct, and issues like the choice of a
profession. The Harvard Society shows were only the beginning of
their relentless support of unprecedented, and often painfully unpopular, notions of beauty.

I V

At the end of the 1920s, it was normal and predictable for modern
art to inspire ire. The Boston journalists represented and reinforced
the prevalent disapproval of avant-garde painting and sculpture. To
the public at large, art was supposed to represent good breeding, and
hence be refined, pretty, and psychologically unthreatening. This
wasn't a class issue. As Lewis Mumford had observed, most everyone believed that paintings and decoration had to conjure European
civilization at its apogee, reached centuries earlier. If rich people—
like Kirstein's, Warburg's, and Walker's families—surrounded themselves with the original artifacts of previous eras, the majority of
Americans could achieve a similar aesthetic with reproductions. The
pervasive preference was to see one's own reflection in Chippendale
mirrors, look at paintings of mythological scenes, and dine off plates

that provided a link, however tangential, with eighteenth-century French royalty.

Not that modernism hadn't already made its wicked appearance here and there. Kirstein, Warburg, and Walker were promulgating a taste that—while repugnant to the public at large—had already made slight inroads. In 1905, Alfred Stieglitz had opened the first of his several New York galleries where he showed John Marin, Charles Demuth, Georgia O'Keeffe, Arthur Dove, Marsden Hartley, and other contemporary painters. Their work represented an unprecedented antihistorical way of looking at things. So did the photography that Stieglitz advanced, with its dependence on current subject matter and technology. Most of the major critics attacked Stieglitz's efforts, but he had his supporters. Then, in 1913, the gates to modern European painting and sculpture had been further opened to Americans with the "International Exhibition of Modern Art" held at the Sixty-ninth Regiment Armory in New York. The crowds flocked in to see work by Cézanne, Van Gogh, Gauguin, Rousseau, Maillol, Bonnard, Vuillard, Laurencin, Derain, Matisse, Rouault, Picasso, Braque, Delaunay, Léger, Munch, Kandinsky, Kirchner, Lehmbruck, Brancusi, and Duchamp. Two hundred thirty-five paintings were sold; the new vision definitely had its proponents.

But what had drawn in the one hundred thousand visitors to the Armory Show was, above all, the venom of the press. The invective proved irresistible. What the influential painter and critic Kenyon Cox called an "insurrection against all custom and tradition" was something that people wanted to see. Even someone as erudite as the Washington collector and critic Duncan Phillips wrote at the end of 1913, "The cubists are simply ridiculous. Matisse is also poisonous."[28] What most people expected of art was the faithful and precise representation of nature. They demanded evidence of ancient standards for technical competence, and of traditional training. The new art was called insane, immoral, ugly, vulgar, destructive, incompetent, egoistic, violent, foreign, and bolshevistic. The Armory Show was parodied in New York with "The Freak Post-Impressionist" exhibition, in which well-known academic painters made paintings for various categories like "psychopathetic," "paretic," "neurotic," and "nutty." In Hartford, Connecticut, the Arts and Crafts Club mounted a "fake" Cubist and Futurist show. When the Armory Show went to Chicago, Matisse, Brancusi, and Walter Pach were burned in effigy. Boston scarcely deigned to give it any reaction at all for its third and final showing. The venue of the Armory Show at the Museum of Fine Arts was the only one to lose money; most of the public was too indifferent to bother to attend.

American taste had not altered significantly in the fifteen years between the Armory Show and the opening of the Harvard Society for Contemporary Art. The show had made its ripples, however. In 1915 the Modern Gallery, backed by the collector Walter Arensberg, opened in New York with an exhibition of Picabia, Picasso, and Braque. The Carnegie Institute began to mount its annual international exhibitions of the type that meant so much to John Walker when he was growing up. By the 1920s there were, periodically, exhibitions of modern art at the Pennsylvania Academy of Fine Arts and the Metropolitan Museum in New York. Commercial galleries for new European painting also began to sprout.

In the two decades preceding the Depression, a few daring collectors—often guided by painters—bought recent European painting. The Americans who patronized modernism while living abroad—Gertrude and Leo Stein, and the Cone sisters—at first had little effect in their native land, but others did. It was to some of these people that Kirstein, Walker, and Warburg were able to turn for loans.

Duncan Phillips was among those who lent work to many of the Harvard Society shows. He had been converted to the new art about ten years after the Armory Show; Phillips had done a complete turnaround on Cézanne and Van Gogh, and had modified his stance on Matisse. In the 1927 edition of his 1914 book, *The Enchantment of Art,* he revised, or totally changed, many of his original pronouncements. In 1921 Phillips and his wife Marjorie, a painter, had opened for the public two rooms of their large house in Washington near Dupont Circle. At first their collection mainly consisted of art from the same periods represented at the Fogg and the Boston Museum—major pieces by Chardin, Monet, Sisley, Renoir, Daumier, and Cézanne among the Europeans; Ryder, Whistler, Twachtman, and Hassam among the Americans. But by the end of the 1920s they also owned some more avant-garde paintings of the type that interested the Harvard Society, and were able to augment the shows above the Coop with key works like the "androgynous" Bonnard.

Then there was Samuel Lewisohn. In his house on Fifth Avenue in New York, Sam's father, Adolph, had filled the vast gallery with paintings by Courbet, Degas, Delacroix, Monet, and Renoir. Then, in the early 1920s, Sam and his wife—the former Margaret Seligman—moved in. Sam wanted the paintings to be part of everyday life, not just objects on exhibition. He had his favorite canvases taken upstairs to the dining room, which Margaret decorated in the latest style, with its walls covered in green metallic wallpaper. The family had made its fortune in copper mining, and Sam was able to expand and modernize the collection. At first he was puzzled by more recent art, but in little time he acquired some major Cézannes and Gauguins, Van Gogh's *L'Arlésienne,* two Picassos, a large Rousseau, and a major early version of Seurat's *La Grande Jatte.* He added the most current work by Braque, Derain, Matisse, Rouault, and Soutine.

It was easy for the Harvard Society founders to get in to see these things. The Lewisohns and Paul Sachs were all part of the same German-Jewish circle. Sachs's parents and Margaret's parents had large Victorian summer villas near each other in Elberon—"the Jewish Newport"—on the New Jersey coast. Moreover, Eddie Warburg was related to Margaret Lewisohn in two different ways. Margaret's aunt (her mother's sister), Nina Loeb Warburg, was married to Eddie's uncle, Paul Warburg, and was also the half sister of Eddie's maternal grandmother. In a world where family links counted considerably, this guaranteed the Harvard threesome not just entrée, but special consideration.

The Lewisohns' and the Warburgs' country houses in Westchester were near each other, and Margaret had been fascinated with Eddie when he would come over to play tennis. Unlike his siblings and parents, he was eager to look at paintings done more recently than the Renaissance. The Lewisohns not only had works by the major names of modernism, but also supported such interesting, little-known contemporaries as Maurice Sterne, who was like a court artist to their family. When Eddie Warburg and his friends asked the Lewisohns if they could borrow several Sternes and an O'Keeffe for the first show, and an important Derain portrait for one they put on a few months later, the loans were instantly forthcoming. That sort of small-world camaraderie is to a large degree what made their exhibitions possible.

In spite of what he owned, Sam Lewisohn was hardly an inspiration for Warburg. As a relative, he was an embarrassment—the cousin who makes you cringe when your friends meet him. He might have a few modern paintings, and one room in the latest style, but for the most part he was cut in the nineteenth-century robber baron style. Lewisohn was gruff and demanding, and imperious

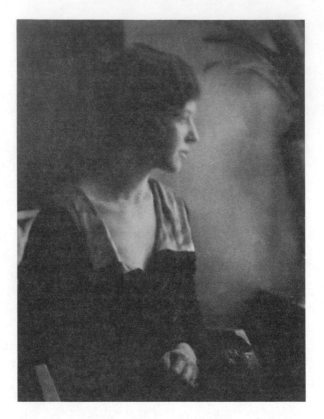

Margaret Lewisohn, c. 1925.

with the help. He treated gallery owners on Fifty-seventh Street like riffraff. His art hung in rooms darkened by wood paneling and velvets and brocades, and cluttered with baronial furniture. Lewisohn was physically unattractive: overweight and toadlike. Younger members of his family typically pictured him humorlessly having the butler pull off a glass jar in which he had gotten his plump hand stuck while trying to extract a peach. Everyone was much more taken with Margaret, a vivacious beauty with dazzling, huge, pale blue eyes, ever chic in her Valentinas. A brilliant hostess and loyal friend, she was so engaging and socially adept that Henry Luce, Walter Lippmann, and Arturo Toscanini would regularly pour their hearts out to her.

Even if Sam Lewisohn was socially uncouth, as a collector and later as a founding trustee at the Museum of Modern Art, he applied the same deep morality with which he and his father had developed a parole system for prisons. There was a story that on one occasion, after he had loudly lambasted a prominent New York dealer for his current show, Lewisohn insisted on paying a thousand dollars for a canvas that the dealer had in his back room—a work by the then unknown Jack Levine—even though the dealer was only asking seventy-five dollars for it. Lewisohn explained that it was far better than the work on exhibition, which was priced at the higher figure, and that the unknown artist needed the money more than the commercially successful one did. In a roman-à-clef written by Lewisohn's daughter Joan, the Lewisohn figure is quoted as saying, "There's more subtle politics and finagling in the art world than there is in Washington. Machiavelli's heirs in America have taken to the arts."[29] Sam Lewisohn and Maurice Sterne would discuss the nuances of Giorgione's style for hours. Lewisohn was always trying to develop his eye further. He wrote extensively, with original viewpoints, about the artists he believed in, ranging from Renoir to Rouault and the then recent Mexicans. He probed the issue of an American style. But he was too coarse, and cocksure, for most people to pay close attention. To most of his associates, he made the idea of the art of people like Rouault and Picasso seem all the more the domain of oddballs. When he bought Cézanne's *Uncle Dominique,* it seemed fitting to most of his acquaintances that this crazy character would be attracted to such muddy working of the palette knife. The passions of someone like Sam Lewisohn would not easily enter the mainstream.

Frank Crowninshield, on the other hand, scarcely could have been more polished or at ease with people. Of the established supporters of modern art in the generation preceding theirs, he was the one with whom the Harvard Society founders could most easily have a close and friendly dialogue. Occasionally Crowninshield took Lincoln Kirstein's advice about what to buy; he regularly lent artworks for the shows above the Coop; and, through his collection, he provided ideas for future exhibitions. Like other wealthy people of the era, the *Vanity Fair* editor dressed in style and surrounded himself with the best of everything, but—unlike many of his cohorts—he believed that "best" meant current, not antiquated. For that reason he greatly admired the pluck of the three students.

Known as Crownie, Francis Welch Crowninshield was part of the circle in which Eddie Warburg's brothers moved, and a favorite extra man at their New York dinner parties. Because Natica Nast—the daughter of Crowninshield's publisher, Condé Nast—was married to Eddie's brother Gerry, the Warburgs were like family to Crowninshield. But it was not only because of the social connections that he could be counted on to be sympathetic to what the Harvard Society was doing. For one thing, painting was in his blood; his father had been president of the Federation of American Painters. Moreover, unlike his father, he was deeply interested in the avant-garde, and eager to advance their cause. He had visited Picasso's Paris studio as early as 1907. He had been one of the organizers of the Armory Show. In his New York penthouse he had eighteen paintings by Segonzac, five Modiglianis, seven Pascins, thirty-six Despiau sculptures, something by virtually every other School of Paris painter, and large holdings of African art. In *Vanity Fair* he reproduced, often in first-rate color, paintings by Matisse, Picasso, Gauguin, Rouault, Braque, Modigliani, Rockwell Kent, and George Bellows, and photographs by Edward Steichen and Cecil Beaton.

Both at *Vanity Fair* and in his art collecting, Crowninshield followed the maxim with which he opened the rule book of the Coffee House, a club he had founded with Robert Benchley: "The first rule is that there are no rules." Fifteen years before the Harvard Society Executive Committee came knocking on his door, Crowninshield had written that one of his new magazine's main purposes was to wean writers "from their still unyielding ways and make them . . . a trifle more fluent, fantastic, or even absurd." Barriers were to be broken: "For women we intend to do something in a new and missionary spirit. . . . We dare to believe that they are, in their best moments, creatures of some cerebral activity; we even make bold to believe that it is they who are contributing what is most original, stimulating, and highly magnetized to the literature of our day, and we hereby announce ourselves as determined and bigoted feminists." True to this dictum, in 1917 he had published Gertrude Stein's Cubist poem "Have They Attacked Mary. He Giggled," and he had lured the copywriter Dorothy Rothschild (later Parker) from *Vogue;* her first caption for him, annotating six photographs of underwear, was "Brevity is the soul of lingerie, as the Petticoat said to the Chemise." He empathized with the Harvard students' wish to support unknown talent; in 1921 he had paid Noël Coward his first dollars for an essay, "Memoirs of Court Favourites," and he had also helped discover or bring to an American readership Max Beerbohm, André Gide, D. H. Lawrence, e. e. cummings, P. G. Wodehouse, Aldous

Huxley, Sherwood Anderson, and Colette. He was one of those people who traveled extensively, knew people who knew people, and always had his receptors open to the latest ideas.

Even when Crowninshield turned people down, he was the quintessential gentleman, with manners of the type the well-brought-up Harvard students greatly admired. Returning a manuscript to Paul Gallico, he wrote, "My dear boy, this is superb! A little masterpiece! What color! What life! How beautifully you have phrased it all! A veritable gem!—Why don't you take it around to *Harper's Bazaar*?"[30] But he appears never to have turned down the Harvard Society's Executive Committee—for loans that today would be unthinkable without an armed guard. Kirstein, Warburg, and Walker had the sort of style and flair Crowninshield always championed.

Coached by Walt Kuhn that modern art was worth looking at and was a good investment, John Quinn had built up remarkable holdings, and by realizing $700,000 the 1926–27 Quinn auctions had demonstrated to a number of people besides collectors like Lewisohn and Crowninshield that this new art had some merits after all. By collecting Augustus John, Jack Yeats, Cézanne, Seurat, Picasso, Rousseau, and the American modernists, Quinn had started a trend. By the late 1920s, America had a small and serious group of collectors of modern art, and however bizarre the larger public may have considered them, many were willing to make their holdings available to the Harvard Society for Contemporary Art. At that time, after all, these paintings were not blue-chip commodities; they were still risky statements in need of approval. Others who frequently lent were Lillie P. Bliss and Mary Hoyt Wiborg of New York, John T. Spaulding of Boston, Frederick Clay Bartlett of Chicago, and Chester Dale of Washington. So did Paul Sachs, as well as the most adventurous New York galleries.

Beyond those with whom Kirstein, Walker, and Warburg had established connections, there were other significant collectors interested in advancing public awareness of modernism. Under the tutelage of the artist William Glackens, the Philadelphia inventor Albert Barnes was acquiring work by Cézanne, Renoir, Matisse, and Picasso. In 1925 Dr. Barnes had formed a foundation—albeit one to which access at first was virtually impossible—for his collection. Another organization promoting the cause of modern painting was A. E. Gallatin's Gallery of Living Art at the Manhattan branch of

New York University on the first floor of One Hundred Washington Square East. Gallatin, a descendant of Thomas Jefferson's secretary of the treasury, was a lawyer by training who had turned himself over to art. Not only did he collect, but he painted, wrote about art, and took excellent studio portrait photographs of contemporary French painters. His Gallery of Living Art was open free of charge at hours that today would boggle any museum director's imagination: Monday to Friday 8 a.m. to 10 p.m., and Saturdays 8 a.m. to 5 p.m. What it showed was Gallatin's own collection: a fine Arp relief, important Cubist Braques and still lifes from the 1920s, a Brancusi drawing of Mme. Pogany, two Cézanne watercolors, a Derain portrait of Matisse, and paintings by de Chirico, Juan Gris, Hélion, Klee, Matisse, Soutine, Utrillo, Vlaminck, and—among the Americans—Demuth, Marsden Hartley, John Marin, and Charles Sheeler. It really was living art. Major Légers exalted the industrial world. Two free-flowing André Massons suggested the unconscious. Miró's 1926 *Dog Baying at the Moon* seemed like a beautiful dream awaiting Freudian analysis—with its fiery semicosmic creature, magical moon, and ambiguous ladder set dramatically against a handsome earthy brown and midnight black. There was an abstract Mondrian, and six important Picasso oils along with numerous works on paper covering a range of his phases from 1906 to 1930.

But although Gallatin's institution was technically for the public and was meant to serve a real role, and although he had marvelous paintings, he lacked the essential ability to communicate their merits to those not so fortunate in their ability to see. He did not reach the general audience with his gallery, in large part because the only way in which he varied the exhibition was by buying another picture. It would take the Harvard Society for Contemporary Art to go beyond one collector's vision and reveal the scope of the current scene.

Another key proponent of some elements of contemporary art was Katherine Sophie Dreier. She was an autocratic evangelist of modernism who crusaded for the new painting much as she championed women's suffrage and their labor laws and trade unionism. Born in 1877, Dreier was one of the great cultural pioneers of her generation. Having started out as both a painter and a social reformer—she was an early director of the Manhattan Trade School for Girls and one of the founders of the Little Italy Settlement House—she had then turned her sights primarily to painting. In 1911 she married the painter Edward Trumbull-Smith, although the match was short-lived once it was discovered that he already had a

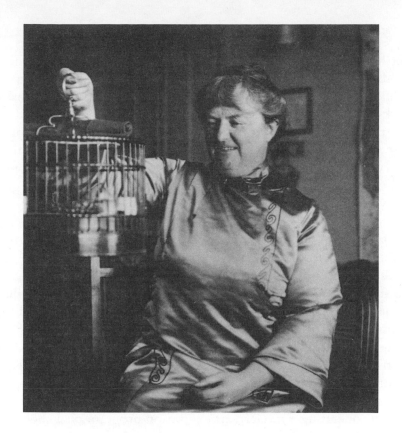

Katherine Dreier, 1922.

wife and children. By that time she had gotten to know Gertrude and Leo Stein in Paris, and John Singer Sargent in London. Then, in 1913, came the Armory Show, in which one of Dreier's still lifes was exhibited. Her commitment to modern art was clinched. In 1914 she founded the Cooperative Mural Workshops, and in 1916 she helped create, along with Walter Arensberg, the Society of Independent Artists, an organization that sponsored large annual exhibitions and through which she met Marcel Duchamp, whose *Nude Descending a Staircase* had caused such a stir at the Armory Show. Duchamp became Dreier's great friend and adviser, and she began to acquire his work. With Duchamp and Man Ray, she established the Société Anonyme, Inc.: Museum of Modern Art 1920. (Having inadvertently borrowed part of that name, the institution now known as the Museum of Modern Art had to issue her a major apology ten years later.) Dreier was the Société Anonyme's main voice. She gave its lectures, organized its exhibitions, and acquired its collection. This sent her to the Bauhaus, where she had a particular admiration for Kandinsky. It also led her to establish a major collection of art that included—in addition to Duchamp's, Man Ray's, and Kandinsky's work—key pieces by Franz Marc, Klee, Naum Gabo, Mondrian, Léger, Brancusi, and Miró, and to finance major exhibitions of the new art. The first Société Anonyme show opened in 1921 at the Worcester Art Museum; from then on, the collection traveled a great deal. But it was primarily a single person's collection, not a program to reveal a full range of new artistic developments.

What distinguished the Harvard Society for Contemporary Art from all these other forays into recent art was that it was concerned with the diverse strains of modernism, not just with one individual's taste, and it had nothing to do with a private collection. Dreier, Phillips, Barnes, and Gallatin were wealthy individuals who had made the acquisition of art virtually their profession. Their wish to share their holdings and awaken the larger public had grown out of their assuming the roles of modern Medicis. Kirstein, Warburg, and Walker, on the other hand, may have come from moneyed families and on occasion bought this or that object, but they were above all college students operating a modern art exhibition program on a shoestring budget. They wanted to present everything that was going on, not to show what they owned or even necessarily what they liked. They would venture into the most avant of the avant-garde; the point was to let the new voices be heard.

V

The network of collectors to whom the Executive Committee had access made it relatively easy for them to schedule one good show after another. Today it would cost a thousand dollars to ship or insure just one of their chosen artworks from New York to Boston and back again—more if a courier required a decent hotel. The paperwork could take days. But in 1929 instead of a detailed loan agreement, facilities report, and insurance certificate there was a handshake over a martini provided by a collector's bootlegger. The owners of the more pioneering commercial galleries in New York— Valentine, Kraushaar, Downtown, Reinhardt, John Becker, and Weyhe—were equally gracious. They were delighted by what the young founders of the Harvard Society for Contemporary Art were doing. Here was an avenue to their future collectors. Besides, these galleries wanted their work shown in any reliable place that would have it. All that was needed was for the students to manage to collect it. The Fogg might arrange shipping via Railway Express; alternatively, Kirstein, Warburg, or Walker would load the paintings or sculptures into the trunk of Warburg's coupe and motor them northward on the Post Road. The costs were minimal. The total expense for the second show, for example, was $415.24, easy to cover by the intake of subscription fees.

The third Harvard Society exhibition was a bit like the catching of one's breath between full-speed sprints. Held in early May, this was a solo show of pictures by Maurice Prendergast: competent, graceful, and noncontroversial. Duncan Phillips, the Kraushaar Galleries in New York, and Prendergast's heirs lent the majority of work. Lillie P. Bliss, one of the New York collectors who a few months later would help incorporate the Museum of Modern Art, also provided a painting. The short essay in the Harvard Society flyer was, for the first time, signed, which meant that it was not by Kirstein; its author, rather, was the distinguished scholar and art historian Walter Pach. Credentials were high and the challenges minimal; the Boston papers once again, as with the society's opening American show, voiced approval. This was a lot easier for Boston to take than the European exhibition had been.

The following show, however, drew gasps even from the society's staunchest defenders. Duncan Phillips and Frank Crowninshield had little problem with Modigliani and Brancusi, but never before could even they have imagined the likes of what the Harvard boys were up to now. Called "4D," it was devoted to the designs of a young man called Richard B. Fuller—known later as R. Buckminster Fuller. "4D" was a reference to the fourth dimension, since Fuller's designing method was from the inside out. The structure that demonstrated that method was called "the Dymaxion House," its name a combination of "dynamic" and "maximum."

On May 17, 1929, the Executive Committee sent out an invitation letter as fearless as it was polite. "This house, built like a tree, with inflatable floors and doors, can be sold for five hundred dollars a ton on a mass production basis. . . . We would greatly appreciate your telling whomever else you think would be interested, and bringing them here to the rooms." By the time the show opened on May 20, they had produced their largest flyer to date to tell the details. On bright lemon yellow paper, the text, set in bold sans-serif type and printed in gaudy valentine red, announced:

A cardboard prototype of this marauder-free, selfishness-resistant structure was installed in one of the rooms above the Coop. Its shape was hexagonal—a form indigenous to nature (and for which Fuller offered copious explanations) and found in honeycombs. It was built out and suspended from a mast according to the same principle of tension used in a suspension bridge. Its sides and ceilings were made of two layers of translucent casein, a fibrous material composed of vegetable refuse. This casein came in hollow triangular modules in which the partial vacuum between the layers served as insulation; these modules were held in place by rubber tubing, which, when filled with compressed air, would tighten to make the enclosure air-tight and of high tensile strength. The large windows were unbreakable glass, the framework duralumin. The floors were inflatable rubberoid units intended to cushion young children. The doors were made of silver balloon silk—suitable because it was both inflatable and dustproof. To close the door, you pressed a button that inflated it; to open it, you pressed one that deflated it. The beds and divans were also inflatable silk.

All the air for the house came in through the top and was drawn out at the bottom "through imperceptible suction." A diesel engine was suspended from the top of the mast to assist in this ventilation and also provide heating and lighting; further illumination was achieved by a system of mirrors and the translucency of the casein walls. The literature accompanying the model explained that to enter a full-scale version of this house you would go through an elevator in the mast. Underneath the neatly suspended structure there was room to store a small airplane.

The red-and-yellow brochure gave further explanation:

> The 4D house casts away the cubical units of contemporary housing, and learning from the strength of crystals, and principles of dynamics, establishes the hexagon as a simplest and strongest unit. . . . The attempt here is to raise architecture from the one tune music box of "frozen architecture," to the infinity of harmony arrived at as in Music today, by conversion from the personal equation to the abstract eternity, via a truthful and standard machine.

For five days, Fuller gave three lectures—morning, noon, and night—promulgating these theories.

Buckminster Fuller with model of his Dymaxion House, photograph in the Boston Globe, *May 20, 1929.*

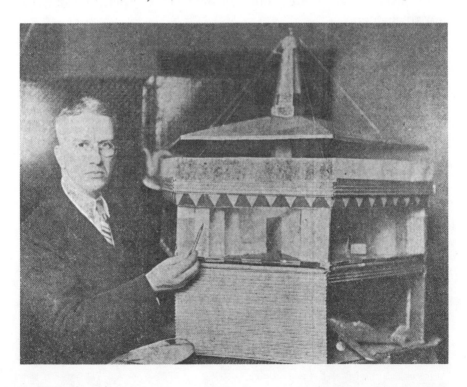

The intention of Fuller's design was to provide the "Best for All," "with no compromise to vanity." It wasn't the first time that members of Kirstein's, Warburg's, and Walker's families had considered the concept of "best for all." In the 1920 presidential election, Walker's grandfather, all of whose peers were staunch Republicans, had voted for Eugene Debs, the Socialist. The senior Mr. Walker explained that, since Debs was unjustly serving a jail term, the only way to get him out was to elect him to the White House. This elegant retiree—at age thirty he had given up work to spend more time reading, fishing, and gardening, while living off his stocks and bonds—delighted in shocking his contemporaries. He insisted on eating only two meals a day; having decided that they should be breakfast and lunch, he adapted a routine that consisted of going to bed at seven every evening and rising at three—in part to minimize the time he spent with his wife. The vote for Debs may have been based more on a deliberate wish to be eccentric than on true social commitment, but whatever the motives behind it, it reflected awareness of the unprivileged. The Warburgs and the Kirsteins, immersed as they were in luxury and good living, had certainly brought up their children to be conscious of helping those less fortunate than themselves. So to all three young men, the idea of mass housing was not an alien one.

But Fuller's ideas went well beyond the acceptable realm of noblesse oblige. They addressed the issue of the greatest good for the greatest number with considerable force. This might not really have suited the senior Walkers, Warburgs, and Kirsteins so well. It did not trouble the young men, however. To make more money than their parents had, or to hoard their inheritances, never seems to have mattered to any of them. They did not skimp on summer travel or in occasionally sprucing up their wardrobes, but neither did they believe in living too high. They saw art and architecture not as the prerogative of the rich, but as something that might potentially benefit larger, and needier, audiences. Such thinking was consistent, to varying degrees, with the social consciousnesses of their parents, but now the benevolence had taken a new form.

To make "no compromise to vanity"—as Bucky Fuller suggested—would be to repudiate every notion of the visual embellishment of life with which the three young men had grown up. Eddie Warburg's mother, for example, at times devoted herself to the acquisition of clothing, jewelry, and household furnishings as if it were her profession. She and the woman who was both her sister-in-law and half aunt, Nina Warburg, were regulars at Cartier's. Belonging to large families, they bought gifts for every relative for every occasion—birthdays, wedding anniversaries, anniversaries of first meeting—and amassed a reassuring clutter of little bibelots, inscribed silver tea caddies, and boxes full of commemorative jewelry. Not that Eddie Warburg or John Walker or Lincoln Kirstein chose to live in a Dymaxion House, but even to promote such an idea was an act of rebellion.

Part of what was so shocking was Fuller's approach to materials. "The standard architectural precept," he said, is that

> the material at hand should control the design; puddingstone houses for Massachusetts, and limestone for Illinois. The machine age says "we can think consciously only in the terms of experience, and every experience involves a material." Therefore if we think in the best terms of experience, a material will always be found for each requirement of the new composition. This is harnessed—not worshipped materialism—true mind over matter—on the road from the complete, stony, compressive darkness of selfish materialism to the infinity of lightful, abstract, harmonic unselfishness.

One cannot be certain how much the three young men pictured the paneled salons of their childhoods as "worshipped materialism" with "compressive darkness," but there is no doubt that in the furnishings of their new exhibition rooms as in their very souls they were seeking a "lightful, abstract, harmonic unselfishness." Visually and psychologically, they craved change. Fuller's ideas suggested that instead of being subject to the dictates of our natural surroundings, we can take control, find what suits us, and call attention to our genuine needs. This attempt both to take charge and to consider everything—as opposed to automatic acquiescence to a preexisting situation, physical or emotional—mattered greatly to the three young men.

Surprisingly, the press was lenient on the subject of Fuller and the Dymaxion House. Commentators stressed first of all—as if it gave the project legitimacy—that Fuller's family had gone to Harvard for generations. Few writers could resist the sheer novelty of his undertaking. The May 20, 1929, *Boston Globe* summed up its lengthy account of these extraordinary developments at the Harvard Society for Contemporary Art with the observation:

> All this and much more sounds freakish. Yet Mr. Fuller is no crank. He is an accomplished engineer. He has served in the Navy and is sane enough to have been entrusted by Uncle Sam. Henry Ford he considers the greatest living artist and, he says, he has done, in evolving his radical theory on housing, just what Mr. Ford did to the automobile.

Long, detailed reports of what the three undergraduates had wrought at Harvard appeared in all the major Boston and New York papers; the events were even considered newsworthy enough to be picked up by the *International Herald* published in Paris.

The Dymaxion show also attracted a new audience for the society. One young man who felt its lure was Philip Johnson, a classmate of Kirstein's, Warburg's, and Walker's. Johnson had not even met the members of the Executive Committee; he had started Harvard three years ahead of them, and had only recently returned to join their class after a nervous breakdown that had caused him to take a considerable period of time off. His major was philosophy, his minor Greek; he never studied art history or got near the Fogg. But he had quite a bit in common with the committee members. Johnson had also been brought up surrounded by an abundance of traditional art. In the family's large, four-story late-nineteenth-century Gothic house on the outskirts of Cleveland, Ohio, Johnson's mother used to show him and his sisters lantern slides of Italian paintings, especially by the Sienese. He too had made a pivotal visit to Chartres with his mother, in 1919 when he was thirteen (Kirstein had been twelve when his mother took him there), an event that he much later called one of the three great architectural experiences of his lifetime, along with trips to the Parthenon and the Ryoanji Temple in Kyoto. In his room at Harvard, Johnson had hung reproductions of work by Simone Martini and Piero della Francesca. But although his sister, a Wellesley student, had recently introduced him to Alfred Barr, Johnson had not encountered the Harvard Society fellows; he simply stopped in to see the Dymaxion exhibition because it was there, and it was new and exciting.

Johnson had a vested interest in Fuller's use of new materials akin

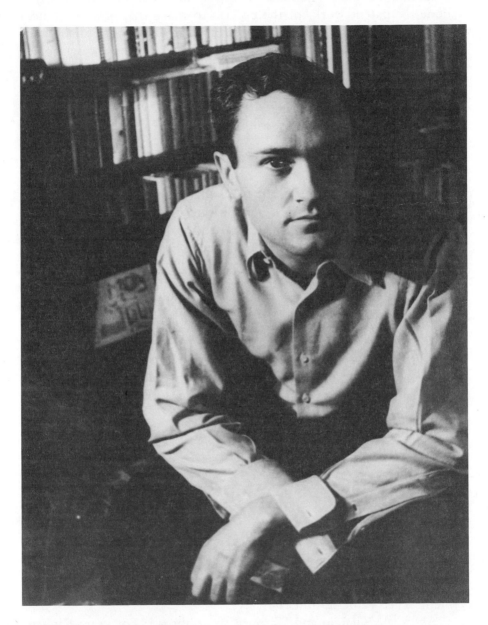

Philip Johnson, photographed by Carl Van Vechten, c. 1932.

to aluminum. Homer Johnson, Philip's father, was a lawyer who had
done the patent work for the process to make that new substance,
and had taken his legal fees in the form of stock in the company that
was to become Alcoa. In 1926, Homer had turned those stock shares
over to Philip, so that his son could have them before they became
encumbered with estate taxes. But whether or not it was financial
concern that drew Philip Johnson in to Fuller's exhibition, it made
"an indelible impression" on him. "That Dymaxion House, I dis-
liked it very much, but that made no difference. You see the point is
. . . that [from it] I learned vast amounts of the potentialities of architecture that I never forgot—from *that* show, not the many shows
that we gave Bucky later, but from that show." (The reference to
"that we gave Bucky later" refers to Johnson's years at the Museum
of Modern Art.) He may have heartily challenged the specifics of
Fuller's design, but equally strongly he admired its startling willingness to try the unprecedented, to kick aside tradition and habit. He
relished the use of new materials and was fascinated by the methods
of construction. He also loved the side of Buckminster Fuller that
would refer to "marauders" rather than mere robbers or thieves.
"You see what people never realized about Bucky, he was a poet with
an Emersonian, Thoreauvian grasp of the English language. He was
a word man, and a delicious one. That poetic presence is what left
the biggest impression on me."[31] To impress other young minds—
especially of those people who might change the look of America—
was what Kirstein, Warburg, and Walker had been hoping to do.

VI

The Dymaxion House was followed by a traveling show of books
and illustrations from modern German presses that had been at the
Grolier Society in New York. After that came art by Harvard graduates, a diplomatic gesture scheduled to coincide with commencement. Then came summer holidays.

As usual, Kirstein and Warburg went abroad. For years Kirstein
had spent those holiday junkets mostly in London. In the summer of
1929, this meant that he could regularly attend performances of
Serge Diaghilev's Ballets Russes. On several occasions, his companion in the audience was Agnes Mongan.

Mongan was spending the summer abroad with her younger sister Elizabeth, also an art historian. Kirstein liked to pass lots of time idling in bookstores and studying shop windows, and during one of his midday browsings, he had encountered her. Neither had realized that the other was in London at that moment. They saw a fair bit of each other at Harvard, but were not close companions; their main link was the friendship with Eddie Warburg. But even if he did not know Sachs's assistant well, Kirstein was delighted to see her; here was someone he might initiate into the thrills of Diaghilev. When he asked her to go to the Ballets Russes with him, she made it clear that she had no idea what this was all about. But she liked the idea of anything new, especially when it was an art form that excited a friend. Besides, as a Degas enthusiast, she always enjoyed the ballet. And so they made the date to go to Covent Garden together.

Kirstein would describe the performance he and Mongan attended in *Flesh is Heir,* a novel he published in 1932. Roger Baum is the Kirstein-like character; Christine Forrester is partially based on Agnes Mongan. When Roger is trying to explain to Christine the idea of this ballet, she asks if Diaghilev is nice. "Nice. I don't know him. I wish I did. Some people call him the wickedest man in Europe." [32]

In the reader's imagination, "wicked" is uttered with more delight than opprobrium. What mattered to Kirstein was Diaghilev's intensity, and the excitement he could provide; anything was better than being humdrum and ordinary, or repressed. Roger Baum tells Christine Forrester about the dancer Nijinsky having "lost his mind." [33] To be mad or evil is complicated, but also thrilling—a way of being more alive. Vitality is what Kirstein and Mongan, like Eddie Warburg, were seeking wherever they could find it. For Kirstein it was in the leaps of the Russian dancers. For Mongan it was in the quick, impromptu sketches of Renaissance masters. For Warburg it was in the energy of Kirstein and, that same summer, in a painting by Picasso. Kirstein's Diaghilev brought a Byzantine, almost hysterical, style to a culture that generally prized tamer modes. Mongan's beloved drawings belonged to the phase of artists' work before they imposed the usual guidelines for balance and order. Warburg's Picasso would, according to the standards by which he was raised, be crude and bumbling. But it was not customary good taste, or rationality, to which these people gravitated. They longed for extremes of feelings: the high moments, sometimes rough, sometimes refined, always ultimate. What counted was to do the unprecedented beautifully.

What captivates Kirstein's Roger Baum is what would move Kirstein in ballet forever after:

> Their thrilling dances then gave me a sharp pang of yearning to get a closer view of things immeasurable and unattainable, such as no poem of Heine's, no prose of Poe's, no fever dream has ever given me, and, since, I have had the same sensation, at once subconscious and acute, which I attribute to the silent and nebulous precision of all they do.[34]

Roger adores the veritable violence of the motion. He is captivated by the hops and leaps and twirls, the sequence of kicks and thrusting limbs. The dancers are described as "fierce and passionate," with "a Mongolian savagery." They revolve and sway and stamp, in "a maelstrom."[35]

The highlights of the performances that Kirstein and Mongan saw together that season at Covent Garden were ballets choreographed by twenty-five-year-old George Balanchine—Balanchivadze, before Diaghilev rechristened him. One of these ballets was *Apollon Musagète*. The music was Igor Stravinsky's, the sets André Bauchant's. Coco Chanel, a friend of Diaghilev's, had designed the tunics that were much shorter in the back than the front. Serge Lifar danced the part of Apollo. The vibrant sounds and sights were different from anything that had ever been heard or seen before.

Then there was *The Prodigal Son,* a new production that season. Here the music was Serge Prokofiev's, the costumes and sets by Georges Rouault. Better than any contemporary newspaper account of Balanchine's choreography is the description in *Flesh is Heir:* "The gestures flowed smoothly and richly into one another like honey into a jar."[36] Again Serge Lifar danced the leading role, with what *The Times* (of London) called "a Blake-like intensity of gesture and expression,"[37] hence conjuring one of Kirstein's favorite artists. For Kirstein, whose artistic heroes were Blake and El Greco, the electric force was irresistible. Balanchine's ballets for Diaghilev transformed everyday reality.

Surprising as they were, the movements, sets, costumes, and music were all grounded in tradition. Balanchine's choreography was strikingly original, yet based on classical steps and movements;

viewing a rehearsal of the production, Diaghilev had been heard to say to André Derain that Balanchine's work was "magnificent. It is pure classicism."[38] Real skill and a craftsperson's sense of discipline were at the core. Everyone knew what he or she was doing, and knew it well. These ballets expanded the boundaries of experience, but there were still boundaries. The radical newness was accompanied by a keen sense of judgment in the interest of achieving grace and beauty.

To be the audience at such an event—and later to be its patron— was to feel empowered. Roger Baum is almost as excited by the other spectators at Covent Garden as by what he sees on the stage. They are like a society of cognoscenti, an exclusive community that shares inroads of knowledge. The narrative in *Flesh is Heir* expounds on their fever pitch: "Sometimes there was a pause in the music and the dancers paused, but the audience never rested for a second, for the gaps in the action were as rich in texture, in feeling as the highest leaps or most sinuous glides."[39] Even the moments of repose have a charge to them.

As for Agnes Mongan—or Kirstein's Christine Forrester—she watches the ballet "like a very happy child." To have such childlike intensity and pleasure was a great achievement: the sort of pure, uncluttered, immediate response that new art forms might provide.

Roger Baum notes that ballet brings together various art forms at once. Diaghilev presents what is most exciting in painting and music as well as in dance. Moreover, he can survive, in fact flourish, on a shoestring budget. The views that Kirstein put in the mouth of his fictional hero were prescient of what would motivate him, and Eddie Warburg, for years to come.

With his admiration for undulating, keyed-up form, Lincoln Kirstein had decided to make El Greco the subject of his senior dissertation. In preparation, he spent August of 1929 retracing the painter's steps from Venice to Rome. In Venice, he again ran into Agnes Mongan. Having written about El Greco in her course with Georgiana King, she was now considering the training which the Greek had received from Tintoretto in Venice. In particular she was looking for the source of El Greco's way of rendering his subjects' eyes so that they seemed to "look beyond this world to another."[40] She believed that the answer was to be found in the painter's early training. El Greco had also worked in the shops of Cretan icon painters; Mongan felt that this was where he had acquired the Byzantine line that led to the elongation of his figures. This was a point on which she and Kirstein differed. Kirstein felt that myopia or astigmatism was the reason for the shape of El Greco's figures. They hoped to resolve this matter by seeing the art at which El Greco had looked in church. So on one blazing hot day, Mongan and her sister Betty and Kirstein went together to the Church of San Giorgio dei Greci, where they assumed their subject to have worshiped.

Approaching San Giorgio, the three art enthusiasts had a surprise. A basso was chanting a service of mourning. Moored on the usually tranquil Rio dei Greci in front of the church was a black gondola with gilded winged angels and a large black catafalque—the sort of structure used for the public exhibition of bodily remains. A red cross was atop the catafalque. There were other gondolas as well—some full of flowers—all part of a funeral cortege that had just made its way "over a green carpet of boughs, twigs, and leaves" strewn there by a violent thunderstorm the night before.[41] The gondoliers were all dressed in black with red sashes. Inside the church the Mongan sisters and Kirstein saw men clad in elaborate uniforms and cocked hats, all black trimmed with gold braid. The mourners included three extremely stylish women dressed entirely in white. In front of the dazzling apse, thick with icons and gold-and-red mosaics, there was a coffin surrounded by an enormous mass of flowers. The Mongans and Kirstein assumed this to be the funeral of a Venetian prince. Agnes Mongan's touch of Boston propriety won out over Kirstein's curiosity, and she persuaded him to leave. Part of her role for her rebellious friends was that she might counsel them not to do things like crash a funeral.

The following day, August 24, the threesome decided to take a train to Padua, where they would hire a car and driver and go in search of a lost Veronese fresco. Kirstein bought the *Paris Herald* for the trip. Reading it on the train, he suddenly screamed. The paper announced that Serge Diaghilev had died in Venice on the nineteenth. Only ten days earlier, Diaghilev had arrived at the Grand Hotel des Bains de Mer on the Lido. One of his favorite places to rest, it was the same hotel where, in the ballroom seventeen years earlier, Stravinsky had played to him the beginning of *The Rite of Spring*. There Diaghilev had taken ill. The doctors had at first thought he was suffering from rheumatism. Serge Lifar, who shared his room, had taken care of him. Diaghilev had summoned his friend and backer Misia Sert, and she and Coco Chanel, who had been cruising on the Duke of Westminster's yacht, had constantly been at the ballet impresario's bedside. What no one realized, until it was too late, was that he was afflicted by irreversible blood poisoning. The funeral into which Kirstein and the Mongans had stumbled on August 23 in the Greek church had been Serge Diaghilev's.

The three women in white had been Misia Sert, the Baroness Catherine d'Erlanger, and Coco Chanel. When Sert and Chanel had visited Diaghilev and his fever had been 105, he had exclaimed deliriously, "Oh, comme je suis heureux! How well white suits you, Misia, who must always wear it![42]. . . Promise that you will always wear white."[43] Diaghilev had repeatedly told his secretary Boris Kochno that Chanel and Sert were "so young" and "so white"[44] when they visited; the mandate for their attire at the burial was clear.

Diaghilev's funeral cortege in Venice, 1929.

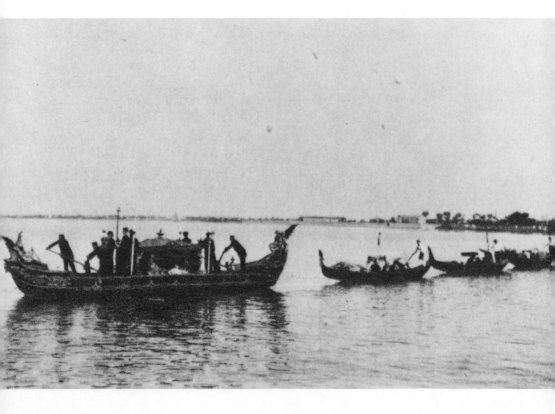

Accounts differ as to whether it was Chanel or Sert who paid for those final rites, but what is certain is that the Ballets Russes was heavily in debt at the time, that one of those two women in white footed the bill, and that the remaining member of the trio—the Baroness d'Erlanger—had organized the ceremony. Not that any of this background was known to Kirstein or the Mongans—or to the writer of the account in the *Paris Herald*. All they knew was that they had rarely seen an event of such magic. Nor could they have imagined a ceremony so different from their usual ken. Funerals in Boston looked nothing like this.

After they got off the train in Padua, Kirstein and the Mongans hired a car and driver to take them back along the Brenta in the direction of Venice. They were lucky in their choice of driver. He knew that the undiscovered Veronese was in the very last Palladian house along the river before they would reach Venice itself—the Villa Foscari, known as "La Malcontenta." This time Agnes Mongan had no qualms about whether they had the right to be there. She was willing to hazard the stop at the villa because she was carrying the document she called her "Dago Dazzler." Bearing the gold stamp of Harvard, this official piece of paper identified its bearer as a worthy and accredited scholar of art history who should be permitted to see any and all artworks, whether they were sequestered in private houses or locked in minor chapels. She presented the document to the doorman at the Malcontenta. He, in turn, disappeared to give it to the owner of the villa, Alberto Landsberg, who was upstairs. Landsberg descended and invited the young Harvard woman and her companions to enter. He obligingly led them into a large, barrel-vaulted hall with whitewashed walls. After staring for a few moments, the Mongans and Kirstein realized that in a few places some of the distemper had been removed, and massive, armored figures were visible. Their host explained that these were the frescoes. In fact they were primarily by Zelotti, Veronese's master, but Veronese may have worked on them. Landsberg said that his efforts to uncover the paintings were slow and laborious, but that he intended to chip away.

Talking with the three students, Landsberg suddenly became quite tense. He nervously announced that friends were coming to tea. The Mongans and Kirstein began to make their farewells. But before they were out of the great room, they caught sight of the arriving visitors. The men were all in black, the women in either black or white. Kirstein recognized the face of the dancer who had been "the prodigal son" in front of the Rouaults at Covent Garden; here in a villa on the Brenta was Serge Lifar. Following Lifar was the rest of the Ballets Russes troupe, the same people they had seen the day before mourning Diaghilev at San Giorgio dei Greci. The owner of the villa with Zelotti's frescoes was in fact an old friend of the great master of the Ballets Russes.

Alarmed, Kirstein blurted to Agnes Mongan, "We've got to get out of here! We've got to get out of here!"[45] She did not understand why, but this was more than he could cope with, and he was desperate to leave. Without good-byes or thanks, the three of them fled out the back door. It seemed like an ending; Kirstein felt with horror that the ballet which he so adored was dead forever. But the way that fate had drawn together the Russian ballet and the young Americans twice in two days was a beginning.

Serge Lifar.

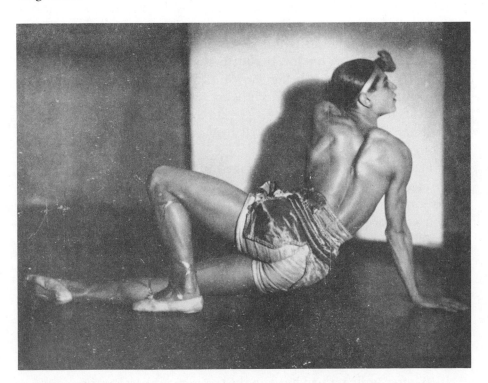

VII

Eddie Warburg was focused above all on painting that same summer when Kirstein and Mongan were on the trail of the Ballets Russes. Eddie's vacation routine was to tour museums and visit his uncle Aby, his other two uncles, and additional family members who were living in Hamburg. Aby was an intriguing character. When, as a younger man, he had declared himself ready to terminate a five-year stay in a mental hospital, the doctors in charge decided that to prove himself able to leave he must give a lecture to the other patients and conduct himself appropriately. Having gone to America to attend Felix and Frieda's wedding in 1895, Aby had been among the first white people to visit the Pueblo Indians; the subject of his lecture was their snake dances and the way in which we employ myth to explain what we don't understand. Eddie was now in Germany, theoretically to follow in Aby's footsteps as an art historian. But he lacked the patience for his uncle's scholarship. Restless after sitting for five hours straight as the great iconographer held forth on "Why the King of England sits in the position of Neptune on the pound note," Eddie took off for Berlin to do the run of galleries where contemporary art was being shown. One of his favorite haunts was the gallery run by Alfred Flechtheim, which he had initially visited with a letter of introduction from Paul Sachs. It was there during the summer of 1929 that he first laid eyes on a painting that would change his life.

Flechtheim's gallery was managed by a likable young man—also from Hamburg—named Curt Valentin. In that summer following his junior year at Harvard, Eddie Warburg complained that the current crop of paintings on exhibition was not up to the standards of previous seasons. Valentin consoled the young American by showing him a painting in the gallery for summer storage but not for sale. This was Picasso's 1905 Circus Period gouache called *Garçon Bleu*— or *Blue Boy*. It belonged to the Fürstin Mechtilde Lichnowsky, widow of a former German ambassador to England. She had bought it years earlier from Flechtheim, who had acquired it from the artist some five years after it had been painted. The painting had been in an important Picasso show at the Moderne Galerie in Munich in 1913, after which it had hung in the German embassy in London; for

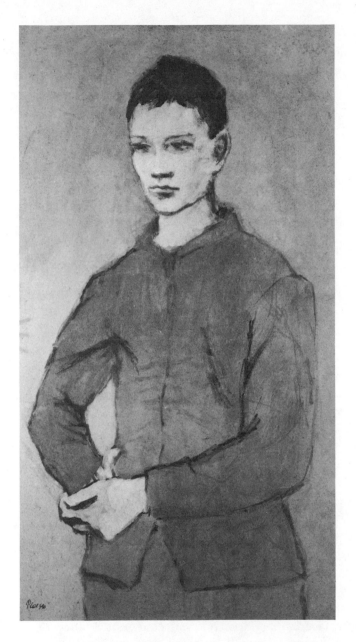

Pablo Picasso, Blue Boy, *gouache, 1905.*

the past fifteen years it had been on loan to the Kronprinzen Palais in Berlin.

In spite of Warburg's eager support of modernism at the Harvard Society, until he faced the Picasso the artworks that moved him the most directly and personally had always dated from earlier centuries. His favorite painting in the world, to which he regularly made pilgrimages, was the fifteenth-century Avignon Pietà at the Louvre. Here at last was a twentieth-century painting with a humanity he had previously found only in older art, now in a fresh and familiar language. This straightforward portrait of a juggler seemed alive.

Picasso's painting has the presence of Roman statuary, but it is uniquely simplified. The content is traditional, the style unaffected and entirely devoid of fuss. The palette consists of nothing more than chalky blue, brown, and tinted beiges. The features of the boy's face are articulated with a few sketchy brown brushstrokes that on close observation are so spare that it seems impossible that they could be so convincing. The broad gashes of paint for the right armpit and the awkward articulation of the right shoulder seem deliberately uncouth. Everything is in shorthand notation and reduced to essentials; one could not take away a single element. The courage of this intense, jargon-free visual language and the new, unburdened methods riveted Eddie. All masking removed, here was a facing up to fundamentals—and a quiet, eloquent honesty.

Blue Boy was stylistically advanced; it also was disarmingly gentle and serene. Whatever Picasso may have been up to in the conduct of his own life, in his art he could be tender and compassionate. The thick-necked, strong-shouldered young man—he appears in many of Picasso's Circus Period pictures, including the famous *Boy Leading a Horse*—is the incarnation of beautiful youth and maleness. He looks almost godlike: not just smooth-skinned and classically formed, but also stolid and confident.

Fancy as the trappings of Edward Warburg's own childhood had been, what made him swoon was not Gainsborough's sort of *Blue Boy* with lace cuffs and velvet waistcoat, not a fancy prince flanked by his polo pony, but an image both universal and humble. Picasso's subject was from a circus family that could probably scarcely make ends meet. His clothing is rudimentary, the setting entirely blank. What matters here is something greater, and simpler, than the props of life. In theme the painting goes beyond all notion of class, position, or background. In style it extols the value of deliberately clumsy candor; consider the proportions of the left arm and the awkwardness of the ear. At home Warburg might look at Anders Zorn's portrait of his mother in crinolines galore, but here at Flechtheim's that sort of puffery had no place.

The measurements of the head, shoulder, and arms correspond almost precisely with those of real young men. Unlike most painted images, this one neither reduces nor enlarges. It is possible to stand up to it as if to a mirror. That honesty of scale makes the image all the more real. At the same time, Picasso's boy is pensive and intense. He has large eyes and a slightly furrowed brow. A gray wash shadows his eyes. Much as he played the role of ham and joker, like all clowns Eddie Warburg was highly introspective too; his and Kirstein's seriousness had an echo here.

But the tone has different facets. Thanks to the terra-cotta colored background, the gouache is not grim. This is the hue of Mediterranean pottery—above all warm and earthy. It belongs to nature and to the sun, to the opposite side of the spectrum from the silks and brocades with which Eddie Warburg had grown up. These colors evoke the solid substance of things rather than their embellishment.

On the right side of the face, in the profile and the indication of the right cheek and the jawline, *Blue Boy* could almost belong to the nineteenth century. It is a realistic, if idealized, form. But on the left the head is flattened out in an entirely modern way. An oddly proportioned, broad expanse of cheek extends to the left ear. The different handling of the parts of the face is accentuated by the division of the surface; the left side is in a brighter glow than the right. This is a case of "seeing the light." It looks like a mental awakening. It is as if the psyche has been divided into areas of greater and lesser awareness. For this reason it would be no surprise if Henri Matisse had seen *Blue Boy* in the six years between when it was painted and when he made the portrait of his son Pierre called *The Piano Lesson*. Both paintings capture the awkwardness—the ill-at-ease, unresolved side—and the brightness of adolescence.

Picasso's juggler is mature and steady, but youthfully tense. His left shoulder is as broad and developed as that of a Bronzino warrior. But he grips his hands as if unsure about what to do with them or with his unchanneled energy. The right side of the face and the left side of the torso are perfect, flawless, classical images, thoroughly resolved; the left side of the face and the right side of the torso are contorted, compressed, suggestive of anxiety and questioning, paeans to stress and restlessness, physical and emotional. That juxtaposition of sedate Classicism and restless, twisting Cubism foreshadows aspects of Picasso's *Demoiselles d'Avignon.* The mix also pertained to the young man gazing at this work in Flechtheim's gallery. Eddie Warburg had fine manners and impeccable bearing; he had been brought up to be a gentleman. At the same time he was not unaware of his own yearnings, discomforts, and anxieties.

Warburg remarked to Curt Valentin that if the Countess Lichnowsky ever needed hard currency, she should let him know. Two days later the negotiating began, and in little time he acquired *Blue Boy* for seven thousand dollars, an amount that required stretching even though he had recently come into some money on his twenty-first birthday. But when his ship docked on the Hudson at the end of his summer holiday, Warburg declared the Picasso at half its value. He knew that there was no duty on works of art anyway, and he could not confront his father and brothers, who were meeting him, with the extent of his extravagance for a modern picture. The customs officer, however, was stunned at even the reduced figure. Upon inspecting *Blue Boy,* he could not believe that anyone had paid $3,500 for it. "Sonny," the officer said to the Harvard student, "I'm going down the dock, and when I come back, you change that figure to $1,000." [46] Eddie's brother Paul, who heard the exchange, explained to the officer that the family found it less expensive to allow the young traveler an occasional bit of reckless spending than to cover the alternative, which was maintenance in a psychiatric hospital.

It was one thing for Sam Lewisohn to own a Picasso, but for twenty-one-year-old Eddie Warburg to acquire one was beyond the realm of acceptable eccentricity. Other Americans had been buying the Spaniard's work for more than a decade—the Stein family, John Quinn, the Walter Arensbergs, A. E. Gallatin, Albert Barnes, and Lillie Bliss had all acquired several examples—but it still just was not mainstream for the Tiffany's/Cartier set. From Felix Warburg's point of view the new purchase could hardly have been less in keeping with the advice he had often given Eddie to savor beauty. When Eddie brought the painting through the foyer of 1109 Fifth Avenue, his mother told him it was completely unsuited for any of the rooms downstairs. Up to the squash court on the fifth floor is where Frieda Warburg sent her child with his souvenir of Berlin. When Eddie returned to Harvard for his senior year, Paul Sachs was delighted to

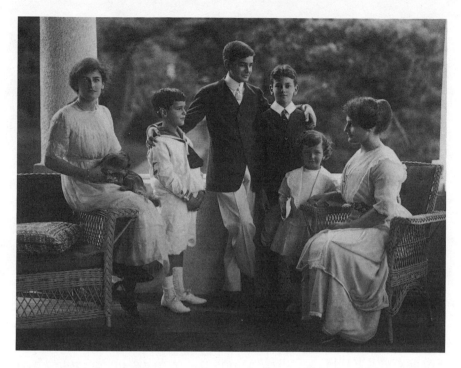

The Warburg family: from left to right, Carola, Piggy, Fred, Gerry, Eddie, and Frieda Warburg, c. 1912.

show *Blue Boy* at the Fogg, but in the family it long remained just another example of why the standard line about Eddie was "Oh my God! What's he done now?"

"Oh my God" is what Eddie's siblings had been saying about him ever since he could crawl. They had always considered him a mama's boy. A smart aleck with a high-pitched voice, Eddie was known to his brothers as "Peeper"—from *Peep Matz,* the German word for a diminutive chipping sparrow, to which one of his nurses compared him. He looked like his mother, while the other three boys resembled their father. Frieda was forty-two when she bore him—late for those days—and since he was considerably younger than the others, she kept him at her side when they were running about. In her memoirs, Frieda made no pretenses about her preferences. "He was my favorite child." [47] His siblings tended to be rough and tumble, but "Edward was always an exemplary child." [48] As a result, Eddie felt like an outsider: "They really felt that I was some kind of disease. They felt I was a fifth columnist probably, as I was much too close to my parents. . . . I was blue-eyed. They were all black-eyed or brown-eyed depending on who hit who first. I was always trying to smooth out troubled waters when my brothers got into trouble or had done something awful. I had to try and explain it or keep mother from getting angry or involving father in the situation in any way. This was not appreciated. They preferred that most of their escapades were without me. I felt very much out of it."[49]

Eddie Warburg has often described himself as wanting above all to be one of the gang. Yet he never acted merely eager to please the sort of people with whom he grew up. He reacted to his brothers in the same way that he and Kirstein responded to the majority of their Harvard classmates: with great independence. They may have felt a twinge of envy, but they were deliberately different.

Warburg's great challenge was to reconcile his simultaneous wishes to be an outsider and an insider. He wanted to fit in, but it took a while to figure out with whom: his brothers and the majority of his classmates, or the modernist elite. By backing the Harvard Society and buying modern paintings, he made his choice. Those moves guaranteed him the usual shocked response of his family and their set; it also garnered loud cheers from a far smaller circle of supporters. That need to affront some people and win the approval of others underlies a great deal of adventurous arts patronage. Rather than acquiesce to the judgments and power of the majority, the patron has chosen to join a smaller group. That need for self-definition can be more of a determining factor than is pure aesthetic response. It is all part of establishing how one fits into the world.

The usual way of fitting in, of course, is to conform to the prevailing tastes—whatever they may be—of one's time. By the time that Eddie Warburg was helping bring Buckminster Fuller to Harvard and carrying a Picasso gouache off an ocean liner, his siblings had all gone from the grandeur of 1109 Fifth Avenue to the pleasant, decorator-designed, flower-patterned interiors suitable for affluent young people of their era. The modus operandi behind the Warburg children's early education had been, after all, that they should *not* make choices. When they were little, the boys' clothing was always laid out for them, and it never occurred to them to question the choice of suit or change the color of necktie or socks. In the country the groom decided exactly the direction in which to ride, and the vegetable garden and kitchen were things to be looked at from afar, not matters in which one was to have any say. It was assumed that art collecting would be handled in much the same way. This was to be young Edward's domain, and the expectation was that he too would buy seventeenth-century etchings and Renaissance paintings. His siblings had stuck to the tried and true; presumably he would too.

On the other hand, it was very much a Warburg tradition to do things one wasn't quite supposed to do. On those special occasions when the children dined with their parents and the pre-meal grace written by Jacob Schiff was recited, each boy would always conspicuously try to blow the floating flower in a perfect circle around his finger bowl. It was the family style to violate the very formality their surroundings appeared to impose. Humor counted in a big way. Once when Felix Warburg was giving a JDC speech in Zurich, a little man had persistently tugged at his sleeve trying to hand him a slip of paper. Felix had thanked him and pocketed the paper, but thought little more of it. Some time later he learned that the man was Albert Einstein, a passionate Zionist. The piece of paper was an autographed summary of the theory of relativity, the only way that Einstein could thank Mr. Warburg for what he was doing on behalf of Jewish refugees in Palestine. When Einstein came to New York, he and Felix grew to know one another quite well, but Felix made no pretense of understanding the scientist's ideas. "I don't understand one word of your theory," he told Einstein. "The nearest I can translate it into terms that make any sense to me is 'everything is relative except relatives and they are constant.'" It was a message he often reiterated to his family.

Felix was an upright philanthropist, but he was also a guiltless dandy and bon vivant who loved both his tiny pony cart and his giant yacht. His family and closest friends called him "Fizzie." He wore a mask of propriety—when his sons, using their favorite euphemism for Felix's philandering, would ask, "Are you going out to ride your bicycle, Father?" as he headed out to the flat of one of the Metropolitan Opera singers or other young women with whom he liked to keep company, he invariably grunted as if he had no idea what they were talking about—but he concealed little. And he was no harsher in his judgment of the whims of others than he would want them to be of him. Fizzie wholeheartedly backed Eddie's involvement at the Harvard Society for Contemporary Art. This mat-

tered a lot to Eddie. For both Kirstein and Warburg—although not
for John Walker—family backing weighed heavily. They thrived on
approval as much as on disapproval. They knew how much their
parents cared about what they did or did not do. Eddie counted on
his father—who met often with Paul Sachs and Edward Forbes
about art matters at Harvard—as his ally. To shock his family may
have been part of his self-definition, but he also depended, especially
in the case of his father, on emotional backing.

Felix's involvement was useful on a practical level. The society
managed to keep in the black, but that is because when it looked as
if there was going to be a deficit, it was Eddie's—and Felix's—to
pay. It was, however, a family tradition to back up one's own. This
had been the case when Frieda Schiff had undertaken her first major
project in her early twenties. Frieda was chairman of the Building
Committee of the Young Women's Hebrew Association in New
York, and her task was to raise money for a building at 110th Street
and Fifth Avenue. Her father, Jacob, said he would provide twenty-
five thousand dollars and not a penny more under the condition that
two hundred thousand dollars be given by other people; it was up to
Frieda to solicit those gifts. When the deadline came, she was still
eighteen thousand dollars short. Knowing how her father stuck to
his guns, she trembled. He was not the sort of person to go easy on
a bargain. Nor could he let his daughter down. "I had a letter from
my father formally addressing me as chairman of the building committee. He had said he had heard that, notwithstanding all my efforts, we were still $18,000 short—and he had persuaded Mrs. Schiff
to give $18,000 for the library in memory of her brother, Morris
Loeb—and the check was enclosed." [50]

Lou Kirstein also was firmly behind *his* son. Lincoln's father didn't
understand far-out ventures like *The Hound & Horn* and the Harvard Society for Contemporary Art, but he nonetheless backed
them. That support was key to Lincoln's ability to proceed against
countless obstacles. As a person of strong impulses who always
thought he was right about everything, it meant a lot that although
his father did not share his views, he never in any way attempted to
stop him either.

Louis Kirstein had, after all, named his son for a great man, and
he wanted to see his son live up to that great man's legacy. What
remains unclear is which of two people the original great "Lincoln"

was. There are those who say it was Lincoln Filene, the founder of
the store Lou ran, but Lincoln Kirstein questions this. Filene's last
name, after all, was bogus; when *his* father had arrived in America
from Eastern Europe, the family name had been Katz, which in the
hands of an immigration authority went to Cats and then to Feline
misspelled as "Filene." So his first name seemed of equally dubious
origin. In Lincoln Kirstein's opinion the Lincoln his father had in
mind was probably Abraham Lincoln, one of Lou's great heroes. It
was Abraham Lincoln's passion for principles that he would carry
forward as part of the family legacy.

Like Warburg, Lincoln Kirstein had strayed from his parents' aesthetics while adhering in other ways to their well-defined sense of
values. In his tenacity and unique way of looking at things, he resembled his mother. When Rose Kirstein returned from a trip to the
Vatican during which, at an audience with the Pope, she had kept a
hundred rosaries under her skirt so that they could be sold at Filene's
Basement, fifteen-year-old Lincoln told her he wanted to convert
from Judaism to Catholicism; her reply was, "Of course. It's all theater." [51] In his rigorous quest for directness and honesty, Lincoln was
his father's son. In February 1925, Louis Kirstein, then vice president
of William Filene's Sons Company, delivered an address before the
annual convention of the National Retail Dry Goods Association
about truth in advertising. He attacked the hype of inflated publicity
claims as vehemently as his son, a few years later, promoted candor
in art and language. Lou Kirstein admonished his audience of retail-
ers "First—to make sure as far as humanly possible that our advertising is *worthy* of belief; second, to *convince* people of this so that
they will read it, believe it and respond to it." If you substituted the
word "art" for "advertising," this could have been the gospel his son
followed.

Louis Kirstein advocated Better Business Commissions as watch-
dogs for truthfulness. They would make sure that artificial silk was
called rayon, and that "fashioned" hosiery would not be confused
with "full fashioned." Kirstein was adamant about the need for clarity in language. "When we say 'fast colors' we are using a loose term.
A waist may be fast to boiling, fast to sunlight and fast to laundering,
but if a customer buys it and perspires the first time she wears it, and
the waist turns color, she doesn't care a hoot about the other claims
and makes up her mind that somebody lied." [52] It's no surprise that a
businessman who could come up with an example like that as his

audience sat back under the glittering chandeliers of a hotel ballroom would bring up a son who would display Donald Deskey's ashtrays on a modern steel counter and make everything from a Hopper tenement scene to Brancusi's ovoid the basis of an art exhibition—all in the interest of honesty. What mattered was to know the truth and speak it plainly.

Of the three young men at the helm of the new organization, only John Walker had separated himself from his family. Not only had he chosen Harvard when his relatives had all gone to Yale or Princeton, but he had taken on the leadership of an art society when the sole organizations with which his father had ever affiliated himself were the exclusive Pittsburgh clubs where he and others of his background could spend afternoons at the card or billiard tables or backgammon board, or on the golf links. The most essential artifact for the senior Mr. Walker was his whiskey and soda, and when he died—largely from drinking too much too rapidly—when young John was seventeen, he left his son "all he had: a Patek Philippe watch . . . and a silver cocktail shaker."[53] John Walker, Sr., may have liked nice things, but to work hard and try to shift public taste was a step of John Jr.'s own invention. And in one way or another, to invent a new self was what these three men and Agnes Mongan were determined to do.

VIII

When they returned in the fall of 1929 to start their senior year, Kirstein and Warburg put their memories of Diaghilev's funeral and the Picasso acquisition behind them. The Harvard Society for Contemporary Art arranged a show called "School of New York, 1920–30" which ran from October 18 to November 1. Its goal was to round things out where the society's inaugural exhibition had left off. The earlier show had brought together a disparate group of relatively established middle-aged American painters and sculptors; here were some younger artists unknown to the broad public. One of them was Stuart Davis, an artist in his mid-thirties who had done more than anyone else to bring Cubism to American painting. What the Harvard Society showed by Davis was no mere fragment; it was his quintessential work of that period, a large and pioneering canvas called *Super Table* that bore the influence of Picasso and

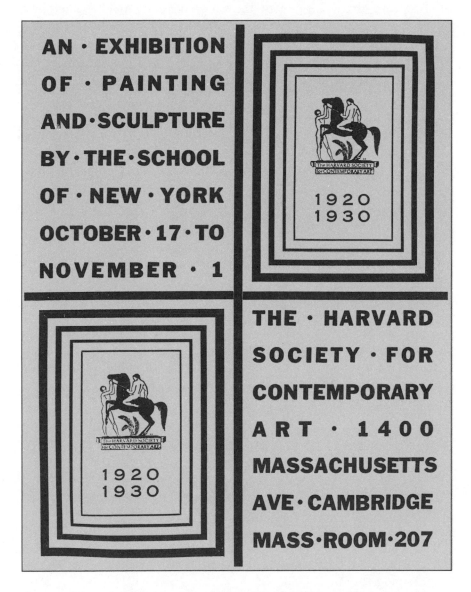

Cover of the exhibition brochure from "An Exhibition of Painting and Sculpture by the School of New York." The Harvard Society for Contemporary Art, 1929.

Léger. The oddly flattened forms reflect a radical geometry in their obeisance to the discipline of the Golden Section. The palette of dusty rose and purplish gray that would in time become part of the everyday vocabulary of Art Deco—and, more recently, of post-modernism—was then as new and startling as Lindbergh's flight. The Davis was one of six works lent by the Downtown Gallery in New York.

Other painters in "School of New York 1920–30" were Peter Blume, Preston Dickinson, Guy Pène du Bois, William Glackens, Walt Kuhn, Yasuo Kuniyoshi, George Luks, Charles Sheeler, Max Weber, and John Walker's beloved John Kane. For sculpture there were pieces by Gaston Lachaise—increasingly one of Kirstein's and Warburg's favorites—the twenty-six-year-old Japanese-American Isamu Noguchi, William Zorach, and the thirty-one-year-old Alex-ander Calder. Calder was represented by two wire pieces—*John D. Rockefeller* and *Dowager* (also called *The Debutante's Mother*)—that characterized those dignified types with a bite sure to raise the eye-brows of many a well-brought-up young Harvard man. The show was a potpourri of some of the most advanced art of the day. Kirstein had also asked Arthur Dove and Elie Nadelman to exhibit, but they declined, ostensibly for lack of work.

Most of this art was too untraditional to be shown anywhere else in Boston, in either museums or commercial galleries. Albert Franz Cochrane in the *Boston Evening Transcript* of October 19 explained why: "The real reason may be that Boston is a bit discriminating as to what it accepts. . . . In art of the past decade we have tolerated mud and distortion. It is time to prune." The main point of Coch-rane's long attack—the critics were allowed many more column inches back then than they are today—was that the so-called ad-vanced art wasn't advanced at all. "When we come to view the so-phisticated childishness of mature men and women, we are prompted to say, 'Take your finger out of your mouth, and act your age!' " It was just the sort of nastiness Kirstein, Warburg, and Walker were hoping for.

The stock market crashed at the end of October, but nothing altered the pace of the Harvard Society. Walker's allowance money remained ample enough so that when he needed to get away from the whirl-wind of his friends and his Harvard social life in order to study for exams, he would take a quiet room at the Ritz where he would park his notes on the mantelpiece and pace up and down committing facts to memory. There's no sign that Kirstein needed to hold back; people still shopped at Filene's. As for the Warburgs, they suffered far less than most of their ilk thanks to the advice of Felix's older brother Paul, also a partner at Kuhn, Loeb. Paul had been nicknamed the Cassandra of Wall Street earlier that year because of his strong premonition that the boom was suspicious and that the smartest thing one could do was to convert assets to cash, advice he had implored the rest of the family to follow. Besides, the Harvard Society ran on a small budget, and although the Executive Committee had to kick in a bit extra from time to time, most of the expenses were covered by the various membership categories. In spite of the vicissitudes of the economy, the roster continued to grow.

The show that ran from November 7 through 27, 1929, delved more into the sort of material shown at the Fogg Art Museum than was usual for the society. It was "Derain Matisse Picasso Despiau"— three painters and a sculptor whose work one *could* see elsewhere. But the paintings shown in the two rooms over the Coop were their most recent, by no means the style for which they were already well known and had gained a degree of approval. Consider the case of Derain. The usual line on Derain was that he was greatest during his brief Fauve period (1906–8), and had never equaled that peak since— the cliché of opinion that prevails to this day. Shocking as the bright Fauve color and splashy forms had seemed when they were first shown, twenty years later they had come to be considered acceptable, even appealing, over one's mantel, but his later work was viewed as inferior. The Harvard Society saw otherwise. They borrowed half a dozen major Derain oils of the 1920s, in addition to the highly animated 1911 *The Bagpiper* from the Valentine Gallery. These later canvases affronted the average viewer. A painting like *The English Woman,* owned by Sam and Margaret Lewisohn, struck most people as strident and gloomy.

In three lucid paragraphs in the exhibition flyer, the Harvard Society—which is to say Kirstein—stated its case. Kirstein unequivocally presented the view that Derain's real achievement began *after* Fauvism. "Derain's first real period can be dated from 1908–1914." Because of World War I, Derain then did not work at all for four years. "His interest has been since [the end of World War I] in the application of paint in formal relations, in the creation of plastic massing, with hardly any reference to psychological insight or a lit-

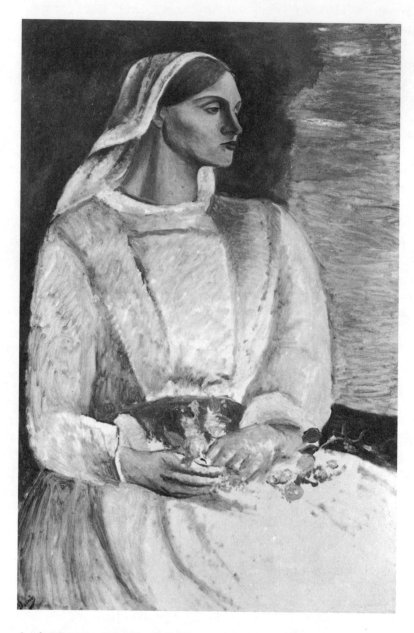

André Derain, The English Woman. *Oil on canvas, 42⅝ × 27½".*

erary subject." Kirstein linked Derain's work to that of the brothers Le Nain and Courbet, and continued:

He is a serious artist more interested in the complex simplicity of his personal problems than in the innovation or in the reorientation of tendencies in painting. He is an academic painter, in the old and good sense, a painter working soberly and strongly with a set of restricting, helpful principles of solidity, economy and precision.

It was, then as now, an unfashionable point of view. But it was no surprise that Kirstein would espouse Derain's relentless search for visual truth and his tireless attempt at the best method for revealing with maximum honesty the appearance of things.

There were eight major oils by Matisse—among them three loans from Valentine—also from the 1920s: *that* artist's least popular period. Assuming Kirstein was the author of the text, he may well have been identifying with the painter when he referred to "the almost ferocious directness of his vision." Kirstein points out that "a freshness of colour surpassing in brilliance even Van Gogh led those used to his perplexing simplicity to call him a wild man, a Fauve." If the deprecating Boston critics had called Kirstein and Warburg "wild men," the two students would have been tickled.

Despiau was represented by six recent bronzes, all lent by Frank Crowninshield. The values the Harvard Society flyer ascribed to his work were synonymous with their raison d'être: "Despiau in all his emphasis on essentials, his sensitive handling of surfaces, his sympathies with human personality, and the intensity and profundity of his personal imagination is surely one of the greatest sculptors of our time."

The sentences on Picasso—who was represented by five major oils, among them the large 1923 *Bathers,* lent by the New York dealer Paul Rosenberg—also suggest the personal goals of the members of the Executive Committee: "He rehabilitated the commonplace . . . His energy is colossal." In addition, Kirstein presciently wrote, "Only the critic of fifty years from now can fully appreciate how profoundly he has altered, controlled, and assimilated European painting of the first quarter of the twentieth century." Yet the three college students recognized this achievement already.

. . .

The next exhibition was a last-minute affair that had not been planned in time for the society's printed schedules, and for which there was no catalog. Running between December 6 and 30 of 1929, it consisted of original drawings by "American Cartoonists and Caricaturists." With Frank Crowninshield as the main lender, a number of these were artists whose illustrations regularly graced the pages of *Vanity Fair* and *The New Yorker*. Among the better known were Peter Arno, Peggy Bacon, Calder, Miguel Covarrubias, Charles Dana Gibson, John Held, Jr., Helen Hokinson, and Rollin Kirby. Their main common denominator was that nothing was sacred—an attitude that suited the Executive Committee perfectly.

What followed was a show that appealed to a very different aspect of their sensibility. It consisted of Japanese and English pottery and weaving. This must have been quite a managerial feat since it included a large number of artists, the best known of whom today is Bernard Leach. The exhibition, which ran from January 10 to 25, 1930, clearly took a lot of forethought, since it was accompanied by an elegant catalog printed on fine Japanese rice paper. The actual event, however, opened with disaster. A number of pieces of Japanese pottery were displayed on the monel-topped table with its ice-cream-shop legs when someone leaned on it and sent everything flying. Many objects broke. The only slight compensation was that the secretary for the society had erroneously overinsured the work, which was for sale, and had valued it at its selling price rather than at the society's cost.

What came next was another of their unscheduled shows, too late for the calendar or a catalog. The Executive Committee had been so impressed with Alexander Calder's contributions to the School of New York and Caricature shows that they asked the thirty-two-year-old sculptor back for a solo exhibition. It ran for scarcely more than a week, from January 27 to February 4.

On January 26, Warburg drove to Back Bay station to pick up Calder, who had taken the train from New York. Warburg was one of the few Harvard students with a car, and Kirstein had dispatched him to pick up the sculptor and the seventeen pieces he was supposed to bring along. Calder arrived, however, with only three coils of wire, some pliers, and a small suitcase. Warburg panicked, having no idea where the show was, but Calder told him to have no fear.

Back in Warburg's room in Holworthy Hall, Calder opened the small flat suitcase. It contained a few pieces of clothing and a stack of wooden boards. He unpacked the boards, took off his shoes and socks, and changed out of his trousers into pajama bottoms. Then he set to work. Using his big toe as an anchor, he looped the wire around, turning and twisting it with his pliers. As Eddie Warburg sat there watching, Calder assembled all seventeen pieces, attaching each to one of the boards, which served as bases.[54]

The subject matter was no more traditional than the sculptural method. Manipulating the wire into a few well-defined curves, Calder crafted *The Hostess*. Rising from the base on the narrowest high-heeled pumps, she sticks out her rear end, which is formed as if clad in skintight silk. One long-fingered hand hangs forward in a limp handshake; the other holds a lorgnette. The socialite's profile—nothing more than the end of a piece of wire—consists of the perfect haughty nose and narrow eye, framed by a series of well-trained curls.

Alexander Calder, The Hostess, *1928. Wire construction, 11½ × 4½ × 11⅞".*

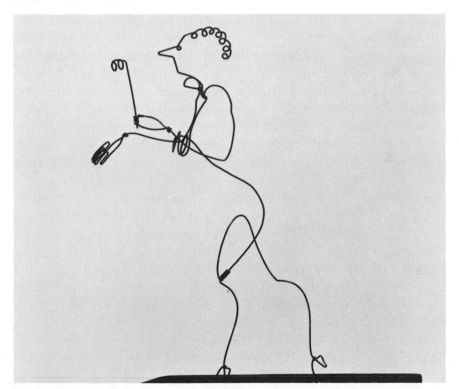

Calder knotted together a somewhat more elaborate group of wires to form his *Cow.* This creature has a quizzical look, floppy ears, and an enormous udder with sofa-spring teats. Directly underneath its hind legs, a truncated coil of wire, shaped like a flattened cone, is her "cow pie."

While he worked away, Calder studied a large photograph of Felix Warburg on Eddie's desk. Again the sculptor began to bend and twist. In little time the high-living philanthropist came to life before his son's eyes. Calder set the head on a wire Star of David base, and then, as a finishing touch, incorporated a test tube to hold Felix's signature boutonniere, which he crafted out of wire as well.

When Calder was sitting on the toilet in Eddie's bathroom, he noticed a gas outlet, no longer in use, on the wall. The cork plugging the bulging metal form reminded him of a nipple. When he got off the toilet seat he chalked in a large voluptuous nude of which the gas outlet became the left breast. That bathroom ceiling and walls became famous all over Harvard. It was the first time that many of America's future leaders saw an actual piece of contemporary art.

The usual notion of art and decoration in 1930 was that they required order and planning. Even if the interior of Eddie Warburg's parents' house at 1109 Fifth Avenue and the places where most of his Harvard classmates were brought up didn't share a common style, they were unified in reflecting forethought and labor. For something to be deemed beautiful, it had to bear the imprint of endless hours of work by well-trained artisans. The molded plaster reliefs that decorated the most ordinary upper-middle-class American suburban houses at that time reflected the schooling and careful measurement that were considered the prerequisites of professionalism. Objects looked as if their makers were one further link in the chain from Vitruvius to Palladio to Sheraton. What was not acceptable was for art to look as if it had sprung from the unconscious. Nor should it be made of materials as rugged as coat hangers. Premeditated was better than spontaneous, imported better than local and convenient. Acceptable beauty in much of America depended on Italian marble, African mahogany (preferably worked in England), and gilded filigree. To construct sculpture with a few spur-of-the-moment twists of ordinary wire was both an act of daring and an act of faith. To be able to enjoy and champion it was nothing less.

The Calder exhibition had more popular appeal than almost anything else the Harvard Society did. Enlarging the respectful debunking that the caricature show had initiated, it had an urbane, good-natured mockery that audiences loved. And to people like Kirstein, Warburg, and Walker, it offered refreshing spontaneity. Here was someone who did not know in advance what he was going to do. Calder did not think it necessary to sketch, plan, or prepare. He did not lean on tradition or other people's ideas for his means of communication; his unadorned forms belonged to as new a language as Brancusi's. No one else had drawn with wire in air. Artists did not usually allow the sheer physicality of their work to be so blatant. To make these steps reflected—and this was a big part of the allure for the young Harvard men—extraordinary faith in oneself.

IX

There was little time to publicize the first public performance ever of Calder's Circus, sponsored by the Harvard Society for Contemporary Art and held at 9 p.m. on January 31, 1930. But a lot of people turned up anyway. One of them was Alfred Barr, for whom it was the first exposure to this artist. Another was the society's occasional visitor Philip Johnson. Even if he avoided the usual run of museum shows, Johnson felt that this was an event not to be missed. He began to enjoy himself the moment Calder handed out peanuts to the assembled audience before the action began. He loved watching the bearlike artist's enormous hands become "nimble, delicate, and skillful" as they pulled the strings of the various circus animals. It was "a kinetic experience," seeing the horse's and kangaroo's hind legs flex as they came over the three-inch-high structure that was the circus ring. Calder pulled the strings at just the right speed to edge the acrobats along their wire and to prompt the cyclists and wheeled cages into action. The scale and timing were so splendid that "everybody burst out in laughter and applause."[55] By comparison, the Circus as it stands now in its permanent installation at the Whitney Museum of American Art in New York is a dead experience. Like Calder's later mobiles, the Circus was designed with motion—never the same twice—as one of its essential elements.

The Circus looked as if it could have been made with materials from a garbage heap. If the miniature animals that Philip Johnson, Lincoln Kirstein, Eddie Warburg, and John Walker had known in their youths had the glaze of Staffordshire, now the stuff of art was

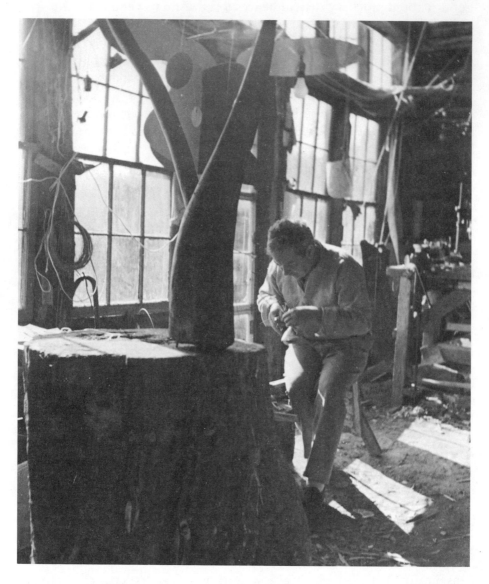

Alexander Calder working on the Circus, photographed by André Kertesz, 1928.

discards of cloth and bent scraps of metal. Each creature looked about as haphazard as it could be while still representing something. Like the Cubists whose work he had studied in Paris, Calder fashioned his images out of the detritus of everyday life. He looked toward the direction of ordinariness, away from the rarefied. What was presumably unimportant could be given new meaning. You could make something out of nothing. Circus visitors—figures a few inches high who had wire limbs and wore striped dresses and floppy hats—were fashioned out of coat hangers and fabric remnants. There were a kangaroo of wood and tin; a stuffed felt elephant whose trunk and tail were constructed from shreds of industrial rubber tubing; a dachshund supported by two small wheels (in fact washers) and

Cowboy *from* Calder's Circus *(1926–31). Wire, wood, yarn, leather, cloth, metal, and string, 10½ × 5¾ × 18¾".*

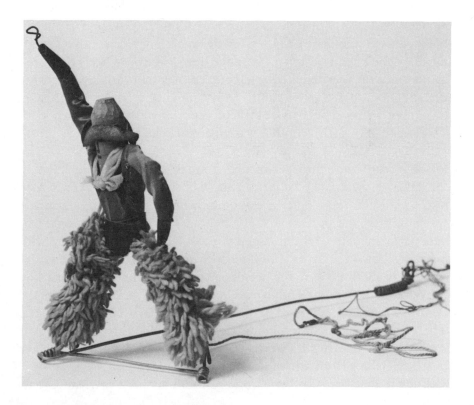

made of rigid macaroni–like ribbed rubber. A cyclist was crafted of tin painted bright yellow. Acrobats and dancers, structured of wire, were covered with stuffing and bright festive outfits made of rags. The garbage-fleshed cast of characters also included Monsieur Loyal, the ringmaster; two stretcher-bearers; a spear thrower; exotic dancers; a cowboy; a sword swallower; the bearded lady; a stilt walker; clowns; a weight lifter; animal trainers; and charioteers. Among the animals were a cow and a bull whose head and torso were fashioned of corks, seals who could bounce a miniature beach ball, and a quintessential lion with a large stuffed head. Each creature was the epitome of its type. The busty, pinch-waisted chanteuse with her rhinestone tiara and choker was the showgirl par excellence. The tin-legged acrobats could scarcely have looked nimbler, the angel in a paper gown and with paper wings more the soul of goodness. For Kirstein and Warburg this epitomized a way of generalizing—a creation of recognizable, ordinary types—that would underlie much of the art they would endorse and bring to the larger public.

The sense of imperfection and frank revelation of flaws were a big part of the charm of all this. The rough twine that held the high wire in place had been knotted and tied and looped all over, as if it had been patched a hundred times. Bits of rags hung from it. The decoration of the bright yellow and orange lion's cage on wheels consisted in part of two mermaids whose cork breasts had nipples that were the roughest splotches of paint. Today none of this may seem startling, but to revel in flaws in 1930, especially for boys born with silver spoons in their mouths, was an act of revolution.

Having first made and performed a small-scale circus in Paris in 1926, Calder had packed it into a couple of suitcases and taken it with him to New York, where he elaborated the circus setting and made more animals and performers. By 1929 he was doing occasional private performances of the enlarged Circus. The first was a party with beer and hot dogs in the Fifty-sixth Street showroom of dress designer Elizabeth Hawes, the person who a couple of years earlier had introduced the young sculptor to Joan Miró. The next was in the Lexington Avenue house of designer Mildred Harbeck and her sister. There the guests included Frank Crowninshield, Edward Steichen, and the gallery owner E. Weyhe. Kirstein or Warburg may well have heard of Calder from any of these people.

But the first occasion when one of them actually saw the Circus was when Lincoln Kirstein attended a performance in the apartment at 270 Park Avenue of the wealthy theatrical designer Aline Bernstein. A detailed fictionalized account of that event is given in Thomas Wolfe's novel *You Can't Go Home Again*. It is presented very cynically by Wolfe, who regarded Calder's work pretty much as F. W. Coburn did: as the plaything of elitist swells.

The novelist calls it "Piggy Logan's Circus," a performance that takes place at "The Party at Jack's." Frederick Jack is a prosperous Wall Street broker. His worldly and stunning wife, Esther, a devoted patroness of the arts with vast social skills, was closely modeled on Aline Bernstein, with whom Wolfe was in the throes of a passionate love affair—and to whom he dedicated *Look Homeward, Angel* the same year that Calder presented his Circus in her home. In earlier writing he had named his Aline Bernstein figure Rebecca Feitlebaum; by changing it he evoked more of her and her husband's characters, since Esther means "star" in Hebrew and "Jack" can signify a knave or maverick.

Wolfe had met Mrs. Bernstein during the summer of 1925, when he was a third-class passenger on the *Olympic*—the White Star Line's sister ship to the *Titanic*—as it made its way from Southampton to New York. A Harvard friend of his had introduced him to two ladies who were traveling first class.[56] Mrs. Bernstein was one of them; the other was Mina Kirstein. Wolfe was poor and unworldly, Mrs. Bernstein a beautifully dressed woman. Part of the same prosperous German-Jewish circle that included the Warburgs and the Sachses, she was a member of the board of directors of the Neighborhood Playhouse, where her fellow directors and close friends included Eddie Warburg's relatives Irene and Alice Lewisohn—Sam's cousins. Mrs. Bernstein moved easily in an echelon of New York life that could make a pivotal difference to the struggling writer; the Neighborhood Playhouse was just in the process of considering Wolfe's play *Welcome to Our City*. Wolfe was then twenty-four years old, Mrs. Bernstein forty-three; he six and a half feet tall, she diminutive. In spite of—or because of—some of these differences, they developed a great liaison. So when Sandy Calder presented his Circus in Aline Bernstein's apartment, with Lincoln Kirstein in attendance, Thomas Wolfe was there too.

On one side of Mrs. Bernstein's living room sat Calder's friends. On another sat Mrs. Bernstein's—by Calder's account "dressed negligently or in negligees."[57] Calder crouched on basketball kneepads as he took the little animals and acrobats along their course. The only comment Mrs. Bernstein made afterward was, "It's a lot of work." The only utterance from her sister, who was associated with Bergdorf Goodman, was a question as to where Calder got the box from that store into which he packed some of the Circus figures.

Thomas Wolfe's lengthy version of that evening pretty much corroborates the chic audience's point of view that there was nothing so great about what had gone on. Wolfe's preference was for the fancy ladies mocked by Calder; in his eyes "beautiful women with satiny backs were moving through the room with velvet undulance." Calder, by comparison, was like a longshoreman. Piggy Logan—Wolfe's Calder character—is

a thickset, rather burly-looking man of about thirty, with bushy eyebrows of a reddish cast, a round and heavy face smudged ruddily with the shaven grain of his beard, a low, corrugated forehead, and a bald head gleaming with perspiration. . . .

Mr. Piggy Logan was attired for his performance in a costume that was simple yet extraordinary. He had on a thick blue turtleneck sweater of the kind that was in favor with college heroes thirty years ago. Across the front of it—God knows why—was seen an enormous homemade Y. He wore old white canvas trousers, tennis sneakers, and a pair of battered knee pads such as were formerly used by professional wrestlers. His head was crowned with an ancient football helmet, the straps securely fastened underneath his heavy jowls.

Wolfe describes the performance of the Circus:

It started, as all circuses should, with a grand procession of the performers and the animals in the menagerie. Mr. Logan accomplished this by taking each wire figure in his thick hand and walking it around the ring and then solemnly out again . . .

Then came an exhibition of bareback riders. Mr. Logan galloped his wire horses into the ring and round and round with movements of his hand. Then he put the riders on top of the wire horses, and, holding them firmly in place, he galloped these around too. Then there was an interlude of clowns, and he made the wire figures tumble about by manipulating them with his hands. After this came a procession of wire elephants. This performance gained particular applause because of the clever way in which Mr. Logan made the figures imitate the swaying, ponderous lurch of elephants . . .

Wolfe writes of the trapeze performance and the sword-swallowing act as well. Here, however, the impressions are of resounding failure. The little wire figures keep failing to catch one another as they hang from the trapeze. The audience, whom up until this point Wolfe has shown to be restless and often bored, is now even more uncomfortable.

> It became painful. People craned their necks and looked embarrassed. But Mr. Logan was not embarrassed. He giggled happily with each new failure and tried again. As for the sword-swallowing, it is even more of a disaster, with Piggy Logan giggling even more nervously as the doll's rag throat resists the hair pin being thrust into it, and the audience responding with blank faces . . . in a puzzled, doubting way. . . . But he persisted—persisted horribly.[58]

The unpredictability was discomfiting to Thomas Wolfe. But Lincoln Kirstein, who was also on Mrs. Bernstein's side of the guest list, didn't just like what he saw; by arranging for the Circus to be presented under the auspices of the Harvard Society, he sponsored its first public performance—as opposed to a showing at an invitation-only party in someone's house.

Today the Mr. and Mrs. Jacks of this world flaunt the Calder mobiles in their bank lobbies and living rooms more proudly than their shares of IBM. The Circus itself is treated as a modern icon: one of the very few objects that never gets moved and is a constant fixture in one of our major museums. Facing the lobby of the Whitney, it is almost always surrounded by as many viewers as Monet's *Water Lilies* at the Museum of Modern Art—more people than generally fill the Rembrandt rooms at the Metropolitan. But in 1930 it was unacceptable to the public at large, and the Boston critics lambasted its presentation at Harvard. Calder signified above all the ability to let go—of ideas about planning, of traditional notions of surface and finish, of the idea that everything had its unvarying position. As ingenuous as child's play, his performance took the supreme courage to do something without being able to foresee how it would turn out. It risked a new language, as unadorned as Brancusi's or Picasso's. Calder dematerialized sculpture, letting the voids, rather than masses of precious material, be the subject. No one else was willing to be as bluntly physical, even clumsy. And if people as astute in many ways as Aline Bernstein and Thomas Wolfe could give so little in return, the palpable glee of a roomful of bright young men and their friends at Harvard and Radcliffe colleges must have given quite a boost.

X

The society published a report of its first year. The document summarized the purpose and content of each exhibition, and presented a meticulous accounting of income and expenditures. Receipts were $7,879.05, and expenditures $7,288.43. The most expensive show had been "Derain Matisse Picasso Despiau" at $724.33; the total cost for the Calder exhibition had been $60.70. The Dymaxion House had been the least pricey of all, at $56.66, with all of the other shows ranging between about $100 and $500. The main expenses were for rent, furnishing, insurance, shipping, printing, and teas.

A small amount of the society's income was from commissions on sales. The society had netted $567.70 for its share of the sale of paintings by Maurice Prendergast, Martin Mower, and Margarett Sargent and of sculpture by Alexander Calder, and $338.02 for sales of prints and decorative art objects. The rest of the income came from membership fees. By the end of that first year they already had thirty-five people in the "more than $10 annually" sustaining member category. Among them were Eddie Warburg and his parents, who were probably the most "more than $10" of anyone. Other sustaining members were Philip Johnson and Mrs. John D. Rockefeller, Jr., and Lillie Bliss—two of the three women in the process of founding the Museum of Modern Art in New York at that time. There were 137 ten-dollar contributing members, and 129 two-dollar Harvard and Radcliffe members.

The society had hired an able part-time secretary who did most of their bookkeeping. Lincoln Kirstein was officially treasurer.[59] But Eddie Warburg was the member of the Executive Committee with the most business sense, and the accounting statement had been his responsibility. This was a triumph, since in spite of the family's financial interests, their knowledge of business methods was slight. For example, once when Eddie had gone off to Chicago, his father both signed and countersigned all his American Express Travelers' Checks. The son, knowing nothing more than his father about the need to have these checks in his own name and to countersign only when cashing them, had tried to use one to pay for his train ticket home. After answering no to the question "Are you Felix Warburg?" he had had to walk, completely penniless, from the train station to the American Express office in search of assistance. At American Express he politely suggested to a clerk that "maybe a telephonic communication might help." The clerk was not about to start trying to ring up some student's father in his New York office. But he couldn't help falling for the deferential tone of voice and earnest look. He agreed to give Eddie enough cash for the ticket, if not a penny more. Eddie got home, even though very hungry. And he began to learn a bit more about how money really changed hands, so much so that by the time he had turned twenty-one at least he could tally the books of the Harvard Society.

The acquisition of Calder's sculptures—*The Hostess, Cow,* and *Felix Warburg*—had been made by Warburg himself. He covered their purchase prices out of his allowance money. This wasn't easy, however. For even if Jacob Schiff's estate in 1920 had been valued at about fifty million dollars—about half the amount Warburg's grandfather had given to charity during his lifetime—that allowance was relatively modest. The family did not believe in indulgence. Another Harvard student—for whom Warburg's parents were paying tuition, room, board, and pocket money—fared far better. He was the son of the director of the New York YMHA, the organization Jacob Schiff had helped establish and Frieda had done her best to perpetuate. Frieda always saw to it that the other young man got more extra money than her Edward did. The idea was to instill energy, not just a sense of well-being, in her children.

The second year of the Harvard Society opened with safe and daring side by side. "Watercolors by 5"—the second-generation American Impressionists Marion Monks Chase, Charles Hovey Pepper, Carl Gordon Cutler, Charles Hopkinson, and Harley Perkins—accompanied bronzes by Noguchi. Noguchi had for a while been living in Paris as Brancusi's studio assistant as well as the gramophone operator for Calder's Circus. There he mainly sculpted biomorphic abstractions out of sheet metal. Then, after having a show that sold nothing, and feeling that he was "too young and inexperienced for abstractions," he had moved to New York and rented a studio on top of Carnegie Hall. At that point, "There was nothing to do but make heads. It was a matter of eating, and this was the only way I knew of making money." [60] He took commissions from friends and friends' friends, one of whom was Bucky Fuller. Fuller was going to be showing an updated version of the Dymaxion House at Harvard, and by the time he was heading to Cambridge with the model for it in the back of his station wagon, he packed several dozen of Noguchi's bronze portrait busts in with it, and invited Noguchi to take the passenger seat. It was these boldly simplified and direct portraits of modernist heroes—among them Fuller himself, Martha Graham, and George Gershwin—that occupied the two rooms above the Coop.

Noguchi's bronzes offered no great shock. They were more intense and streamlined than the portraits people were used to, but at least they resembled their subjects. Their presentation, however, raised eyebrows. Most of the public was appalled. The Harvard Society had installed the busts on pedestals made of lengths of shiny new galvanized furnace pipe. The February 28 *Boston Transcript* summed up this affront to the usual way of doing things: "One just can't see the fire for the smoke."

The showing of the updated model of the Dymaxion House took place on March 12, 13, and 14. This time the model was erected in the courtyard of the Fogg. It included a laundry that could wash and dry clothing within three minutes (unfortunately none of the contemporary accounts explain how this worked), a revolving hanger large enough for thirty overcoats, and a semicircular closet that could hold up to fifty dresses. The "everyone" for whom Fuller intended his structures apparently consisted of people with ample wardrobes.

Time and again the Harvard Society was the first institution ever to deem something worth showing. They assembled artworks that the public had never before seen, either individually or grouped. From today's perspective the exhibition list doesn't seem particularly unusual, but at the time it offered one innovation after another. From March 21 to April 12 the society presented "Modern Mexican Art," an assemblage culled from several New York galleries. The key painters included Jean Charlot, Carlos Merrida, Diego Rivera, José Clemente Orozco, Rufino Tamayo, and David Siqueiros. What had been identified as the quintessential values of art in the catalog essays for the "School of Paris" and "Derain Picasso Matisse Despiau" shows were now out of favor. The text about the art from south of the border espoused some entirely new ideas.

At least for Kirstein, who was probably the author of the unsigned flyer, each undertaking was like a rebirth. He and Warburg—Walker was by now even less involved than before—were always looking for the major answers to life. With each event they sponsored, the answers changed. The urgent writing about the Mexican show rings like salvation, even if salvation this month had a very different form than it did last month. The text—based largely on Anita Brenner's *Idols Behind Altars,* a book published the previous year—gave politics and social values the supremacy that a season earlier had been awarded to humor, and before that to the purely formal qualities of art.

> Art for Art's sake, and Pure Painting as practiced in Montparnasse have no place in Mexico. Drawing and painting became the language adapted for the teaching of all subjects—from geography to hygiene. The expression of a religious and political tradition in art is the living breath of the land, and it tastes of the soil whatever the form that period and locality define . . . It is not improbable that future historians will find in Mexico City, in the fusion of architecture and painting, illustration and decoration, an actual renaissance, a rebirth of original values, far exceeding in importance the sterile ingenuities of the followers of contemporary Paris.

No one seemed troubled by the contradiction with the previous adulation of the art of contemporary Paris and of the American art that mimicked it.

The Mexican exhibition evoked a range of responses. As usual, *The Christian Science Monitor* championed the activities on the second floor of 1400 Massachusetts Avenue. Referring to "the courageous Harvard Society for Contemporary Art," it pronounced that "the freshness of art uncorrupted by foreign influence is welcome." The *Boston Herald* took the middle ground. Its stance was mainly that this Mexican foray was an event to reckon with; they covered it extensively, but without judgment. An unsigned editorial pointed to "Modern Mexican Art" as a major political statement, "made by revolutionaries for the revolution's sake" and revealing Communist ideology. It was certain to prompt "letters to editors denouncing the young gentlemen of the Harvard Contemporary Society for bringing such an exhibition into this country."[61] But precisely what those editors thought was unclear.

The society's next exhibition was "Modern German Art." The German art historian William Valentiner had organized the first contemporary German show at the Anderson Galleries in New York in 1923, and subsequent exhibitions had been arranged by Katherine Dreier for the Société Anonyme by the collector Galka Scheyer, by A. E. Gallatin at the Gallery of Living Art, and by J. B. Neumann in his New York gallery. But the Harvard Society's show was still a milestone. Because of the strong anti-German attitude that had prevailed ever since the end of World War I, this was the first time in more than fifteen years that an extensive showing of German art of any period at all had been presented in the Boston area. Besides ten major paintings by Paul Klee, there were works by Max Beckmann, George Grosz, Erich Heckel, Karl Hofer, Ernst Ludwig Kirchner, Oskar Kokoschka, Georg Kolbe, Otto Mueller, Emil Nolde, Max Pechstein, and Karl Schmidt-Rottluff, as well as the lesser-known Anita Ree, who was represented by a portrait of Eddie Warburg called *The Tennis Shirt.* The sculpture in the exhibition included another piece from Warburg's burgeoning collection—Kolbe's *Kneeling Figure,* a souvenir of one of his summer sojourns to visit his uncle Aby—as well as a Lehmbruck. Other lenders of this modern German art included a number of new sources for the society—among them Mrs. John D. Rockefeller, Jr., Jere Abbott, J. B. Neumann, and above all W. R. Valentiner, who had become a close friend and adviser to both Paul and Felix Warburg. But what Valentiner sold to the older generation were Dürers and Rembrandts. The art that Eddie and his friends were borrowing for the rooms over the Coop was the fire of their times.

XI

At the same time that the three college students were showing Brancusi and Bucky Fuller in their two rented rooms over the Harvard Coop, Mrs. Rockefeller and Miss Bliss—along with Mrs. Cornelius Sullivan—were busy making plans for their new museum of modern art to open in the middle of Manhattan. In November of 1929, nine months after the Harvard Society had presented its first show, they opened their doors in rented quarters on the twelfth floor of the Heckscher Building on the southwest corner of Fifth Avenue and Fifty-seventh Street. Like the Harvard Society, they opted for a startlingly simple setting, and had the walls covered in light beige monk's cloth.

At the advice of Paul Sachs, the founding trustees had selected Alfred Barr as the Modern's director. Barr wanted to open the museum with a show much like the inaugural exhibition his advisee Lincoln Kirstein had organized for the Harvard Society nine months earlier, which Barr himself had reviewed so enthusiastically for *Arts*. But his trustees insisted on something French, and a bit more time-tested. Their opening exhibition was a more traditional form of recent art than the first shows in the two rooms on "Mass. Ave." The premiere of the new Museum of Modern Art consisted of paintings by Cézanne, Gauguin, Seurat, and Van Gogh. This could be classified as modern, but not contemporary.

It is difficult to assess the precise role that the Harvard Society for Contemporary Art played in the early development of the Museum of Modern Art in New York. But in April of 1930 the Modern's trustees did invite the three undergraduates, along with Philip Johnson, onto its newly formed Advisory Committee. This new committee, consisting of "young people interested in the Museum,"[62] was intended to propose ideas to the trustees. Starting in July it held monthly meetings on the Tuesday before the trustees' meeting. The chairman of the Advisory Committee and three of its members periodically met with the regular board, and one member of the board attended Advisory Committee meetings. Agendas for the trustees' meetings were sent to each member of the Advisory Committee. Kirstein, Warburg, Walker, and Johnson were not the only members

of the inaugural crew; Mrs. Charles Payson, John Nicholas Brown
(the Harvard Society trustee), James Johnson Sweeney, Mrs. James
Murphy, Mrs. Porter Chandler, Mrs. D. Percy Morgan, Mrs.
Charles Russell, Howard Sachs (Paul's cousin), Miss Elizabeth Bliss,
Nelson Rockefeller, Miss Ethel Hawes, and George Howe were also
on the Advisory Committee. But the four Harvard men were strong
and significant voices.

Newspapers of the era made much of the connection of the Harvard Society Executive Committee with the Junior Advisory Committee. The *New York Evening Post,* on March 3, 1932, summed up
that bit of recent history by reporting,

> The almost instantaneous success of the Society for Contem-
> porary Art was followed before many months by the founding
> of the Museum of Modern Art in New York City, more preten-
> tious and with more substantial backing than the Harvard So-
> ciety, but identical with its Cambridge predecessor in its basic
> aims.
>
> The undergraduate directors of the Harvard organization
> were elected to the directorate of the New York museum—ac-
> knowledgement of how much the latter owed to the germ of
> that idea born at Harvard.

A few years later the *St. Louis Post-Dispatch* unequivocally called the
Harvard Society "the germ of the Museum of Modern Art" both for
the way it had sponsored startling exhibitions and for the overlap-
ping cast of characters of the two institutions.[63] The *Dispatch* pointed
out that both Alfred Barr and Jere Abbott, who was the associate
director of the Modern, had been Lincoln Kirstein's advisers at Harvard College and had closely observed the Harvard Society. (It might
also have been said that some of Kirstein's taste was attributable to
his tutor's guidance.) Moreover, by the time this article appeared,
Eddie Warburg—identified as "the bad boy of Harvard Yard"—was
a regular trustee as well as secretary and treasurer of the Modern's
new film library, and Kirstein had been the instigator of several major exhibitions.

It's a far reach to say that the Museum of Modern Art was begat
entirely by the venture over the Harvard Coop. But there is no doubt
that the founders and many of the other principal characters of the
Museum of Modern Art were profoundly impressed by what Kirstein, Warburg, and Walker achieved. As sustaining members of the

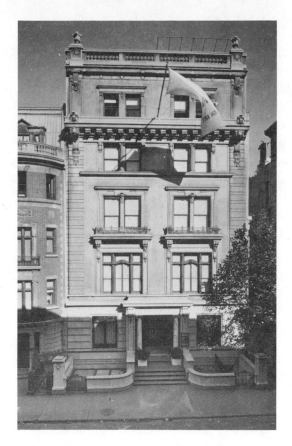

Town house at 11 West Fifty-third Street, home of the Museum of Modern Art, New York, 1936.

Installation view of the exhibition "Cézanne, Gauguin, Seurat, Van Gogh," November 7 through December 7, 1929. The Museum of Modern Art, New York.

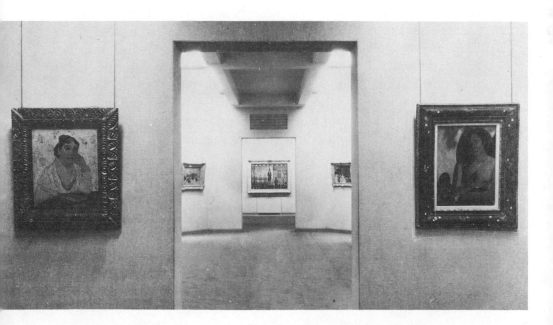

society, Mrs. Rockefeller and Miss Bliss were particularly attuned to
what was going on there. In addition, at least two of the Modern's
three founders had attended the society's opening exhibition.[64] Barr
and Abbott were contributing members of the society; Philip Johnson, who went to work at the Modern shortly after its founding,
was in the "sustaining" category.

The worlds of the two organizations overlapped constantly. When
Felix Warburg took the *Olympic* home from England in June of 1929,
one of the people meeting the liner at the pier in New York was A.
Conger Goodyear, who had recently become the first president of
the Modern and was at that point planning its opening. Goodyear
wanted to be there when the *Olympic* docked because Paul Sachs was
also on board. Goodyear was desperate to ask Sachs to be on the
museum's founding committee. Goodyear and Felix Warburg talked
eagerly as they waited for Sachs to finish arguing with customs
officials about some of the art he was bringing in; Felix was un-
doubtedly regaling Goodyear with accounts of young Edward's
carryings-on in the two rooms over the Coop. Within a year, Goodyear would become a trustee of the Harvard Society.

One of the reasons Mrs. Rockefeller, Miss Bliss, and Mrs. Sullivan had asked Conger Goodyear to head their new institution was
that as chairman of the board of the Albright Gallery in Buffalo he
had been so vociferous in his support of modern art that his fellow
trustees had thrown him off its board. He had committed two major
crimes. One was that he had taken a loan show from Katherine
Dreier's Société Anonyme. The other was that he had purchased for
five thousand dollars Picasso's *La Toilette,* a Rose Period painting not
unlike the one Eddie Warburg would buy later that summer. Chatting on the dock, Goodyear and Felix Warburg looked like rule-
abiding upper-crust gentlemen, but their lives were beginning to be
touched by bohemianism and new approaches to vision and thinking
more than most of their fellow businessmen could ever have imagined.

In addition to Mrs. Rockefeller, Miss Bliss, Mrs. Sullivan, Mr.
Goodyear, Professor Sachs, and Mrs. W. Murray Crane, the founding committee for the Modern included Frank Crowninshield.
Moreover, when the initial Museum of Modern Art board was
formed that October, not only did Sam Lewisohn become one of the
first trustees, but so did Chester Dale of Washington—a regular
lender to the Harvard Society—and Frederick Clay Bartlett of Chicago—who had lent de Chirico's *Twin Steeds,* as well as a Dufy and

a Vlaminck, to the pivotal second exhibition. Bartlett was a sustaining member of the Harvard Society.

In its early years the Museum of Modern Art would echo the Harvard Society in many ways. There was no comparison of scale, of course; the museum's first annual budget was $100,000, about fourteen times that of the Harvard Society, and the monthly visitor tally during its second exhibition was as high as forty-seven thousand. But in program it often mimicked the Harvard Society. For example, the second Museum of Modern Art show, "Nineteen Americans," was based on a similar premise to the exhibition with which the Harvard Society had opened its doors ten months earlier. It showed work by many of the same artists, among them Edward Hopper, Rockwell Kent, John Marin, Georgia O'Keeffe, John Sloan, Eugene Speicher, and Maurice Sterne. The "Painting in Paris" show held at the Modern at the beginning of 1930 echoed the Harvard Society's second exhibition, and depended largely on loans from the same people who had already sent works to Cambridge, such as Chester Dale and Sam Lewisohn. The patterns would be repeated. Within the next few years the Modern would follow the Harvard Society in showing Diego Rivera, German Expressionism, Bauhaus design, recent photography, and American folk art. The subject matter may have been totally new to the broad public that walked through the doors of the Heckscher Building and into the Modern's subsequent locations, but to people who had climbed the stairs of the Harvard Cooperative Building a lot of it was already familiar. In the case of the Bauhaus, for example, the Modern's exhibition— which has historically been treated as having been the first in America—came eight years after that of the Harvard Society.

The Museum of Modern Art mirrored the Harvard Society not only in what it showed, but in the nature of the critiques some of those choices inspired. The "Can you believe this idiocy?" running commentary that A. J. Philpott and A. F. Cochrane had repeatedly spewed to the broader readership of Boston was now put forth by many of their prominent counterparts in New York. Above all, Royal Cortissoz—in the *New York Herald Tribune*—went at the Modern constantly, so much so that A. Conger Goodyear, in his official history of the museum, while not actually deigning to name him referred to "our pessimistic castigator . . . of the Royal memory."[65] Reviewing the "Painting in Paris" show on January 26, 1930, Cortissoz described Picasso's *Seated Woman* as "merely grotesque and repulsive," and when the Modern showed some Paul Klees several months later he characterized them as "queer unintentionally amusing scrawls of childish effort." His comment on the 1931 show of contemporary German art was more acid than anything the Harvard Society's similar show had evoked a year earlier: "The collection of paintings here is the crudest, most raucous and least interesting of modernistic groupings we have seen in a long time." [66] But in general the Museum of Modern Art was tamer than the Harvard Society and had been formed in a more sympathetic city. Public support was its lifeblood, and in general it won high praise. Audience tastes had to be accommodated; the museum had its charter from the Regents of New York State, and it had consequent obligations.

By focusing on nineteenth-century paintings in its inaugural exhibition, the museum had opened on a modern but noncontroversial tack. There was Cézanne's *Still-life with Apples,* Van Gogh's *L'Arlésienne,* Seurat's *Parade,* and Gauguin's *The Spirit of the Dead Watches*— fine paintings to be sure, but also relatively safe ones. It was little wonder that *The New York Times* referred to "the rewards so lavishly spread before a visitor's eye." The values being promulgated were more established than the Harvard Society's in Boston; hence the congratulations were more readily forthcoming. Not that Royal Cortissoz was the only voice of dissent. The Modern's "Painting in Paris" show prompted W. B. McCormick in the *New York American* of January 26, 1930, to say that Matisse and Picasso "show to the full how thin is their art, how empty they are of ideas savoring of anything like originality of art." But Picasso was sufficiently mainstream in some circles that the *New York Sun* the day before had referred to one of his paintings as "an acknowledged miracle of art." The local and national press generally endorsed the new museum, which is why by the end of its first season the Modern had drawn in 170,000 visitors.

This isn't what the Harvard boys wanted. The Modern had opened with Seurat and Van Gogh; they had charged forward with the likes of Bucky Fuller, Calder, and Brancusi. Nothing could get them to compromise. They were ardent about what they showed, and didn't give a hoot about pleasing the crowd. Extreme reactions were just fine. In time, of course, Kirstein and Warburg would do their best to engender a bit of controversy at the Museum of Modern Art, but at least at the start "the young Turks"—as the most loud-mouthed of the Advisory Committee members were called—let the New York institution emerge peacefully, and confined their ranting and raving to greater Cambridge.

XII

A month after they had been appointed to the Advisory Committee at the six-month-old Museum of Modern Art, Lincoln Kirstein, Edward Warburg, John Walker, and Philip Johnson were graduated from Harvard. Even more so than the others, Warburg went out in rare style.

In September of 1926, shortly after Warburg had started freshman year, his father had written him a letter addressed to "Dear Teddy, Most learned of gentlemen!" It began:

> Perhaps by this time you have imbibed so much wisdom that I am taking you away from your serious labors for the purpose of reading this letter, but you may take my apologies for that.
>
> I was awfully glad to learn that Paul Sachs has been so cordial to you and I know that if you show any sign of reaction this will mean a friendship and an inspiration and a guidance for life to you.

By Warburg's senior year, however, things were no longer going precisely as his father had intended. The young modernist had indeed shown a "sign of reaction" to Paul Sachs, but it was not the type to guarantee friendship for life. Warburg had begun regularly to voice his view that art history courses focused too much on facts and identification. He attacked their indifference to judgments of quality in art. To ridicule the methods by which monuments were memorized he pointed out that Cefalu Cathedral could always be spotted because all the university photographs of it had a dog defecating in front. He and Lincoln Kirstein made up a painter called "Bebi di Papa Daddy" and convinced several fledgling art historians that Bebi was for real.

Then Warburg ignited the situation further. He made it public that he and a friend, Thomas Howe—the future director of the California Palace of the Legion of Honor who, in the *Crimson,* had shown rare sympathy for the Harvard Society's "School of Paris" show—had skipped classes for an entire month of winter term, during which they had sailed to and from London to see the exhibition of Italian Renaissance painting at Burlington House. Not a single faculty member had detected their absence. Moreover, the journey had in no way harmed their grades. Simply by reading their professors' books, they were able to prepare themselves for exams as thoroughly as if they had attended the lectures.

The final stroke was the speech Eddie Warburg gave as class orator at commencement in June of 1930. To speak one's mind was a Warburg family tradition. When Eddie's great-grandmother Sara Warburg, a close friend of both Heinrich Heine and Prince Otto von Bismarck, was annoyed because Bismarck's court chaplain had made an anti-Semitic pronouncement, she ceased her regular practice of sending Bismarck his annual Passover cookies, forcing the prince to deploy an emissary to her to try to make amends. Eddie could hardly be expected to bite his tongue when he felt strongly about something. His oration was an attack on the Harvard tutorial system. Speaking in Memorial Hall to his classmates, their parents, and much of the Harvard faculty, he depicted the great professors as remote and lazy. He pointed out that the only faculty with whom students had any direct connection were the tutors and section leaders who were more interested in their own graduate work than in teaching.

> Who are these section men and tutors upon whom the main responsibility of stimulating the interest of the students rests? Too often they are simply young men whose main aim is working for their doctor's degrees, or doing research for a future book. This is not so peculiar, since after all they depend on their books or their Ph.D.'s for recognition and promotion, and *not* on their ability to *teach*.

Eddie Warburg said that the professors and assistant professors—those unapproachable eminences who gave the actual lectures—very often merely repeated what they had already said year after year and had previously published in their books. More than teachers they were status-seekers—a category of sinner for which he and Kirstein had particular contempt. Before the assembled group of people who had so much invested in the experience of the past four years, Warburg amplified: "In an attempt to keep up its prestige as far as other colleges and the outside world is concerned, Harvard finds itself lamentably lacking in teachers and rather overloaded with authorities."

The oration was discussed a few weeks later in an unsigned editorial in *The Nation*,[67] where the names on the masthead included

Oswald Garrison Villard, Heywood Broun, Lewis S. Gannett, H. L. Mencken, Norman Thomas, and Carl Van Doren. Under the title "Fair Harvard," the piece began: "Only fair, according to Edward M. Warburg, senior orator at the Class Day exercises . . . That great institution, it seems, has grown too fast. The teachers, alas, are gone." It quoted Warburg as saying, "'The time of stimulating discussion between student and professor in the classroom is a thing of the past,'" and went on to analyze that development in some detail, reflecting that it was symptomatic of an overall degeneration in college education throughout America. *The Nation* cited a student at another prominent university who claimed that "the old-time contact between professor and student was entirely gone . . . but after all it didn't matter, because there were no teachers left among the professors—none of them cared for anything but research." The editorial concluded by quoting Warburg's assertion that Harvard was

> . . . lamentably lacking in teachers and rather overloaded with authorities. Mr. Warburg is right, and Harvard is in the same boat with most of the good colleges in the country . . . We congratulate Mr. Warburg, then, on making a frank and outspoken criticism of his Alma Mater, and we congratulate Harvard on training sons ready to criticize as well as praise.

The editors at *The Nation* may have been impressed, but Paul Sachs was livid. Sitting next to Felix Warburg, he could hardly control himself. When Eddie called on Sachs a few days later, Sachs exploded. His rage drove him to tears. Felix Warburg's youngest son, however, was incorrigible. Eddie told Sachs that he would demonstrate the proper role of a conscientious tutor by taking the post himself, gratis. Sachs's response was anything but a thank you. He considered this the most presumptuous suggestion he had ever heard.[68] Before young Warburg could dream of showing his face at Harvard again, he would have to begin his teaching experience elsewhere.

As usual when he was at loggerheads with Sachs, Warburg turned to Agnes Mongan. She had not only her familiar easy laugh and soothing voice, but a specific solution. "Hark the herald angels sing, Here's to Georgiana Goddard King," she intoned. She completed the verse: "Who is this who knows each thing, Yet she has no wedding ring. Peace on earth and mercy mild, Has she ever had a child?" King had told her Bryn Mawr students that she had had every experience known to women; the only one they could not imagine was her having given birth. But surely there was nothing about Eddie Warburg—oration, joking ways, modern art shows, and all—that King could not handle. Mongan arranged for Warburg to interview for a position. With a bit of Fizzie-style charm, he got a job. When King asked him why he had come to see her, Eddie "fell back defensively, and using one of Father's gallantries, responded, 'To meet one of America's few intelligent women.'"[69] She said that he should study in Europe for a year and then return to Bryn Mawr to teach a course in nineteenth- and twentieth-century painting and a second course in a still undetermined subject.

There was a hitch, however. Bryn Mawr lacked the funds for another art instructor. When Warburg volunteered to teach for nothing, King said that was out of the question. To teach without a salary would violate the school's standards and jeopardize the entire profession. But she did suggest that if she were to receive a check for one thousand dollars from an anonymous donor, that salary would be taken care of. Eddie Warburg's reply was to ask if she wanted him to sign it right away, and they shook hands on the deal.

By early fall Eddie Warburg had agreed that the second course should be a history of sculpture from the Renaissance to modern times. He headed for Paris to begin to prepare himself by looking at art and collecting slides. John Walker also went to Europe that fall following college graduation, to work with Bernard Berenson in Florence. Of the three members of the Executive Committee of the Harvard Society for Contemporary Art, only Lincoln Kirstein remained in Cambridge.

Kirstein had plenty to do there. *The Hound & Horn* was still going full force. So was the Harvard Society. He continued to mount exhibitions that launched trends that have had a lasting impact on American public taste. From October 15 to 31, the Harvard Society held an exhibition of American folk art that made it the first modern art organization to recognize the aesthetic relevance of these older objects. The show presented late eighteenth- and early nineteenth-century portraits, landscapes, mourning pictures, still lifes, and ship pictures in oil and watercolor on materials ranging from canvas and paper to wood, glass, cardboard, and velvet. This unacademic native art was more spontaneous than tutored. Generally unsigned, and of little interest to most art historians, it had many of the values prized in the more adventurous contemporary art.

The unsigned catalog essay—presumably Kirstein's—dealt as before with the issues of truthfulness and authenticity of feeling.

> The great charm of provincial and folk painting is its freshness, its surprising closeness to all that is directly necessary to the initial development of a culture. . . . A growing nation without the benefits of absolute despotism or state patronage has little chance for a broad artistic development, but on these walls, considering the artist's limited range, we have several qualities displayed without which the most sophisticated work is useless—a purity of linear handling, a deep psychological insight in portraiture, a freshness of color combined with the use of original media and an honesty that is as gracious as it is disarming.

Whether in Eddie Warburg's oration or in the stovepipe bases for Noguchi's sculpture, that high regard for candor was at the crux of things.

From November 7 to 29 the society put on a photography show. Again the concept, not unusual by today's standards, was pioneering for the time and place:

> The present exhibition attempts to prove that the mechanism of the photograph is worthy and capable of producing creative work entirely outside the limitations of reproduction or imitation, equal in importance to original effort in painting and sculpture.

The participants, most of them quite young, included Berenice Abbott, Eugene Atget, Margaret Bourke-White, Walker Evans (he was then twenty-seven), Charles Sheeler, Edward Steichen, Alfred Stieglitz, Paul Strand, and Edward Weston. There were unsigned aerial and astronomical views—the latter lent by the Harvard College Observatory—and press photographs, among them two shots of motor accidents lent by the *Boston Herald*. The show also included X rays, with titles ranging from "dislocation of the ulna" and "a bony tumor within the frontal sinus" to "skull fractured by baseball." In this way the Harvard Society further elevated the notion of truth—this time medical and biological—as an essential component of art.

. . .

In December 1930 and January 1931, the first Bauhaus show ever held in America was installed at 1400 Massachusetts Avenue. It was the only such exhibition outside Germany that took place while the experimental German school linking arts and crafts was still in operation. The Cambridge show—and its subsequent venue at the John Becker Gallery at 520 Madison Avenue in New York—was pivotal in introducing the American public to art and ideas that have since penetrated our society.

There were paintings, drawings, and prints by Erich Borchert, Lyonel Feininger, Johannes Itten, Wassily Kandinsky, Paul Klee, Gerhardt Marcks, Oskar Schlemmer, and Lothar Schreyer—lent primarily by John Becker and Weyhe. There was typography by Herbert Bayer, and an array of objects—plates, a lamp, an ashtray, a scarf of rayon and silk—all lent by Philip Johnson. And there were lots of photographs and Bauhaus books lent by Jere Abbott and Alfred Barr. Barr and Johnson had both visited the Bauhaus in Dessau, which is how Kirstein had come to know enough about the school to mount an exhibition.

The society issued a handsome catalog that credited Mr. Alfred V. Churchill, Mr. Philip Johnson, and Helmuth von Erfa as sources of its information. Von Erfa had been a pupil of the Bauhaus at Weimar. Churchill, head of the art department at Smith College, had become something of an authority on the school thanks in part to his close friendship with Feininger, the one American-born artist who taught at the Bauhaus. The authorship of the catalog was not cited, however; nor was there any indication of the name of the designer of the cover. This was a brilliant Bauhaus-style abstraction along the lines of the sand-blasted stained-glass constructions that Josef Albers was making in Dessau at the time. Later when the cover design and entire layout were reprinted for the John Becker Gallery, Lincoln Kirstein's name was given as both the writer and the designer.

Kirstein's task was to present the Bauhaus to an audience that had never before heard of it. With precisely the sort of clarity that the school was striving for, he wrote, "The exterior should directly echo the interior in lack of ornamentation and use of rigid economy in material and labor." He elaborated on that idea with a statement about the Bauhaus's third and final director, the architect Ludwig Mies van der Rohe—a name then scarcely known in the United States:

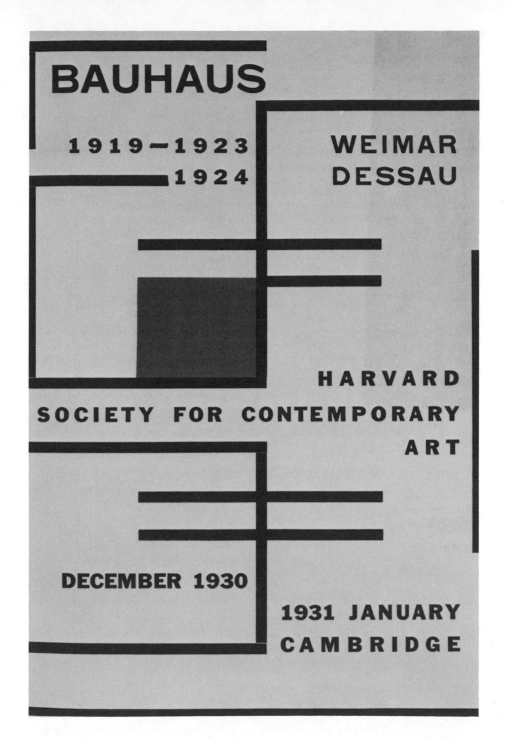

Cover of the exhibition brochure from "Bauhaus, January, 1931," The Harvard Society for Contemporary Art, 1930.

Mies wishes to make the best school in the world for those who are interested in architectural development, based not on aesthetic, historical, or Beaux Arts points of view, but founded on the principles of functionalism, of materials that are necessary and indigenous to the present, regardless of tradition, with an eye always open to social implementation.

The anonymous Kirstein cited objects that exemplified these principles. He mentioned Albers's glass work, Breuer's chairs, Gropius's architecture for a theater in Jena, and Moholy's photography. In time all four of these people would end up in America, teaching a generation of disciples and redesigning the look of the country; Gropius would eventually teach architecture within a stone's throw of the Fogg. This exhibition and Kirstein's essay put these names before a new public for the first time.

Kirstein, of course, did not simply fall at Gropius's feet. As with the American, French, and Mexican shows, he latched on to new ideas with considerable enthusiasm and prescience about future American cultural trends, but he also had his own point of view. He expressed this with the unabashed certitude that he revered in others. Kirstein admired the honesty of the man who had founded the Bauhaus in 1919, but made no bones about his views of Gropius's shortcomings:

Gropius had an extraordinary effect on everyone who came in contact with him. A brilliant publicist and theorist, he had the astounding faculty of making men of small parts outdo themselves when working for him. His influence was everywhere, in everything, in the painting, in the typography, and of course in the architecture. Gropius had the fundamental fault of being obsessed by the problems of technic. Primarily an artist he has the romantic fallacy of feeling that he must talk like an engineer, not like a designer—that if a wall is made of brick, a plaster facing is a dishonest facing.

Here was an instance in which Kirstein had put on an exhibition that did not necessarily follow his own taste. He preferred bravura to austerity; he liked evocative figurative art more than purist abstraction. But he valued integrity above all, and this is what he found in the Bauhaus. Moreover, he had developed a special regard for Philip Johnson, who had introduced him to this material.

Above all, the Harvard Society's Bauhaus show emphasized paintings. As in the modern German art show, they assembled an exemplary collection of Paul Klee's work. The catalog praised Klee for being "conscious of the extraordinary power of the poetry of simple intentions, the lyric of the pure primitive." As in so much else that the Harvard Society backed, what mattered was the idea of getting to the core. To attain knowledge and beauty one must peel away the coverings. The ideal was to know one's true instincts and to have the courage to be spontaneous. It was the concept that Sigmund Freud was at the same time doing so much to perpetrate in other ways.

At the start of 1931 Kirstein organized a Picasso exhibition, primarily with loans from the John Becker Gallery, Paul Sachs, and John Nicholas Brown. He then put on shows of work by Harvard graduates and of recent American art. Walker and Warburg had become "ex officio" on the Executive Committee, but Kirstein still had a strong board of trustees, to which he had added A. Conger Goodyear. But funding was getting to be more and more of a problem, especially without Eddie Warburg there to be the most sustaining of the sustaining members. Kirstein sent out a letter saying that it would be necessary to increase membership and contributions, or else to close.

Operating with limited funds, he slowed down the pace of exhibitions. At the end of March he presented modern art from the British Isles, but after that there was nothing on view in the two rooms at 1400 Massachusetts Avenue until November. Then came "Modern Painting in Review," which included major work by Monet, Seurat, Renoir, Cézanne, Van Gogh, Gauguin, Degas, Matisse, Picasso, Derain, Kandinsky, Marin, and Léger. More along the lines of what was being shown at the Museum of Modern Art, a bit less risky, it was meant to attract new blood to the society. The following exhibition was simply called "Abstraction." It was announced by a startling flyer the cover of which is dominated by a bold solid black square. In the white space on top of the square, "ABSTRACTION" is written vertically in black upper-case sans-serif type, bisected horizontally by "The Harvard Society for Contemporary Art" in red. Kirstein gave the rationale for the content of the show. What the works had in common was that independence from subject matter was their pervasive quality. Their underlying qualities were "simplification and stylization," "distortion," or "pure pattern." With those criteria, the selection included a fifth-century B.C. Greek white lekythos, an Egyptian limestone relief, a late fourteenth-century Sienese

Madonna, an El Greco painting, Russian icons, a notebook by Ho-kusai, Negro masks, Mexican santos, and work by Archipenko, Chagall, Léger, O'Keeffe, Lachaise, Gris, Masson, Picasso, de Chi-rico, Braque, Moholy-Nagy, Mondrian, Brancusi, and Gauguin. This exhibition was conceived as a swan song. On the back of the flyer it was announced that the gallery would close at the end of the exhibition because of lack of financial support.

News of the society's closing also appeared in the *Harvard Crimson* and the *Boston Transcript*. So did a significant letter of protest. Alfred Barr, as director of the Museum of Modern Art, wrote to the *Crimson* to voice "his astonishment and utmost regret . . . I have admired the courage and alertness of its directors both in their choice and presentation of exhibitions. Very frequently they have been in ad-vance of any other organization in the country in presentation of new phases of modern art. . . . If the Harvard Society for Contem-porary Art should die in the wealthiest academic community in the world it would be little short of disgrace." [70] Barr's and Kirstein's efforts paid off. Students came up with $900.33. In addition, $400.17 was pledged, $500.16 was contributed by people outside the college, and $700.00 was given by an anonymous donor.

So 1932 got off to a running start. There was another Picasso ex-hibition, this time of original drawings, copper plates, and etchings for Ovid's *Metamorphoses*. When the same exhibition had been at the Marie Harriman Gallery in New York the previous month, Henry McBride had said it was "exceedingly difficult, and for that reason will greatly please those already in the cult, and violently repel those who are not." [71] That was exactly the sort of material the Harvard Society longed for. And the cult appeared to be growing. A new student executive board was formed with three members of the Har-vard class of 1933 and a Radcliffe sophomore. The first show at the society after their induction demanded even more of a personal taste than the Picasso had. This was an exhibition of Surrealism that in-cluded three major works each by de Chirico, Dali, and Picasso, four Max Ernsts, and a range of drawings, books, and periodicals. It was the third venue of the exhibition, which had been organized by an-other former Paul Sachs student—Julien Levy—who had a gallery in New York. But the Harvard Society put its own special slant on it. They issued another striking flyer; its cover brandished the word "Surrealisme" with each individual letter backward—which made it far more puzzling than a perfect mirror image, with the entire word in reverse, would have been. Then there was Kirstein's succinct explanation of what the show was all about. What could have been intimidating material became palatable:

> The Surrealiste artist is interested in externalizing the experience that takes place in the remote spaces of consciousness. He attempts to reclaim for painting the regions that lie beyond logic. He is experimenting at the very edge of the expressible and the communicable.
>
> Surrealisme . . . uses a vocabulary of recognizable images and it links them in a purely subjective sequence. . . . It has the triple lure of the unexpected, the censorable, and the remote; and at its best it is embarrassingly comprehensible.

The society was back in full swing. From March 21 to April 2 there was a show of architecture and interiors with models and photographs of work by, among others, Gropius, Howe and Lescaze, and Frank Lloyd Wright. On its heels came another exhibition of recent American painting. Then, following the summer break, Kirstein presented twenty-three gouaches by Ben Shahn for *The Passion of Sacco and Vanzetti* and ten of his depictions of the Dreyfus case. This was risky stuff. One of the people depicted as a henchman of Sacco and Vanzetti was President A. Lawrence Lowell of Harvard, with whose nephew—Francis Cabot Lowell—Kirstein had roomed during his freshman year. At the order of the Harvard Yard police, the posters for the show were torn down from bulletin boards of dormitories and other college buildings—the official claim being that there had been no application for permission to hang them. It took courage to challenge the larger establishment in this sort of way, but here again Kirstein's ways were consistent with his father's; out of sympathy for what had happened to the two Italian immigrants, Lou Kirstein employed Sacco's son as his chauffeur.

Next came another photography show and an exhibition of designs for the theater. But even if Kirstein had managed to keep his art society alive and well, his own focus was shifting. He handed the reins of power over to J. P. Coolidge and R. P. Heller. The Harvard Society lasted awhile longer—even expanding its ranks to include sustaining members like Bernard Berenson—but in little time it faded. Kirstein moved to New York to be closer to his old friends and to be where he could see more art and ballet. He left Cambridge the legacy of a great literary review and a pioneering public art gallery.

XIII

Eddie Warburg's Bryn Mawr preparation program was no hardship. If he saw an artwork that would be instructive to his students, he often simply bought it. Curt Valentin helped guide his purchases. When Valentin visited Paris from Berlin, they would lunch together with the new young art dealers whose wares Valentin felt Warburg should consider. They owned galleries off the beaten track, as opposed to places like Durlacher or Wildenstein where Warburg might have run into his relatives or his parents' New York friends. After a sufficiency of sweet Anjou wine to wash down the special green and white oysters known as "marennes moyennes," Warburg invariably picked up another experimental drawing or piece of German Expressionist sculpture.

Equipped with addresses from Valentin, Warburg also traveled through Germany to see and in some cases acquire sculpture and drawings by Georg Kolbe and Gerhard Marcks. In Lübeck he looked up Professor Carl Georg Heise, a former student of Aby's whom he had met in Hamburg several years earlier. Heise was a great patron of the sculptor Ernst Barlach. Warburg bought several major Barlach bronzes, including a very dramatic and boldly formed *Head* and a poignant beggar leaning on crutches. He visited the Folkwang Museum in Essen, where he was even more excited by a loan exhibition of Gauguin than by the German collection. A wooden figure, barely ten inches high, moved him to distraction. Roughly whittled, stained red and black, and resembling a piece of folk art, this graceful statue—called *Woman on a Stroll* or *The Little Parisienne*—was made in 1880, at the very beginning of the artist's career. It is to Gauguin's work as *Blue Boy* is to Picasso's: a rare moment of innocent charm and loveliness. Again Warburg turned to Curt Valentin for intervention. The piece was on loan from Gauguin's widow, who lived in Copenhagen. Dollars were magic in those years, and Warburg became the owner.

At almost the exact time that the Bauhaus exhibition was filling the rooms at 1400 Massachusetts Avenue, Warburg called on Paul Klee at the Bauhaus in Dessau. Having admired Klee's work at Flechtheim's, he bore a letter of introduction from Curt Valentin. He arrived eagerly at Klee's doorstep, but stopped at the sound of the

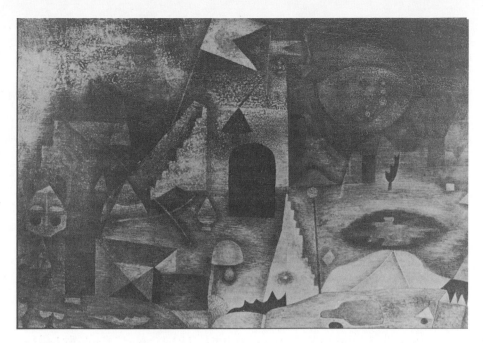

Paul Klee, Romantic Park, *1930. Oil and watercolor, 33 × 50 cm.*

artist playing Bach on the violin. He waited to knock until the sonata
was over. Once inside, he was even more riveted by what he saw
than by what he had heard. First there was the sight of the intense,
dark-eyed artist in the sort of white coat worn by surgeons. Then
there was the art as fresh and spontaneous as any statement Warburg
had previously encountered in any form.

The young Harvard graduate began to look at works on paper.
When he attempted to detour one of Klee's many cats from walking
across a watercolor he was holding, the artist urged him to let the
animal do as he liked. Warburg said he was afraid the cat would leave
a pawprint; the watercolor was still wet. Klee laughed and replied
that many years henceforth such a footprint would be a great insol-
uble mystery for art historians trying to figure out the technique
with which it had been achieved.

It was all a revelation. The art with which Warburg had grown up
left no room for happenstance. Here was someone who believed in
flowing with life rather than imposing artificial strictures. In little
time, Warburg became enchanted with an oil called *Departure of the
Ships.* In his experience boats were either Felix's hundred-foot yacht
or ocean liners where one's valet laid out one's evening clothes; Klee's
canvas of ships presented the idea of seagoing vessels in its greater,

more generalized form. The painting reveals motion itself. It illustrates wind. Its sails could be any type, anywhere, in the moonlight. Like *Blue Boy, Departure of the Ships* presents its subject as universal rather than specific, in all its humble grandeur. The young collector was equally fascinated by Klee's *Romantic Park,* a complex, dreamlike painting full of banners, lamps, jagged staircases, upside-down heads, and half-ornamental, half-real forms charged with inexplicable motion. It took the idea of staircases out of their 1109 Fifth Avenue mode and into their more Freudian aspect. In its complexity and the readings that it invited, it reminded Warburg of paintings by Hieronymus Bosch. This imaginative way of seeing things was irresistible, and at about eight hundred dollars a picture, he acquired the pair.

While Warburg was traveling around Europe buying Barlachs and Klees, most of his college classmates had gone the route of what Fizzie called "the money-mad crowd." Those who hadn't headed to graduate school had generally gone to work for banks and brokerage firms. Eddie's brothers Fred and Piggy fit into the mold by entering the financial world. Recognized by every headwaiter in New York, they adapted easily to the life of the rich. His brother Gerald, however, had also taken an alternate course. He became a professional cellist. If Eddie fulfilled one of Felix's missions by linking up with Sachs and the Fogg and making full-time work of his father's hobby of art, Gerry performed the same role in music. Fizzie didn't only collect Renaissance art; he also collected Stradivariuses. He owned four, which Gerry put to good use by founding the Stradivarius Quartet. On one occasion the Music Room at 1109 Fifth had the unique distinction of housing an all-Stradivarius octet when the Warburgs' four were joined by Herbert Strauss's.

Gerry annually bowed Kol Nidre during Yom Kippur services at the Temple Emanu-El, New York's bastion of German Jewry. On the other hand, his family's connections and fortune sometimes worked to his detriment. Determined to make the most of his musical career, he got his father to arrange an audition with Fritz Kneisel, the brilliant violinist who was head of the Kneisel quartet. When Felix asked Kneisel (in German), "Has the boy got talent?" the reply was, "Talent he's got, so long as he's ready to starve for it." "That," Felix replied, "is the only thing I can't provide." To many musical aficionados, what made the difference between Gerry's being merely a good cellist and a great one was that he never had to push himself enough. Not only did he not have to find the income to make ends meet, but he often couldn't get jobs performing because everyone knew that he didn't need the money; besides having his own income, he was married to Condé Nast's daughter. Especially in the 1930s, when so many people were struggling, it seemed unfair to deprive others of work.

Eddie Warburg may have also seemed like a rich young dilettante in the eyes of the world, but when he began to teach at Bryn Mawr in the fall of 1931, the students hung on his every word. He felt that his main job was to teach people *how* to see. By never proselytizing and by sprinkling his comments with humor, he managed to explain alien concepts to educated but unadventurous people. Warburg's students had traditional notions of the function of art; he knocked down their preconceptions and opened them to new possibilities. They considered verisimilitude a prerequisite of art; he showed them that abstraction was equally viable.

Having attacked the dependence on slides at Harvard, Warburg did his best to teach with actual objects. He had most of his art collection in his two-room apartment at the Bryn Mawr Gables on the Montgomery Turnpike. He often brought examples into the classroom. He also regularly squeezed as many students as possible into his Packard roadster to ferry them to the Philadelphia Museum. Georgiana King called Warburg into her office to heap praise on him. He responded by telling her that in that case he would give himself a raise.

King decided, however, that the young lecturer needed a real salary. Since she could earmark no more than five hundred dollars, adequate for only half a course, she proposed that Warburg return the following year for spring term. During the 1932 fall term he accompanied Professor Arthur Upham Pope, an authority on Near Eastern art, to Persia. Pope had asked Warburg to join him as a general assistant and adjunct photographer.

To get to Persia they went by train from London to Warsaw and then to the Soviet Union. They spent several weeks in Moscow. When Jacob Schiff's grandson looked out of his shabby Red Square hotel room at Lenin's tomb, he had to ask Pope who Lenin was. But ignorance of the history of Communism did not keep him from being sympathetic to its possible value. In a letter he wrote to his family from Leningrad on October 18, a description of miserable accommodations, greasy food, and his "second dose of fleas," was followed by the conclusion:

> All this sounds pretty terrible, but despite it all, I am *all* in favor of the life and all that goes with it. I have never felt better and I have never understood what went into pioneering before. It is a real thrill!! . . . The propaganda against Russia, that even I had become a victim of, is so fallacious as to seem humorous. . . . The figures on literacy, health, employment, and harnessed natural resources are all in favor of the Soviets.

The critic of Harvard's tutorial system and teacher of privileged young women at Bryn Mawr at last saw an education program that impressed him.

> I wish I could have had some of my students, world-weary friends, and depressed family, along with me on my trips to the schools and clubs. The cheerful, eager attitude exuding from those audiences was not only a tonic but a lesson. Everybody is on their toes and in sharp competition with his neighbor. . . . For the first time I witnessed education administered to fulfill a genuine *demand* from the students. Here they got what they wanted, and they not only knew what they wanted, but wanted lots. . . .
>
> Imagine groups of sailors and soldiers asking the museum to supply them with a guide who will tell them about the works of Art exhibited. Imagine the Hermitage having eight times the attendance it had before the revolution and its directors busy lecturing in the lunch hour in the steel mills. Imagine a nation educated to believe,—AND BELIEVING—, that culture is a necessity in this race.

Warburg may have been charged by the fervor for art in Russia, but he hadn't forgotten who the readers of his letter were any more than who his lecture audiences were.

> I could go on for many more pages but I can just see and hear the skeptical snickers these lines will arouse and the pitying tolerance you will all feel for me—"for having been pulled in like a sucker". I am no parlor-bolshy but I certainly am glad I got

bitten by fleas in this country and thereby got the chance to see Life from the side of a worth while, exciting adventure.

Don't worry. I won't bother you with all this when I get home.

Fondly,

Edward

He never minced words about his faith or tastes, but he always knew how far he could go.

Warburg and Pope encountered long delays in the Caucasus Mountains while they waited for equipment to arrive and paperwork to clear. When they reached Azerbaijan, Pope suffered from acute food poisoning. Warburg stuffed his shirts into a samovar to make hot compresses to apply to his mentor's stomach for two days until he could get him to a doctor. Both men were periodically ill, the plumbing primitive at best. But they continued happily past Teheran, to the site of an excavation on the Caspian, and then to Isfahan. There, urinating on a minor mud-covered tomb, Warburg inadvertently uncovered some key inscriptions. This unstandard technique revealed such fascinating ornament that he and Pope cleaned off the rest of the tomb—with more traditional methods—to reveal what was later considered a major monument of Persian art, fragments of which ended up in the Teheran Museum.

Next they went to Baghdad by way of a region where the American minister had recently been captured by brigands. Officials advised them to have a military escort. Warburg and Pope drove it alone, however, continuing on to Jerusalem. There Frieda Warburg and one of Eddie's cousins awaited them. Eddie had escaped his realities for long enough. He wanted to discuss Persia; his mother wanted to talk about family. Family won. There was also a letter from Georgiana King. She had only been able to raise fifty dollars toward his salary. In her attempt to come up with more she had written to people ranging from his father's fellow philanthropists to his own friends with the appeal, "Won't you please help save Mr. Warburg for Bryn Mawr?" Warburg was embarrassed; it was no one's priority to feed a Warburg at the peak of the Depression.

Despite the lack of funding, Warburg returned to Bryn Mawr for one more term. But after that he decided he had had enough. In his teaching he was too often quoting what he had said the previous year—the very shortcoming of which he had accused the Harvard faculty. But what was most discouraging were the passive students eager only to score well on exams. Warburg found them pretentious, interested only in appearing cultured. He missed the broader popu- lace that had moved him so in the museums of Moscow. Looking for the American equivalent of that general audience, as well as for more social life than he could find on the Montgomery Turnpike, he re- turned to New York.

For Eddie Warburg, the new Museum of Modern Art was the center of New York life. He had traveled there often from Bryn Mawr, including one occasion when he gave the first public lecture at the museum, on Matisse. What drew him primarily was the magnetism of Alfred Barr and of Philip Johnson. After Harvard, Johnson had traveled around Europe looking at modern art with Henry Russell Hitchcock, and in the fall of 1930 he had started a Department of Architecture at the museum. His terms of employment were like those of Warburg at Bryn Mawr, except that in addition to his own salary, he also paid his assistant's and, in time, that of the museum's first librarian. He too was caught up in the fervor for modernism, willing to do what it took to abet the new cause.

Warburg, Johnson, and Kirstein saw one another all the time. Among other things, they met at meetings of the Modern's Advis- ory Committee. Here again, Kirstein was full of ideas. It was time for the Modern to stop getting its customary pats on the back and to make a few waves as the Harvard Society had. He proposed a show called "Murals by American Painters and Photographers." Not only had he long admired the murals at the Boston Public Library, but in 1928 he had painted some murals of his own—in a geometric/ representational style akin to that of Stuart Davis and Gerald Mur- phy—for the Harvard Student Liberal Club. Organized by the Ad- visory Committee under Kirstein's direction, Kirstein's show was scheduled for the spring of 1932, to launch the museum's new head- quarters in the former Rockefeller town house at 11 West Fifty-third Street.

Kirstein asked each of sixty-five painters and photographers to take "The Post-War World" as their subject and to do designs on different scales. One of the works, by a little-known painter named Hugo Gellert, was called *Us Fellas Gotta Stick Together*. It showed Al Capone entrenched behind money bags and operating a machine

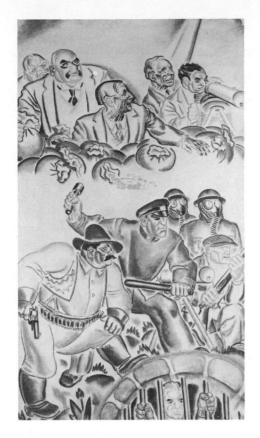

Hugo Gellert, Us Fellas Gotta Stick Together, *chalk on celotex sized with plaster, 7' × 4'.*

gun, with President Herbert Hoover, J. P. Morgan, John D. Rockefeller, and Henry Ford at his side. It was fine with Kirstein, but most of the powers at the Modern were enraged. The Advisory Committee members who were the liaisons to the Modern's board begged Kirstein to do something. Kirstein's reply was that if the museum refused to show this work, he would organize the same exhibition elsewhere and focus maximum publicity on what had happened.

It took another contemporary of Lincoln Kirstein's and Eddie Warburg's to save the day. The same year they finished Harvard, Nelson Rockefeller was graduated from Dartmouth. Having become closely caught up with activities at the museum his mother had helped start, he was chairman of the Advisory Committee. As a grandson of the tyrant portrayed at Al Capone's side, he discussed the matter with both his father and J. P. Morgan. Although some of the trustees wanted Kirstein fired, Rockefeller and Morgan agreed that the show should go on as planned. The public flocked to see it.

The murals were more than the critics could fathom, however. Generally a staunch supporter of the avant-garde, the *New York Sun*'s

Henry McBride called the exhibition "simply terrible. It is the saddest event of a none too cheerful winter."[72] Edward Alden Jewell in *The New York Times* wrote, "The exhibition is so bad as to give America something to think about for a long time"; it was "easel painting glorified into an ignominious failure."[73]

Nelson Rockefeller did not waver, however. And Kirstein did not go down quietly. In an essay called "Contemporary Mural Painting in the United States" in the July–September 1932 *Hound & Horn,* he applauded the new works at the Modern as the best of their kind. First Kirstein evaluated two well-known murals at The New School for Social Research; the Orozco, he opined, "has the advantage of his medium's earthy palette, but suffers from the awkward proportions of the place and an iconography which has not been wholly resolved." Thomas Hart Benton's New School mural was "more a documentation than a decoration," its colors unduly harsh. Then he defended the dining room murals by José Maria Sert at the Waldorf-Astoria, works that most critics had attacked. "Architecturally speaking, the building is a monument of mediocrity and false chic, but that is no reason for the fashionable condemnation of the murals along with it, for they are another thing." The Sert Room, Kirstein felt, reflected tradition and competence, and the reason they had been slandered was that these values were out of favor, much to Kirstein's dismay. He then addressed the issue of the recent Museum of Modern Art show without naming its curator. "The Museum of Modern Art, with a gesture of courage which has not yet been fully appraised, attempted to do what it could for mural painting." The show was "an excitement and a stimulus" for artists; since for most of the painters this was a first attempt, they warranted further opportunity to work on a large scale. Ben Shahn's *The Passion of Sacco and Vanzetti* was a model of straightforward eloquence. Even more successful was Philip Reisman's *The Post War World.* It illustrated farmers setting fire to wheat they could not market and pouring full milk cans into a brook, and members of the Ku Klux Klan hanging a victim. As for the critics who objected to this or Hugo Gellert's revelations of the class struggle in America, Kirstein's conclusion was that "The panels were very efficient. They provoked violent anger." Addressing McBride's remark that "The murals lack ideas, they lack beauty, they lack interest" and Jewell's assertion that they were "violations of even the most catholic conceptions of good taste," Kirstein belittled the notion of "good taste." What mattered was that statements had been made.

HARTFORD, CONNECTICUT

The year that Kirstein and Warburg entered Harvard, Edward Forbes's teaching assistant was A. Everett Austin, Jr.—"Chick" to his friends. His background was solid and educated, if less glamorous than that of the Harvard Society boys. His father was a prominent Boston-area physician and professor of medicine. His mother was a devout churchgoing member of the Daughters of the American Revolution whose most notable quirk was her rare penchant for collecting things—like the 321 side chairs, from a range of periods and countries, she amassed in the attic of their country house in New Hampshire.

Like Philip Johnson's, Lincoln Kirstein's, and Eddie Warburg's parents, the Austins spent quite a bit of time in Europe. By the time he was a teenager Austin knew the monuments of Vienna and had gone to schools in Dresden and Paris. Then, after attending fine Boston private schools and Phillips Academy in Andover, in 1922 he was graduated at age twenty-two from Harvard College. After that he joined a year-long expedition to Egypt and the Sudan during which he worked with the archaeologist George Reisner, much as Warburg later apprenticed to Arthur Upham Pope.

In Egypt, Austin helped uncover important collections of ancient artifacts that ended up at the Boston Museum. In the shadows of the pyramids some thirteen hundred miles south of Cairo, he also took up painting and developed a passion for looking at pictures. After Egypt he gave himself six months in the museums of England, France, and Belgium. Then he returned to Harvard where he studied architecture and at the same time took Forbes's course in the techniques of Italian painting, which in 1924 he began to assist teaching. In the summers he would travel to study fresco technique, first in Siena and then in Mexico at Chichén-Itzá, and in his spare time he painted tempera panels in the old Italian manner, as well as mild-mannered lyrical watercolors.

It was those rather tepid watercolors that Lincoln Kirstein reproduced in *The Hound & Horn* in 1929 and that the Harvard Society for Contemporary Art included in several of its exhibitions. By that time Austin was living in Hartford, Connecticut, where he had become the director of the Wadsworth Atheneum. Most everyone in America who needed a museum director in those days turned to Edward Forbes or Paul Sachs. In 1927, when Charles Goodwin, the Wadsworth's president, had sought advice on filling a vacancy in his institution—the oldest public art museum in America—Forbes and Sachs concurred that Austin was unquestionably the best candidate. They had considered recommending Alfred Barr for the post—in his letter to Goodwin, Forbes referred to Barr as "the man who is interested in Modern Art." But Austin, "an attractive man with brains and good taste," was best of all. He was, according to Philip Johnson, "the most charming man in the world. He could charm the birds off the trees without any trouble at all." Goodwin, whose father, the Reverend Francis Goodwin, was a first cousin of J. Pierpont Morgan, Jr., was the sort of person who hired and fired people easily, and without wasting the time to interview anyone else he appointed Austin to the new post in October of 1927.

Hartford was "the insurance city," and the moneyed people there—many of whom helped run Aetna, Travelers, and other similar firms—liked to do things carefully. As a precaution with regard to their new museum head, they made Austin acting director for his first year, with Edward Forbes as advisory director. By 1928, however, they decided that he had made the grade, and they gave him his reins.

Austin moved quickly. He opened 1928 with a group show that included a range of work from Egyptian Saite reliefs to a Van Gogh flower painting, intended to stimulate local private collecting. Then he turned to his mentor Paul Sachs for a loan show of drawings. From Sachs's private collection the Atheneum borrowed works by Tiepolo, Tintoretto, Holbein, Dürer, Degas, Ingres, Renoir, and Picasso. People were pleased. But what Hartford prized even more than great art was good parties. This suited Austin to a tee. On April 20, 1928, six months after he arrived in Connecticut, a "Venetian fête" was scheduled as a benefit for the Atheneum. The young acting director went to work designing and painting the scenery. He transformed the central tapestry hall of the Atheneum's Renaissance-revival Morgan Memorial, one of its main buildings, into the hall of a palazzo. This seventy-five-foot-long, thirty-foot-high barrel-vaulted space was ideally suited. Through doors to smaller galleries, the palazzo-for-a-day opened to vistas of the churches of Santa Maria della Salute and Santa Maria Maggiore, the Piazza San Marco, the

Grand Canal, the Bridge of Sighs, winding streets, and canals populated with gondolas.

Nine hundred of Hartford's lawyers and bankers and insurance executives and their wives danced away in the lavish make-believe setting to the music of Wittstein's orchestra from New Haven. Then, at 10 p.m., they assembled for a grand pageant. In ravishing costumes they swept down the grand staircase—decorated for the evening to resemble the grand staircase Pietro Longhi had designed in the Palazzo Stucco on the Grand Canal. Most of them wore colorful tricorns and voluminous skirts designed by Austin and made locally by the Royal Skirt and Coat Company. Mr. and Mrs. H. Bissell Carey, Mr. and Mrs. J. Ellicott Hewes, and Mr. and Mrs. Heywood Whaples were among the "strolling players and characters from Goldini's plays." In the true tradition of eighteenth-century Venetian masquerades as illustrated in paintings by Longhi, "Umberto the Hippo" was in the procession as well. The ferocious life-size animal, drawn by a young Ethiopian page and bearing Mrs. Philip Roberts as a scarlet-and-black Columbine, moved on castors. Made of plaster of Paris fashioned on a skeleton of barrel hoops, the hippo had a vast mouth that opened to reveal a frightful crimson gullet.

After the Goldini characters and their hippo came thirty-four Venetian dancers with very un-Italian names like Mr. and Mrs. Waldron Faulkner, Lucy Goodwin, Gertrude Robinson, Sage Goodwin, Hamilton Maxim, Frederick Pingree, and Charles Strictland. The dancers were followed by the Comedy Group, among them Mr. Dexter Coffin and Mr. Burton Cornwall, who must have been an extraordinary blend of Ivy League and Longhi in Austin's costumes. Next was the Carnival Group—students from the Hartford Art School, which was located in the Atheneum at that time—followed by the Promenaders of the Plaza. Miss Anne-Carolyn Bissell, Mr. Varick Frissell, Mr. Lauder Greenway, and Mr. Winthrop Saltus then entered as Venetian Glass Figurines, after which came characters from Longhi paintings and others representing the Compagnia del'Opera Veneziana.

What followed must have been very grand indeed. Imitating a rite observed annually by Venetian aristocrats in the eighteenth century, some of the local gentry enacted the marriage of Venice to the Adriatic. The ceremony symbolized the dependence of Venice on the sea. Venice was Mrs. Austin Dunham. Preceded by two lantern bearers and a blackamoor, she arrived in a regal sedan chair, which

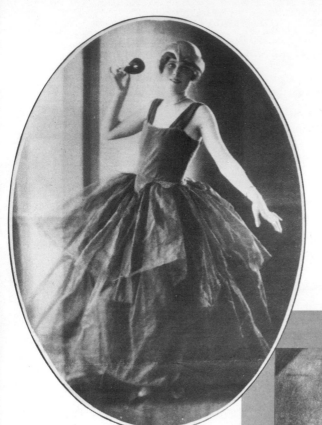

Miss Barbara Farmer at the
Venetian Fête. Hartford
Courant, *April 22, 1928.*

Cover of program for the
Venetian Fête, April 20,
1928.

PROGRAM
—
VENETIAN FÊTE
WADSWORTH ATHENEUM
APRIL 20, 1928

A. Everett Austin had designed for the evening and which was carried by two liveried servants. Mrs. Dunham wore a gown in a range of pinks and oranges that suggested the colors of the sunset. Following her chair came a group of people dressed in gowns and suits in shades of yellow, blue-green, and blue that symbolized the Adriatic Sea. Next came some of the most prominent local attorneys and civic figures in The Murano Group, followed by more executives of local industries and insurance companies and their wives as the Ladies and Gentlemen of the Ducal palace.

Finally came the most elaborate entrance of all. Charles Goodwin—the president of the Atheneum and the man who had hired Austin—was Doge Marca Foscarini. Generally seen in nothing other than a proper dark suit or evening clothes, Mr. Goodwin donned a flowing, fur-trimmed costume of red-and-silver damask. Mrs. Goodwin, the Dogaressa Isabella Foscarini, wore a gown of brilliant red-and-golden-yellow brocade. They were attended by standard-bearers; chamberlains; a cardinal; the artists Giovanni Battista Tiepolo, Francesco Guardi, and Pietro Longhi, and the composer Domenico Cimarosa—most of whom sported brocade vests, knee breeches, and powdered wigs. Their ladies-in-waiting were in heavily embroidered gowns of pale blue brocade and mulberry velvet.

Of the twenty-six members of the doge's retinue, almost half had the last name of Cheney. And wherever you looked in Venice that night, someone had the last name of Goodwin. Establishment Hartford consisted of just a handful of families, and, at least initially, they were all happy to dance to the tune of Chick Austin. They reveled for hours. In the early morning they took their supper in a clammy dungeon he had made for the occasion by using iron grilles, lanterns, and heavy furniture to transform the basement underneath the grand gallery. If it was Austin's wish, Hartford would gladly down its bouillon, salads, ices, and coffee in the ancient gaol where prisoners were incarcerated before making the trip across the Bridge of Sighs.

The event wasn't mere frippery, however. It appeased New England guilt by serving a very real purpose. The Venetian fête raised over three thousand dollars—not just pocket change for a benefit in 1928—so that the Atheneum could begin to take loan exhibitions and attract visiting lecturers. Austin's goal was that "the reputation of Hartford's artistic vitality will spread even to the foreign cultural centers." [1]

The exhibition that opened with the Venetian fête and ran from

April 20 to May 5, 1928, was, like the Sachs collection show, an attempt to put Hartford on that map. It presented a group of paintings by modern artists that included Braque, Cézanne, Derain, Degas, Raoul Dufy, Gauguin, Laurencin, Matisse, Modigliani, Morisot, Picasso, Redon, Rousseau, Toulouse-Lautrec, Utrillo, Van Gogh, and Vlaminck. The lenders were almost all New York or Paris galleries: Wildenstein, Durand Ruel, Reinhardt, Knoedler, and Weyhe. This was closer to the acceptable modernism already shown at the Fogg and other major museums than the sort of avant-garde pickings the Harvard Society would put on view, but it was daring nonetheless. Most of these artists had been shown in America before. But their work was still rare in public institutions, and nothing like it had been shown in Hartford.

In 1927, before Austin had taken the helm, the major shows at the Atheneum had included titles like "Exhibition of Valentines," "Exhibition of Scottish Clan Tartans," "Exhibition of Linen Damasks," "Exhibition of Printed Cottons," along with solo shows of work by the artists Gifford Beal, Edith Briscoe Stevens, Paul Saling, Russell Cheney, and Ruel C. Tuttle—Beal being the only one who isn't highly obscure today. Austin turned everything around. Following the Modern French exhibition, he displayed twelve of Edward Hopper's watercolors. They weren't just aesthetically avant-garde for 1928. They were also daring for their focus on the sides of American life on which the West Hartford insurance set generally preferred to turn its back. Moreover, Austin managed to acquire two of the Hoppers for the museum that year, along with works of two other American contemporaries, Preston Dickinson and Charles Demuth. A man named Frank Sumner had left his fortune in the form of a bequest to the museum. Mrs. Sumner's death in 1927, the same year that Austin arrived in Hartford, had freed over two million dollars for the Ella Gallup Sumner and Mary Catlin Sumner Fund—named for Sumner's wife and sister-in-law—which enabled Austin to begin a major acquisitions program.

Austin was not as relentlessly contemporary as the Harvard Society founders. Nor was he as deliberately eager to make waves as Kirstein was. He was, after all, a salaried employee working under the eyes of watchful trustees. The same year that he was buying Hopper for Hartford, he used Sumner money for important paintings by Fra Angelico, Tintoretto, and Daumier, and two drawings by Goya. His heart was in the seventeenth and eighteenth centuries as much as the twentieth. What he liked was for something to be quintessentially whatever it was.

A few months after he had transformed a nineteenth-century American public space into an eighteenth-century Venetian palazzo, he redecorated his own private apartment, about a mile from the Atheneum, in the epitome of the latest modern style. The week before Christmas, it was opened up for public viewing. In Hartford you might have a modern toaster or the latest model of radio, but proper domestic style meant objects like lamps with eagle finials and maps of the Thirteen Colonies wrapped around their bases. Unless they had peeked into one of the more forward-thinking New York department stores, few of the locals had ever seen anything quite like what their museum director had done with his rooms. The usual knotty pine paneling and imitation Georgian everything was nowhere. Austin was making the startling suggestion that it might be possible to have some other prototype for style than eighteenth-century England or Colonial America. One did not have to look backward at all. The furnishings—many of which had previously been in an exhibition of modern decorative art at Lord & Taylor's in New York—were mostly of the type that had been shown by the Wiener Werkstatte and in the "Exposition International des Arts Décoratifs et Industriels Modernes" that had taken place in Paris in 1925 and had recently given birth to the name "Art Deco."

Austin's study had one black wall and three in different shades of gray. The carpet was a neutral yellow-brown. Its wrought-iron and palisander wood "couch hammock" consisted essentially of a brown upholstered cushion supported by a platform suspended from the ceiling. It was backed by heavy tan-and-ivory rayon hangings that had been handwoven in Paris. There was an unusual adjustable wall mirror that slid up and down, and a nest of triangular mahogany stacking tables on which a modern pewter and glass lamp rested. The man who had designed the couch hammock—Chareau—had designed the desk as well. Also made of wrought iron and palisander wood, it was a crisp arrangement of cantilevered planes. Nearby stood one of the first of Marcel Breuer's Wassily chairs ever seen in America, with the original gray canvas stretched across the steel tubing. The rug was chenille, the fabric on the large and stylish Art Deco armchair a beige whipcord. Paintings were by Juan Gris and Ossip Zadkine, while works by Marie Laurencin and Charles Sheeler hung on the checkerboard wood veneer walls of the enclosed porch.

Then there was the salon. Austin had painted its walls battleship gray, and covered its floor and ceiling in jet-black carpeting. The wallpaper was a hand-blocked black, white, and gray design of ladies surrounded by exotic birds and foliage, the draperies oyster white celanese. A modern silver and rosewood coffee set by Jean Puiforcat of Paris was on the coffee table, and pieces of Lalique glass sparkled from here and there. A German ceiling fixture that was an amalgam of flat planes of frosted glass, silver, pewter, and iron cast suitably cool and even light.

The couch in the salon was by Ruhlmann. Upholstered in silver gray velvet, with ivory and hyacinth blue triangular cushions that gave the room one of its rare color accents, this modern adaptation of Empire style suggested sheer languor. Here soignée ladies might recline alongside decadent Parisian noblemen or Oscar Wilde dandies.

If black, white, and gray could be shocking, so could their opposite. In the hallway, the woodwork was painted lime green. Its walls were covered with German wallpaper in broad vertical stripes of a chartreuse and lemony yellow. The background for a large Elsie Driggs canvas of smokestacks, a John Marin, and a Yasuo Kuniyoshi, these walls accented the daring modernism of the paintings. The bathroom, with its rough chartreuse silk shower curtain and draperies and its orange, yellow, and green wallpaper, was equally vivid.

Lewis Mumford was right about American taste in general, but there were exceptions. Austin's rooms and his defense of their new machined appearance forecast the rationale that four years later would govern the International Style Exhibition at the Museum of Modern Art, a show that would be organized by Philip Johnson and Henry Russell Hitchcock. At the time Austin refurbished his apartment, Hitchcock was a twenty-five-year-old assistant professor of art at Wesleyan University in Middletown, Connecticut—not far from Hartford. Having been graduated from Harvard in 1924, he had been a tutor of fine arts there when Austin was assisting Sachs and when they had all come to know Alfred Barr. Hitchcock had become one of the greatest proponents of the new architecture, and Austin one of his most loyal friends and disciples.

The next spring Austin remodeled his office in the Atheneum's Morgan Memorial along the same lines as the apartment on Farmington Avenue. It resembled the latest interiors at the Dessau

Bauhaus, with solid-colored panels that turned it into a sort of three-dimensional Mondrian. The leanness stopped people in their tracks. What have become design clichés today—like Breuer's Wassily chair—began to seep into the mainstream of American life.

Austin was giving people more to talk about all the time. In 1928 he had created an organization called "The Friends and Enemies of Modern Music," a subscription society that gave six concerts a year in private houses. At its first get-together Clifton Furness and Elliot Carter had performed music by Stravinsky, Milhaud, Schoenberg, Poulenc, Ives, Satie, Hindemith, and Antheil. Austin "believed in the importance of the contemporary composer and felt more or less with him the sad plight of all modern creative spirits who have, alas, so limited an audience. I wanted to find him a small but sympathetic and intelligent audience in Hartford."[2] Before long there were evenings like one on which Roy Harris, Aaron Copland, George Antheil, Paul Bowles, and Virgil Thomson all played work by one another.

Meanwhile Austin continued to jump from century to century. Within a month of inviting the local population to see streamlined contemporary design in his apartment, he mounted a show of French eighteenth-century art. The loans from Sir Joseph Duveen, Wildenstein & Co., Jules Bache, P. W. French & Co., and other fine collections included major paintings by Boucher, Chardin, Fragonard, Greuze, and Watteau; drawings by most of the same artists; Royal Beauvais tapestries; and exquisite examples of Louis XV and XVI furniture. But Austin's eye was not for the urbane and fancy alone. While these pre-Revolutionary French masterpieces filled the Morgan Memorial, an exhibit of work by "American Negro Artists" occupied the Atheneum Annex. Presented by the Race Relations Committee of the local YWCA in cooperation with the Race Relations Commission of the Federal Council of Churches and the Harmon Foundation, it showed the work of twenty-seven virtually unknown black artists. One canvas illustrated the spiritual "Swing Low, Sweet Chariot"; others ran the gamut of themes. There was very little Austin wouldn't consider.

On July 11, 1929, Austin married Helen Goodwin, the niece of the man who hired him and a daughter of the Reverend Dr. James Goodwin. She had been one of the gowned aristocrats at the Venetian fête, and a month prior to that party she had been one of the ladies ladling out punch for the opening of the Sachs collection show. Helen and

Chick were two beautiful, capable, and stylish people. Like characters in a Noël Coward play, each called the other "Cunning." They were wed in the American pro-Cathedral in Paris, much as Alfred Barr and Margaret Scolari would be married less than a year later at the American Church on the Quai d'Orsay. For art lovers, Paris was less out of the way then than now, and lots of Helen and Chick's friends and relatives sailed to Europe to attend their wedding.

That same year, Austin acquired for the Atheneum a major Goya, two Luca Giordanos, a Salvator Rosa, and a Cézanne watercolor. In the fall he put on a second show of contemporary French art. With Picasso, Matisse, and Derain at its core, it also presented such oddities as four paintings by de Chirico. Here the defender of the cause was Henry Russell Hitchcock. Like Kirstein, Warburg, and Austin, Hitchcock had the rare ability to put new and potentially disturbing ideas into readily comprehensible language. Like theirs, his voice was calm and patient. In an essay in the *Hartford Times,* he explained that "Chirico is a painter of dreams and his subject matter, like that of a dream remembered, has a depth of emotional tone not easily traceable to specific or analyzable causes."[3] Statements like these helped take the threat out of the new art.

Not that Hartford lapped up modern art with a spoon. A few months after the second Modern French show, a cartoon in the local paper bore the caption "Trying to Get the Right Angle on the Modernistic Painting at the Memorial." It showed a bedraggled and anguished spectator attempting to stand on his hands, obviously hoping that by seeing the paintings upside down he might glean some meaning from them. Tears fall onto his hat, which, also upside down, lies beside him on the floor. The cartoonist's paintings look faintly Cubist, and almost entirely abstract. One bears the title "Nude Ascending Staircase." It wasn't, apparently, a poke at the Atheneum alone, but at all of modern art—going back to Marcel Duchamp's *Nude Descending a Staircase* that had caused such a ruckus at the New York Armory Show in 1913. The target of this cartoonist's humor was beginning to rear its head everywhere. The "modernistic painting at the Memorial" was part of a trend; the Museum of Modern Art had recently opened. Chick Austin, in fact, had a painting in its fifth exhibition in the Heckscher Building, which was devoted to work by men and women under the age of thirty-five. What was the object of derision on one front was rapidly becoming the stuff of worship on another.

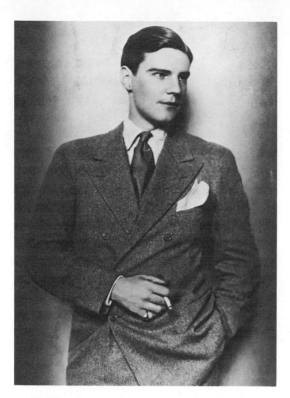

Chick Austin, 1927.

A. E. Austin's office in the Morgan Memorial of the Wadsworth Atheneum, 1930.

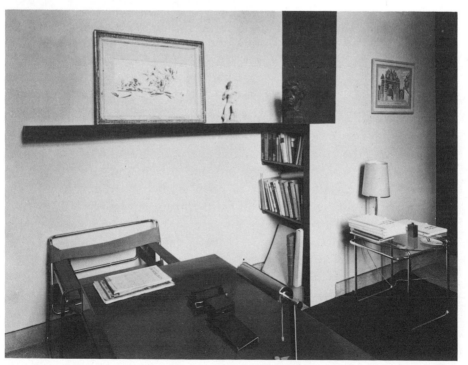

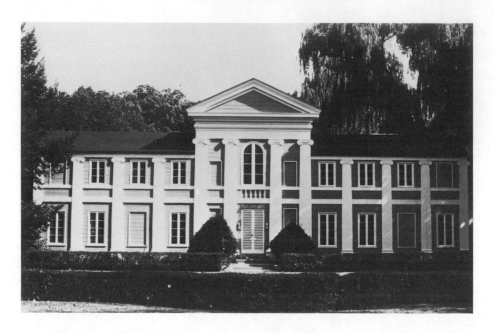

Helen and Chick Austin's house on Scarborough Street, 1932.

Whatever the voice of opposition, Austin had hit the stride he would keep up for another decade. In January of 1930 he put on the first important American exhibition of Italian Baroque painting, another of his passions. An unpopular style at the time and generally considered decadent, this work did not take in Hartford, but it further established the Atheneum as an institution of international significance. Visitors came from some distance, and the national art press gave favorable reviews. While the catalog did not sell as well to the local populace as the museum had anticipated, after the show closed it practically sold out to people who ordered it from elsewhere in the United States and from Europe, most of all Germany. The exhibition attracted the interest of cognoscenti everywhere. Even if the locals weren't enthusiastic, Austin had his mandate. He acquired for the Atheneum key seventeenth- and eighteenth-century paintings, then still quite unrecognized and hence inexpensive, at a clip. In 1930 it was a major Caravaggio—the next year important works by Tiepolo, Strozzi, Longhi, and Bellotto. He would maintain the pace for quite some time.

. . .

Meanwhile, shortly after they were married, Chick and Helen built an extraordinary house on Scarborough Street, a wide boulevard divided by a lovely stretch of grass and trees. This was in the most desirable residential area of Hartford, at the edge of West Hartford and a short walk from the Connecticut governor's residence on the city line on Prospect Avenue. The new house went up quickly and looked like a stage set. The other residences in the neighborhood were the usual neo-Colonials and imitation English Tudor or Gothic country houses preferred by affluent Americans. Brick or stone, they represented solidity, and assured their inhabitants the security of Anglo-Saxon tradition. The Austins' house, on the other hand, looked like an outrageous bit of frippery that could be blown over with one good gust. It was one room deep—twenty feet wide—but nearly a hundred feet long. Seen from the road, from which it was set back at considerable distance at the bottom of a formal lawn, it resembled a cardboard facade; the material was actually wood painted gray and white. The style, however, of this sequence of tapered columns topped with a templelike pediment was Palladian.

Working with an architect named Leigh French, Austin had based his new residence on an Italian villa on the Brenta River between Padua and Venice. He had seen it from the window of a train and sketched it on the back of an envelope near the place where Agnes Mongan and Lincoln Kirstein had encountered Diaghilev's mourners. Austin wasn't bothered that the Hog River, which flowed behind *his* villa, was neither as wide nor as long as the Brenta, and wound its way through the poorer sections of Hartford rather than through the northern Italian countryside. The house, after all, was like an illusion. Austin loved to perform magic tricks at social occasions; the landscape could require a stretch of the imagination as well. If the surrounding residences asserted rank, affluence, and above all solidity, this one was a song lyric announcing that life should be as amusing as possible. It was like the large bright pocket handkerchiefs Austin sported in an era when his neighbors and trustees would scarcely allow a discreet point of white to accent their dark pinstripes.

Austin's mother put up most of the eighty thousand dollars needed for the house and its interiors. He furnished it in a panoply of styles. Lavish scrollwork and gilded cherubs abounded. The living room had a French Regency–period door mantel and mirror. Its walls were covered with tempera panels of seascapes painted in Turin in about 1720. The foyer, furnished with Venetian eighteenth-century furniture and silks, was decorated with Chinese figures. One end of the dining room was occupied by an Austrian Rococo sleeping alcove—or "bed-niche," as it was then called. There were elaborately carved Baroque doors that Austin had found in a French country house, and walls hung with Italian blue-green brocatelle. Austin himself had marbleized the woodwork of the dramatic spiral staircase that ascended in the middle of the house in a well topped by a dome.

On the other hand, some surfaces were totally lean. The dressing room was based on one in Walter Gropius's house at the Dessau Bauhaus. Its walls were cream, cocoa, brown, and blue; its furniture glass and steel. One of the bedrooms, based on designs by the contemporary German architect Bruno Paul, resounded in greens and yellows. The bar in the basement was painted with solid planes of color in the same manner as the apartment Austin had shown a couple of years earlier. It had modern German lighting fixtures and a swinging hammock by Chareau.

Everyone who picked up the local papers followed Austin's carryings-on. What was happening at the local museum, and the latest forays of its colorful director, were as much a part of everyday life as foreign news and sports and tales of Hollywood stars. Day after day the local press had described in detail the costumes and decor of the Venetian ball. Now the *Hartford Courant* devoted a full page of photos to the interior of Chick and Helen's new house, which was opened for public tour to members of the Atheneum. The *Courant* and the *Hartford Times* gave purchases of important paintings front-page coverage. The reporting never included dollar amounts; it tried, rather, to put more of a true cultural perspective on the latest acquisition. Journals carefully explained ideas like "Baroque" and "Renaissance" to the larger population. Given the exigencies of the period, this was both education and entertainment. It was a much-needed lift.

A mile or so from Austin's Palladian villa, along pleasant suburban roads of large houses with big lawns, the scion of one of Hartford's prominent manufacturing and tobacco families was living in a more expected way on Westwood Road in West Hartford. James Thrall Soby had built a French provincial house in keeping with acceptable suburban style. But even if his house resembled others in the neighborhood, Soby had set his sights higher than most of his friends had. No more at ease in country clubs than Kirstein, Warburg, and Austin were, he opted for other areas of diversion. In 1928 and again in 1929, he had been overwhelmed by Chick Austin's exhibitions of recent French painting. Here he got to see, firsthand, art of the type he had known mainly from illustrated books and from the trip he had taken to Paris with his mother after his sophomore year at Williams College. He admired the French artists' reaching for new forms of expression, and enjoyed their wholehearted embrace of the life before them. By January of 1930 he could no longer resist the temptation to take down the Connecticut Impressionist canvases that filled his living room and replace them with the more avant-garde paintings from France.

So the twenty-four-year-old James Thrall Soby drove to New York and on a raw winter day went to Valentine Dudensing's gallery on Fifty-seventh Street. He bought two paintings recently back from a show at the Harvard Society for Contemporary Art—Henri Matisse's *The Red Sofa* and André Derain's *Head of a Woman*—and Moise Kisling's *Bateaux*. The Matisse cost seven thousand dollars, the Derain four thousand dollars, the Kisling a pittance. It was more money than he had ever dreamed of spending for artworks, but he was sure he wanted them, and he drove back home to West Hartford with the three canvases that same afternoon.

Within the next couple of days, however, Soby began to get cold feet. His friends couldn't believe what he had bought, and his bankers told him he was out of his mind. So he got into his car and drove downtown to the Atheneum. He asked for Chick Austin, whom he had never met before but whose taste he knew from the two French painting shows.

In those days it was possible to get in to see a museum director without an appointment. Soby was ushered into Austin's stream-lined office. He immediately described the purchases and his recent trepidation about them. Austin could not believe his ears. He had been desperate to buy a Matisse of a ballet dancer for the Atheneum a year earlier after it had been in his contemporary French show, but his Acquisitions Committee had scoffed at the twenty-thousand-dollar price tag. Their reaction to the news that a major New York collector (Stephen Clark) had an option on it was to say that New Yorkers were noted spendthrifts. The museum director grabbed the young collector's arm, told him to get into his car, and raced up Hartford's Asylum Avenue past the imposing corporate neo-Classical palaces of insurance and other safe risks to the suburban living room where the exemplars of French modernism were still leaning on the mantel.

Austin was thrilled. Not only were these wonderful paintings, but someone out there in the community had cared enough to buy them. And Soby was buoyed up. Here was one individual who wasn't say-ing he was crazy. The Soby/Austin alliance would have a lot in com-mon with Warburg's and Kirstein's. Soby could state Austin's case to people who wouldn't hear it from the man himself, and so provide him with a foothold in the acceptance world of Hartford; Austin could nourish Soby with an intellectual vitality and spiritual courage that the young acolyte found nowhere else. Like Alfred Barr, Chick Austin was an indefatigable teacher—and Jim Soby his most atten-tive student.

James Thrall Soby was a handsome and affable gentleman who may have had eccentric tastes but whom most everyone liked. Old photos show him confident but never cocky, impeccably dressed without being foppish, looking as if he is having a supremely good time being alive. In almost all those pictures he wears classic, thin horn-rimmed eyeglasses. In time Soby would ally himself with some fairly avant-garde tastes, but he never thought there was anything wrong with being an easygoing gin-and-tonic-swilling Connecticut gentleman. He fit in well with the world from which he came. As a boy he could ride his mare Easter Belle at a full gallop while bending down to use his teeth to pick up a handkerchief from the ground. At Lawrenceville he played all the right sports, and when he completed his prep years at a day school called Kingswood in Hartford, he was captain of the football, basketball, and baseball teams. He may have opted out of the country club set, but he had the advantage of plenty of money and entrées pretty much wherever he wanted to go.

Family connections enabled Soby to be a liaison with the conservative power structure embodied by the museum's trustees. Hartford was like an old boys' club, and he belonged to the inner sanctum; Austin may have married into it, but that wasn't exactly the same thing. When Soby was a boy growing up and his father was president of the Connecticut State Fair, the family had a box in the middle of the grandstand section. Frank Sumner, who had endowed the Atheneum's acquisitions fund, held the next box. He was one of Charlie Soby's closest friends, and every year he would lean over and offer Charlie a huge sum of money, compounded annually, for Jim and his brother Ralph. Sumner, who was childless, claimed that these were the sons he had always wanted. Soby had similar connections with many of Austin's other key donors and trustees. These acquaintances could not totally shut out certain modern ideas if he was the one who posed them, and he came to function as a sort of one-man advisory committee. He was the young voice to whom the older stalwarts were willing to pay attention.

Like Philip Johnson, Soby was able to enjoy the good life because his father had, early on, acquired stock in a new and untried product that contributed unprecedented ease to everyday American life. Charlie Soby had backed an eccentric inventor named William Gray who had come up with the idea for a coin machine that made pay telephones possible. The device meant that money which someone had deposited could be returned if the call wasn't completed. Charlie Soby had put up most of the money for the factory that made the money box, and he shared the patent with Gray. He earned most of the profits, which were substantial.

In addition, Charlie Soby manufactured cigars. Charlie's father-in-law had been a great tobacco expert. By the time Charlie joined the business the family owned excellent fields—many of which were next to fields owned by their good friend Joseph Alsop—in which a high quality of tobacco leaf was being grown from Cuban seed. That Cuban-style leaf was used for the wrappers of Charlie Soby's two top-sellers: the five-cent "Bachelors" and the ten-cent "German Lovers."

If Eddie Warburg's brothers were forced to use the marble amphora in their house as a spittoon, Charlie Soby used the real, and very large, spittoon in his house to catch barely smoked cigars after he had tested each new batch with as few puffs as possible. He believed in making money from people's smoking, but he didn't believe in smoking for himself or for his two sons. One pleasure he did approve of, however, was the possession of beautiful objects. For Charlie that meant such heavy artifacts as the spittoon and a small collection of nineteenth-century academic paintings. Among these was the work of an unknown artist of the Dusseldorf School, *The German Lovers,* for which Charlie's top-of-the-line cigar was named. After Charlie sold his cigar business to a New Haven firm, the new owners immediately changed the name to "Soby's Lovers." World War I had recently ended, and anything German was taboo. The name "Soby's Lovers" was more than Charlie Soby's wife could bear, however. It made her feel like a scarlet woman who had borne her two sons out of wedlock. Charlie sued the New Haven firm, and won. "German Lovers" returned to the marketplace and sold in spite of the forces of nationalism.

The Dusseldorf School painting had long been the trademark of Charlie's company. It was reproduced on his cigar boxes and on the horse-drawn lorries that carried his wares. When Jim Soby was growing up, he considered that painting a key to the family's financial success, and part and parcel of their identity in the world. He put great store in the role that art could play in one's life.

So by the time he was in his second year at Williams College he began to surround himself with pictures. By then he was beginning to be a bit less like one of the guys. As a freshman he had written short stories and poetry for *The Williams Graphic;* as a sophomore he had started the year with "a rather severe nervous breakdown"[4]— not requiring as long a home leave as Philip Johnson's had, but forcing some substantial time off nonetheless. When he returned to school he tired of the array of college banners with which he had decorated his room. He acquired a lot of large color reproductions of Maxfield Parrish paintings from a secondhand furniture dealer in Williamstown, and covered his walls with them.

Soby associated the emotional pitch and intensity of the Parrish reproductions with the way his own mind worked. "Their saccharine romanticism complemented the drooling poems I was then writing," he later wrote. His favorite among these Parrishes "showed a young girl, nude but sensibly misty, on a swing a few feet above an Arcadian terrace. I was spellbound by the picture and its carefree, mild eroticism."[5] Pictures could connect in an essential way with one's personal emotions.

Next Soby began to buy illustrated books. After starting with Rockwell Kent and other Americans, he moved on to the volumes being published in Paris by Ambrose Vollard that showed the most recent French art. Once he had absorbed the work in reproduction, Soby was desperate to see the real thing. He asked his mother, who by then was widowed, to go to Paris with him at what should have been the start of his junior year at college. He tirelessly haunted the bookshops and galleries near the Seine, and spent endless hours in the Louvre, where he developed a passion for Géricault and Delacroix. Next the mother and son headed south so that Jim could have his first taste of the glories of the south of France.

The few months of travel obliterated any sense of the value of school. Soby and his mother returned to Hartford, but nothing could get him back to Williamstown. On December 24, 1927, he turned twenty-one and came into his full inheritance. Two days later he married a beautiful eighteen-year-old Hartford girl named Elmina Nettleton. Shortly thereafter he built the small château on Westwood Road.

Once the house was completed, Soby had to figure out what to do with his life. From his point of view, "The problem, as it so often is for the young with independent income, was what kind of work to do. . . . Our chief problem was for me to find some occupation, since both our parents had told us that a man with a wife should work, whether or not he made any money at it."[6] First Soby tried being a playwright. He went to the Yale Drama School, but lasted there only until he was told that he had to start out by learning to paint scenery, less literary an undertaking than he would entertain. Next he took an office in West Hartford center. His intention was to write, but nothing happened. A neighbor asked Soby to join him in his brokerage firm. In that office, however, he couldn't make head or tail of all the shouting. The numbers baffled him; he quit after three days. There was nothing left to do but ensconce himself in his third-floor study on Westwood Road and read everything he could put his hands on about modern art.

Soby immersed himself in the writings of Roger Fry. He eagerly awaited his monthly issues of *Cahiers d'Art*. Above all, he read Clive Bell. Bell championed Matisse, Picasso, and Derain; Soby had admired their paintings both in Paris and at the Atheneum. That was the point when he took his Connecticut landscapes off the wall and drove back from New York with the Matisse, Derain, and Kisling in the trunk of the car. Heading up the Post Road, with Manhattan fading and Hartford looming, he had imagined "officials in bank-ruptcy proceedings awaiting me with guns drawn at my front door." Instead, he met Chick Austin.

III

Chick Austin regularly frequented the Harvard Society for Contemporary Art. He had first met Lincoln Kirstein at an evening party given by Edward Forbes and his wife in their country house at Gerry's Landing a few miles from Cambridge. Austin was older than Kirstein and Walker and Warburg, but he had probably heard a lot about them from Alfred Barr, Jere Abbott, and Russell Hitchcock. He became a member of the Harvard Society, and had had paintings in its show of art by recent Harvard graduates.

Austin had received his traditional education in Cambridge, and now he was to get a lot of his ideas about the avant-garde there. He was so impressed by what he saw in the two rooms at 1400 Massachusetts Avenue that he arranged for several shows that originated there to travel to the grander halls of Hartford. In March of 1930, after the second version of Bucky Fuller's Dymaxion House made its appearance in Harvard Yard under the auspices of the Harvard Society, Austin arranged a subsequent venue in the stately Morgan Memorial. It seems unlikely that any of Hartford's insurance executives would have agreed to write a policy for it. Nor would one of their wives be inclined to store her floral-print dresses on its rotating clothes hangers. But at least no one stood in Austin's way. A month later, the "Modern Mexican Art" show that the *Boston Herald* had considered exemplary of "communist ideology" had a two-week run in Hartford directly after it closed in Cambridge. "Modern German Art" took the same route immediately afterward, as would "Contemporary Photography" later in the year.

Both the Mexican and German shows were surprisingly well received by the Hartford press. The local critics gave them extensive coverage; inspired by the exhibitions, they provided their readers with detailed accounts of the development and nature of modern art in both these countries. They praised Austin for giving the public a chance to see the new work. In many ways it was a warmer reception than either exhibition received in its initial presentation in Cambridge. And since the source of the shows was never mentioned, Austin got credit as if he had originated them.

The next of Austin's forays into the contemporary was an old-fashioned museum practice applied to a modern painting. It was an exhibition of a single artwork. The notice read:

THE WADSWORTH ATHENEUM AND MORGAN MEMORIAL

ANNOUNCE THE EXHIBITION OF AN

EARLY MASTERPIECE BY

ANDRE DERAIN

"LE JOUEUR DE CORNEMUSE"

LENT BY MR. AND MRS. JAMES T. SOBY

IN THE GREEN GALLERY UNTIL JUNE 21

A month after he had bought the Matisse *Red Sofa* and the Derain *Landscape,* Soby had purchased Derain's *Les Oliviers*—for $5,130—from the dealer Henry Reinhardt in New York. Then, the next month, he returned the *Landscape* to the Valentine Gallery and used the credit of $4,000 against the purchase of Derain's 1911 *Le Joueur de Cornemuse*—or *The Bagpiper*—a painting that the Harvard Society for Contemporary Art had borrowed from Valentine a few months earlier. With the hefty price tag of $14,000, *The Bagpiper* was a large—74 × 59 inches—oil on linen. Derain's Paris dealer, Kahnweiler, had sold it to John Quinn, from whose estate Valentine had bought it. It was a monument of the art of the time, and to buy it was a major statement.

The Bagpiper had many of the qualities that would attract James Thrall Soby in paintings from that point forward. With considerable painterly grace, it made real a totally imaginary experience. Derain had by chance seen a shepherd playing a bagpipe out in the fields in the region of Carrière Saint Denis, where in the summer of 1909 he had spent quite a lot of time with Braque. For *The Bagpiper* he depicted the actual landscape of that region, but clothed the piper in a medieval costume a jester or troubadour might have worn: a wide-brimmed hat, flowing cape, and ruffled garters. The creature, standing firmly with a wide-angled stance atop a mound of earth in the lower left-hand corner of the large painting, looks as if he has just alighted from another time and another place. His cape looks like a pair of wings. In a void of sky over his head, there is, in profile, a bird that Derain has painted in a subtle, mysterious way. Its details are washed out by the sun, but its shape and high-angled wing make it otherworldly and seemingly holy—like the dove that oversees Piero della Francesca's *Baptism of Christ*. Even the tree that dominates the scene, painted as a dramatic massing of light and shadow, has something unreal and mystical about it. Perhaps it has just sprung up, full-grown, only a moment before the bagpiper landed. Yet everything else, like the road and distant houses and cove, has been there for a very long time. An amalgam of unexpected occurrences and revelations, accentuated by the ambiguity of costumes and disguises, the painting abounds in themes that were enthralling James Thrall Soby more and more.

Austin's showing of *The Bagpiper* must have given Soby a terrific boost. It was a complete turnabout for the young collector whose first purchases had made him the object of opprobrium only six months earlier. Suddenly a single canvas in his possession was deemed worthy to be the sole subject of a prestigious exhibition. His impetuous dash to Austin's office had changed everything.

This presentation of *The Bagpiper* was also a rare opportunity for the public. Rather than facing an impenetrable blockbuster or being dizzied by crowded walls, they could focus on one extraordinary picture. The local newspaper reproduced it and devoted a major article to the painting and its creator. The single-canvas show must have had special meaning in light of the economic situation that spring. It suggested that one did not need a lot of art; a unique, key example might suffice. The strange sight of the medievally clad bagpiper, looking as if he had just landed from a cloud in the modern landscape, was a powerful statement of hope and high spirits. The jesterlike piper lightens the atmosphere. Looking at him, we believe that it takes nothing more than a simple musical instrument to raise hopes and put beauty in the air. The setting looks magical. The tree and bird are enchanted. A lot in the world may have been shattered in the previous ten months, but it remained a time for believing.

In the second half of November that year, the Atheneum mounted a show of ten paintings from Jim and Mimi (everyone's name for Elmina) Soby's growing collection. *The Bagpiper* again left Westwood Road for the pleasure of the larger audience, as did three more Derains, two Matisses, a Marie Laurencin, a Jean Lurçat, an André Lhôte, and the Moise Kisling. Except for *The Bagpiper,* all but one had been painted in the previous five years. With Chick Austin behind him, the man who a year earlier had been looking for something to do had become a real somebody. Not only pictures of his

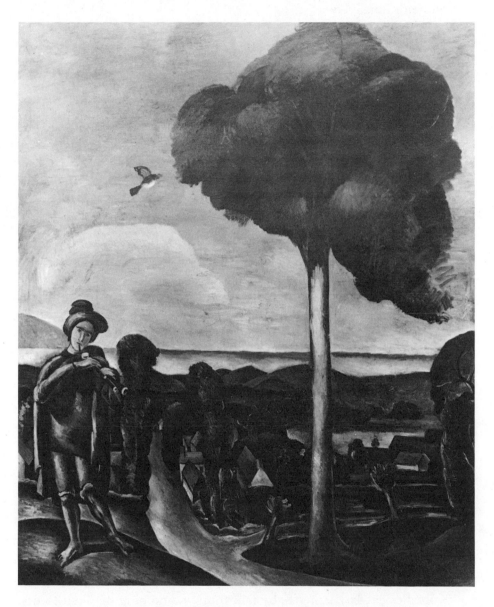

André Derain, The Bagpiper, *1910–11. Oil on linen, 72¹⁵/₁₆ × 59⅛".*

pictures, but pictures of Soby himself, filled the local papers. He was quoted extensively.

Henry Russell Hitchcock, Jr., applauded Soby's collection in the *Hartford Times*.[7] And Chick Austin did far more than simply show it. He lectured enthusiastically about Soby's activities. At every turn he praised not only the pictures but the act of collecting them. Private collectors, he told the newspapers, were of indispensable significance in bolstering their local museums. "These private collections, even though they may be owned by one individual, become in some strange way the property of the whole city,"[8] Austin explained.

The Soby collection was not shown at the Atheneum on its own. Also on view were twenty-six paintings by de Chirico, lent by Demotte Inc in New York. That juxtaposition sowed important seeds for the future; James Thrall Soby would in time become one of de Chirico's greatest champions in America, the curator of his most major exhibition and author of its catalog. The de Chirico pictures were more controversial than Soby's School of Paris group. Even as forward a thinker as Henry Russell Hitchcock referred to the works as "difficult to appreciate" and having a "repetitiousness" and "a perverse pomposity and a sinister humor which become rapidly tiring." But in presenting literary and metaphysical aspects of painting that few people had previously considered before, they had no little effect.

From then on, Soby kept swapping and buying paintings. Just before the Hartford loan show, he had acquired, again from Valentine, a Matisse pastel of a nude; in January of 1931 Soby returned the Matisse pastel. That same month he bought an important Matisse *Odalisque,* but ten months later he returned that as well. He also traded in Derain's *Les Oliviers,* but acquired Derain's *Monastery* and a still life. In October of 1931 he was thrilled to purchase Daumier's small oil *Les Avocats* from Valentine, but a month later he swapped it at Wildenstein toward Degas's *Woman Putting on Her Gloves;* he had no extra funds, since that same month he bought a large Picasso drawing on canvas and Douanier Rousseau's *The Goatherd* from Knoedler. At last James Soby had found something he liked to do. He wasn't just shopping; he was engaged in a relentless search for quality and meaning. At the Atheneum, he began to assist Austin on the catalogs and labels for shows. Like Philip Johnson at the Museum of Modern Art and Eddie Warburg at Bryn Mawr, he was happy to work without pay as long as he could abet the cause of pioneering art.

Even Edward W. Forbes called Chick Austin "careless . . . and un-businesslike."[9] The local manufacturers, attorneys, and insurance magnates were not unequivocally thrilled to have Austin in their midst. It wasn't just Austin's pocket handkerchiefs or lack of business sense that were getting hard to take. Some of his exhibitions and purchases seemed incomprehensible. Not that Austin was following a single path. He ended 1930 with a show of four contemporary painters—Aaron Berkman, Clinton O'Callahan, Russell Cheney, and, of greatest interest, Milton Avery—and started 1931 with a crowd-pleasing assemblage of landscape painting from Sassetta to Rembrandt and Gainsborough. His purchase of Corot's lovely pastoral *View of Rouen* that January was front-page news to which no one could object. But in the spring came a group show of the neo-Romantic artists Tonny, Tchelitchew, Bérard, Berman, and Léonide. These young artists working in France, little known in the United States and never previously grouped, had an eerie vision that was not to everyone's liking.

In the last two weeks of May, Austin borrowed a group of Picasso drawings from John Becker's gallery in New York. In June the So-bys' expanding collection went on view. But what really stunned the locals that year was the exhibition Austin put on from November 15 to December 6. Called "Newer Super-Realism," this was the first Surrealist show in America. Although the 1927 Carnegie International had included three works by Salvador Dali, this was the first presentation of Dali's art in depth, and also included a range of work by André Masson, Max Ernst, Miró, and Picasso that had never before been seen on the western side of the Atlantic.

How much credit Austin should get for the Surrealism show is, however, a tricky issue. In his Director's Report in the 1931 "Report of the Wadsworth Atheneum," he mentioned that "A similar exhibition, containing many of the pictures shown in Hartford, was later successfully received at a New York art gallery."[10] Although true enough, that statement fails to present the whole story. The exhibition of Surrealist objects, literature, sculpture, and painting had been entirely organized by Julien Levy, another of the students who had taken Paul Sachs's museum course at Harvard, and who had opened a gallery in New York earlier that year. Austin may have slightly varied the New York exhibition by adding or deleting a few objects, but essentially it was Levy's show. Yet no publicity acknowledged this fact, any more than information about the modern Mexican, German, and photography shows made mention of their having originated at the Harvard Society for Contemporary Art.

Julien Levy represented all of the artists in Austin's neo-Romantic show, and had provided a number of the loans for that exhibition. He had felt greatly bucked up by Austin's interest in the work he was showing, not just in Tchelitchew, Tonny, Berman, Bérard, and Léonide, but also in Joseph Cornell, Dali, Ernst, Man Ray, and Pierre Roy. It gave him great encouragement to know that a museum man associated with as venerable an establishment as the Atheneum was behind him. So having arranged the first Surrealist show in America and scheduled it for the beginning of 1932, he acceded to Austin's request "to let Hartford have it first, to give the Atheneum the prestige of America's first exhibition of the kind."[11] Levy discusses its presentation at the Atheneum in his memoirs. "It had been to strengthen its impact, to lend it museum authority, but above all to do a favor for one of my best and most stimulating friends, Chick Austin, who begged to have it, that I lent him the whole group of paintings and drawings so painstakingly collected."[12] And of course it would do Levy's artists no harm to have their work shown in a public institution.

Austin gave the show its own name for its venue in Hartford. Alfred Barr, who was also interested in Levy's artists, had opted for "Super-Realism." Levy felt they should stick to the French "Surréalisme," which he felt was untranslatable. Austin, however, chose "Newer Super-Realism." The name, of course, suggested that there were older superrealists. The painters Austin probably had in mind for the category were people like the sixteenth-century Italian Arcimboldo, with his heads made of intricate combinations of flowers and vegetables, and the nineteenth-century American trompe l'oeil painters like Harnett and Peto, whose illusory and mysterious paintings of objects hanging on grainy doors and folded dollar bills make the viewer feel as if the creases can be touched. Austin's term did not stick in the long run, but at least it put the artists in a context that the public might understand.

Levy did well to give the show to Austin. The Atheneum director served the new cause admirably. His irrepressible enthusiasm was

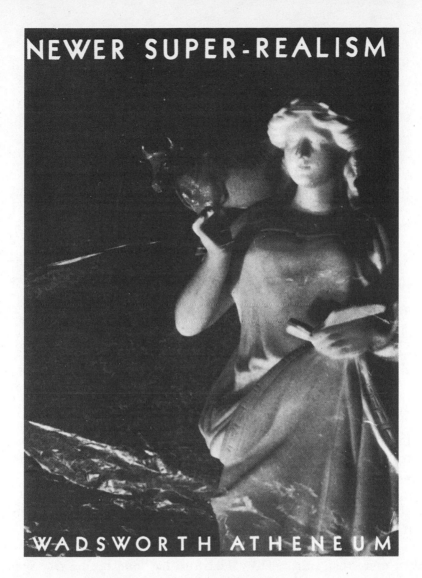

Cover of an exhibition flyer for "Newer Super-Realism," 1931.

catching. Like Eddie Warburg, he may not always have been the originator of an idea, but he was a splendid spokesperson. He lectured often, and advocated the new art to the press, putting things on a level readily comprehensible to the larger public. He explained that Super-realism represented

the more exquisite reality of the imagination, of the dream, even of the nightmare—the desire to push reality beyond the visual actualities of most painting. In it there is much of Freud of our contemporary interest in the subconscious mind. Meta- physical ideas, too, play a part. The artist seeks to create an effect of surprise and astonishment, made breathtaking by the juxtaposition of strange and disparate objects. Sensational, yes, but, after all, the painting of our day must compete with the movie thriller and the scandal sheet. As a matter of fact super- realism is not unknown in this country. We have all met it and some have recognized its spirit, more diluted and popularized in "Mickey Mouse" and the "Silly Symphonies," which for pure nonsense, imagination, and a sense of speed, remain in the field of the motion picture to be surpassed. Visitors have, in reality, a fight to find excitement in the museum too, as well as in a movie theatre.[13]

This was the sort of thing that really drew people in. A journey to the local art museum could be as much fun as a night at the flicks. But sometimes Austin could go over the edge:

Fashion in art is very much like fashion in dress. Most of our clothes are bought with the idea of ultimately discarding them. . . . Yet we do not hesitate to dress in fashion because we fear that next year the mode will alter. We . . . feel pride in knowing that we are in style.

These pictures which you are going to see this month are chic. They are entertaining. They are for the moment. We do not have to take them too seriously to enjoy them.[14]

Even more than other places, Hartford has long been a city where how you dress is who you are. Austin was trying to get people where their hearts were. He was dealing with a populace whose reigning aesthetic passion was in matching shoes to clothes. For people who spent more time in haberdasheries than in museums, the link to styles of dress might win their attention. But whatever the reasons to link fashion in art to fashion in clothing and hence justify the trendiness, this was a strange move. One would expect a diatribe crying for art to have deeper, more lasting values, not an extolment of its momentariousness. To use the adjective "chic" in a laudatory rather than a pejorative tone was an affront to intellectualism as much as to stodginess. But even if Austin's lack of curmudgeonliness, his love of pleasure and of the new, reflected his limitations, they were also his greatest asset.

According to Julien Levy, the Surrealism show had a totally different impact in its two settings. Levy felt that, coming directly from the inner recesses of the mind, the art did far better in the close confines of his gallery than in the august exhibition spaces of the Morgan Memorial.

> The museum's exhibition, just before Christmas, 1931, was extensive and solemn. Mine had the advantage of intimacy and enthusiasm, partly due to the limited size of my just two rooms in a building no wider than a New York brownstone. It was packed with the force of the unconscious, of our secret desires, of that iceberg of which only the smallest fraction shows, the bulk remaining submerged and powerful. Perhaps forced compression increased the impact.[15]

Hartfordites could wander in solitude viewing the new art in its institutional setting, while New Yorkers crowded into Levy's Gallery. But both audiences of the first Surrealism show were in for a startling experience. Inexplicable, often disturbing, images of dreams were here crystallized as art. The paintings had none of the visual ambiguity of Cubism or abstraction—on one level the subject matter was perfectly clear—yet it was impossible to understand the juxtapositions. The realistic painting technique gave the expectation of plausibility, but closer inspection made viewers feel as if the rug had been pulled out from under them.

Take Pierre Roy's *Electrification of the Country,* a canvas Austin had bought a few months earlier for the Atheneum's permanent collection. Even sixty years after its first showing in Hartford, the Roy is puzzling. The painting has an unreal glow. Its particular blue and green seem unimaginable before the era of color movies and television. The colors are distinctly artificial—like a mix of chemicals—and distant. They appear to be behind a mist, or, to modern eyes, a Plexiglas screen. The subject matter, while entirely legible, is completely implausible. A round, flat piece of wood stands in the foreground with two goblets on it. In relation to the size of the goblets, the wood should have the dimensions of a cheeseboard. But considered in scale with the power line and towers that are in the distant

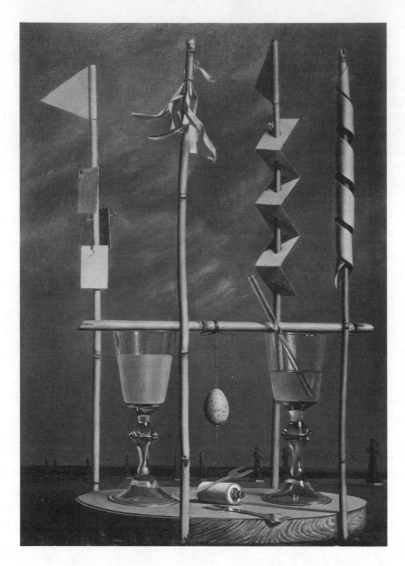

Pierre Roy, Electrification of the Country, *oil on canvas.*

background, it would have to be about the size of a football field, and about twenty feet—rather than a couple of inches—high.

Spaced around the piece of wood there are four sticks that seem either about two feet or eighty yards high. These could be, variously, parts of an electrical experiment[16] or gigantic staffs of the type knights might brandish in our dreams. There are some specific references to electricity—a glass rod in one of the goblets, which is filled with water; and parts of a battery—but also allusions to everyday domesticity, like a goblet filled with milk. An egg hangs by a string from a stick that appears to float. It could have any of a number of meanings: it may refer to a similar image in Piero della Francesca's *Brera Madonna,* it may represent flawless natural packaging, it may symbolize order. The fastidious painting technique suggests precision and comprehension; the array of subjects provokes dismay. That acceptance of the incomprehensible, and the elevation of mental puzzles to high art, was what this exhibition was all about.

Dali's *The Persistence of Memory*—or "the limp watches"—was also in this exhibition. Dali had painted this 9½- × 13-inch oil on canvas a few months earlier, and Levy had bought it from Pierre Colle for about $250. This was its first public viewing. Its flaccid pocket watches—hanging over a tree branch, draped over the edge of a large wooden block, resting like a saddle across the back of a frightening, imaginary sea creature—were totally disconcerting. They oppose usual notions of reality: watches are meant to be rigid, just as time is meant to proceed at a regular pace. Dali's imagery suggests that the normal flow of time has lost its power, and we feel a loss of power as we look at the painting. It's a disturbing jolt.

To the Hartford viewers, who ruled their lives by their pocket watches as best they could, this was scary stuff. The seashore was supposed to be like their family enclaves on the Connecticut shore at Fenwick or across the sound on Fishers Island—where the Atheneum trustees occasionally held their meetings. There you knew who and what you would see. There was no danger of whiskered amorphous blobby creatures or bizarre bits of furniture appearing on a beach. Even the light was relatively predictable; it would never be the eerie tone of Dali. What the Spanish painter had wrought was mind-boggling, as were the other objects Levy had assembled.

Besides *The Persistence of Memory,* there were six other Dali paintings and two drawings. There were also four works by Giorgio de Chirico, thirteen by Max Ernst, three by André Masson, five by Joan Miró, and seven by Picasso—all major paintings of those artists' Surreal periods. In addition, there were two further Pierre Roys, three works by Leopold Survage, and a painting called *Ambiguous Subject*—attributed to an "Unknown Master" but in the manner of Arcimboldo—that belonged to Mr. and Mrs. Alfred Barr.

Surrealism had already begun to make inroads among the upper echelon at the Museum of Modern Art. Levy had sold one of Dali's paintings—*Le Sentiment de Devenir*—to Mrs. W. Murray Crane, and another—*Au Bord de la Mer*—to A. Conger Goodyear, to whom he had also sold two drawings. Mrs. Stanley Resor, another museum trustee, would soon buy *The Persistence of Memory* for the Modern's collection (at a price reported to have been $350). There were a few other private collectors who had ventured into the troubling territory of the Atheneum's exhibition; three of the Max Ernsts belonged to Berenice Abbott, and two works each by Max Ernst and Joan Miró came from Katherine Dreier's Société Anonyme collection. But, beyond that, most of the work in "Newer Super-Realism" belonged to Mr. and Mrs. Julien Levy or Levy's Gallery, or to other galleries or their owners: Pierre Matisse, Valentine, and Wildenstein in New York, and the Pierre Colle Gallery in Paris. This meant that a lot of the work was available for purchase. Austin bought Dali's *La Solitude* for the Atheneum's permanent collection for three hundred dollars. He might have acquired more, but to get this work approved was an uphill battle, and there were only so many he could fight.

The title *Electrification of the Country* inadvertently had a lot to do with both Austin's and Levy's intentions for their startling exhibition. Levy wrote, "We hoped that this was a prophetic title, and joked about it without foreseeing that, although there were to be a few power failures, Austin's illumination would become an international glow long before most of his Connecticut countrymen saw the light." [17] The reaction on Austin's home front was mainly static. But here and there this pioneering approach to painting was moving people to consider some new and fascinating possibilities.

V

James Thrall Soby was one person who seemed perfectly at home with the Surrealism show and all that it represented. He may have been the paradigmatic New England gentleman on the surface, but even before he started collecting art he had already developed a Surreal mentality. Soby's background was full of good things—kind and moneyed parents, fine schools, social niceties, fun and games—but it had also had its share of odd twists. By the time he had entered Williams, Soby recognized that life did not always go as it seemed it should, that reality could be stranger than dreams and that dreams could have an odd echo in actual events.

The first bit of nightmarish reality that had indelibly impressed Soby occurred when he was seven. He was a student at Miss Wheeler's Outdoor School, near his parents' house. Miss Wheeler was, in Soby's later memory, "a tall thin woman with incredibly long fingers and a most stern brow" who believed that children benefited from fresh air and who had them sit on an open porch no matter what the weather. In the winter the youngsters wore heavy wool suits made for Eskimos. One day Miss Wheeler "poked her bony forefinger" at the shivering young Soby and asked why he wasn't writing his lessons. He replied that he couldn't write because the ink was frozen and the inkwell was on the wrong side of the desk for him. She thundered at him. Miss Wheeler was not a woman to be intimidated by the weather, and she certainly had no intention of relocating her inkwells "just to please a few southpaw spastics."[18]

The seven-year-old Soby fled. No one saw him until much later that cold day, when his father found him whimpering in a vacant lot. His parents called in doctors. They removed him from Miss Wheeler's to the care of a tutor and eventually to a newly formed private school. But the experience haunted him forever after as one of the pivotal events of his childhood.

So did another event a few years later when Soby was at the Lawrenceville School. One December night, in the middle of exam time, he had a dream that his father had been killed in an automobile accident. Waking early the next morning, he was so shaken that he skipped the day's exams. That afternoon his housemaster called for him, and without any preamble blurted out, "Your father has died and they are sending for you."

Soby replied that he knew this already. He calmly explained that his father had died the previous evening in a car accident, which is why he had failed to take his exams that day. The housemaster was openmouthed. The essential fact was correct even if the details were wrong. He told Jim that Charlie Soby had died of pneumonia after spending time at the Connecticut shore in an empty, cold house he had wanted to rent for his family for the coming summer.

Soby began to have memorable nightmares. By the time Surrealist art and poetry appeared before his eyes, its bizarreness, both real and imaginary, seemed natural to him. Surrealist film charmed him especially. For this reason, one late autumn evening in 1931 when most of his West Hartford neighbors were playing cards or listening to the radio in their stone and brick Tudor or clapboard neo-Colonial houses, Jim and Mimi Soby provided a very different form of entertainment.

Downtown at the Atheneum Jim Soby had helped Chick Austin

with the flyer and labels for "Newer Super-Realism." In the course of their work they learned about a film called *L'Age d'Or* made by Salvador Dali and Luis Buñuel. It was the second film on which Dali and Buñuel had collaborated. The first, *Un Chien Andalou,* had been a minor cause célèbre because of the sequence that appeared to show a human eyeball (in actuality the eye of a dead pig) being dissected by a razor blade.

When working on *L'Age d'Or,* Dali had written to Buñuel, "Let's have a few blasphematory scenes, if you will, but it must be done with the utmost fanaticism to achieve the grandeur of a true and authentic sacrilege!"[19] The film had already caused a furor in Paris. Because of it, one of its principal backers, the Vicomte de Noailles, had been threatened with excommunication from the Catholi ` Church. When it was shown in a place called Studio 28, the audience threw blobs of indelible ink at the screen, broke the theater seats, and slashed the Surrealist paintings in the foyer.

In spite of that, neither Austin nor Soby was worried about what a carefully selected small audience of their chums might think or do. Although Austin had arranged for René Clair's *Le Million* and the films *Surf and Seaweed* and *Mechanical Movement* to be shown in conjunction with the superrealism exhibition, clearly *L'Age d'Or* was not for the community at large. Still, he and Soby were desperate to show it.

Since Soby's living room on Westwood Road was bigger than Austin's on Scarborough Street, that was where they held their screening.[20] As many people as could squeeze in sat on folding chairs that Jim and Mimi borrowed from a funeral parlor. Russell Hitchcock gave an introduction. Then most of the assorted guests sat spellbound as they watched Dali's and Buñuel's sequences. They saw a blind man get abused, a dog squashed, a son murdered by his father, and an old lady slapped. The heroine rapturously sucked the naked big toe of a statue of a pope. Priests climbing a rocky hillside were transformed into praying mantises, a species that fascinated Dali because of the female's habit of killing and eating its mate immediately after they have mated. Near the end of the film, the Marquis de Sade's protagonist from *Les 120 Journées de Sodome* appeared in the guise of Jesus Christ.

Whether because of good manners or true intellectual fascination, few of the viewers flinched. "Nobody knew what to say"—one way or the other.[21] The projectionist, however, was in terror. Jim Soby had hired him from a local movie theater. Desperately afraid that the police would come and arrest him and take away his professional license, he spent the entire performance with his eyes focused on the front door. In addition, some devout Catholics who were there that night found it too much to take. Shortly after *L'Age d'Or* began, they headed down to the Sobys' basement bar to fortify themselves with Prohibition liquor. They soon began shouting upstairs that if someone didn't stop the film they would come up and destroy it. Soby simply placed one of his more broad-shouldered friends at the top of the narrow cellar stairway to keep the rebels back. He succeeded in blocking them, but not in muffling their battle cries, which were the background noise to which the rest of the audience viewed Dali's and Buñuel's work.

It wasn't just conservative newspaper critics who would excoriate this sort of thing over the next couple of years. In the April 8, 1933, *New Yorker,* Alexander Woollcott gave a summary of *L'Age d'Or* after which he wrote, "I hereby submit their synopsis in full for preservation in the archives of wonder, whereby posterity may know that, in addition to evolving Adolf Hitler, Aimee Semple McPherson and Al Capone, the twenties and thirties also produced this sort of thing." George Orwell opined that *L'Age d'Or* showed that "the artist is exempt from the moral laws that are binding on ordinary people. Just pronounce the magic word 'Art', and everything is O.K. Rotting corpses with snails crawling over them are O.K., kicking little girls in the head is O.K.; *L'Age d'Or* is O.K." [22] To James Thrall Soby, A. Everett Austin, and at least a few of their friends in that West Hartford living room, this wasn't just moral torpor, however. If to many of the brightest minds of the day Dali's scenario represented a lassitude of normal decency, to them it had some greater strength. More than its shock value swayed them. The new art may have been frightening and disconcerting, but it also allowed for the human imagination to have a fuller voice. Life could be cruel, and people predatory; the frank revelation of uncomfortable experience gave superrealism the ring of truth.

Superrealism was just the sort of thing that got Chick Austin in trouble with the old-timers in town. Even if Soby was Austin's partner in crime, as part of old Hartford he had the chance to back the museum director up. On one occasion two men who were long-standing Atheneum trustees—and whose sons had been at the

Kingswood School with Soby—took Soby off for a fine lunch in New York to try to get him to see things their way. When they told him he was acting "like Chick's stooge," he responded, " 'You flatter me,' "[23] and the conversation ended.

Soby was bothered that Austin wasn't more of a reader and was too restless for scholarship, but he had come to revere Austin's eye. The same year as the Surrealism show, he witnessed a key example of the director's connoisseurship when Austin acquired a commanding, dynamic seventeenth-century painting by Bernardo Strozzi, *St. Catherine of Alexandria*. Austin had bought the large Baroque canvas in Italy. When the crate containing it arrived at the Atheneum, he zealously opened it as Soby and others stood watching. But before he had seen little more than a corner of the picture that had been sent, he exploded, "That's not the painting I bought in Italy. It must be a copy." He was right, and after some nasty communication between Hartford and Italy the correct picture arrived.

This sort of discernment rendered Austin heroic for Soby. Besides, Soby was also shocking his confrères. In April of 1932 he acquired, from Valentine, Picasso's *Seated Woman* of 1927. If people had found Eddie Warburg's gentle, accessible *Blue Boy* and Conger Goodyear's lyrical *La Toilette* hard to take when they had bought them a few years earlier, here was a painting that could really raise hackles. It had already inspired one of Royal Cortissoz's diatribes when it was shown at the Museum of Modern Art. This 51- × 38-inch complex rendering of disconcerting images in oil on wood, which is today a signature Picasso, was then, for most people, unbearably scary. Alfred Barr later described the painting by saying that "Picasso's power of inventing masks is here remarkably demonstrated: a great curving band sweeps upward to terminate in the frightening white profile which is then both intersected and magically extended by the black, axe-bladed, disc-eyed shadow."[24] Such images may have intrigued a person of Barr's sophistication, but they were beyond the taste of most people, however well educated. When a local banker who had been a friend of Charlie Soby's saw the Picasso reproduced in one of the Hartford papers shortly after Soby acquired it, he drove out to Westwood Road and demanded that the young collector return the painting immediately. Insisting that "Picasso" was some sort of obscure Italian word, the banker accused Soby of throwing away his inheritance by spending sixteen thousand dollars on this purchase. The money man was adamant: "Take that

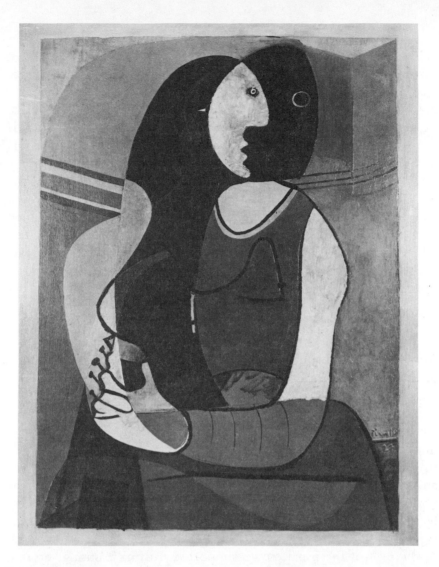

Pablo Picasso, Seated Woman, *Paris, 1927. Oil on wood, 51⅛ × 38¼".*

horrible thing back to the dealer, no matter what you can get for it, which I assume to be about a tenth of what you paid for it," he ordered. "I can't have you squandering your father's money in this way!"[25] Soby replied that the bank no longer handled his money, and that the banker would do well to remember how much a painting— *The German Lovers* that had been the trademark of Charlie Soby's cigars—had contributed to the family's success.

Picasso's *Seated Woman* was one picture Soby would not swap. He

held on to it through thick and thin. Over the years, the height of
the thin occurred when he lent it to the Smith College Museum after
Jere Abbott had become its director, and one of the Northampton
newspapers said that as fitting retribution for his owning this piece
of heresy a cavalry regiment should ride over Soby with swords
drawn. The thick must have been when Alfred Barr wrote his commentary on the work. In his pivotal 1939 book *Picasso: Forty Years of
His Art,* the ultimate verdict was that *Seated Woman* was "one of the
most awe-inspiring of all Picasso's figure paintings." By Soby's own
account, he would not have had the courage to buy the Picasso had
it not been for "the enthusiastic backing of Chick Austin and Jere
Abbott." [26] In the same way that Eddie Warburg knew that his parents and brothers would equate his Picasso acquisition with whole-
sale lunacy but that Agnes Mongan and Lincoln Kirstein would pat
him on the back for it, Soby could count on his allies.

In February of 1932 the Brummer Gallery in New York put on a
show of Chick Austin's paintings. Kirk and Constance Askew lent a
painting of Venice. So did Mr. and Mrs. Edward Forbes, who also
lent a view of Toledo. Philip Johnson lent a work called *Murano,* and
Henry Russell Hitchcock provided *The Bridge at Budapest.* These
were from Austin's old phase. He also had a newer superrealist style
not unlike the mysterious arrangements of imaginary forms painted
by Pierre Roy. *A New Leaf* combined ambiguous cylindrical forms
and musical notation. *Materials for Celebration* had a paper party hat
under an oversized firecracker and related but unidentifiable objects
held in place by a rope. The Sobys lent a painting of this more recent
type.
　　But even if the usual crowd supported Austin's painting, no one
raved. Given that catalog essays by artists' friends generally enthuse
endlessly, the text by Austin's pal Henry Russell Hitchcock was
hardly the norm. "Mr. Austin is not original or profound," Hitchcock wrote. His conclusion about these paintings was "Their function is merely to please the aesthetically literate, not to reveal to them
a new type of art or to revive a fundamental tradition." [27]
　　What everyone admired was Austin's diversity and energy. The
same week that he had lectured on superrealism, he had also given a
talk on *La Traviata.* Having loved magic ever since his childhood, in
April he began to give magic shows in the tapestry hall of the Morgan Memorial. He made an unsupported electric light move across

the stage. He escaped from locked handcuffs and a locked trunk. A pile of tied handkerchiefs and an untied pile changed places without any visible help. Not only did the fine entertainment draw people in, but ticket sales raised money for supplies for children's art classes.

Austin continued to present extraordinary exhibitions. In April and May of 1932 he borrowed the pioneering "Modern Architecture: International Exhibition" that Henry Russell Hitchcock and Philip Johnson had mounted at the Museum of Modern Art. Having traveled around Europe together looking at modern buildings, Hitchcock and Johnson had been Barr's natural choice as organizers of this show devoted to the latest building design. Their exhibition presented models and photographs of the most revolutionary utilitarian architecture of the recent era, and gave "the International Style" its name. The major architects represented were Le Corbusier, Ludwig Mies van der Rohe, Walter Gropius, and J. J. P. Oud. Above all, the work shared a lack of ornament and an emphasis on function. The presentation of these men's work as a unit changed the face of architecture the world over. For the Atheneum to be the third institution on a nationwide tour was a significant honor for Hartford.

Austin was working hard toward the creation of a new building for the Atheneum, the Avery Memorial. He intended it both to embody the visual and emotional clarity of the International Style and to augment his program. He was also busily strengthening the Atheneum's permanent collection with the addition of work ranging from a group of Coptic weavings to an important painting by Piero di Cosimo. Austin was always offering new approaches; after the architecture show he mounted an important exhibition of children's art. This extolled the naive and primitive beauty of pictures done by boys and girls mostly between the ages of ten and fifteen, both by putting it on view in the auspicious spaces of the Morgan Memorial and by reproducing it in the Atheneum Bulletin alongside work by Louis Le Nain, Tiepolo, Longhi, and Picasso.

In August the Soby collection again went on view at the Atheneum for six weeks while its owners traveled in Europe. In addition to some of the paintings like *The Bagpiper* that had previously been exhibited, there were new works by Pierre Roy, Eugene Berman, Tchelitchew, Léonide, and Tonny. By now Soby had returned Matisse's *The Red Sofa,* but had acquired his *Green Blouse* and *Rose.* He had also added a Rousseau and a Cocteau. But the painting that attracted the most attention this time was Picasso's *Seated Woman,* now considered the most important work in the collection. Hartford critics were surprisingly sympathetic to it, perhaps in part because they had the high praise of Alfred Barr to quote whenever they discussed the work. Moreover, a few months later, *Seated Woman* and *The Bagpiper* were lent to the "Century of Progress" Exposition in Chicago, which warranted extensive newspaper coverage and further reproductions of the Picasso. What Charlie Soby's banker friend was saying by now remains unknown, but a lot of people were beginning to think twice before calling this modern art stuff such folly.

Austin, Soby, and Hitchcock worked together on a show called "Literature & Poetry in Painting since 1850" that ran from January 24 to February 14, 1933. It contained paintings of the previous eighty years that revealed the direct effect of fiction and poetry. Soby, who loved literature as much as he loved painting, considered it "a more difficult and courageous venture" than "The Newer Super-Realism" show that had taken place thirteen months earlier.[28] It was in his eyes even more of a breakthrough in the acceptance of emotionalism in painting. The show accorded the visual arts an intensity of feeling usually confined to literature. "The object of the exhibition was perhaps to relieve all the arts of shame in their intimacy." That eradication of shame, and the acceptance of levels of feeling previously deemed unacceptable, was for Soby and Austin an imperative. It was what Agnes Mongan cherished in drawings and what Kirstein and Warburg admired in the work of artists as different as Calder and Lachaise.

The forces behind "Literature & Poetry in Painting" had some front-line defending to do. Both Soby and Austin spoke to the local press, and Hitchcock wrote the catalog essay. He opened his "Explanation" in the "Literature & Poetry" catalog with the sentence, "The modern attitude toward nineteenth century painting has emphasized manner rather than content." The statement could equally apply to what these various young men felt to a large degree about their parents' generation's approach to life in general. One of their major tasks was to get beyond mere style.

Hitchcock credits Surrealism with the revival of interest in the sort of subject matter—ranging from "the late Romantic musings of Gérôme" to "the Freudian dreams of Dali"—pivotal to this exhibition. The new raison d'être was the stimulation of emotions, in preference to the more purely formal sides of art. His essay lacks the succinctness or comprehensibility of the explanations Kirstein wrote for the Harvard Society, but it makes some interesting points. Hitch-cock suggests the possibility that contemporary art can reflect the content of contemporary song lyrics by people like Ira Gershwin and Noël Coward, that "Who Cares?" and "Some Day I'll Find You" are fertile philosophical themes. He and Soby and Austin were also reacting to pure abstraction and the trend of nonobjective painting taking hold elsewhere in the most advanced reaches of the art world. "A black circle on a black ground may be a possible ultimate of the art of painting, but so, also, is a mother and child."

The emphasis on theme led to an interesting assemblage of art-works from a variety of cultures and of historical periods. Drawing heavily on Soby's and the Atheneum's own collections, there were works by artists ranging from Bouguereau, Cézanne, Corot, Ingres, and Rossetti to de Chirico, Ernst, Klee, Roy, and Tchelitchew. The three Rousseaus included the Sobys' *Pastorale,* and among the five Picassos were their *Le Soupir* and Eddie Warburg's *Blue Boy.* The joining of pre-Raphaelites, Impressionists, post-Impressionists, Ital-ian Futurists, American Realists, and Surrealists through their em-phasis on storytelling and thematic content pointed out how emotions can transcend era, culture, or artistic style. "Literature & Poetry in Painting" elevated emotional content in a new way. In link-ing the qualities of narrative and art, it paved the way for much that the Atheneum would do in the near future.

Individuals like Jim Soby and Eddie Warburg might remain largely untouched by the Depression, but public institutions could not. Even with Austin's clever fund-raisers, the Sumner bequest, and money from J. P. Morgan there to help, the Atheneum was feeling the pinch. After a special board meeting in March of 1932, Charles Goodwin announced salary cuts of 15 percent on top of the 10 per-cent voted the previous year. Publications were ceased, and the ex-hibition program curtailed. The basement in which the Wallace Nutting furniture collection was exhibited was closed on weekdays. Austin continued, however, to do his best to break into new terri-tory. It was too late to cancel plans for the solo exhibition of Pierre Roy that April. A group of local supporters—the Austins, the So-bys, Austin's assistant Paul Cooley, and others—helped foot the bill of trucking the show from New York and insuring it.

Austin also continued to work away on the details of the Avery Memorial and its 299-seat theater. Not only would the new building

house pioneering art, but it would provide a setting for performances of theater, music, and film. Wanting the Avery interior as
streamlined as possible, he needed to overcome the Beaux Arts taste
of the building's architects as well as of many of its patrons. Pleading
his preference for Spartan form and utilitarian details of the type
being made at the Bauhaus, Austin informed his trustees, "I believe
that I am competent as a critic and as a creative personality to establish my conception of contemporary beauty in a museum building. . . . Later the ornament I eschew for good reason because it is
ugly, can be applied again at no great cost, if the taste for mediocrity
and vulgarity persists in this country."[29] Times might be rugged, and
tastes tough to change, but little would keep him down.

A BALLET SCHOOL

I

A taste for the literary side of painting, a tenacity about modernism, the will to prevail, a soupçon of arrogance: this was what Lincoln Kirstein admired. On July 16, 1933, Kirstein wrote Chick Austin a long letter from Batt's Hotel on Dover Street in London that began,

Dear Chick, This will be the most important letter I will ever write you as you will see. My pen burns my hand as I write: words will not flow into the ink fast enough. We have a real chance to have an American ballet within 3 yrs. time. When I say ballet—I mean a trained company of young dancers—not Russians—but Americans with Russian stars to start with—a company superior to the dregs of the old Diaghilev Company. . . . Do you know Georges Balanchine? If not he is a Georgian called Georgei Balanchivadze. He is, personally, enchanting—dark, very slight, a superb dancer and the most ingenious technician in ballet I have ever seen. . . . He is 28 yrs. old—a product of the Imperial schools. He has split from the Prince de Monaco as he wants to proceed, with new ideas and young dancers instead of going on with the decadence of the Diaghilev troupe, which I assure you, although it possesses many good, if frightfully overworked dancers, is completely worn out inartistic-Commercial. . . . I proposed the following and they are willing and eager to do it. To have a school of dancing, preferably in Hartford: it is distant from New York— plenty of chance to work in an easy atmosphere. Balanchine is socially adorable—but he hates the atmosphere both of society, as such (Lifar loves it) and the professional Broadway Theatre. For the first he would take 4 white girls and 4 white boys, about sixteen yrs old and 8 of the same, *negros*. They would be firmly taught in the classical idiom—not only from *exercises* but he would start company ballets at once so they would actually *learn* by doing. As time went on he would get younger children from 8 yrs. on. He thinks the negro part of it would be amazingly supple—the combination of suppleness and sense of time superb. Imagine them, masked, for example. They have so much abandon—and disciplined they would be *nonpareil*. . . . Now, if you could work it he could use your small theatre: a department of the museum [where] a school of dancing could be started. . . . It would be necessary to have *$6000* to *start* it. That guarantees them for one year with passage back and forth. I count this sum as dead loss—though it won't be at all because by February you can have four performances of wholly new Ballets in Hartford. Balanchine is willing to devote all his time to this for 5 yrs. He believes the future of Ballet lies in America as do I. I see a great chance for you to do a hell of a lot here. The expense can be under*written,* say I glibly—but you must realize how much this means—so I have to be arrogant, by Phil *Johnson,* who is willing, myself, *Jim* Sobey [*sic*], Jere, the Lewisohns . . . and I feel sure there are others. . . . It will not be easy. It will be hard to get good young dancers willing to stand or fall by the *company. No* first dancers. No *stars*. A perfect *esprit de corps.* . . . He is an honest man, a serious artist and I'd stake my life on his talent. . . . He could achieve a miracle, and right under our eyes: I feel this chance is too serious to be denied. It will mean a life work to all of us. . . . It will not be a losing proposition. . . . I wish to God you were here: that you could know what I am writing is true. That I am not either over enthusiastic or visionary. Please, Please, Chick if you have any love for anything we do both adore—rack your brains and try to make all this come true. . . . Please wire me, give me some inkling as to how you will receive this letter. If not I can't sleep. I won't be able to hear from you for a week, but I won't sleep till I do. . . . We have the future in our hands. For Christ's sweet sake let us honor it.

> Yours devotedly
> Lincoln[1]

The sixteen-page-long paragraph was filled with accounts of the dancers who might come with Balanchine; of ideas for American ballets with subjects like *Moby Dick, Custer's Last Stand, Pocahontas, Uncle Tom's Cabin,* and *Defense of Richmond;* and with more on Balanchine's independent stand against the decadent remnants of Diaghilev's original Ballets Russes.

Kirstein and Austin had stayed in touch ever since the Harvard

Society days. They periodically encountered one another in the New
York galleries like Julien Levy's and John Becker's where one could
count on seeing the most interesting current art. They also met frequently in the key salons of that era. One of these was in the home
of Muriel Draper, who for a number of years had been at the center
of the contemporary music world in London. Muriel Draper "knew
everyone in New York," and sat in a sort of throne.[2] She was married
to Paul Draper, a singer and man about town. At one time or other
she had been the mistress of Arthur Rubinstein, Paul Robeson, and
Bernard Baruch. Her skill as a saloniste came in part from her uncanny ability to link the right people, and to become everyone's in-
timate within moments of first meeting. The other great salon was
the East Sixty-seventh Street brownstone of Kirk and Constance
Askew. Kirk, who had also taken Paul Sachs's course at Harvard,
was a small, alert man with chiseled features who directed the distinguished Fifty-seventh Street gallery Durlacher Brothers, where Austin often shopped for Baroque paintings. Constance was a wealthy
New Englander whose serenely beautiful face Virgil Thomson lik-
ened to Greta Garbo's and John Houseman compared to that of a
Greek goddess; her ample bosom and coils of silvery-blond hair were
the talk of the town. Kirk was in London for about half the year, but
when he was in New York, he and Constance always held Sunday
afternoon "at homes" in their opulent Victorian drawing room with
its tall windows overlooking a fine garden. Throughout the week,
they also routinely offered tea at five, cocktails at six, and dinner at
seven-thirty. Dinner meant dressing, and there were dinner guests
every night except when the Askews were dining out. More people
came after dinner, and at around midnight those who had stayed late
often headed toward Harlem. All evening long people would talk
animatedly, above all about art. The going drink was homemade
Prohibition gin—which during cocktails would be shaken with non-
alcoholic vermouth, and after dinner would be mixed with soda or
ginger ale. Along with the other regulars like Austin, Kirstein, and
Thomson, the people there often included Houseman, Aaron Copland, Joseph Losey, Carl Van Vechten, Emily Hahn, Archibald
MacLeish, Gilbert Seldes, Henry McBride, e.e. cummings, Agnes
de Mille, and assorted young curators and painters. Art dealers like
Marie Harriman, Pierre Matisse, and Valentine Dudensing were also
in attendance.

Seeing each other in the galleries and at Muriel Draper's or the

Askews', Kirstein and Austin liked each other's enthusiasms, but were very different types of people. In many ways Kirstein considered Austin a bit of a lightweight.

> Although I must have talked about books with him, I never imagined him reading any. . . . He did not consider himself an intellectual and had contempt for the rather solemn group of young critic teachers-to-be that awed me. He was already playing quite hard; he made a business, or rather a professional career, of playing—playing at pictures, at theater, at museum administration. This was somewhat disturbing, at least in the serious and dedicated context of the heirs of Ruskin. . . . I wanted to be a professional poet, painter, novelist and dancer. But professional. Chick did not deign to dignify his dilettantism. . . . He was anti-intellectual by policy. By intellectual, I suppose one means a person capable of analysis on a comprehensive or consecutive basis. Chick was not notoriously analytical, or rather he judged ideas and objects by enthusiasm rather than in sequence. His antennae vibrated at large, in all directions at once; his nostrils sniffed new smells from afar; he heard advance blasts from distant trumpets minutes sooner than the sentries who were supposed to be permanently alerted.[3]

In spite of their intellectual differences, that extraordinary receptiveness was ample ground for making Austin the target of Kirstein's urgent letter.

Kirstein had long felt the sway of anything connected with Diaghilev, and he had often admired George Balanchine onstage. But he had only finally met the dancer—in the kitchen of a house Kirk Askew had rented that summer in London—a few days before he wrote to Austin. His thoughts were all new and unformed. He had, however, picked the right person to pour them out to. In his search for a foothold for Balanchine and the new ballet company, Kirstein was better off with a spirited amateur in a position to help than with a fellow bookworm. Austin wasn't even halfway through the letter when he brushed everything else off his desk and burst out, " '*This* is the only thing that's of any importance. We've got to get them, we've got to get them.' "[4] In little time he was charging around to his more sympathetic trustees. Within weeks a new School of American Ballet—with George Balanchine as its director—had the promise of a home. The lecture room of the old Morgan Memorial would do perfectly for practice, and in a few months time the small theater in the new Avery building would be ready for performances. This would be a national school of dancing—along the lines of the great Russian imperial academies—reapplied to the American idiom. It was all set.

Fortunately, though, Austin wasn't the only ally back on American shores to whom Lincoln Kirstein turned that summer. There was one person he did not even bother to name in that list of patrons because he was so much his soulmate that Kirstein knew he could count on him even more than on his own loyal father. Even before he had mentioned his dream to anyone, he had known that he could depend on Eddie Warburg.

That confidence in Warburg's support had been one of his mainstays in some pivotal early discussions Kirstein had had in Paris before he actually met Balanchine. The seeds of the future undertaking had been planted early that summer in the French capital when Kirstein had told the artist Pavel Tchelitchew of his wish to create an American ballet company. Tchelitchew, who was doing sets and costumes for Balanchine's *Errante,* had proposed Balanchine as the choreographer for this hypothetical entity. Following Diaghilev's death four years earlier, Balanchine had helped found the Ballets de Théâtre Monte Carlo. But since then he had been at loose ends. Kirstein thought this possibility of backing him made sense, and went off to see Virgil Thomson about it. Thomson had been graduated from Harvard a few years before Kirstein, and they had come to know each other at the Askews'. Thomson was very direct with him about the need to think first of all about money: "Whose? How much? How certain?" Kirstein's response was to think, "I had an ally as far as money went. . . . It was he who made my presence in Paris and my conversations with Thompson and Tchelitchew not entirely irrelevant."[5]

So when Kirstein wrote to Austin, he also wrote to Eddie Warburg. Warburg was someone whose intellect Kirstein held in no higher esteem than he did Chick Austin's, but like Austin he was kind and generous, he believed in supporting the arts, and he was a true friend.

Kirstein was desperate. At the same time that Balanchine was entertaining this idea of going to America, he had other offers. There were invitations to become maître de ballet in Copenhagen, to stage a Stravinsky–André Gide opera at the Paris Opera, and to take on other European projects. Wanting above all to go to the United States, the Russian needed only transportation and living expenses. The question was how to secure them. Kirstein had the impetus, but not the funds.

In little time, however, Austin and Warburg as his support system made everything possible. Austin guaranteed institutional support for the ballet; Warburg wrote to say he'd cover the steamship fare. This meant buying tickets for both Balanchine and his business manager, Vladimir Dimitriev. Dimitriev, who had been in Nijinsky's class at the Imperial School in St. Petersburg and in 1924 had organized the flight of the Ballet Russe troupe to Western Europe, was considered an essential part of the program. What was required were two round-trip tickets; the Russians didn't want to be stuck in America if Hartford didn't work out. By August 12, Kirstein felt free to send Austin a cable from Paris:

> DERAIN BERARD TCHELITCHEN [*sic*] BALLETS CAN BE PRESENTED HARTFORD BY JANUARY FULL OF NEW PLANS JUILLARD [*sic*] COPENHAGEN PARIS BIDDING OR [*sic*] BALANCHINE BUT HE WANTS US ALONE ANNOUNCE NOTHING YET DON'T GET COLD FEET   LINCOLN.[6]

The moment Kirstein's boat docked in New York at the end of that summer, he headed out to White Plains to Warburg's parents' country retreat. It was a noticeable change from Kirk Askew's kitchen and from the theaters and hotel lobbies in which he had been negotiating with Balanchine in London. To Kirstein it was "a tract of land as large as a duchy" in which "the Warburgs held state in considerable grandeur."[7] Called "Woodlands"—although Eddie's uncle Morris Loeb had suggested "Moneysunk"—the estate had started on thirty acres that in little time had grown to six hundred as Felix and Frieda did their best to keep the neighbors from encroaching on their privacy. Woodlands had come into being before Edward was born. Felix and Frieda used to take their children to the nearby Century Country Club on Sunday afternoons, and the older boys were so noisy that the Warburgs had decided to buy some adjacent land for them to run around on without disturbing anybody. Then one Sunday it had rained, so Fizzie realized that he had better build a roof over their heads. The result was an enormous, rambling, multitur-

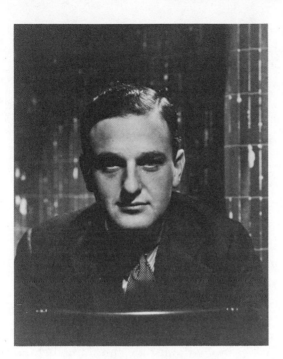

Edward Warburg, photographed by George Platt Lynes.

Woodlands.

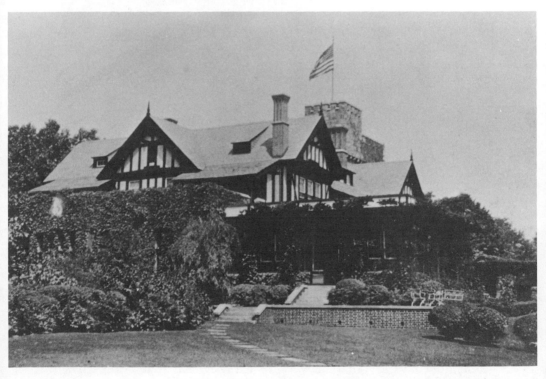

reted Tudor-style house with a three-story-high fieldstone tower topped by a crenellated parapet. Eddie had been born in the house, in his parents' large first-floor bedroom overlooking the woods. There had been some grumbling at White Plains Hospital by those who felt that Frieda had called for the doctor like a page—she had sent a horse and buggy for him—but it was easier for him to make the trip than for her, and she had arranged a nice guest room for him.

In addition to the usual spaces a large family with a lot of friends might want for living and entertaining, Woodlands had an indoor swimming pool and a squash court, which, unlike the one in town, was used for squash. A hothouse grew the carnations for Fizzie's signature boutonnieres. Fizzie had a passion for sweeping vistas, so he periodically cut down pieces of forest to open up splendid views of the surrounding countryside. Felix Warburg always thought big; after Frieda suggested that they rent a couple of cows to provide milk for the children, he bought a herd of Guernseys, hired a herdsman, and named the cows for family members. He also built a rambling half-timbered stable and silo that looked as if they should be behind a vast château in the Barbizon forest. There were more than a dozen horse-drawn carriages available to meet family and guests at the White Plains train station. The boys skied and skated in the winter, and in the summer they played tennis on the grass court with Helen Wills, Alice Marble, and other participants in a nearby tournament who regularly stayed over in the big house. There was never any danger of not having a place to play, since there was a second, all-weather court on the other side of the house. There were also almost seven miles of bridle paths, and a polo field that was generally used for football. There was no saying with whom one might play football; on one occasion the Warburg boys were joined in a game by the entire police escort there to guard British Prime Minister Ramsay MacDonald when he was inside visiting their parents. Not every visitor was interested in a game, however; when Alfred Knopf brought Thomas Mann to meet Felix, the boys were told to keep as quiet as possible.

It was walking past the stables and tennis courts and polo fields as they headed through the pristine gardens out into the Warburgs' private woods that Kirstein poured forth the details of his scheme. Eddie was all ears. He had been delighted ever since his old friend had telephoned to say that he was on his way. Kirstein's calls always meant the prospect of something new and interesting; this time he knew the subject was dance, and he wanted to hear more. Back at Harvard Warburg and Kirstein had spent endless hours questioning how an artist in any medium could make enough money to survive. They had bemoaned the struggle of any serious composer, painter, dancer, or musician who lacked family money and needed to make ends meet. Even then, Kirstein had championed the idea of ballet. As he had pointed out to Agnes Mongan, this was the art form that brought together the greatest range of creative people—composers, costume and set designers, musicians, and dancers—in a single undertaking out of which everyone might receive a cut from the box office.

From Warburg's point of view, the plan that Kirstein outlined as they wandered through the fields and woods at Woodlands was the dream at last. Here was a way that he might really help those less fortunate than he. His father had told him to have "all the noblesse oblige that station requires." The style with which he would have it might be very different from Fizzie's, but at least he would be lending a hand.

It was, after all, a tradition of Eddie's childhood milieu to back the arts. In 1907, Otto Kahn, one of his father's and uncle's partners at Kuhn, Loeb (although no friend of Felix's), had gone from being a leading shareholder of the Metropolitan Opera to becoming chairman of its board. It was Kahn who lured to New York the general manager of La Scala, Giulio Gatti-Casazza, and with him the new maestro Arturo Toscanini. Kahn was instrumental in getting Enrico Caruso to give his first performances. If Eddie Warburg in 1933 knew little about the ballet itself beyond the concept of its ability to reap the greatest benefits for the largest numbers, he understood the idea that people lucky enough to have money could do a great deal. Moreover, he never could resist an adventure, whatever the risks or possible embarrassments. Walking around Woodlands, Eddie Warburg guaranteed further funds and agreed to head a corporation. With Balanchine as artistic director and maître de ballet, he would be "director general" of Ballet Productions, Inc., the producing company of the School of American Ballet. It would all be legal and correct. The future New York City Ballet was under way.[8]

It was necessary to raise as much money as possible before Balanchine and Dimitriev actually set sail for Hartford. Beyond the round-trip tickets, Warburg came up with a thousand dollars right

away. Kirstein, generally more inclined to tap than to give, contributed two thousand dollars. Philip Johnson gave five hundred. The
poet Cary Ross contributed fifty. Jere Abbott was good for two hundred, Kirk Askew and his wife for fifty, A. Everett Austin's mother
for twenty-five. Austin himself gave a hundred. More importantly,
Austin knew to whom he could turn in Hartford. His assistant, Paul
Cooley, gave five hundred dollars. Pretty much as Kirstein had pre-
dicted in his letter, the other five-hundred-dollar donor was Jim
Soby.

Under advisement from Connecticut 1st District Congressman
Herman P. Kopplemann, Balanchine's importers applied for a visa
for the dancers. Its four guarantors were Lincoln Kirstein, A. Everett
Austin, James T. Soby, and E. M. M. Warburg. They provided suitable references: Lee Higginson Trust Company of Boston for Kirstein, Phoenix State Bank and Trust Company of Hartford for
Austin, Hartford National Bank & Trust for Soby, and Kuhn, Loeb
for Warburg. On September 1, 1933, the four men wrote the American consul general in Paris. They wished not just to have Balanchine
and Dimitriev come to the United States, but to bring in three dancers—Roman Jasinsky, Tamara Toumanova, and Madame Toumanoff—as well. The four young supplicants had deposited three
thousand dollars in George Balanchine's account at Lloyd's Bank "to
pay for the passage of the members of his troupe to this country and
for their return passage to France." They "jointly and severally"
guaranteed that Balanchine, Dimitriev, Jasinsky, Toumanova, and
Toumanoff "shall not become public charges either of the United
States or of any State, County or City therein while they remain in
the United States." They promised that if the three thousand dollars
was insufficient for the return passage of any of these individuals,
they would be responsible for the remainder. Their guarantee would
"be operative until the departure of everyone of the above named
people from the United States." The three dancers never made the
journey, but for George Balanchine that return passage would never
be necessary.

Vladimir Dimitriev and George Balanchine, then twenty-eight years
old, sailed from London to New York on the *Olympic*. When Felix
Warburg and Paul Sachs had sailed home on that ship two years and
four months earlier, they had been traveling in first-class cabins. But
as Eddie Warburg, Lincoln Kirstein, and Chick Austin waited at the

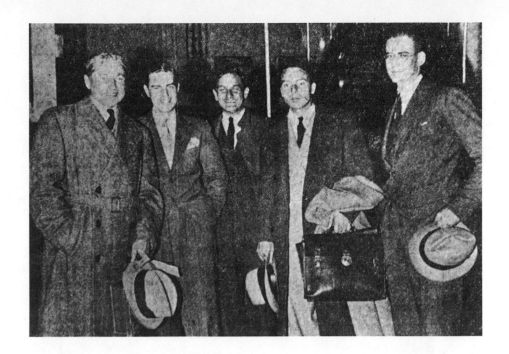

Photograph from the Hartford Times, *October 18, 1933. The caption read
"Coming to Hartford to Direct Ballet. Georges Balanchine (second from
right), famous ballet choreographer, and Vladimir Dimitriev, teacher and
manager, were met when the* Olympic *docked in New York last evening by
three members of the corporation which is responsible for bringing the
Russians here under the auspices of the Morgan Memorial in Hartford. In the
picture are, from left to right, Dimitriev; A. Everett Austin, Jr., director of the
museum; Edward M. M. Warburgh [sic] of New York; Balanchine; and
Lincoln Kirstein of New York, editor of* Hound and Horn."

dock to meet the two Russians, they had no idea what class their
visitors were traveling in—even though Warburg had paid the fare.
The three young Harvard graduates desperately scanned the crowd
for the slim, dark Balanchine and his gray-haired, monocled business
manager. Then Kirstein spotted them in Tourist. But they appeared
not to be getting off the ship; as one newspaper reported, "Passenger
after passenger came down the gangplank, but no Balanchine and
Dimitriev." Through the din of unloading the greeting party could
barely make out Balanchine's voice saying that they could not disem-
bark. They would have to stay on the boat overnight and go to Ellis
Island—"not a very pretty place," Balanchine later informed the
press.

Advertisement for the School of American Ballet, Stage, *January 1934.*

The problem was that the Russians had a six-month visa and a year-long contract; in addition, Balanchine had lost his landing card. Warburg briefly disappeared. "By the magic of a name, Mr. Warburgh"—the journalist covering this may have thought the name magical, but did not know how to spell it—"made his way on board, and settled the difficulties, and soon the two men came down the gangplank, smiling and very happy to be at last in America."[9] The date was October 17, 1933.

The two Russians quickly got a taste of the new life. After checking into their rooms on the thirty-fourth floor of the Barbizon Plaza they had dinner in the hotel dining room. Although he spoke only Russian and French himself, Dimitriev complained because the menu was in French; he wanted "everything American, because . . . there is going to be a great American ballet in Hartford." Balanchine, who had picked up quite a bit of English since his discussions with Kirstein that summer, kept saying that everything was "swell": it was "swell" to be in America; Eddie Warburg was "a swell guy." Over dessert he exclaimed, "Ice cream is good. And ice cream soda!" But ice cream wasn't all that was needed; the two émigrés were whisked off to the Askews' in hope of finding some Prohibition vodka. The next evening Kirstein and Warburg took them to Radio City Music Hall. Afterward they took their visitors to the top of the RCA Building so that they could see the skyscrapers at night. Looking at the lacy flamelike tower of the nearby American Radiator Building, Balanchine exclaimed, "Mon Dieu, on a déjà des ruines ici!" ("They already have ruins here!")

On October 19 Kirstein and Warburg drove Balanchine and Dimitriev to Hartford, where they stayed at the Austins' house on Scarborough Street. There's no saying exactly what the Russians thought they would find in America, but the neo-Palladian villa could not have been less typical. Their expectations were hardly the norm either. A day or two after the pair reached Hartford it was Jim Soby's task to help them find a place to live. Cruising past brick apartment buildings and tree-lined streets of Victorian and neo-Colonial wooden houses, Balanchine saw nothing he liked. Finally he told Soby, "in his mild, gracious way . . . that what they really wanted was an eighteenth-century apartment. It was rather difficult to explain to him in French that people in Hartford did not build or live in apartments in the eighteenth century." [10]

This was just one of the many difficulties the American Ballet School was having in the insurance city. Another concerned Soby's role in general. Austin told Soby that Kirstein objected to Soby's presence at meetings about the school's plans because he felt that Soby knew too little about dance. Soby couldn't have agreed more. The only ballet he had ever attended had been the Ballets 1933 in Paris, and he had only gone to that because he wanted to see the sets and costumes by Bérard and Tchelitchew, two young artists who interested him greatly. Austin, however, wouldn't hear of excluding his greatest aide-de-camp, whatever Soby's own views were, and said he would bail out if Soby didn't remain. That settled, the situation exploded when an announcement appeared in the Hartford papers saying that there would be no tuition at the new ballet school at the Atheneum. For one thing, Balanchine was irked by the idea that in a museum that bore the name of Morgan he would earn little more than a pittance. It wasn't that he expected to take in a lot of money, but he found the attitude denigrating. The idea that the school would be run on a nonprofit basis also raised hackles from the outside. In the *Hartford Courant,* two sisters who headed a local dancing school publicly attacked Austin for thus enabling a tax-exempt institution to support their competition and thereby help put them out of business. And James Thrall Soby's cousin, Walter Soby—who for Charlie had been the black sheep of the family because he had become a professional dancing teacher and headed a Hartford institution called Soby's School of Dancing—added his eager voice to the opposition. Walter, who had the distinction of being national secretary-treasurer of the Dancing Masters of America, Inc., presided over a meeting of some twenty dancing teachers. He pointed out that "free dancing lessons"—which is how the new program was regarded—were "unfair competition and a violation of the DMA program."[11] All local dancing teachers "should have been consulted and called into conference for advice and suggestions."

Chick Austin responded by publicly guaranteeing that the ballet school would take at most two dozen pupils—most of whom would come from Boston or Philadelphia. There would only be full-time pupils, and hence few Hartford residents would even qualify. He appealed to his dissidents by voicing his hope for "a true American ballet [that] would give an opportunity to American composers and artists . . . in an attempt to express through this art those native literary and artistic ideals which have never been developed to their fullest extent. The artistic prestige of Hartford," Chick Austin proclaimed, would be established "not only nationally but internationally."

The Hartford dancing school contingent wouldn't calm down, however. Walter Soby called Jim and carried on about "Russian freeloaders." And the hostility of the fox trot set was not the only problem. The Russians and their backers could not come to grips with the tuition issue. The *Hartford Times* gave the story.

It is Mr. Austin's contention, and that of James T. Soby, one of the members of the managing committee, that the school here should have been maintained on a non-commercial basis. The plan was to keep the school as a purely artistic project and to make it an opportunity for the training of a genuine American ballet. This would involve the admission of pupils without tuition and an intensity of training not equalled in any other school. The school was to be practically an endowed institution and to be operated as a non-profit making program.

Despite the fact that all the preliminary plans were in accordance with this idea, Mr. Balanchine and Mr. Dimitriev objected to this proposal after they reached Hartford.[12]

This was not their sole objection, but the local paper could hardly be expected to say that the Russians had found Hartford to be a hostile environment and that they were longing for eighteenth-century housing and better restaurants. In any event, less than a week after it had arrived, the American Ballet School left Hartford.

Hartford did not have sustaining power, but without it, the new ballet would never have progressed beyond the drawing board. Austin and the Atheneum had given the ballet the legitimacy that enabled Warburg to guarantee sufficient funds and that persuaded Balanchine that he was really heading somewhere. It was the Hartford area congressman who cleared the paperwork. But the only place where the new enterprise had a real chance was New York.

Balanchine and Dimitriev might not find an eighteenth-century apartment in Manhattan, but at least they could go to the Russian Tea Room. Not only was Eddie Warburg willing to pick up their tabs there, but he also paid the rent checks for the ballet school's new premises in Isadora Duncan's former studio at 637 Madison Avenue. Balanchine had its walls painted the gray-blue that he remembered from the Imperial Academy. Everything was coming together at last. A new corporation was formed, in which lawyers who usually concerned themselves with the problems of Kuhn, Loeb and the legacy of Jacob Schiff now turned their energy to the needs of a fledgling ballet company. Official letterheads were printed for the School of American Ballet, Inc., with Georges (in this case using the *s*) Balanchine as its artistic director, Edward M. M. Warburg, president, Vladimir Dimitriev, vice president, Lincoln E. Kirstein, secretary-treasurer. Advertisements appeared in the *New York Herald Tribune* and the *New York Times* telling future students how to register and explaining that the purpose of the new institution was to develop a national ballet created by American artists to express an American tradition. The curriculum constitutes a complete education in the art of the dance and has been designed to train a permanent company of American dancers whose productions will be presented by the school.[13]

On December 11, 1933, the School of American Ballet opened its doors.

II

In November of 1932 the trustees of the Museum of Modern Art elected Edward M. M. Warburg, who had recently turned twenty-four, to join their ranks. The only other person that young in the same position was Nelson Rockefeller. Warburg took an office in the museum's new building, which had just opened on West Fifty-third Street. He paid for his secretary out of his own pocket, and began to give art objects and books to the museum. Rather than take a salary, he made an annual contribution of five thousand dollars. The museum had an operating budget of about sixty-five thousand dollars a year, and Warburg also went after his parents to make regular gifts beyond his own. To achieve this, he wrote them letters of solicitation, even though he was still living at home. With great tact he would acknowledge their distaste for modern art and confess his own expenditures on the museum's behalf, before appealing to their generosity on the basis that it was above all an educational institution.

The 1932–33 season on Fifty-third Street opened with a show of Persian frescoes organized by Arthur Upham Pope, in large part a result of the trip on which Warburg had accompanied Pope. At the start of 1933 there was an American folk art show that was like an expanded version of the one the Harvard Society had done. But what interested Warburg above all was the need of the museum to reach the larger public. In addition to his pioneering lecture on Matisse, he gave a radio talk about abstract painting on WNYC. Every week he sent long reports to Alfred Barr on his idea for further lectures and for a broadcast series. The speakers would include Lewis Mumford on architecture, George Gershwin or Kay Swift—a com-

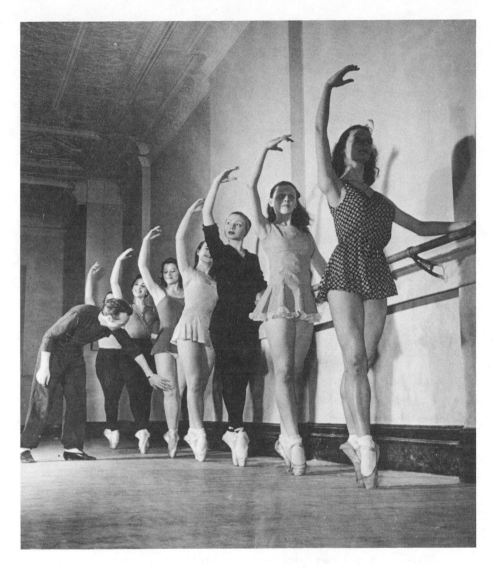

Balanchine and students at the School of American Ballet.

poser married to Warburg's cousin James Warburg—on music, Philip Johnson on arts and crafts, Gilbert Seldes on the movies, John Mason Brown on the theater, and Lincoln Kirstein on the dance. To spread the gospel of the new to the greatest number of people, he proposed a national radio hookup. But that wasn't all that was on his plate.

On August 31, 1933, Eddie Warburg wrote the following letter to Alfred Barr:

Dear Alfred:

I want to tell you about another project that I have been playing with during the last few weeks.

One Mr. Rice came into my office several weeks ago and told me that he had formerly been connected with Rollins College in Florida and that due to a disagreement with Dr. Holt, the president, he and several other professors resigned (9 to be exact) from Rollins College. And some twenty students resigned with them. The argument, it seems, concerned itself with progressive education. . . .

Rather than wait around for jobs that might be offered from more conservative organizations, they banded together. They found a place in North Carolina that is used by a conference centre in the Summer by the Young Men's Christian Association, and which, with very little change, could be turned into a college during the Winter months. They decided to rent this place and with a $20,000 guarantee which they have collected, and thirty students, they are opening up this Fall.

The members of the faculty will receive no salary for the first year and are pooling their own personal libraries for the benefit of the students. . . .

Mr. Rice came in to see me about finding a man to head their Fine Arts Department, and both Phil and I immediately thought of Albers. We have written him a letter to find out whether he and his wife would come over here, and we received a cable to the affirmative.

The problem now is how to get them into this country. Phil, Mr. Rice and I went down to see Mr. Duggan of the International Institute for Education, and he informed us that the Immigration Authorities demand that the invitation for any professor who has taught for a minimum of two years prior to application, must come from an accredited institution. As Black Mountain College (the proposed name for their college) is not yet on the list as an accredited institution, this does not apply to them. However, Mr. Duggan felt that if it were possible to guarantee a salary of $1500. to Albers, and his wife as well, that Col. McCormick, the head of the Immigration Bureau, would be perfectly willing to let him in. And we are now trying to figure out where we can get $3,000. . . .

Unfortunately, Albers's not being a Jew, my usual contacts are fairly useless as my friends are only interested in helping Jewish scholars. The Christian people who might be interested, have given towards foundations and the foundations are usually a bit scarey of new organizations.

I would like to know from you whether you think it would be diplomatic and right for me to place this whole matter before Mrs. Rockefeller.

I cannot help but feel that getting Albers into this country would be a great feather in the cap of the Museum of Modern Art. . . .

With Albers over here we have the nucleus for an American Bauhaus!

What do you think of the whole scheme?

As ever,

Eddie[14]

"Phil" was Philip Johnson. Johnson had met both Anni and Josef Albers on his visits to the Dessau Bauhaus. Josef was active in furniture design, typography, metalwork, photography, and above all in the glass workshop, where he had developed an elaborate technique for making the sand-blasted glass constructions so similar to the vibrant abstraction Kirstein had designed for the Harvard Society's Bauhaus show. Josef Albers was also deeply immersed in Bauhaus theory about the nature of form and the teaching of art. He was the first Bauhaus student to have been elevated to the status of "Master," and had become an important teacher of its preliminary course in material and design. In 1930 he had been appointed the school's assistant director.

The placid-faced Albers—with his narrow eyes, fair skin, and blond bangs he looked like one of Memling's saints—had started at the Bauhaus when he was thirty-two. That was in 1920—one year after the school was founded in Weimar. This meant that he had been affiliated with the institution longer than anyone else. Albers was a working-class Catholic who had previously taught public school in his hometown of Bottrop, a bleak industrial city on the River Ruhr. In 1925 he had married Anneliese Fleishmann, one of the star weavers and textile designers at the school. Anni—in keeping with the new style, she had made even her name simpler and more functional—was from a very different sort of background. Her parents were both Jewish, albeit the sort of German Jews who didn't enter a synagogue; one branch of the family had had a group conversion (some eighty members of the family baptized together one Sunday at the end of the nineteenth century), and her parents had had her confirmed in Berlin's fashionable Protestant Kaiser Wilhelm Gedachtniskirche. Her father's family were successful furniture manufacturers; her mother's, the Ullsteins, were prominent publishers. Her maternal grandfather owned one of the first telephones in Berlin, but wouldn't answer it "because bells were only for domestics." When she had told her father that she wanted to attend the experimental "Bauhaus" in order to pursue "the new style," he had replied that there were no new styles; there had already been the Renaissance and the Baroque, and everything else just repeated them. But Anni had persisted, and even if her Ullstein uncles sometimes mortified her by visiting Dessau in their Hispano Suiza, she had plugged away as a young Bauhausler, working diligently at both designs for yard materials and the creation of bold, abstract, rigidly geometric, and simplified woven wall hangings.

A couple of months prior to Eddie Warburg's writing Alfred Barr, Philip Johnson had run into Anni Albers on a street in Berlin. Anni's father was helping the young couple by paying rent on an apartment they had stripped to the barest white and furnished with their own art and the leanest chairs and tables they could find, and where they served water from chemists' flasks in order to avoid ornate decanters. Anni invited Johnson to come up and to see the place as well as their recent work, and to have a cup of tea.

The Bauhaus had just closed. Under the directorship of Mies van der Rohe, the school had a year earlier moved from its large Dessau campus to an old Berlin building that formerly housed a telephone company—in an effort to cut costs as the Nazis stepped up pressure against them. National Socialism had little use for abstract art and the new design, or for the sort of people that made them. But in spite of the move to Berlin, faculty salaries at the start of 1933 were still paid by the city of Dessau. Then, on June 15 of 1933, the Oberstadtinspektor of the Dessau City Council had written Josef Albers a letter in which he stated that the Bauhaus was "a germ-cell of bolshevism." Moreover, as a member of the Bauhaus faculty, Albers was reminded that he "did not and [would] not offer any guarantees that [he would] at all times and without reserve stand up for the National State." [15] Therefore Dessau was discontinuing his salary. A month later, the Gestapo padlocked the doors of the school. On July 20, the faculty, at a meeting in which Albers was one of the seven participants, voted to dissolve the Bauhaus. So when Anni Albers invited Philip Johnson up for tea, she wasn't just being gracious; she was also picking up any thread that might lead to her husband's finding a new job.

Anni Albers was a personality to reckon with. A painting owned by James Thrall Soby gives clear evidence of that fact. In 1931 Soby had acquired a small Paul Klee called *Gifts for I.* As Eddie Warburg and Philip Johnson had done before him, Soby had called on Alfred Flechtheim in Berlin. Chick Austin, who had been in the gallery a short time before, paved the way for him. Knowing that Soby would be coming in and was above all interested in Paul Klee's work, he had Flechtheim take out approximately fifty of the best Klee oils and watercolors he had to offer. Soby wanted everything in sight, but he was out of money. He had acquired Picasso's *Seated Woman* earlier that year, and en route to Berlin had bought a Bonnard and a Gris in Paris. Unable to purchase the lot, he settled happily on *Gifts for I,* which shows a large head on its side and some ambiguous objects descending from above it.

Soby saw the painting as representing the sort of scene he knew well from West Hartford. "It records a party for a friend of the painter. In the picture I assume it is the friend's head which rests horizontally on the floor, and above him are the festive table, champagne glass and salt and pepper shakers." [16] Had Soby ever gotten to know Anni Albers, he could have been put straight on this. If its American owner thought the painting depicted a drunken partygoer passed out cold on the floor with the remnants of a celebration tumbling toward him, Anni knew better from direct experience. She had helped organize Klee's fiftieth birthday party in 1929, and that is what *Gifts for I* really showed.

Klee was Anni's "god at that time"; he was also her next-door neighbor. Although the Swiss painter was, in her eyes, aloof and unapproachable, she admired him tremendously. She had even bought one of his watercolors—an unusual move for a Bauhaus student. As her god approached his major birthday, she had the idea—along with three other students in the Dessau weaving workshop—of hiring a small plane from the Junkers aircraft plant, not far from the Dessau Bauhaus, so that they could have this mystical, otherworldly man's birthday presents descend to him from above. Klee's presents were to arrive in a large package shaped like an angel, for which Anni made the curled hair out of tiny, shimmering brass shavings. Various Bauhaus people made the gifts the angel would carry: a print from Lyonel Feininger, a lamp from Marianne Brandt, some small objects from the wood workshop. Anni was in the small plane from which the angel descended. As the cold late October air penetrated her coat, and the pilot joked around with the four young weavers by doing complete turnabouts as they huddled together in the open cockpit, Anni was so obsessed with abstract art that what struck her most was her sudden awareness of a new visual dimension; she had been living on one optical plane and now saw it from a very different vantage point. Then she spotted Klee's house, next door to her own. As planned, they let out the gift. It landed with a bit of a crash. But Klee was excited nonetheless, and memorialized the unusual presents and delivery in the painting that later went to Jim Soby. What Soby thought were the accouterments of his habitual sort of social encounter were in fact souvenirs of the Bauhaus workshop and part of a new and adventurous world in which Anni Albers was an enthusiastic player. The figure on the ground was the gift-bearing angel. Soby's idea of a champagne glass was in actuality an inverted parachute.

When Johnson was in the Alberses' new flat, he was as intrigued by Anni's personality and work as by Josef's. She wove simple, unadorned yard materials in which the fibers themselves and the structure with which they were linked constitute their entire design. At the same time, she made abstract geometric wall hangings that made a claim for textiles as a high form of art, as serious in intention as her husband's glass constructions and the oils and watercolors of Klee and Kandinsky. Johnson was fascinated. He was also intrigued by a bit of injustice of which he became aware in the Berlin flat. On that summer afternoon he looked at several fabric samples that, a few months earlier Mies van der Rohe's mistress, Lily Reich, had represented to him as having been hers. These were Anni's, and Johnson realized that Anni Albers was not only exceptionally talented on the basis of what he knew she had done, but also on the basis of what he had been led to believe someone else had done.

· · ·

Johnson had his visit with the Alberses in mind when, shortly after his return from Berlin, Warburg invited him to join the meeting with John Andrew Rice in the museum's offices. Rice had gone to see Warburg at the suggestion of Margaret Lewisohn. Margaret was especially aware of what her young relative Eddie was up to those days because Sam Lewisohn was then secretary of the museum board. The reason Rice had approached Margaret Lewisohn was because of the mother of a young man named Theodore Dreier.

Ted Dreier, who had been seven years ahead of Warburg and Johnson at Harvard, was the nephew of Katherine Sophie Dreier. His father, Henry, was the only one of Katherine's four siblings to bear children. Aunt Kate also was childless, so Ted grew up with an especially close connection to her. He saw her often and heard her discussed all the time. It wasn't just her art collecting that gave the family plenty to talk about. At one formal Sunday dinner, Katherine made a particularly strong impression on the children by scratching her back with her knife. Her explanation was that the conversation was getting a bit dull.[17] Like a number of the Warburgs, she made a point of misbehaving in the dining room as well as challenging the usual way of doing things out in the world. Ted took easily to this notion that it was important to violate a few rules on many fronts.

Ted Dreier's own interests were outside the art field. What impressed him most in the family legacy was the idea of rebellion and the spirit of good works. Another of his aunts headed the Women's Trade Union League. His mother was chairman of the Women's Suffrage Party of Brooklyn and the Women's Committee for Mayor La Guardia's Re-election, and she had politicized the Women's City Club of New York City. What moved Ted above all were causes to better humanity.

Although Aunt Kate had made him more cognizant of Surrealism and other modern art developments than were most Harvard undergraduates of the day, Ted had had few overlaps with the world of Paul Sachs and the Fogg Museum crowd. At Harvard he majored in geology, before studying electrical engineering at Engineering School. At Rollins he was teaching physics when he met Rice, who was a classics professor. Then, as Eddie Warburg had intimated to Alfred Barr, Rice was fired by Rollins's president, Dr. Holt. Holt claimed that, among other things, Rice had "called a chisel one of the world's most beautiful objects, had whispered in chapel, . . . had an 'indolent' walk, had left fish scales in the sink after using the college's beach cottage, and . . . wore a jockstrap on the beach."[18] Two other faculty members were fired shortly after Rice. Sympathetic to their cause, Ted Dreier had been the next to resign.

Almost immediately, this group of outcasts set about forming Black Mountain College, with Rice at the helm. Their progressive coeducational institution stressed free inquiry, gave faculty the control of educational policy, eliminated grades, emphasized participation in community life, and elevated the arts as the focal point of the curriculum. Rice was particularly glad to have Ted join him in the new venture. In his eyes the young Harvard graduate was "a sweet person, a very endearing dreamer—one of those strange creatures that the rich families produce every now and then; they want to repudiate the whole thing."[19] In addition, his coming from one of those wealthy families would do the new school no harm. Not only did his relatives have money, but they had friends with money. Of the fifteen thousand dollars in contributions required to get Black Mountain off the ground, Ted's friends Mr. and Mrs. J. Malcolm Forbes had anonymously provided ten thousand, and his parents had given two thousand.

When Ethel Dreier told Ted some of the things she had learned from Margaret Lewisohn about what the people at the Museum of Modern Art were up to, it was only natural to go knock on the door. In little time he and John Rice were looking at photos of the folded paper experiments done in Josef Albers's introductory course at the Bauhaus. They both immediately felt that it was precisely what they were looking for. The Black Mountain founders were especially eager "to break the tradition of the idea that it was effeminate to be in the arts,"[20] and felt that this sort of work could only help advance that point.

Philip Johnson had various reasons for wanting to help Black Mountain get the Alberses. He thought that Anni was "the best textile designer [he'd] ever met." He admired the honesty and rigor of her work. In his own designing, he was advocating the aesthetic of exposed radiator pipes in preference to brocades. He believed in acknowledging the truth of things: that's where heat comes from; that's what the material is made of. It was time to stop disguising. Johnson believed that Anni Albers's presence in the United States would improve textile design in general, and that she and Josef would help the museum.[21] Shortly after Eddie Warburg wrote to Alfred Barr, so did Johnson:

Eddie is writing to you about Albers. . . . But I know he is thinking of paying his way himself if he has to. He also got $500 from Mrs. R. for him. Personally I wish no responsibility for him, but I can't think better [sic] person could be got from the lot of ex Bauhaeusler [sic] than Albers. He could be very useful in all the industrial arts and in typography.[22]

Barr, who had met Josef if not Anni at the Dessau Bauhaus—and had written him a long letter (in German) four years earlier—was sympathetic.

When Eddie Warburg had written Barr about his scrambling for the funds to get the Alberses over from Germany, Black Mountain College was still five hundred dollars short of the minimum amount it needed to get started. Rice may have told Warburg that they had received a twenty-thousand-dollar guarantee and were opening in the fall, but in truth they weren't there yet. Moreover, although Warburg was able to wangle things with the immigration authorities and Johnson was able to negotiate with Albers so that all that was needed to get the Alberses to America was a guarantee of fifteen hundred dollars for the combination of Josef's salary for one year and his and Anni's fare over, no one was coming up with the necessary money. Warburg did indeed go to Mrs. Rockefeller and get five hundred dollars from her—whether this was with or without Barr's clearance remains unclear—but he had no choice as to what to do about the remaining sum. He gave it himself.

According to Ted Dreier, without that gift from Eddie Warburg, "Black Mountain College would never have started."[23] Dreier had promised the Forbeses that he would abandon the whole venture unless he got five thousand dollars in addition to their ten thousand. He had managed to scrape together forty-five hundred, but had reached his deadline without seeing how he could possibly raise another penny. Warburg's own contribution, along with the one he raised from Mrs. Rockefeller, entitled the school to receive the Forbes money, in addition to guaranteeing that Josef Albers—whose thousand-dollar salary would be the only wage paid to a Black Mountain faculty member that first year—could come to the United States.

In November of 1933 Anni and Josef Albers landed in New York on the S.S. *Europa*. Philip Johnson was waiting at the docks. The following day, he and Eddie Warburg took them to 1109 Fifth Avenue for a tour of the collection of Rembrandt and Dürer etchings. Then they crossed the street and walked downtown a few blocks to the Metropolitan Museum, where the Alberses marveled at the eager crowd—as they had at the energy and dynamism on the city streets. Two days later, Anni and Josef were at Black Mountain College. At first things were hard to get used to. A thumbtack attaching a notice to an Ionic column at the school's Robert E. Lee Hall was difficult to fathom; in Germany, columns were made of marble. There were new notions of aristocracy. Back at home people of Ted Dreier's and his wife Bobbie's social and economic class might have spent their holidays taking the waters at Baden-Baden; the Dreiers' idea of a vacation was to go backpacking. If their German counterparts would have whiled away the hours playing baccarat, Ted and Bobbie joined the road crew. But Anni and Josef Albers fit in soon enough. Once Warburg had got them across to America, they would never again leave except for brief travels.

III

Late in 1932, when Kirstein took Warburg to the New York studio of Gaston Lachaise, the French-born sculptor was practically penniless. Lachaise had been one of the favorites of the Harvard Society for Contemporary Art. He had been sporadically helped by a handful of patrons, but he was unable to hold on to money. The previous year, Kirstein had posed in the nude for Lachaise—for a sculpture that Gertrude Whitney bought for twelve hundred dollars. Kirstein had periodically done what he could to help. Now Warburg commissioned a portrait bust of himself. He wanted to understand the processes of sculpture, and he wanted to provide funds.

Lachaise regularly recounted his daily struggles at that time in letters to his wife Isabel and his stepson Edward Nagle, who were in Maine while he was in New York. Suddenly, on April 3, 1932, he wrote a letter to Nagle in which the tone of the correspondence changed completely. He gave his address for the next week as "c/o EMM Warburg Esq., Hotel Greenbrier," in White Sulphur Springs, West Virginia. After months of sitting for the portrait (he posed sixty-five times in all) Warburg had wanted some variation in the routine. At the lavish resort where Lachaise was Warburg's guest, they followed their three-hour morning work session with Lachaise

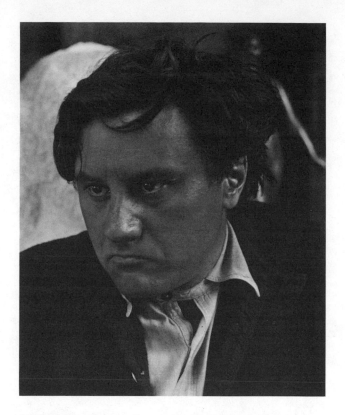

Paul Strand: Gaston Lachaise, Georgetown, Maine, 1927.

sunbathing and Warburg playing tennis. The afternoon and evening sittings were framed with pleasant walks, fine meals, and the occasional swim. Lachaise carried the life-size Plasticine head around in a cardboard box in which it was suspended between large nails at the top and bottom so that its surface never touched the sides. Warburg was highly amused to be accompanied by someone carrying his head in a box.

Throughout 1933 and 1934, Lachaise's stream of correspondence to Isabel—in scrawled pencil script alternating between French and English and a blend of the two—was packed with references to projects with the young Warburg. From White Sulphur Springs the report was that his patron had a "nature tellement agreeable & aimable."[24] He was, at the very least, patient; the commission took seven months to complete. From New York in the ensuing weeks came a cycle of statements that the bust was almost done and then that it wasn't. First Lachaise wrote that he would be casting it in

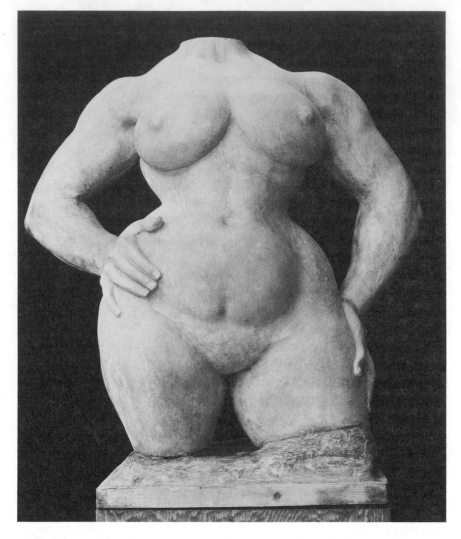

Gaston Lachaise, Torso, *1934 (front view), plaster, 45 × 41¼ × 21¼".*

bronze within a day or two. Then he was back at work on it. Again he was about to cast it, but in the next report he was refining it just a bit more. So it continued. Finally, on May 1, he wrote Isabel, "Pour moi, et pour lui, c'est un success." The same day, he informed Edward Nagle, "I finished Warburg portrait in Plasticine it is a great thing. I do like Warburg very much the more I know him, almost as much as Joe Gould which I know for many years and which as you know is a great friend for me." On May 9 the sculptor wrote to Isabel that this could go among the best portraits ever made, on May 10 that it was "le portrait d'un jeune Empereur." The letter of May 11 said not only that Warburg had taken it home and Felix was pleased, but also that Eddie and Lachaise had visited the Museum of Modern Art together. By the end of May, Warburg—who had paid a thousand dollars for the bronze—had agreed to a second version, for four thousand, in pale English alabaster.

Lachaise's goal wasn't primarily physical resemblance. What he was after, in his own words, was "a likeness with the skin removed." [25] It scarcely mattered when Henry McBride told the sculptor that Eddie Warburg's features were not quite right, that "the nose was too high on the head, not the Semitic two-thirds but Roman proportions." The bronze, even more than the alabaster, is the essence of the young art patron it portrayed: pensive yet outgoing, reflective, fervent.

If McBride was correct, and the well-defined features lack perfect verisimilitude to Warburg's appearance at the time, they nonetheless make a good pass at his rather exotic good looks that also show up in photographs. And Lachaise has arrested Warburg's features in a moment of intensity. Under strong light, the bronze is as smooth and shiny as Bellini's paintings and School of Fontainebleau enamels—the art with which Eddie Warburg was essentially the most comfortable. The veneer is flawless, the patina refined and elegant. But there is no bland perfection. Lachaise's Warburg, subtly asymmetrical, has the irregularity of living form. The bust is an exquisite object, but it reflects the complexity of human feelings. The face looks hungry for a purpose, engaged in a relentless search for the meanings of existence. Formed like a statuesque god, it is also tortured. Eddie Warburg may have prepped with impeccably bred American upper crusters and palled around with the right Wall Street boys, and he may have been brought up with perfect scrolly monograms, but this image shows someone unable to cut off the darker sides of life. This is a person who recognizes suffering, both in himself and in others. Sixty-five sittings may have seemed like a lot, but Lachaise was getting somewhere. His subject is as questing and restless as he is handsome, rich, and empowered.

By the time all three versions of the portrait bust were complete, Warburg had become Lachaise's primary benefactor. He had started early in 1933 by buying the powerful, intensely simplified marble *Knees*. In a letter to Isabel, Lachaise described Felix's and Frieda's reactions to that purchase. Lachaise stated, in French, "He showed the knees to his father and mother—his father liked them—his mother said I have knees better than those—showing her knees—his father said no"—and continued in English "and Warburg say that a family affair started."[26] Frieda thought even less of what followed. Eddie's next purchase was a highly sensuous, smooth-surfaced marble sculpture of bulging breasts with their firm, disproportionately high nipples jumping like exclamation points. Then he acquired the grossly exaggerated twelve-inch-high marble *Torso* in which vastly oversized breasts and buttocks—and nothing else—emerge from a rough block. Celebratory or deprecating, the voice of these works is certainly obsessional. The woman who vetoed *The Knees* and thought Picasso's *Blue Boy* too daring for the living room now thought her son had gone mad. Eddie's brother Fred's only comment, uttered repeatedly, was that he would be buying kneepads for *Knees* and a bra for *Breasts*. This was the sort of stuff Eddie had to put up with all the time.

Frieda Warburg went into a state over the enormous plaster Lachaise figure that Eddie gave to the Museum of Modern Art in 1934. Shortly after the presentation of his gift had attracted the attention of the national press, he took his mother to see what the excitement was all about. She could only see the piece as a mockery of her own need to drop some weight. "All I can say, Edward, is that I take this as a personal insult,"[27] Frieda balked audibly in the midst of the crowd on West Fifty-third Street. Two years later, however, Eddie turned her reaction to good advantage. The occasion was Frieda's surprise sixtieth birthday party at 1109 Fifth Avenue. Eddie gave a slide show of artworks that represented his mother's life. A Cubist Picasso portrait suggested her confused. The Lachaise represented Frieda before one of her pound-shedding visits to Elizabeth Arden's Maine Chance Farm, while a Malvina Hoffman sculpture of Pavlova portrayed her after her stay there.

The larger public, though stunned by the new Lachaise at the museum, saw it as more than a commentary on diet. The sculpture was the first major work by an American sculptor to be given to the museum's permanent collection.[28] *Time* magazine showed a photograph with the caption "huge steatopygous torso of a woman labeled COLOSSAL." This novel notion of female beauty was national news.

Warburg was buying both big and small. Having acquired La-chaise's bronze *Dolphins,* he commissioned—for $350—a nickel-plated dolphin as a radiator cap for his Packard. This prompted one of Lachaise's finest French-English blends, in a letter of March 6, 1933, to Isabel: "je travail pour lui a un radiator cap pour son car an open big touring packard." Warburg also periodically bought draw-ings. On one of his regular visits to Lachaise's studio, he noticed a new development in the recent pencil sketches. He told the sculptor that he had a sense that there was one particular work to which everything else was leading but which he had still not seen. The ob-servation prompted Lachaise to show Warburg the plaster version of *Dynamo Mother,* hitherto unknown to anyone else. The vivid and daring sculpture, although only eighteen inches long, was in many ways the culmination of the sculptor's work. It shows a highly ex-aggerated female form in a pose that suggests both the sexual act and the process of giving birth. Her erect nipples are as big as limbs. The head and legs are reduced in scale, the breasts and buttocks enlarged, the enormous labia pushed forward. Even today there are few collec-tors who would dare get near such a thing. But Lachaise wrote to Isabel on September 25, 1933, "He told me that the finest thing you have done of all these," and that Eddie Warburg wanted it. The sculptor promptly made a single casting of the piece into bronze— "It is the most powerful thing I have ever done"[29]—and Warburg bought it immediately.

What motivated Eddie Warburg to make the purchase is difficult to assess. Lachaise's account makes it a matter of an immediate, in-stinctual response. Warburg's own evaluation is less kind:

> To a certain extent I think it was my ambition to be considered "daring." And there never was anybody less daring than I was. I was a timid guy wanting very much to be included. And wanting to be part of the gang. The gang that I wanted to be part of was the young enthusiastic art followers and collectors. Somehow I felt that by owning these things and having had the courage to purchase them I thereby established my creden-tials.[30]

This may be a case of relentless self-denigration. It may be a valid commentary on the motives behind a lot of pioneering art collecting. In either case, the acquisition of *Dynamo Mother* was a brave step that gave the artist essential support, both emotional and financial.

By the middle of 1934, Warburg had signed the lease for Lachaise's studio at 42 Washington Mews and was paying the monthly rent. He had taken on the sculptor's needs as his personal problem. Sometimes this meant writing to him as a father might to a recalcitrant son. Consider the letter of May 15, 1934, on Museum of Modern Art stationery:

> You have been very considerate in sparing me the details of your financial condition. At the same time this prevents me from really helping you solve it. Until I know the exact amount you need to take care of your past debts and your future maintenance, I cannot cope with the situation.

Warburg goes on to request a statement of all obligations and expenses, to remind Lachaise that his wife and stepson will take on his debts when he dies, and to urge him both to get a job and to work on the more salable side of his sculpture. But after instructing his beneficiary to "face the cold facts," he closes by saying that his motive is "to solve this impossible financial muddle so that the work of America's foremost sculptor, Gaston Lachaise, may continue under the most favorable conditions."

Warburg would often start out tough and then go easy. On October 11, 1934, he wrote Lachaise that he could no longer pay his rent. The main reason was the demands on his funds "partly caused by the European situation and partly by the world-wide depression." It was no false claim; he had begun to sign further affidavits and to come up with more people's ticket money, and he could hardly turn his back on the escalating needs of his parents' pet organizations like the Joint Distribution Committee. So Warburg wrote Lachaise, "It is only right . . . that in view of the contracts you have for the coming year that a certain amount of this [rent] money, if not all, be paid back to me." But he crossed out his secretary's typewritten "if not all," and a paragraph later changed his tune: "I am perfectly willing to let bygones be bygones, and to forget all past debts as long as I do not have to meet any new obligations." He moved from his hard line even more readily than Jacob Schiff had with Frieda over the YWHA. In fact, Warburg did not stop paying Lachaise's rent at that point. That occurred only with a letter written five months later, in March of 1935—this time on a letterhead of the American Ballet. Warburg had reached his limit. Declaring that Lachaise's ideas on money were "completely impractical and therefore impossible in the civilization in which we live," and calculating that he had spent seventeen thousand dollars on Lachaise's work—"for which I have received in return many of your finest pieces of sculpture"—he finally gave up the lease on Lachaise's studio.

Besides buying Lachaise's sculpture and paying the rent, Warburg brought other collectors to the sculptor, intervened for Lachaise's getting commissions for Rockefeller Center, and steered grant money his way. He also lectured about Lachaise. In a talk at Vassar, he had to project the slides on a sheet hanging freely in a doorway. Winds blew in, and the sheets began to billow. His back turned to the makeshift screen, Warburg could not see what was happening. But his audience of young women was overcome by laughter. Never before had they seen naked women with such buxom figures dancing so freely.

Warburg and Kirstein worked in tandem on Lachaise's behalf. Warburg laid much of the groundwork for the retrospective show the sculptor had at the Museum of Modern Art in February 1935; Kirstein made the selection and wrote the catalog. The show was a success. To accommodate more conservative visitors, the museum paired it with an exhibition of work by the nineteenth-century American George Caleb Bingham, but while the Bingham show sold 101 catalogs, Lachaise sold 371. The combination of the two exhibitions drew in over twenty-five thousand people in thirty-four days.

As usual, it was Warburg's job to handle the nuts and bolts while Kirstein attended to more esoteric matters. Just before the exhibition was scheduled to open, a marshal of the City of New York served notice on Lachaise, care of the museum, for $78.92 that the sculptor had owed one of his marble suppliers for the past three years. The supplier was going to lay claim to one of the sculptures in the show if the debt wasn't settled. It was not the sort of expense for which the museum had ready funds. A letter from Alfred Barr to Eddie Warburg—at the offices of the ballet—tells what happened:

Dear Eddie:
    You were more than angelic to leap into the breach with your check in payment of Lachaise's debt to the Tompkins-Kiel Marble Company. I have made the check of $78.92 over to Albert Hohauser, marshal no. 48, who brought the notice of levy.

Lachaise does not know who has saved him though he may guess. I will tell him if you wish me to.

You may have saved the Museum considerable embarrassment since a sale of Lachaise's work on the premises might easily have been given an unfortunate publicity slant.

Now for the great event.

Expectantly,

AHB[31]

Henry McBride, in Lachaise's obituary eight months after the exhibition, listed as the sculptor's admirers e. e. cummings, Gilbert Seldes, Lincoln Kirstein, and Edward Warburg. The one he singled out was Warburg.

It was probably due to the influence of the last named that the astonishing one-man exhibition of the Lachaise sculptures occurred in the Modern Museum last winter, an exhibition so overwhelming in its appeal that you would have thought the whole world must have succumbed to it; but there were no signs of such a submission.[32]

Four years after the artist's death, Warburg wrote a letter to Isabel Lachaise—this time on the streamlined Art Deco letterhead of his private office at 30 Rockefeller Plaza. He was responding to her proposal that he "select some work of Gaston's in payment of past indebtedness."[33] From his point of view he had been "more than amply repaid," having bought work at prices "far from adequate" although Lachaise had insisted they were "fair and just. . . .

I in no way feel that you or Mr. Lachaise's estate owe me anything. As a matter of fact, I am really grateful for the privilege of not only possessing such fine examples of his work, but for the warmth of his friendship, and for the insight into sculptural problems as well as the problems of the sculptor, which I gained from him.

1934

I

Chick Austin and the Wadsworth Atheneum pulled themselves together quickly after the ballet debacle. There was the new building to finish, shows to mount, parties to plan. Nineteen thirty-four was going to be a big year for them, and nothing would get in the way.

Others anguished while Austin rallied. On October 26, 1933— just days after the ballet had left Hartford—Philip Johnson wrote Austin to say that while he "was very happy to join a non-profit making venture to further the interests of ballet in this country" and regretted having been able to give no more than five hundred dollars toward the Hartford undertaking, he would have nothing to do with the school as it was being planned in New York.

> Concerning the new upset I know nothing at all, only that the School is to be founded in New York, is to be a paying venture and is to attempt to route a ballet to regular theaters throughout the country. This is not at all what I understood on our first conversation or Lincoln's word from Europe, and I regret very much that I will be unable to contribute financially in any way to the new plan. I wish it, as I wish all ventures in the ballet in this country, success, but don't feel, under the circumstances, that it is much more worthy of support than others which already exist in this City.
>
> Please believe that I am thoroughly in sympathy with anything which you attempt in Hartford and that I will do anything that is within my power to help you personally and your theatre.[1]

Eddie Warburg had a lot to explain back at 1109 Fifth Avenue. Why had Peeper put so much money into something that had only lasted a week at its first location? Did he really think it would do any better in New York? Shouldn't he consider just taking a good solid job, like Freddie and Piggy? Why was he always listening to Kirstein, instead of to nice sensible people?

As for Kirstein, he felt "an anguish of embarrassment having put everyone involved in a false position. . . . I was whipped and sullen, disappointed and ignorant. . . . I smoldered."[2] The turmoil took its toll on Balanchine too. Shortly after moving to New York he fell extremely ill. He spent much of the end of November and the beginning of December in Northampton, Massachusetts, being nursed back to health by Mina Curtiss. Kirstein, Warburg, and Balanchine all managed to rally for 637 Madison Avenue, but not without some reassessment and spiritual recharge first.

On December 2 Austin announced the acquisition of Serge Lifar's collection of original designs for scenery and costumes for Diaghilev's ballet company. The last of Diaghilev's great male dancers, Lifar was Diaghilev's heir. Having heard about Lifar's holdings, Julien Levy had met the dancer in New York. He bought the collection of ballet art in its entirety, knowing that Austin would want it for Hartford. Using ten thousand dollars from the Sumner Fund—an extravagance in the eyes of his trustees—Austin thus obtained the complete assemblage of sketches, pen-and-inks, watercolors, and gouaches. It included many works by Léon Bakst, including his 1911 portrait of Nijinsky dancing in Michel Fokine's *The Spectre of the Rose;* four Braques; twenty-four de Chirico costume and set designs, most of them for the 1929 production of *Le Bal* that George Balanchine had choreographed in Monte Carlo; Jean Cocteau's 1931 pencil portrait of Lifar; ten André Derains, mainly designs for the 1926 Paris production of *Jack in the Box* choreographed by Balanchine to music of Erik Satie orchestrated by Darius Milhaud; five works by Max Ernst; four by Juan Gris; four by Fernand Léger; a Matisse curtain sketch; two Mirós; six splendid Picassos including pencil drawings of dancers and a sepia ink set design for the production of *The Three Cornered Hat* that Léonide Massine had choreographed in 1919; Rouault's sets for *The Prodigal Son* that Balanchine had choreographed in 1929; and nine works by Pavel Tchelitchew. There were also numerous pieces by André Bauchant, Alexander Benois, Christian Bérard, Paul Colin, Naum Gabo, Natalia Goncharova, Marie Laurencin, and various lesser known artists. Most were for performances produced by Diaghilev to music by the leading composers of the day.

Austin wanted to stage his own great artistic collaboration. With his new Avery Memorial Building opening on February 6, 1934, he had the chance. In 1927 Virgil Thomson had asked Gertrude Stein to write the libretto for an opera for which he would compose the music. Thomson felt that her sort of language would do well sung.[3] Stein took on the task. She based the opera mainly on the lives of her two favorite saints, Saint Teresa of Ávila and Ignatius Loyola.

Although its cast eventually consisted of fifteen saints in addition to those in the chorus, and it had a prelude and four acts, she called it *Four Saints in Three Acts*. Its themes were "religious life—peace between the sexes, community of faith, the production of miracles,"[4] set to melodies by Thomson that evoked Christian liturgy. Gertrude Stein's evaluation of it in *The Autobiography of Alice B. Toklas* was "It is a completely interesting opera both as to words and music."

Thomson, who was living in Paris, regularly performed parts of the new opera. He sang the various roles himself. In December of 1928, when he was visiting New York, he gave one of those solo performances at Carl Van Vechten's apartment. One of the people who heard it there was Mabel Dodge Luhan, who commented, "This opera should do to the Metropolitan what the painting of Picasso does to Kenyon Cox."[5] Cox, who had been among the opponents of the Armory Show, was a portraitist and mural painter who had died in 1919. His academic style had won him great favor with the most conservative critics of his day. But the powers at the Met were not yet ready to be jostled from their Cox-like stance by the musical equivalent of Picasso.

Meanwhile, Henry Russell Hitchcock had heard bits of *Four Saints* in Paris. He raved to Chick Austin about it. Alfred Barr and Jere Abbott, who also knew it from jaunts to the French capital, concurred. That was enough for Austin. In the winter of 1932–33, he decided that the perfect event with which to inaugurate the auditorium of the new building would be the world premiere of *Four Saints in Three Acts*. So five years after Mable Dodge Luhan made her prediction, Thomson had occasion to orchestrate the opera.

From Thomson's point of view,

> Chick went ahead with the opera plan in the same way that he accomplished other things, not by seeing his way through from the beginning but merely by finding out, through talking of his plan in front of everyone, whether any person or group would try to stop him. Then once inside a project, he would rely entirely on instinct and improvisation. For he considered, and said so, that a museum's purpose was to entertain its director.[6]

This time, there was no one to stop him. The local dancing schools—or for that matter the opera guilds—felt no threat from the production of *Four Saints*.

Not that the failure of the ballet in Hartford didn't interfere. Chick originally intended to produce *Four Saints* "under the auspices of the American Ballet." [7] He expected Thomson to orchestrate some new ballets for Balanchine, and Balanchine to choreograph a ballet especially for *Four Saints*. It was only five months before the premiere that Thomson arrived in New York from Paris and upon walking into the Askews' apartment discovered that the American Ballet Company had left Hartford almost as soon as it had arrived there. But Austin had already found a solution. For one thing, Eddie Warburg, who felt bad about how things had turned out for the ballet considering all the trouble Austin had gone to, gave five hundred dollars. The Sobys and the Askews and Jere Abbott also contributed generously, with the Julien Levys, the Alfred Barrs, the Paul Sachses, the Edward Forbeses, John Walker, and other people giving as well. And for most of his funding—the budget for the production was ten thousand dollars—Austin could count on the support of The Friends and Enemies of Modern Music.

Thomson had a lot of ideas about the staging, but needed a director. In November he met John Houseman at one of the Askews' Sunday afternoons. Houseman was at that point an unsuccessful playwright, and had never directed anything, but Thomson recognized him as the person for the job. The next morning the composer got Houseman to go to his hotel room, where he had a piano. For almost two hours he banged away and sang arias, recitatives, and choruses in "his thin, piercing tenor voice." [8]

He performed lines like the opening:

> "To know to know to love her so.
> Four Saints prepare for Saints
> It makes it well fish.
> Four saints it makes it well fish."

In one passage Saint Ignatius sang about

> "Pigeons on the grass alas. . . .
> If a magpie in the sky on the sky can not cry if the pigeon on
> the grass alas can alas and to pass the pigeon on
> the grass alas and the magpie in the sky on the sky
> and to try and to try alas and the magpie in the
> sky on the sky and to try and to try alas on the
> grass alas the pigeon on the grass the pigeon on
> the grass and alas." [9]

Houseman was convinced. When Thomson asked him to work on the production—gratis—the playwright accepted happily.

Together they set about to find a cast, rehearse, and coordinate. Thomson asked the artist Florine Stettheimer to do the sets. Wanting a good choreographer, he persuaded Frederick Ashton to come from London. The production had enough money for third-class fare. The Askews could offer a free bed. The only people who could be paid were the singers and the orchestra.

Thomson specified that the performers were all to be black. Contemporary newspaper accounts present both his reasons for this decision and their own startling evaluations of it. The *Hartford Courant* reported:

> In the selection of a Negro cast, Mr. Thomson believes that he has overcome obstacles which otherwise would have lessened the quality of the performance in several directions.
>
> Because of the libretto, it was highly essential to have English speaking singers. So great is the verbal or phonetic importance that it would never have done to employ singers to whom English pronunciation and phrasing was not native or instinct.
>
> The choice of singers therefore was immediately limited to American or English. Mr. Thomson felt that the vocal characteristics of these nationalities—pure head tones, flutey but hollow—lack the sonority which is completely essential to the music. Through process of elimination, Negro voices were all that was left.
>
> Thus far the selection of a Negro cast was negative. There was, however, an entirely positive phase to the selection.
>
> The Negro voice is sonorous. Its diction, contrary to expectation, is clear and easy in enunciation. Moreover, the Negro is noted for real style in singing—the power of the race to throw itself completely into song, its traditional resort to song on all occasions, makes singing a national medium of expression, and one which has therefore by now been highly developed.
>
> Then too, the Negro cast has no intellectual objections to the advanced nature of the libretto. Not once, said Mr. Thomson, has any member giggled over the arrangement of words—a condition which the composer believes he could not duplicate among any other singers. The completely serious, unbiased and non-self-conscious acceptance of the text on the one hand, and the natural clear enunciation on the other, enables the cast, in

Mr. Thomson's words, "to pronounce the words as if they did mean something."[10]

To an interviewer from the *New York World Telegram,* Thomson explained, "Negroes have the most perfect and beautiful diction. . . . I have never heard a white singer with the perfect diction and sense of rhythm of a Negro."[11] Blacks represented both an ideal spontaneity and nonjudgmentalism for him. He had always liked Negro church choirs. Helped by a talent scout who specialized in black performers, he began to stage auditions in the Askews' drawing room. After filling the lead roles, he went to Harlem to hear future choristers. Soon enough, he had assembled a cast. He also found Miss Eva Jessye—who had been training Harlem choirs for years—to work with them in her studio on the second floor of a local brownstone. Then for the final preparations Thomson and Houseman rented a rehearsal hall in the basement of St. Philip's Episcopal Church on 137th Street.

Meanwhile there was no end to the sweeping generalizations made on the subject of this "all-Negro" cast. After hearing the actual performance in Hartford, Carl Van Vechten evaluated its effect as having been precisely what Thomson had anticipated:

> There is a simplicity and a distinction about this singing, a clearness in the enunciation, a complete lack of self-consciousness in the involved and intricate action of the piece, which completely justifies his decision in this direction. . . . There is nothing Negro in the gestures or singing speech of this remarkable company. After ten minutes it is possible to forget altogether (unless you perversely prefer to pleasantly remember) that these are Negro singers. . . . I may say in all truthfulness that on few previous occasions have I encountered such a perfect mating of cast and work.[12]

If Lincoln Kirstein had written Austin that Negro ballet performers in Hartford would be "nonpareil," from Thomson's point of view they were just that:

> The Negroes proved in every way rewarding. Not only could they enunciate and sing; they seemed to understand because they sang. They resisted not at all Stein's obscure language,

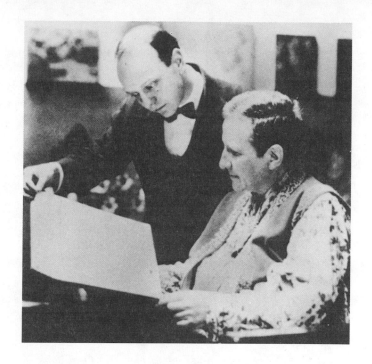

Above: Virgil Thomson and Gertrude Stein look at the manuscript of Four Saints in Three Acts in 1934. Below left: Frederick Ashton, photographed by Lee Miller, 1934. Below right: Florine Stettheimer, c. 1925.

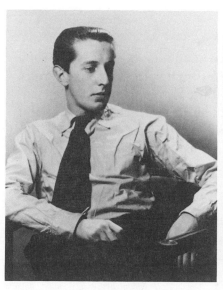

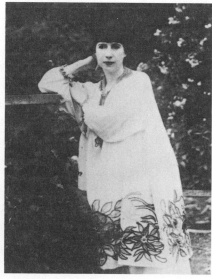

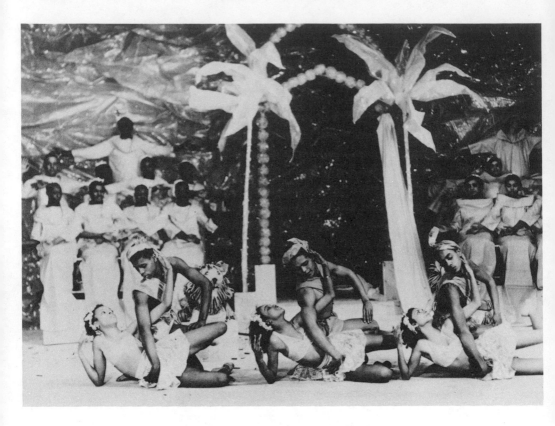

Performance of Four Saints: *angels dancing.*

adopted it for theirs, conversed in quotations from it. They
moved, sang, spoke with grace and with alacrity, took on roles
without self-consciousness, as if they were the saints they said
they were. I often marveled at the miracle whereby slavery (and
some cross-breeding) had turned them into Christians of an
earlier stamp than ours, not analytical or self-pitying or romantic in the nineteenth-century sense, but robust, outgoing, and
even in disaster sustained by inner joy.[13]

Here again the goals were naturalness and freedom from inhibitions.
To be able to respond to one's own instincts was far better than to
bow to artifice and the imposition of form.

. . .

The presence of blacks was troublesome for Florine Stettheimer, however. She claimed that their hue threw off her color scheme, and asked that their faces be painted white. In this she did not prevail, although she did get the cast made up to an even shade of light brown, and put into white gloves. About most everything else, Miss Stettheimer got her way entirely. Saint Teresa wore crimson velvet, while the chorus was clad in long blue robes and silver halos. There were trees made out of feathers. A seawall at Barcelona was constructed from shells. The sky was made of fifteen hundred square feet of blue cellophane mounted on cotton mesh. For a procession scene there was a baldachino made of black chiffon, framed in bunches of black ostrich plumes. Joseph W. Alsop, Jr.—who had been graduated from Harvard in 1932, and whose father was a Hartford insurance executive as well as a prominent tobacco farmer with land next to Charlie Soby's in the Hartford suburb of Avon—would report the effect from his first journalistic post at the *New York Herald Tribune:* "Two yellow cloth lions reclined before a sort of bower of cellophane, on either side of which two cellophane palms with magnificent cellophane plumes rose gracefully." [14]

For the last three days of rehearsals, Miss Stettheimer and her sister Ettie stayed at Hartford's elegant Hotel Heublein, as did Carl Van Vechten and his wife and Henry McBride, who was covering the event for the *New York Sun.* The cast, on the other hand, stayed in black households and those hotels where blacks were permitted. This was arranged by the Negro Chamber of Commerce, who also greeted the bus which transported the singers from New York. Thomson, Houseman, and other staff members filled the guest rooms of Helen Austin's mother's house.

The weather reached sixteen below zero. But everyone was too excited to care. During one rehearsal, Frederick Ashton grew so upset with Alexander Smallens, Leopold Stokowski's assistant in Philadelphia and the conductor of *Four Saints'* orchestra of twenty, that he stormed outside after exploding, "I have worked with Sir Thomas Beecham! A genius! And he never spoke to me as you have!" [15] The temperature sent him right back in, though; nothing would stop this production.

The Avery Memorial officially opened on February 6, 1934. *Four Saints in Three Acts* had its "honorary dress rehearsal" the next night, and its world premiere on February 8. There was a program de-

signed by Henry Russell Hitchcock, its shocking pink cover presenting both a poem by Richard Crashaw about Saint Teresa of Ávila
and a photograph of Bernini's dramatic *St. Theresa in Ecstasy*. Inside
was a musical portrait of Gertrude Stein by Virgil Thomson, a prose
portrait of Virgil Thomson by Gertrude Stein, reproductions of
painted portraits of both of them by Christian Bérard, and a reproduction of Kristians Tonny's highly offbeat, elaborate portrait of
Thomson. In addition there were startling photographs by Lee
Miller of the opera's directors and cast. Formerly an assistant and
mistress to Man Ray, Miller was one of the regular Surrealist exhib-
itors at Julien Levy's gallery. She revealed her subjects in telling
ways. Chick Austin has his head cocked dramatically. John Houseman has that look of erudition that would later become his trademark. Frederick Ashton, wearing what must be the world's widest,
horizontal-striped tie, is the epitome of an inspired and intense choreographer. Virgil Thomson appears serious and intense to the core
but sports a checked pocket handkerchief the size of a bistro napkin.
There are also a number of members of the black cast, one face more
richly beautiful than the next, all looking devout to the point of rap-
ture. In addition, there was one photograph by Man Ray himself—
provided by James Thrall Soby, who was working at that time on an
album of Man Ray's photos. It shows Gertrude Stein looking like an
idol, someone who unquestionably knows everything.

The people who attended paid ten dollars a ticket. For the most
part they were fashionable out-of-towners who came for the combination of the Avery opening, the opera, and the Picasso retrospective that Austin had arranged to coincide with these events. The
New Haven Railroad added extra parlor cars to shuttle New Yorkers
to these great happenings in Hartford. Mrs. Harrison Williams, considered one of America's best-dressed women, had ordered a special
dress that she could keep at cocktail length on the train and unfasten
to full length for the reception and performance. Others who lacked
such an easy means of switching from day to evening changed in the
lavatories at the Heublein, conveniently en route between the Hartford train station and the Atheneum. Kirk Askew and Julien Levy
didn't object in the least to dressing in such close quarters, although
Francis Henry Taylor—who a few years later would become director
of the Metropolitan Museum of Art—thought far less of it. Standing
in his gray flannel underwear he excoriated the "unfeasability of
Chick."[16] But most people were thrilled to be there. When a shiny

black vehicle "shaped like a gigantic raindrop"[17] arrived at the museum itself, it deposited Buckminster Fuller flanked by Dorothy Hale and Clare Boothe in their shimmering evening gowns. The bizarre automobile was Fuller's first Dymaxion car.

A sizable press corps also attended. There were critics from all over the East, and representatives from the major wire services. In many ways this was a national event. The society columnist Lucius Beebe gave a lengthy account in which he reported that "Since the Whiskey Rebellion and the Harvard butter riots there has never been anything like it, and until the heavens fall or Miss Stein makes sense there will never be anything like it again."[18] The opera was broadcast on radio throughout the country. Readers of the *New York Herald Tribune* were treated to Joseph Alsop's account of the performance the next day. Of the introduction to *Four Saints,* Alsop wrote:

> It made no sense in logic. Words were repeated, sentences were broken off and phrases kept popping back into the song like corks rising and falling in a bottle. Nevertheless, from the very first Miss Stein's curious rhythmic verse, which the singing made more clearly audible than is usual at operatic performances, had an effect all its own. There were two or three bursts of laughter when the chorus, in long blue robes and diamond-studded gloves, repeated some especially startling phrase, but it was evident that a receptive audience liked the much-discussed words of the matron saint of art of Paris.

Alsop was as interested in the audience as in the opera. His report also covered the intermission following the first act:

> The curtain went down on a finale with the phrase, "they never knew about it" for its theme, and the audience trooped into the foyer of the theatre to chatter, gaze at one another and talk of the play. Mrs. William Averell Harriman and her sister, Mrs. William Lord, discussed it in one corner. Henry McBride, critic, was not far off, next to a woman with heliotrope hair, who was congratulating Virgil Thomson. A. Everett Austin, Jr., director of the Wadsworth Atheneum's Museum, to which the theatre is attached, and president of the Friends and Enemies of Modern Music, stood by a punch bowl, receiving congratulations. Alexander Calder, sculptor, turned out in a tweed coat

and dusty boots, ignored the highly full dress appearance of the rest of the company. Carl Van Vechten, author of "Peter Whiffle"; Alfred Barr, director of the Museum of Modern Art in New York; and Mrs. Muriel Draper were scattered in the crowd. They all gossiped and smoked until the second-act curtain rose for a new revelation.

Of the second act, Alsop wrote,

> The lighting, arranged by [Abe] Feder, bathed the set, on which all the saints this time were in white, in a special luminousness. With the light and the color and the form, at once complicated, amusing and lovely, the setting seemed to give the note for the whole performance. There were elements in it that were merely smart, and therefore valueless, and there were other things about it of deep charm. . . . The ballet of six young Negroes emerged for the first time in the second act, rather startlingly naked for so saintly a gathering, but quite effective enough to deserve St. Ignatius's "thank you very much" at the end of their dance. The choreography of the whole opera, which was done by Frederick Ashton, ballet master of the Camargo Society of London, was an important part of the general effect. It, too, like the setting and the words, managed to be baroquely witty and handsome in one breath.

Alsop's overall evaluation of Gertrude Stein's text was that "they made no sense, yet sung they were lovely." Discussing a sequence in which the key words are "magpie in the sky," he wrote,

> In print the excerpts from the aria seem incomparably silly, but sung its foolishness was forgotten, and the handling of rhythm and sound in it, that talent which Miss Stein has been able to pass on to Ernest Hemingway and Sherwood Anderson, had its full effect.

Not everyone in America was focused on the black tie opening of an experimental opera that day. While the society column set was descending on Hartford in parlor cars and limousines, Eleanor Roosevelt spent the day at a ceremony held at the Hotel Governor Clinton in New York. The event had originally been scheduled for the

Waldorf-Astoria, but a strike of waiters and cooks had forced the change. She used the occasion to sew an NRA label to a straw hat and promise a "better day for all of us." Joseph Alsop, for one, was cognizant of how rarefied the Hartford audience was. "What a less hand-picked public, less interested in smart art, will think of the production remains to be seen," he wrote. Indeed, half a century later, *Four Saints in Three Acts* is not a part of the standard opera repertory. But at least to three hundred people for each of six nights in Hartford, Connecticut, and to subsequent groupings in Philadelphia and New York, these were rich pickings.

And for those of the inner circle, this was cause for celebration. There were dozens of curtain calls. Russell Hitchcock, smashing his opera hat and tearing open his shirt, got Austin to take a bow. People applauded Virgil Thomson. And then the same crowd who had had cocktails at the Sobys' before the performance repaired to the Austins' afterward.

In the Rococo living room of the Palladian villa, Salvador Dali sat in a love seat next to Mimi Soby. Staring at the mother-of-pearl buttons on the bosom of her dress, he politely asked if they were edible. ("Madame, ces boutons, sont-ils comestibles?")[19] Nearby, Nicholas Nabokov—a composer who had recently fled Russia—banged out Russian folk songs on the piano while Archibald MacLeish and other guests sang along. Not everyone was quite so festive, however. Julien Levy waxed rhapsodic to Virgil Thomson, but Thomson would have none of it. "Oh dear, Julien, didn't you notice that the trumpets came in a beat late at the beginning of the second act?" he complained. Replying "Oh, Virgil, don't split hairs!" Levy gave Thomson "a small push" that sent the composer out of balance and into a fragile antique chair made of gold bamboo; the chair fell into splinters and Thomson landed on the floor. Sandy Calder—whose red flannel shirt had caused quite a stir among the black-tie crowd that night—saw all this. He enveloped Levy "in a tight bear hug" and, asking if he was drunk, carried the art dealer upstairs and put him to rest in a quiet bedroom.[20]

Shortly after, Carl Van Vechten wrote to Gertrude Stein to say, "Four Saints in our vivid theatrical parlance is a knockout and a wow. . . . I haven't seen a crowd more excited since Sacre du Printemps. The difference was that they were pleasurably excited."[21] Van Vechten also wrote an essay entitled "How I Listen to Four Saints in Three Acts" that appeared in the souvenir program of the opera's

six-week run—the longest engagement to date for an American opera—at the 44th Street Theatre in New York. He recommended an
approach to the performance that could apply equally to a session of
psychoanalysis. "It is better to take your seat in the theatre where
Four Saints is being performed without expecting or hoping or desir-
ing for anything," suggested Van Vechten. That posture of openness
and receptivity was no small task. Even if a number of Van Vechten's
readers were in the habit of trying for it on their analysts' couches, it
was tougher to achieve in a theater seat. But the goal was central to
what people like Warburg, Kirstein, Austin, and Soby were all
working for in various ways: a willingness to approach experience
unarmed.

This was the point of view Stein put forward in a radio interview
she gave later that year:

> If you go to a football game you don't have to understand it in
> any way except the football way and all you have to do with
> *Four Saints* is to enjoy it in the *Four Saints* way which is the way
> I am, otherwise I would not have written it in that way. Don't
> you see what I mean? If you enjoy it you understand it, and lots
> of people have enjoyed it so lots of people have understood it.

Of the "Pigeons on the grass alas" sequence, Stein explained,

> I was walking in the gardens of the Luxembourg in Paris it was
> the end of summer and I saw the big fat pigeons in the yellow
> grass and I said to myself pigeons on the yellow grass, alas . . .
> and I kept on writing until I had emptied myself of the emo-
> tion. If a mother is full of her emotion toward a child in the
> bath the mother will talk and talk and talk until the emotion is
> over and that's the way a writer is about emotion.[22]

Carl Van Vechten wrote of the *Four Saints* performance, "If the
auditor demands a plot, he will be disappointed, but why should he
demand a plot? It is like looking at a painting and demanding a
story." An approach free of the usual demands and expectations
would reap rewards. Astute listeners could enjoy "the great skill
with which Virgil Thomson has written for the voice, following its
natural inflections so instinctively that the music proves to be more
consistently singable than many other operas written by the most

celebrated composers. Miss Stein's words always sound better than they look." Moreover, "to compensate for the lack of story in the accepted sense, there is abundant action, action which is witty, beautiful, suggestive, and full of entrancing double meanings."

By suspending old-fashioned, traditional criteria and by allowing oneself to revert to primary instincts, there was a new access to the enchantment of unexpected truths. The requisite was the deceptively difficult feat of relaxation and of letting down one's guard.

> If you will lounge in your chair and permit the words of Gertrude Stein, the music of Virgil Thomson, and the imaginative action of Frederick Ashton against the extraordinary decorations of Florine Stettheimer, to sink into your consciousness, play as they will on your emotions, you will perhaps find yourself, to your own surprise, actually enjoying this strange work of art, enjoying it very much indeed, in fact.

Van Vechten was among those proponents of modernism capable of such pleasure: "The performance of *Four Saints,*" he concluded, "is just about as perfect as would seem humanly possible." The benefits of an open mind and relaxed posture were vast.

II

To some people the *Four Saints* premiere marked a change in the course of Western civilization. However, at least one person considered it with a different historical perspective.

Agnes Mongan felt a distant connection with Gertrude Stein, who had been a Radcliffe classmate of Paul Sachs's sister. In a review she later wrote of Stein's book on Picasso, Mongan pointed out that Stein's deliberately tendentious approach always achieved the author's goal of "an aroused, alert, attentive reader."[23] That awakening was a worthy goal. Thus Mongan could write Austin a perfectly correct, tactful letter about the premiere: "All of us who were at your historical opening agree that we have never had better fun. It was a grand two days. Your stage setting for the whole was superb."[24] Yet this was short of the gusto with which Mongan might describe a Poussin sketch. Even if the Stein-Thomson opera made for a nice occasion with "the old gang"[25] from the Fogg, she did not regard it as the same apotheosis they did. The person to whom she confessed this reserve was her mentor Georgiana King. G.G. had of course known Gertrude Stein since before Austin and Hitchcock were born, and had periodically reviewed Stein's books. But like Mongan she was immersed in the culture of previous centuries, and from this vantage point might sympathize with Mongan's view that what was an amusing adventure was not much more. So on February 15 Mongan—who rarely wrote to her former teacher—suddenly poured out her heart to "Miss King":

> The Hartford opera was great fun. I would not have missed the opening for anything less than pneumonia—but I did miss, even though I followed it intently, the significance of many things. I wish you had been there. Certainly you would have known how seriously Miss Stein intended it to be taken. I was content to have it a Baroque conceit, as I heard it called, until a bright young man whom I asked about "There are pigeons in the grass, alas, there are pigeons in the grass" said in superior tones, "Why that is the whole of Spanish iconography." If his answer was correct there are things you did not teach us about Spain, Miss King, or else I was sadly lacking in attention. . . . The scenery, all wrapped in cellophane, glittered and shone in the shifting lights. Yet in the end I wondered how it would fare in New York as a professional production. The whole thing seemed to have the gaiety and intimacy and spontaneity of an amateur performance done in the presence of sympathetic friends. That was largely the reason it was such great fun to see and hear it. Edward Warburg doesn't in the least agree with me. You may hear his opinion when he lectures at the Deanery [at Bryn Mawr], as Miss [Charlotte] Howe tells me he is going to do.[26]

Meanwhile, the other key event of the Avery Memorial opening presented artworks of more certain long-term significance. Mabel Dodge had said that *Four Saints in Three Acts* would do to the Metropolitan Opera what Picasso would do to Kenyon Cox. Stein and Picasso were thought of in tandem back then. The Avery auditorium had opened with the sort of modern music and modern writing guaranteed to put stalwarts of tradition on their ears; its exhibition space naturally had to be launched with art that was equally new and audacious. Picasso's paintings were the answer. Like Stein's and Thomson's collaboration, not only were they pioneering, but they also represented the hotbed of creativity that was centered in Paris at the time.

A Picasso retrospective was a wise choice to show to advantage the interior court of the new Avery Memorial. The building's exterior, in deference to its donor's wishes, was of the same marble and bronze as the adjacent Morgan Memorial, and compatible in style if updated in tone. The interior, however, was pared down and streamlined. The aesthetic advocated by Philip Johnson and Henry Russell Hitchcock had made its mark. The cantilevered balconies over the Avery court were clean and fresh uninterrupted expanses of white plaster. The bold architecture called for daring, forthright art.

The courtyard had a lean but adventurous display of recent sculpture. There was Brancusi's *Blonde Negress,* lent by Philip L. Goodwin, as well as a number of pieces that Eddie Warburg provided, among them the little wooden Gauguin and works by Epstein, Lachaise, and Lehmbruck. Upstairs on the second-floor balcony and in galleries paneled simply in pine, the Wallace Nutting Collection of seventeenth-century American furniture and objects was put on view to rare effect by Henry Russell Hitchcock. These rough-hewn pieces dramatized life in an era when experience had of necessity the immediacy and high pitch that many modernists were now seeking by choice. There were two other loan shows: "French Art of the Nineteenth Century" and "Museums One Hundred Years Ago"— an exhibition of photographs and plans also organized by Hitchcock. But the real drawing card was the Picasso exhibition, which was on the third-floor balcony and in the adjacent large exhibition room.

Picasso had had solo shows in America before, mostly in New York. The first was in 1911 at the *291* Gallery. Then came a 1914–15 show at the Photo-Secession Gallery, and in 1923 an exhibition of his new "neo-classic" works at Wildenstein. The pace had stepped up at the end of the 1920s and beginning of the 1930s, with fairly regular shows—mostly of drawings and gouaches—at the John Becker, Reinhardt, Demotte, Marie Harriman, and Valentine galleries. But these were all private gallery exhibitions of work for sale. The only nonprofit institutions to do solo Picasso exhibitions were the Chicago Arts Club—with two small shows in 1928 and 1930— and the Harvard Society for Contemporary Art, where Picasso's

work had been shown in both 1931 and 1932. The Atheneum's Picasso exhibition was in a different league altogether.

There were seventy-seven paintings, and an equal number of
prints and drawings. The oils ranged from the small 1895 *Mother and
Child* to some of Picasso's most recent work, like the enormous 1931
Large Still Life from Paul Rosenberg's collection in Paris and the 1932
Woman Before a Mirror. As part of the collection of the Museum of
Modern Art this painting would eventually become synonymous
with the artist's name, but in 1934 it was still in Picasso's personal
collection and largely unknown.

The Atheneum's show put on public view for the first time a number of paintings that have since become widely familiar—reproduced
on cards, posters, and T-shirts, and in countless Picasso books.
Many of these artworks would again be seen in the Museum of Modern Art's major Picasso show in 1939 and in scores of subsequent
exhibitions, but prior to 1934 they had been available only to a small
and exclusive audience. Lent by some of the most adventurous, prescient American art collectors and galleries of the era, these paintings
and works on paper showed all Picasso's major developments to
date. Adolph Lewisohn provided the brushy and Impressionistic
Courtesan with a Hat from 1901, the same year as Dr. and Mrs. Harry
Bakwin's *Fille Au Chignon* and M. Knoedler & Co.'s *At the Moulin
Rouge*—three paintings that showed Picasso still under the influence
of Toulouse-Lautrec and absorbed with music hall life. From the
year 1903 came some of the most evocative portraits of the artist's
Blue Period: the Art Institute of Chicago's *Old Guitarist,* Jere Abbott's *Les Misérables,* and A. Conger Goodyear's *Vieille Femme.* Felix
and Frieda Warburg may have thought that Picasso's *Blue Boy* be-
longed on the squash court, but the Wadsworth Atheneum was more
than happy to have it on view for a second time and to reproduce it
in the catalog along with other 1905 landmark works like Sam and
Margaret Lewisohn's *The Harlequin's Family,* Mr. and Mrs. William
Averell Harriman's *Woman With a Fan,* the Marie Harriman Gallery's
Woman Combing Her Hair, and *La Toilette*—the painting that had cost
Conger Goodyear his relationship with the Albright Art Gallery in
Buffalo and hence freed him for the Museum of Modern Art. It is
hard to imagine a group of pictures that could better convey the
blend of Picasso's classical grace and tranquillity with an indefinable
mystery.

A. E. Gallatin lent a 1906 *Self-Portrait* with boldly chopped-out
features that attacked the issue of human appearance in an entirely

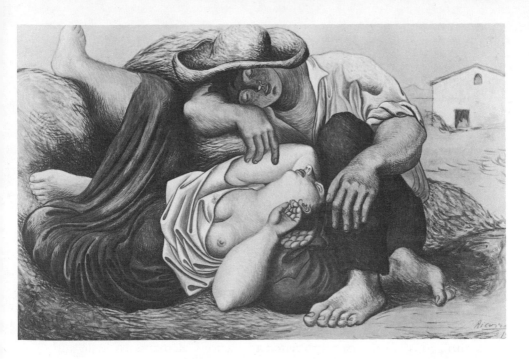

Pablo Picasso, Sleeping Peasants, *Paris, 1919. Tempera, watercolor, and pencil on paper, 12¼ × 19¼".*

different way from the work of the preceding year. The Marie Harriman Gallery and the artist George L. K. Morris supplied Cubist still lifes. Paris collectors lent generously as well. The Baron Fukushima provided various major works, including the wonderful 1919 *Sleeping Peasants*. Alfred Barr would eventually call this small colored ink and crayon drawing of two exhausted lovers in the hay "one of the earliest and most memorable of Picasso's compositions in the 'colossal' style"; today it is one of the artist's most popular works at the Museum of Modern Art.[27]

Another work that would in time become a focal point at the museum and that Barr came to regard as one of the two paintings "which are perhaps the high point of synthetic cubism" was the 1921 *Three Musicians* lent by Rosenberg.[28] Other key works of the same style had come from nearer by, like the large *The Table* that was at Smith College. The Atheneum show was also rich in paintings from Picasso's neoclassical phase. There was Philip Goodwin's 1920 gouache *The Rape*, Pierre Matisse's 1921 *Legend of the Source*, and a range of canvases that measured at most six by eight inches each but loomed large. These included the Atheneum's own 1922 *Nude Woman,* Mr. and Mrs. James Thrall Soby's 1923 *Mother and Child,* and *Maternité* and *Jeux Familiaux*—both from the artist's own collection.

The curvilinear Cubism of the 1920s was represented by a range of large and important canvases lent by the Sobys; by the Wildenstein, Valentine, and Becker galleries in New York; and above all by Paul Rosenberg in Paris. There were also some fairly disquieting works from the later 1920s: the Sobys' *Seated Woman,* a large canvas that belonged to the New York collectors Mr. and Mrs. Sidney Janowitz, and more paintings from Rosenberg. And bringing it all up to date there were some paintings from the artist's Surrealist phase. These ranged from A. E. Gallatin's playful 1929 *Bathers at Dinard*—a remarkable small canvas that showed highly abstracted figures in striped bathing suits ecstatically throwing a ball on the seashore—to an unsettling 1929 *Composition* depicting a head that is a unique assemblage of forms closely related to various elements of male and female genitalia. One can hardly imagine what the local insurance executives and their wives made of these recent canvases in particular. For people to whom the seashore meant martinis on the veranda, and dreams meant something you didn't talk about at breakfast, the Surreal phase was the most startling of all.

This first solo Picasso exhibition in a major American museum evoked little of the hoopla begat by the *Four Saints* premiere. Newspapers mentioned it, reviewers and the public attended, but there was no significant outcry. None of the major national magazines gave the show any attention at all. Nor were the newspapers especially engaged. The *New York Herald Tribune* did not deem it worthy of a separate review. Joseph Alsop mentioned it briefly at the end of his big February 8 piece on *Four Saints,* calling it "an exhibition of Pablo Picasso which experts concede to be the finest ever arranged of the great modernist," but he treated it essentially as a news item, significant mainly because of its comprehensiveness and the distance the paintings had traveled.

In *The New York Times,* comment on the Picasso show in Hartford was confined to a short article in the lower-left-hand corner of page twelve of section nine that same Sunday. Ambiguously titled "It Makes it Well Fish" it would have attracted the attention of only the most assiduous of readers; it certainly did not appear to be an exhibition review. "It Makes it Well Fish" was Edward Alden Jewett's take on all that had happened at the opening of the Avery. He was amused by *Four Saints,* although he called it a "succès fou" and pointed out that "Cellophane is only cellophane and a museum is for the ages." As for the Picasso exhibition, it warranted one paragraph, predictably condescending toward abstraction and sided toward the artist's classical, nonconfrontational phases. Equally predictably, the text included the names of the more prestigious lenders—as if this was what was necessary to give the event a bit of clout. It wasn't negative, nor was it much else. What received far more notice in all the papers that day were Orozco's new murals at Dartmouth College and a big Prendergast show at the Whitney; these were the paintings reproduced when Picasso's were not considered deserving of illustration.

The one New York critic who did the show justice was Henry McBride. Unlike his counterpart at the *Times,* he did not wait until a couple of weeks after its opening to bother to mention it. While the other papers relegated Picasso to a position of little significance in spite of all the attention they awarded to *Four Saints,* McBride's coverage in the February 10 *New York Sun* dignified the Picasso show as a significant event. He made much of the new building and the opera premiere, but his general take was that the Picassos were "the whole thing of the occasion."

The Picasso show had other champions among the small circle already committed to modernism. Austin and Soby lectured around town and at the exhibition itself, trying to drum up enthusiasm. The specialized art press gave the show attention. *The Art News* put a large reproduction of one of the paintings on its first page and reported that this was "an occasion not to be missed at any cost." Its critic said that there was no "parallel in Western art for line such as one finds already in 'Garçon Blue' from the collection of Mr. E. M. M. Warburg," referred to the "amazing" solidity of form of *Woman Combing Her Hair,* and credited the small neo-classical canvases with "a monumentality that is amazing, and the intensity of old masters." She was less enthusiastic about Picasso's recent art— the 1929 works were "empty of meaning," and "regarding those of 1932 even less can be said"—but at least she cared enough to comment.[29]

The occasional visitor, too, was deeply moved. The person with whom Agnes Mongan had driven down from Boston for *Four Saints* and the Picasso opening was Nathaniel Saltonstall, a Boston architect who was a trustee of the Museum of Fine Arts. On the way back Saltonstall told her that they really ought to be doing the same sort of thing on their home territory. He later spoke with his mother about the possibility of a fund-raising performance on behalf of a new organization to advance contemporary art. She offered the use of her drawing room overlooking the Charles River for a concert. Saltonstall knew just the person to give it—a bright young friend of his, a Harvard undergraduate who played the piano beautifully. And so Leonard Bernstein's first public performance was arranged.[30] It helped to launch a Boston branch of New York's Museum of Modern Art—the Boston Museum of Modern Art—which initially held exhibitions at the Fogg and at Harvard's Germanic Museum. To a degree this organization tried to pick up where the Harvard Society for Contemporary Art left off. Soon to evolve into the Institute of Contemporary Art, it opened in 1936 with Saltonstall as its president, and Alfred Barr, Paul Sachs, and Mongan on its board. The first director was James Sachs Plaut, a nephew of Paul Sachs who had been on the staff of the MFA and felt inhibited by its strictures against buying or showing the work of living artists.

But not everyone got the message. A contemporary account of the Hartford exhibition reported

> Confronting one of Picasso's abstractions one hears a conversation rather like this: "Is or is that not a chair? Is somebody sitting on it? This must be a man because the title says so." And finally the spectator finds himself furious with both himself and Picasso because he has been wasting his time on unimportant matters.[31]

This was the dominant American view, captured above all by Thomas Craven, whose widely read book *Modern Art* was published three months after the Atheneum's Picasso show. Craven's views on Picasso represented majority opinion in America in 1934:

> This small, sly, uneducated Bohemian is the king of modern painting; by common consent the master of the modern School of Paris. And a master he is—but not of art. He is a master of methods.
>
> Picasso's career is a masterpiece of strategy. . . .

Bothered by no deep convictions which try the souls of bigger men, he has patiently cultivated the enigmatical . . . His art is perfect because it offers nothing; pure because it is purged of human content; classic because it is dead. . . .

His subjects . . . are artificial forms manufactured in the studio; they are devoid of vitality and meaning; they have no basis in the observed facts of life, or in the behavior of man. He uses a stock expression for all faces; his figures are all alike—all concepts, curiosities, isolated trash. There is not, in the whole lot of them, a single convincing human being. . . .

Picasso's cubes and cones—give them as many titles as you please; disguise them, if you can, by esoteric riddles and psychological balderdash—remain cubes and cones, congested particles of dead matter. . . .

Picasso is a perfect specimen of the artist reared in the atmosphere of an international Bohemia. He is neither Spaniard nor Frenchman; his art reflects no environment, contains no meanings, carries no significance beyond the borders of the Bohemian world of its birth. The content of his art, where any is to be discerned, pertains to those vague generalities by which youth unconsciously betrays its ignorance of life.[32]

A year before this publication came out, Lincoln Kirstein had written to Agnes Mongan, "I am pleased to get Craven sore, if possible, for he is such a son of a bitch."[33] On the other hand, a lengthy review in *The New York Times Book Review* legitimized Craven as a writer by comparing him to Thomas Dewey in his cry for living experience as the content of art.[34] In a major front-page piece in the *Herald Tribune*'s Sunday Book Review, Frank Jewett Mather, Jr., called Craven's book "a much needed tract for the times."[35] Closer to home for Chick Austin, the *Hartford Courant* devoted an unusually extensive piece to Craven's book, endorsing the critic's diatribe on the sort of people who supported Picasso:

On the whole our museums are gilded show places stuffed with inferior old masters and directed by soft little fellows from the Fogg factory who use pictures to titillate mischievous erotic appetites. Some of them support little communities of retainers, traders, esthetes. They cater to tail coats, bored women, and kept radicals.[36]

Those who bought and showed Picasso at that point in history might congratulate one another, but opprobrium and mockery were still what they could expect from the public at large.

III

Like Philip Johnson and Eddie Warburg, Jim Soby didn't mind working without pay, and became honorary curator of modern painting and the librarian of the Atheneum. Austin had limited funds for loan shows, but often he needed to do nothing more than walk down the hall to ask Soby to lend his holdings. From May to October of 1934, the Atheneum did its third show of the Soby collection. By now there were four Picassos: the diminutive *Mother and Child* and *Bather,* and *Le Soupir*—all from 1923; and of course *Seated Woman*. The count of Derains was currently at four. Above all, there was now a surfeit of the neo-Romantics: thirteen paintings and six drawings by Eugene Berman, and works by Bérard, Léonide, and Kristians Tonny. In October, Jim Soby provided a different exhibition entirely—his collection of photographs by Man Ray—about which he had recently completed a book.

Things were lively at the Museum of Modern Art as well. Philip Johnson put on an exhibition called "Machine Art" that consisted of kitchenware, lighting fixtures, adding machines, gasoline pumps, springs, propellers, and other machine-made objects. Josef Albers, from his studio at Black Mountain College, helped design the catalog cover. In 1933 Eddie Warburg had become chairman of a committee to study the possibility of a film library at the museum, and the following year they arranged a showing at the Wadsworth Atheneum of films made between 1914 and 1934. The program, prepared by Iris Barry, who was the Modern's librarian, was a success. The Modern organized similar programs elsewhere and decided to establish its Film Library, run by Barry, with John Hay Whitney as its president and Warburg as its treasurer.

The School of American Ballet was also moving forward. Kirstein ran the show, Balanchine instructed, and Warburg kept an eager band of journalists supplied with information on the ballet's progress and purposes. In addition, Warburg had commissioned a new home for himself. For this he had turned to Philip Johnson. Johnson was not an accredited architect; in fact he had never before designed anything for a client. But it was clear from what he was doing at the Modern that he knew a lot about architecture and design, and Warburg admired and liked him.

It's no surprise that by the end of 1933 Warburg was beginning to feel he needed a space of his own. Even if he would have to keep *Dynamo Mother* in the closet wherever he lived, he needed a more sympathetic setting for *The Knees* and *Breasts* than the squash court at 1109 Fifth. Johnson found him a fourth-floor walk-up in an old brownstone on the river side of Beekman Place. He told Warburg they should wreck it completely and start all over again. Where there were two small windows overlooking the East River there should be a wall of glass. Every last drop of ornament had to go. If at 1109 Fifth Avenue Warburg was used to rugs on top of rugs, now he would walk on linoleum. Instead of brocades and velvets, the draperies would be fishnet.

Besides their major exhibition, Johnson and Hitchcock had also written a book about the new International Style. Johnson's own first apartment, around the corner from Warburg's at 424 East Fifty-second Street, had been designed by Mies van der Rohe and executed by Lily Reich. The lines were spare and elegant, the atmosphere assertively modern. There were Barcelona chairs, solid raw silk curtains, Chinese floor matting, and austere metal lighting fixtures. Then, early in 1934, Johnson designed a duplex for himself and his sister. There and in Warburg's rooms on Beekman Place, he tore out many of the interior walls of the existing apartment, put down pale ecru linoleum, and focused on the beauty of severe, solid planes at right angles to one another. Rooms had more than one function—a dining room in the living room, a bedroom–sitting room—and everything was physically and visually light. Johnson was violently against surface decoration of any sort. He selected everything for his client, and kept it all as lean as possible. Along with furniture designed by Mies, there were Johnson's own pigskin-covered bucket chairs and sofa, his tubular wastebasket, two of his lamp designs, and the fishnet curtains, all arranged with utmost rigor.

The Warburg apartment was a bold statement. The lack of ornament was a self-conscious assertion of the patron's sense of his own progress. The visual austerity suggests that he could do without what was silly and superfluous. Both Johnson and Warburg were fully aware that this radical aesthetic would shock others, but that was part of the thrill. They were extolling frankness both in what they chose and what they rejected, and they knew the effect it would have. Wishing desperately for change, they achieved it in the declaration of their aesthetic difference from their families.

There is, however, an unresolved attitude toward luxury in Warburg's apartment. Adolf Loos, the Viennese architect, had at the beginning of the century put forward the view that ornament represented wasted effort and wasted material, and hence the unnecessary use of capital. The new simplicity, as it was first conceived, was intended as a vehicle for economic saving. In fact, part of what Warburg's family would find offensive at 37 Beekman Place was the frugality that the visual leanness suggested. But this austerity, in fact, was high-priced custom work. What was deliberately spare and saving was—in this incarnation of the new simplicity—also quintessentially luxurious. There may have been exposed radiator pipes, but there were also those slabs of the perfectly buffed ebony that had been imported at no little cost from Indonesia. There may have been fishnet curtains, but other coverings were raw silk. And the unencumbered setting was a stage for some very fine art objects: a bronze by Jacob Epstein, Lachaise's marble *Knees,* Picasso's *Blue Boy*— which at least to some people was already a treasure.

From Johnson's point of view, the young museum trustee was an ideal client. Warburg made no demands. He never asked either about the schedule or the cost.[37] This was very much the approach Warburg advocated at museum board meetings; if you believed in the people you had hired, you should do everything within your power to nurture and support their creativity without interfering. To trustees like Sam Lewisohn, who at times carried on like frustrated museum directors, he screamed an unpopular "hands off."

Johnson was still unknown, his ideas unproven. Warburg's willingness to give him a start overwhelmed him. "How did he know what I would do? I had never had a commission before. But he trusted me, just as his father trusted him. Eddie has a great sense of style and of patronage. He knew that he was supporting an up-and-coming artist, and he took a big chance."[38] So he went along with that exposed radiator, the unframed mirror with clips, and the frankly industrial furniture. They appealed to him in the way that Calder's wire figures and *Blue Boy* did: they were utterly direct and to-the-point.

Felix Warburg, as usual, did his best to be gracious. At risk to his failing health, he climbed the three steep flights to visit. He tried to like the austerity of the two rooms. But a few minutes after Fizzie arrived, he leaned over to use the phone, and as the metal strap runners of the desk chair slid out from underneath him, his jaw crashed onto the desk. When Eddie rushed over to help, his aging father simply said, "That's what I like about modern art. It's so functional."

Eddie himself had mixed feelings about the place. The Macassar ebony screen walls were beautiful to him, as were the birch dining table and the black lacquer coffee table. The neutral colors and overall simplicity made a striking setting for the art. The view was wonderful. For five years he would live well with the combined living and dining room; central core with kitchen, bathroom, and closets;

The living room of Edward Warburg's apartment on Beekman Place.
House & Garden, *January 1935.*

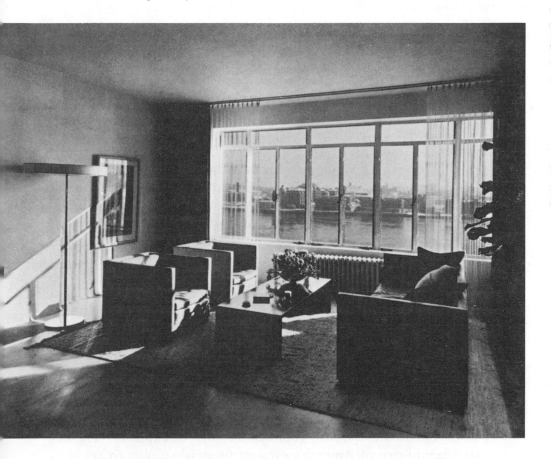

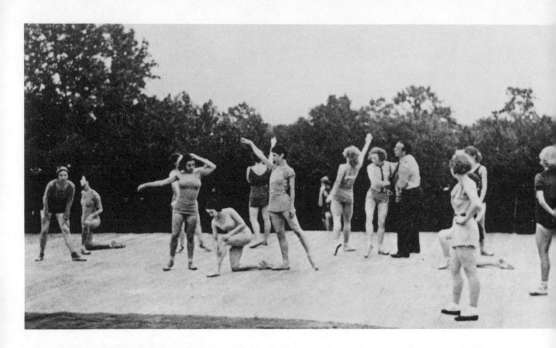

Dance rehearsal at Woodlands.

and the bathroom/study. But the pigskin chairs often gave their occupants a mat burn. And "it was a bit monastic for me. I was uncomfortable with the coldness of it . . . I always felt that when I came into the room I spoiled the composition. The discipline was so violent. If you moved an object an inch, it threw everything off kilter. If a magazine was not at right angles with the coffee table, you felt that the room hadn't been cleaned up. Acoustically it was awful. You dropped a spoon on the table and thought a pistol shot had gone off." Yet he admired the visual grace and fine proportions as well as the textural play. And it pleased him to be, for Philip Johnson, "an angel."

I V

The March 15, 1934, *Town & Country* told its eager readers that "the classes which everyone in New York seems to want to watch" were those being conducted by George Balanchine under the auspices of the "two young Harvard graduates who have made their mark in the arts." But Eddie Warburg could think only of expenses. The descendant of two of America's greatest financial families found himself struggling with bills for tutus. They were indicators of the master's current state of health. When Balanchine, who had had tuberculosis, was feeling frail, he would have the dancers lie down on the floor a great deal, covering their tutus with sticky rosin in the process. When he was heartier he would have them jump around—which kept their tutus clean. Warburg was pleased to save on the cleaning bills.

The first place to see the new ballet company in full performance was at Warburg's twenty-sixth birthday party. In its first few months, the company had developed three ballets, all choreographed by Balanchine. Two of these—*Mozartiana* and *Dreams*—were revivals of works that had been staged in June of 1933 by the "Ballets 1933" at the Champs Elysées Theatre in Paris. The music for *Mozartiana* was Tchaikovsky's arrangement of a minuet, the *Ave Verum,* and a theme and variations by Mozart; the costumes and decor were by Christian Bérard. *Dreams* had music by George Antheil and "themes and costumes" by André Derain. The other ballet, *Serenade,* was an entirely new piece danced to music by Tchaikovsky. All of these works needed a trial presentation in America.

Woodlands seemed the perfect place for that first performance. Eddie's birthday in June would be as good an occasion as any. After all, there was very little that Frieda and Felix wouldn't do to keep their youngest son happy. If a herd of Guernseys and a cowherd were required for their children's milk, then a full-scale ballet premiere and dinner for 250 people—and a repeat event the next night when the first was rained out—were in order for Edward's celebration.

Fizzie had taught his sons to dance by putting on a Victrola record and kicking their feet from under them to get them in time with the music. So why not have a dancing party—even if the steps were made by others? Amusing parties were a family tradition. In 1898, when Frieda Schiff had turned eighteen, her parents gave a celebration at which Walter Damrosch, standing in a tin tub full of water, sang a parody of Wagner's Rhine Maidens.[39] When Felix and Frieda had celebrated their twenty-fifth wedding anniversary in 1920, a silver-coated oak tree had been built in the gold room at 1109 Fifth; it was covered with silver acorns, each of which opened to a different photograph of the five children. The Warburgs didn't care so much for masked balls or the usual society parties, but milestones in the family could not be celebrated too grandly.

No tin tub would do, of course, for the American Ballet Company. Dimitriev designed a bare pine dance platform that was built in a half-circle of lawn framed by cedar trees. Frieda and Felix agreed that the lawn could always be replaced. It was a perfect spot—at the bottom of a gentle slope from the rambling half-timbered multigabled house. Some of the audience could sit on cushions on the grassy bank. Others could watch from the flat lawn at the top of the hill. For this space the Warburgs borrowed folding chairs from the nearest undertaker, just as Jim and Mimi Soby had done for their showing of *L'Age d'Or*. The swimming pool changing rooms became dressing rooms for the seventy-five dancers who arrived by bus. Spotlights were put in the third-floor dormer windows, and Steinway pianos concealed in the bushes.

The event was scheduled for June 9. *Mozartiana* went perfectly. But then came *Serenade*. This ballet seemed almost destined for trouble. In rehearsal the piece had had one sequence with all arms stiffly raised in a way that had reminded Warburg so strongly of a Nazi salute that he had had to persuade Balanchine to change it. Now, at the birthday party, just after Tchaikovsky's music began and the dancers raised their hands heavenward for the opening, the clouds burst.

The crowd was not easily daunted, however. A few people threw some tarps down on the stage, and everyone headed inside for dinner. Eddie's relatives mixed easily with guests like David Mannes, Malvina Hoffman, e. e. cummings, Muriel Draper, Paul Draper, Agnes Mongan, and Philip Johnson. Then Lincoln Kirstein suggested to Eddie's parents that they continue the event the next night. Houseguests repaired to the sleeping porches, and the dancers took their bus back to Manhattan. Frieda consented to come up with another dinner for 250, and everyone else agreed to return the next day.

The next morning, however, nerves failed at breakfast. Eddie suddenly became anxious. Desperately eager to talk with Kirstein, he ran around crying, "Where's Lincoln?" It was Agnes Mongan who heard Eddie's brother Fred sally, "Booth shot him." But whether nervous, mocking, or undaunted, everyone pulled through; Frieda's purveyors came up with a second meal, and the American Ballet Company again tried its demonstration-debut, this time completing *Serenade* and *Dreams* as well as *Mozartiana*. Balanchine's choreography introduced a new form of beauty to its young American audience.

Not that the new ballet company would ever enjoy an event entirely devoid of problems. While Eddie's guests were filling their plates at two nights of buffets in the dining room, the cast was fed in the garage. A cinder-block construction heated and attached to the main dwelling, this structure was in fact one of the rare features of Woodlands—a first of its kind, and initially an anomaly for the insurance company, which hadn't wanted to cover a house with a gas-powered engine within its walls. But in spite of this uniqueness—and although Frieda had done the place with style: red, white, and blue bunting; flowers and candles everywhere—Dimitriev was not impressed. According to Kirstein, Balanchine's manager performed "one of the grandest denunciation scenes since Chaliapin's in *Boris Godunov*. Were artists to be fed like pigs in a barn? He had known we were dilettantes with no comprehension of art, but were we under the gross illusion that good artists were serfs to be served in a filthy stable?" [40] This was just the start of Dimitriev's many furies.

In spite of such problems, from most viewpoints the American Ballet premiere was a success. It looked as if the new company might really get off the ground. Eddie Warburg agreed to cover in advance the expenses of the next six months as well as an additional eight thousand dollars "for costumes and scenery for future ballets." [41] A public debut for the American Ballet was the next step. And what it required was a new ballet with a uniquely local and current theme.

V

Warburg and Kirstein had said from the beginning that it wasn't enough to use the word "American" in the name of the new ballet company and to employ American performers; they needed contemporary American subject matter. A fan of Owen Johnson's *Stover at Yale* and Ralph Henry Barbour's tales of college life, Warburg opted for 1920s stadium life as the theme of a new ballet for which he wrote the book. He named it *Alma Mater*—literally "nurturing mother"—and hence well suited to his tongue-in-cheek attitude toward the rah-rah set. The ballet would be a ludicrous parody of the world dearest to Ivy Leaguers. The main characters would be a punch-drunk halfback and a dizzy young woman who wore striptease-style panties under her Salvation Army uniform. The way in which teams had posed against the old Yale fence for sepia photographs thirty years earlier would set the style. Dancers would move from huddles to maneuvers on the field. The men would wear raccoon coats, or shoulder pads under Yale sweaters of the type

Sandy Calder had donned for his Circus performances. The women would be stylish flappers.

Warburg and Kirstein picked John Held, Jr., to do the costumes for the young football crowd. They could hardly have latched onto someone better able to evoke the American 1920s style they wanted to satirize. Up until the stock market crash, Held had been one of the most successful popular artists in the country. He had illustrated the 1922 edition of F. Scott Fitzgerald's *Tales of the Jazz Age*. His drawings for *Vanity Fair* and *The New Yorker* had helped fix the look of the era. In 1925 Held had made the cover of a "Football Number" for the issue of *Life* magazine that came out on November 19—just in time for a Yale-Harvard game of the type that was the butt of Warburg's parody. The cover presented a flapperesque cheerleader. Her long strand of pearls is flying, her dress stretched tight, her garters at her ankles. Holding her heavily lipsticked mouth as wide open as possible, she is shown to be shouting "Hold 'Em." Two years later Held illustrated the program of a Yale-Princeton game. He knew the types that *Alma Mater* was all about.

By the time Kirstein and Warburg approached him, however, Held was off his pedestal. He had lost a fortune in the stock market crash and suffered the breakup of a marriage and the effects of a bad horse-riding accident. The former rage of the twenties was now living in relative seclusion at the Hotel Algonquin in New York. He was pleased to get a job, and made the most of it. In addition to putting one key character in the classic raccoon coat—the production simply borrowed Eddie Warburg's, so it didn't cost them a thing—he gave the fellow a white boater with a broad blue band into which an oversized blue feather was stuck. The feather brandished a large white *Y*. Held captured that uniquely American way of flaunting one's alma mater that can make well-educated and otherwise rather tasteful people resemble a cross between a billboard and a savage. He gave the Ivy Leaguers the look of the most maniacal alumni who totter through the streets of New Haven on reunion weekends, discarding their usually conservative attire for all the style and subtlety of the souvenir nut dishes sold at the local eating clubs. If Eddie Warburg and Lincoln Kirstein never quite fit in with Ivy League stereotypes, now they would mock them as well as shock them, with John Held, Jr., their perfect accomplice.

Held's watercolor sketch for the villain of Warburg's story shows the fellow with a bright red face. He may have picked up the color sitting in the stadium on a windy day. But more likely his broken corpuscles came from overimbibing from his hip flask. The man looks a total dolt. He is no more animated than a hat rack: his hands entirely limp, his legs straight sticks, his neck a narrow twig supporting his massive globelike head. The hat, which is too small, is squashed in place, while the oversized coat dwarfs the rest of his body. He is the ultimate foolish and ineffectual "Old Blue."

Held also did a telling sketch of the Salvation Army girl over whom the halfback and villain will do battle. Her vermilion lips are painted even wider than those of the cheerleader on *Life*'s football number. On one level, however, she is the image of propriety. She wears the full-brimmed bonnet and long modest skirt required of her station. But the skirt has a deep slit in it. Red garters and brief lacy underwear are in plain view. This is exactly the way that Warburg and Kirstein saw the world: nothing is as it appears to be.

Held depicted people either as ambivalent or with singular characters grossly exaggerated. His bridesmaids for *Alma Mater* are the bridesmaids to beat them all, with dainty white gloves and enormous hats. His photographer is the quintessential photographer of the time period: a short character in baggy striped pants, frantically working his camera. His "boy babies"—the halfback's children—are the ultimate Ivy League offspring, their nightshirts flaunting enormous Princeton *P*s.

As for the generic type Held simply labeled "girls": they look like the sort of women who could easily dance the night through. Their hair is the brightest blond, their eye shadow and lipstick thick as oil paint. Their clothing—and their trim, fabulous legs—make them very much like the woman who composed the music for *Alma Mater:* Kay Swift.

Kay Swift was a slightly airy—"comely," according to one gossip columnist of the day—young woman accustomed to playing the piano before just about any audience. Seventeen years earlier, when she was the twenty-year-old Katharine Faulkner Swift, she had charmed the summer crowd with her playing at Fish Rock camp, Isaac Seligman's place on Upper Saranac Lake in the Adirondacks. Margaret Lewisohn, Isaac's daughter, had recently discovered her, and had imported her for the rest of the family to enjoy. Among the people most enchanted were Eddie Warburg's aunt Nina and her daughter Bettina. They could hardly wait to tell Bettina's brother James, then a young naval cadet flyer, about this ravishing young woman. With her brown laughing eyes, delicate nose, and fine jaw, the petite Katharine would be irresistible to him. She was quick, she was game, and she had musical talent besides.

Katharine had begun studying piano at age seven. Her father had been the music critic for the *New York World*. Following his death when she was a teenager, she had helped support her mother and brother by giving piano lessons in people's homes. After winning a scholarship at the school that is now Juilliard and attending the New England Conservatory of Music, she had toured with a trio. When twenty-one-year-old Jimmy Warburg met her at a dance in New York, his mother's and sister's impressions were more than confirmed. The naval cadet and the musician decided to get married.

Eddie's branch of the family didn't think so highly of the match, however. This was the first time a Warburg had married a non-Jew. When Jimmy and Katharine announced their engagement, Jacob Schiff telegrammed, "I wish you joy to your happiness but cannot refrain from telling you that I am deeply disturbed by your action in marrying out of the faith in view of its probable effect upon my own progeny."[42] Since Schiff was a director of Western Union, it didn't cost him anything to send his warning. Nor did it get him anywhere. In 1918, the war over, and Jimmy having become a banker, the pair was married.

In the 1920s Katharine and Jimmy Warburg lived the high life. They bought two adjacent houses on East Seventieth Street between Madison and Park avenues and knocked down the connecting walls to create rooms large enough for entertaining and raising three daughters. When the decorators came in to make changes, they simply moved family and staff around the corner to the Westbury Hotel so that work and play could run as usual. Hardship for Jimmy was to arrive at the bank exhausted after a long night playing poker with Franklin P. Adams, Alexander Woollcott, Marc Connelly, Herbert Bayard Swope, Harold Ross, and Raoul Fleischmann.

Katharine and Jimmy regularly attended musical evenings at the home of Walter Damrosch, where they grew to know George and Ira Gershwin, as well as Richard Rodgers and Lorenz Hart. Rodgers gave Katharine a job as rehearsal pianist for *A Connecticut Yankee,* after which she took an interest in popular music and decided she wanted to try her hand at composing songs. Jimmy wrote the lyrics. However, as a vice president of the International Acceptance Bank, he didn't want to upset his depositors with his involvement in a profession they might consider undignified. So James Paul Warburg called himself Paul James, and Katharine Swift Warburg became Kay Swift.

Paul James and Kay Swift's first big hit was a torch song called "Can't We Be Friends?" that Libby Holman sang in the 1929 *First Little Show*. They decided to keep going. Donald Ogden Stewart had written the book for a full-length musical comedy for the slapstick comedian Joe Cook, and Swift and James were hired to do the music and lyrics. It was called *Fine & Dandy*. When the producers went broke just before the opening, Paul James simply took up his Jimmy Warburg side and came up with the necessary funds—aided by two of his best friends, Marshall Field and Averell Harriman, who had liked the new musical in rehearsal. Although the three investors never saw cash returns on the project, the show was a great success, running for more than 250 performances, and earning the accolade from the critic John Mason Brown that it was "one of the best musical comedies New York has seen in a blue moon." Moreover, two Swift and James songs, "Fine & Dandy" and "Can This Be Love?", entered the mainstream.

In Kay and Jimmy's enormous living room, underneath the ornate, cherub-covered wooden ceiling and the rows of dark Dutch seventeenth-century portraits, there were two back-to-back concert grand pianos. Sometimes George Gershwin would play with Oscar Levant or Sigmund Romberg; sometimes he would play with Kay. Then, at Kay and Jimmy's eighty-acre farm in Greenwich, Connecticut, he occupied the guest cottage for an entire summer. It was there that Gershwin, who had grown up in New York's poorer neighborhoods, learned how to live upper-class American life. He rode horseback for the first time, and acquired the right clothes for the country. In addition, he worked with Kay on orchestration. Lacking her professional musical training, he benefited greatly from her technical expertise. Gershwin would try new rhythms and melodies; she would suggest the harmonic treatment. Working with her in this way, he composed *Rhapsody No. 2* and *Porgy and Bess*. Often he dictated, and Kay wrote the music down; half of the original score of *Porgy* is in her hand.

Meanwhile, Jimmy Warburg was busy providing the scheme that led to the reopening of the nation's banks, traveling to London as financial adviser to the American delegation at the London Economic Conference, writing a widely distributed book called *The*

Money Muddle, and corresponding regularly with President Franklin Roosevelt. He and Kay drifted apart. Not only had Jimmy's interests kept him away from home, but Kay's involvement with Gershwin had gone beyond the confines of music. It was in the midst of the breakup of her marriage and the burgeoning of her new romance that Kay Swift was busily playing away in George Balanchine's rehearsal hall.

Balanchine had first wanted Jerome Kern or George Gershwin to write the music for their new ballet. Eddie Warburg asked Gershwin, who said he was too busy but recommended Kay Swift. She seemed a fair choice; not only was she a gifted composer, but she was one of Eddie's favorite family members. Where most Warburg wives spent most of their time planning menus, organizing the servants, and shopping for gifts, Kay was both gay and brilliant. It was she who had persuaded Felix that music was the right vocation for Gerry. Family members, including the man Kay was about to divorce, thought the arts were good hobbies but not professions; she prized them more highly. She had spark, and so did her music. When *Alma Mater* opened that December, she may have been second choice, but no one was disappointed in what she came up with. The audiences as well as most of the critics loved what they saw, and above all what they heard.

The *Alma Mater* premiere was the first public performance of "The American Ballet of New York," a small troupe of graduates of the School of American Ballet. Balanchine had progressed well with his year-old school of seventy students. He was "enthusiastic about these lithe American girls and boys." They were "better built than the youngsters of other nations and, while they may be slower to yield themselves to discipline, they were quicker to learn and eager beyond measure."[43] The sixteen girls and seven boys he had selected to show what the new enterprise was all about were mostly ages fourteen to sixteen.

Kirstein and Warburg opted to return to Hartford for this premiere. Not only had the Wadsworth Atheneum given them their start, but in the year since they arrived there with Balanchine, the new auditorium had allowed it to step up its activities beyond art exhibitions. Above all, there had been the *Four Saints* premiere, but the Atheneum had also become the home of the film screenings with which Warburg was involved from his office at the Museum of Modern Art. In a series in March and April, Jean Cocteau's *Le Sang d'un Poète,* Sergei Eisenstein's *Thunder over Mexico,* and René Clair's *A Nous La Liberté* were presented. In October, another series had opened, with further work by Eisenstein and Clair as well as motion pictures by D. W. Griffith, Charlie Chaplin, Fritz Lang, Josef Sternberg, and Walt Disney.

Chick Austin bore Kirstein, Warburg, and Balanchine no grudge, even if the ballet school for which he had slaved no longer had anything to do with Hartford. Warburg had given money for *Four Saints;* Kirstein had come to lecture on the Russian ballet. When they again asked Austin to get involved, the Atheneum director was happy to have the facility serve, as he had once dreamed, for a performance of Balanchine's choreography. So it was in Hartford's new Avery Memorial auditorium that *Alma Mater* was scheduled for its world premiere that December 6. Along with the new football ballet, two other works would be performed. At the Friday evening premiere and Saturday matinee they would be *Mozartiana* and *Transcendence.* On Saturday night, *Serenade* would replace *Transcendence.* *Mozartiana* and *Serenade* were both known to those who had attended the party at Woodlands, but had never before been seen by the general public. *Transcendence,* new to the repertoire, had music by Franz Liszt, arranged by George Antheil, and costumes and sets by Franklin Watkins.

Chick Austin and Eddie Warburg attended to most of the nuts and bolts. They obtained a special permit for one of the girls dancing *Mozartiana* since she was under sixteen. They arranged to move the sets up to Hartford. Above all, Warburg managed the public relations—according to one newspaper, with "the eyes of a zealot and the manner of a co-ordinator." [44] The Atheneum didn't have the money to advertise, and Austin was worried that without publicity it would be hard to sell seats, since tickets—at prices from $1.50 to $7.00—cost more than for concurrent performances of the Ballets de Monte Carlo elsewhere in Hartford. So Warburg had the ballet company fund a few ads saying that for tickets you could telephone Wickersham 2–7667 in New York or write directly to the Atheneum. Then they got lucky. *The New York Times* and the *New York Herald Tribune* both devoted major articles to the upcoming premiere. Lucius Beebe whet his readers' appetites for the event, saying that "the whole daffy shindig" promised to be "one of the most epic lunacies of the generation." [45] The best publicity was free, and suddenly it emerged full force. By the time December 6 rolled around, the premiere was sold out.

Those who flocked to the insurance city included some return visitors from the *Four Saints* premiere, and new faces as well. In part because of Warburg, a lot of Museum of Modern Art people were there: Sam and Margaret Lewisohn, A. Conger Goodyear, Mrs. Nelson Rockefeller, Philip Goodwin, Mrs. Cornelius Bliss, and Mrs. Bliss's daughter, Mrs. John Parkinson. There were assorted Hartford locals, among them Katharine Hepburn. Archibald MacLeish and his wife, who lived in nearby Farmington, also attended. So did the artist Pavel Tchelitchew, who had just arrived from Paris. Others at the Atheneum that night included Salvador Dali and his wife Gala, George Gershwin, Katherine Dreier, Mr. and Mrs. Pierre Matisse, the Julien Levys, Constance Askew, Jere Abbott, Mina Kirstein Curtiss, Sol Hurok, the Wallace Harrisons, Louis and Rose Kirstein, John Held, Jr., George Antheil and his wife, Joseph Alsop, and Dr. and Mrs. Harvey Cushing. Then there were the Cushings' daughters Barbara (the future "Babe" Paley) and Betsy, the latter accompanied by her husband, James Roosevelt, the son of the president.

The New York set convened at Grand Central Station in their evening clothes at five in the afternoon. Then they boarded a train marked "Ballet Special," organized by Ellen Harrison, who was related to the Rockefellers and whose husband, Wallace, was chief architect of the skyscrapers they were building in midtown Manhattan. These pilgrims for culture made quite a sight. The *New York World's* "Mme. Flutterbye" reported that Mrs. Roosevelt "had on one of the most effective evening dresses seen this year . . . [the dots are Mme. Flutterbye's own] it was stiffened white chiffon with lines of gold thread and completely tucked with tiny pin tucks. Mrs. Roosevelt, who is the former Betsy Cushing of Boston, completed her gold and white ensemble with gold slippers and gold finger nails . . . which is certainly a radical departure in the Roosevelt family." Mrs. Roosevelt's mother, meanwhile, was in "a lovely pale blue evening dress pleated from shoulder to hem." Mrs. Harrison, on the other hand, had managed to arrive in a street dress; once on board she simply turned it inside out in order to be clad in a platinum lamé evening gown.

When the train was out of Grand Central, "George Gershwin broke out a hamper of chilled champagne"—this report thanks to Lucius Beebe, who devoted his entire *Herald Tribune* column the fol-

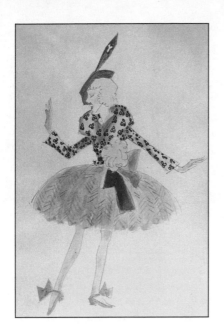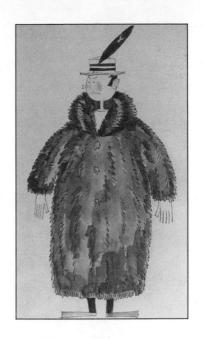

Alma Mater: *costume design by John Held, Jr., for (left) "The Girl" and (right) "The Villain."*

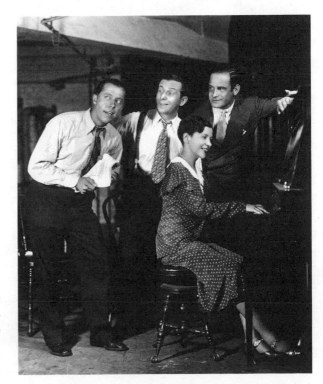

From left: Joe Cook, Dave Chasen, Kay Swift, and Jimmy Warburg in rehearsal for Fine & Dandy, 1929.

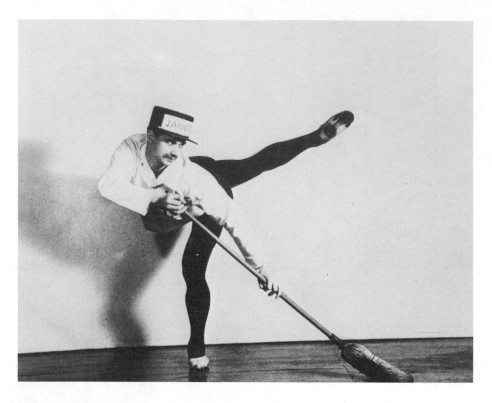

Alma Mater: *"The Janitor"* (above) and *"Portal 6⅞ A."*

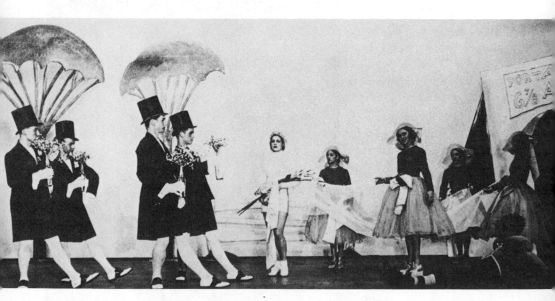

lowing Sunday to the ballet. Then, tended by porters and maids, the New Yorkers enjoyed a buffet supper as they moved northward, and those who hadn't had a chance to change earlier on did so now, causing the smoking compartment, according to Beebe, to take on "a peculiarly Y.M.C.A. atmosphere, with fifteen gentlemen trying to dress at once and getting their arms into the sleeves of other folks' boiled shirts."

The first piece performed that night was *Mozartiana*. The dancers included Dorothie Littlefield, William Dollar, Ruthanna Boris, Leda Anchutina, Holly Howard, and Charles Laskey, clad in Christian Bérard's lovely eighteenth-century costumes. They danced joyfully to Tchaikovsky's reorchestration of four Mozart dances in Berard's bright sunny setting. According to one critic, T. H. Parker of the *Hartford Courant,*

> M. Balanchine has created a ballet summing up the spirit of the classic dance and that of Mozart as well as visualizing the composer's melodies. To the choreography he has brought an elegance, a courtliness, a simplicity and joyousness drawn not only from Mozart but from the times as well.[46]

Alma Mater followed the entr'acte. The ballet opened at a stadium entrance. The dancers emerged in front of "Portal 6 ⅞ A." This ridiculous gate was flanked by tall parodies of New Haven elms, with a section of the Yale fence nearby. Yale had just won a game, and the crowds cheered the punch-drunk, handsome halfback who rode in on his admirers' shoulders. Flappers desperately tried to get his autograph. The impression was of a mad whirl, danced to Kay Swift's jazzy takeoffs on college songs like "Boola Boola" and "Bright College Years."

Next the hero draped himself in a series of classic poses against the Yale fence, while a photographer snapped shots. This was followed by a "snake dance and rah-rah bacchanale"—terms that must have been as alien to Balanchine as they were familiar to Eddie Warburg's college chums. The idea was total Ivy League havoc. The dancing football spectators went so far as to pull out the goal posts. The overall impression of the scene was "Boola, boola. Bam, bam, bam."—this according to the *Washington Post* review of the opening-night performance.[47]

Then the villain arrived in his—which is to say Eddie Warburg's—

raccoon coat. His charger was a bicycle built for two. What Warburg's book calls his "cock-eyed girl friend" and the *Washington Post*
refers to as "the beautiful but dim-wit heroine" was seated behind
him. The halfback plucked daisies for the heroine, as a result of
which the villain "socks"—one imagines the efforts to translate this
word from the book for Balanchine—the halfback. But virtue
triumphs; "we are transported to a rag-time dreamland, a paradise
of Rover Boys at College and the girls of Standish Hall." The halfback gets his "pantied bride" and they are celebrated in a triumphal
march on the gridiron, to wedding music with the ring of a football
song.

From then on this parody of 1920s American collegiate style took
the tone of a Surrealist drama. The images piled on top of one another, some with a bitter twist. Eddie Warburg's text gives the sequence: "Dozens of children emerge from the union to kill their
nightmare pa. A Janitor with a Phi Beta Kappa key sweeps up the
pieces. The villain is confounded in the midst of a rotogravure forest." A duel ensues, and then a final snapshot is taken, for which the
instructions simply are "Smile, Charlie: make Mamie hold her head
up." In conclusion, "the storm breaks and the little photographer is
swept up in the parachute of his umbrella." It may all be pretty rah-
rah, but there are no winners. As far as Warburg and Kirstein were
concerned, it was perfectly fine if for once the football crowd didn't
come out on top. The audience concurred, laughing and cheering as
the ballet went on. When *Alma Mater* ended, they greeted it with
stormy applause.

But *Transcendence* was by many accounts the aesthetic high point
of the evening. It didn't make for as colorful retelling as *Alma Mater*—which *Time, Newsweek,* and newspapers all over America would
describe with delight in the ensuing days—but to serious ballet devo-
tees it was with this final piece that the new company had really
arrived. The book of *Transcendence* had been written by Lincoln Kirstein. Its theme was the pursuit of virtuosity in the era of Liszt and
Paganini. George Antheil had scored Liszt's music accordingly. To
Liszt's *Mephisto Waltz,* the dancers enacted frustration in the quest
for art and love. Then came a "mesmeric" interlude, followed by a
frolicking peasant dance done to a compilation of the composer's
rhapsodies. Franklin Watkins, whose murals Kirstein had so esteemed and who two years earlier had won the Carnegie International Award for his picture *Suicide in Costume,* designed the offbeat
and sinister costumes and setting. Watkins, with Austin's and Kir-

stein's help, had finished painting them only the night before the first performance, but the bare tree branches echoing the pattern of dancers' arms were highly effective nonetheless.

What followed all of this were loud hosannas—in the audience that evening, and in the newspapers for the next couple of days. The dancers were brought out for a dozen curtain calls. Even the reluctant thirty-year-old Balanchine was made to take a bow, as were twenty-six-year-old Warburg and twenty-eight-year-old Kirstein. Kay Swift was not there—she was fulfilling her Nevada residency requirement in Reno in order to get as quick and easy a divorce as possible—but at least she had the solace of a phone call from George Gershwin, who raved.[48] The public may not have gone as wild as they did after *Four Saints,* but they still shouted "Bravo" and "Balanchine" for quite some time.

After the ballet premiere, the Dalis and others of the inner sanctum went out to the Sobys' West Hartford house where *L'Age d'Or* had been shown three years earlier. Then they taxied back to Hartford's Union Station, from where private sleeping cars returned them to New York. Today the way to designate sophistication in Hartford, Connecticut, is to say one bought, or ate, or saw, something "in New York"; in 1934, what counted was what people first encountered in Hartford. According to critics all over the country, the ballet performances at the Wadsworth Atheneum that December represented a milestone in American culture. And as far as George Balanchine was concerned, now he had adapted to his new country. The name of the dancer William Dollar had clinched that fact. "See how American I've become," he boasted to Eddie Warburg; "I even put a Dollar Bill on stage."

There were two primary strains in American culture at that point in the country's history: the novels, films, and plays that focused on the grim realities of Depression life, and those that provided an escape from it. Although much art at the time took the form of social protest, the need to counter the downside was equally strong. *Alma Mater*—and the lives of the people who made it—offered great diversion. At a time when Americans were standing in food lines and selling pencils on street corners, this was all fun and games. The economic situation had most people feeling constrained and even immobilized, but Balanchine's dancers could kick their legs with full vigor. Just to know about this offered a form of relief. Even if only a small privileged minority attended the actual performances, the public at large craved news of them. All over the country, they read about *Alma Mater*—and to a lesser degree the other ballets—in news coverage, critiques, and gossip columns. What gave that Balanchine premiere such color was not just the dancing itself, but the idea of the New York swells who had the wherewithal and mobility to create this sort of thing. For many readers, it was like a fantasy. Here were people who really lived like characters in Cole Porter's musicals and in Fred Astaire movies.

One of the reasons the Kay Swift/Eddie Warburg ballet had such broad public appeal is that these were the ultimate carryings-on of the smart set. The lead of *Time*'s piece began, "Eight years ago there were two Harvard freshmen who used to stay up nights to moon over ballet. One was short, one was tall but both were rich." *Newsweek*'s photo caption was "A ballet in which Harvard satirizes Yale." The idea of the "in" crowd mocking others of their station was irresistible. Newspapers made the most of the mischief. One referred to the "wicked wicked cleverness,"[49] another to the "handsome lampooning of all that is rah-rah and collegiate in American life."[50] The *Washington Post* described the "saucy, irresistible" humor,[51] claiming that of the ballets performed, *Alma Mater* would be the most popular—for its spirit of "good, mean fun." What were noteworthy were Held's "tweed tutus and panties for the cuties and coonskin coats and silly sweaters for the rah rahers," and Kay Swift's "lively music" in which the composer had "managed to thumb a nose and stick out a tongue at every sacred college melody." The *Post* captured that element so vital to Eddie Warburg and his cohorts: "Irreverence is the middle name of the entire production." What mattered wasn't plausibility, but insouciance: mockery with charm. At a time when most of the country was struggling to survive, here were people who had the means and time to poke fun.

Not everyone was impressed with *Alma Mater,* however. For one, Eddie Warburg was disappointed. He felt that the real spirit of *Stover at Yale* and *Winning Your Y* did not emerge in the new art form, that Balanchine had merely reworked standard sight gags and had not adequately evoked Ivy League living. He was annoyed that Balanchine had never gone to a real football game because he always had to rehearse on Saturday afternoons. Kirstein, however, considered the new ballet a breakthrough. Above all it offered signs and portents by which the ballet idiom might be removed from the elite or epicene European atmosphere to gain a public, not equally but at least approaching a mass audience as something less than a snob attraction. . ... It was Balanchine's unprejudiced catholicity in musical taste which was to give our repertory its special savor; this commenced with *Alma Mater*.[52]

Even if for Eddie Warburg the atmosphere of the new production wasn't all he had hoped for, *Alma Mater* completed the transformation of an art form that only ten years earlier had maintained the style of prewar St. Petersburg into something that now was entirely at home in America.

THE LOVER
OF DRAWINGS

I

In the summer of 1929 when Agnes Mongan and Lincoln Kirstein had inadvertently attended Diaghilev's funeral, they had made great efforts to meet the sixty-four-year-old Bernard Berenson. Mongan had written Berenson's secretary, Nicky Mariano, to set up an appointment to see the renowned connoisseur at I Tatti, his villa near Florence. Set among olive trees and cypresses on Settignano hill in the village of Fiesole, this large building had masterpieces of Italian Renaissance art and an incomparable art history library packed within its thick plaster walls. It was a mecca for scholars and connoisseurs. Because of Berenson's travel schedule and some renovation work at the villa, the rendezvous had to be at an alternate location on a date after Kirstein's departure. Mongan ended up going with her sister Elizabeth, a print specialist whose scholarship in her field rivaled Agnes's in drawings, and on that first encounter they met Berenson in his summer residence, a former hunting lodge near Vallombrosa, high in the hills above Florence. But there would be many future get-togethers at I Tatti itself.

The suggestion to make that initial visit to Berenson had come from Paul Sachs. Mongan had no idea that Sachs had an ulterior motive, although Eddie Warburg might have told her. Eddie had been present when Sachs informed Felix Warburg that Agnes Mongan was the person he was grooming to be the chatelaine of I Tatti after Berenson's death, when the villa was slated to become Harvard's property and, as such, an outpost for scholars.

Berenson had attended Harvard, and had remained loyal to the university ever since. A few years prior to Mongan's visit, Bella da Costa Greene, the curator of rare books and manuscripts at the Morgan Library in New York—and a mistress of Berenson's, who was twenty-seven years her senior—had recommended that Berenson leave his collection to the Fogg, and had raised the issue with Sachs as well. It was an idea that appealed to both sides.

Berenson and his wife Mary had not always looked kindly, however, on the German-Jewish banking community with which Sachs was associated in New York. James Loeb, the brother of Eddie Warburg's aunt Nina Loeb Warburg, had been a college classmate of Berenson's, and although Loeb was an esteemed classics scholar and founder of the Loeb Classical Library, Mary Berenson had characterized him as "a handsome, fat, prosperous philistine Jew: . . . in with all the rich Jews in New York" who were unfortunately Bernard's clients on whom he depended for income by doing attributions for paintings in their art collections.[1] Not much respect extended in the opposite direction, either. Aby Warburg, who in 1891 had written his doctoral dissertation on Botticelli, had lived in Florence from 1897 to 1902 and was active in the German Art Historical Institute there. Just as Berenson deplored Aby's sort of iconographic scholarship, Aby put down Berenson as part of a group of "enthusiastic art historians," specifically his type six of the category: "the connoisseurs and 'attributionists' . . . desirous of protecting the peculiar characteristics of their hero." Aby labeled Berenson and others like him as "the whole noisy tribe . . . hero-worshippers . . . only inspired by the temperament of a gourmand. The neutrally cool form of estimation happens to be the original form of enthusiasm peculiar to the propertied classes, the collector and his circle."[2]

Aby's brother Felix, however, did better with Berenson. In 1926 Felix and Frieda had visited I Tatti, at which point the two men talked of their wish to build up the Fogg. Felix gladly functioned as an ambassador of Harvard, writing Berenson after the visit to thank him for his interest in the university, and referring to himself as "a fellow workman in the same field from an entirely different angle."[3] Felix sent Berenson photographs of the works in his collection and wrote to him about Eddie's study of art history; he also naively suggested that Berenson ought to meet Aby in Hamburg at some point. Fizzie made characteristic light of B.B.'s propensity to give questionable attributions. In 1928, with Paul Sachs at his side in his New York office, Fizzie handwrote Berenson a letter just to say that he had heard a story that "a celebrated Italian painter was received by St. Peter in heaven." When St. Peter asked his name, the painter answered, " 'How should I know? Ask Berenson.' "[4]

In many ways, Paul Sachs could have picked no better ambassador than Agnes Mongan to link Berenson's world with his and with Harvard. Berenson had at one point converted from Judaism to Catholicism, and although he had ceased practicing by the mid-1920s, he was still very sympathetic to its adherents. The achievement of which Berenson was proudest was the large two-volume, folio-size *The Drawings of the Florentine Painters,* a work that unlike his other writings to date had no connection with his art dealing. Berenson was more comfortable with his scholarly side than his commercial bent, and in Agnes Mongan he met someone closely attuned to just the sort of work he had done on these draftsmen, and detached from the moneymaking aspect of art. From that first encounter until Berenson's death in 1959, he and Mongan had a close friendship and mutual dependence.

Mongan was enchanted from the start. In Berenson she found someone who had successfully made her own passion his life's work. Connoisseurship, issues of authorship, and the lusty appreciation of Renaissance art were the basis of Berenson's life. Agnes and Elizabeth were so keyed up after their call at Vallombrosa that in the next several days they raced to San Gimignano, Siena, Arezzo, Perugia, and Assisi to visit museums and churches. Then, from Florence, Mongan wrote Berenson a letter that evinced both her characteristic tact and her intense engagement with the master's way of thinking—to which she had first been exposed less directly in the courses of Georgiana Goddard King:

> It was more than generous of you to let us descend—or rather ascend—as we did. I only hope we did not weary you by staying too long. I was so interested in what you were saying that I quite forgot about time.[5]

From then on they corresponded regularly; Berenson counted on Mongan to supply him with photographs and reprints from America, and she posed questions to him as she worked on the Fogg drawings catalog.

Paul Sachs was happy to see the relationship take hold, in part because of the role for which he intended Mongan, but also because of his fantasy that he could turn her into his personal Nicky Mariano—the quintessential assistant. In the spring of 1933 Sachs wrote Mongan from I Tatti,

> What a place *to live & work!* And I am interested to see *how* Miss Mariano works *for* & with him. I begin to realize that poor Agnes is not the only one who does 9/10's of the labor & when she—Miss M—has done all the terrific, endless work & gathering of material that you also do she presents it on a "silver plate" as you do and he "decides."[6]

But the person whom Mongan emulated at I Tatti was not Nicky Mariano; it was Berenson himself. She wrote to Berenson that she wished to visit him again "to see what I can learn of concentration & system."[7] In fact she was already acquiring Berenson's sort of organizational skills, as well as his eye. Throughout the 1930s, Mongan and Paul Sachs were preparing their catalog of the Fogg's drawings collection, and most of the research was hers to do. To develop a feeling for attribution, she looked at as many drawings as she could put her hands on. She studied originals, photographs, and reproductions in books. When she traveled abroad, not only did she take along Sachs's famous letters of introduction, but she also took photographs of the drawings at the Fogg, so that she could make comparisons in the hope of establishing authorship. Beyond the ability to recognize authenticity, she acquired a sharp discernment for what was first rate and what was not.

Mongan quickly mastered special areas of expertise. One had to do with left-handed artists. She herself was left-handed; it was another of her traits that made her feel slightly outside the norm. She recognized that in paintings if the light comes from an open space at the left, the artist was generally left-handed. In drawings, the hallmarks are that the strokes progress from upper left to lower right, and that shading comes from the left. Moreover, the most facile mirror writing is generally done by lefties; their hand does not get in their own way, as it does for people using their right hand. Hans Holbein and Leonardo da Vinci were among the best-known left-handed draftsmen. Her awareness of what this meant to their work gave Mongan further means of confirming or disputing attributions to these and other left-handed artists.

Not long after she had talked her way into Paul Sachs's employ, Mongan's eye for the authorship of drawings began to make her a clearinghouse for all sorts of information concerning questions of authenticity. She was a stickler for accuracy. When an error-laden survey of Italian art was published in France in 1930, it was Mongan who pointed out the carelessness in the *Saturday Review of Literature*.[8] That a painting should be attributed to Filippo rather than Filippino Lippi and the Fra Angelicos of San Marco listed as being at the Uffizi represented a level of sloppiness she found intolerable. In 1930, K. T. Parker of the British Museum, aware of her scholarly meticulousness, had asked her to help with his catalog of Watteau drawings by documenting all of them in the United States. Parker knew her account would be flawless and thorough. Information of the sort he was seeking had not been published anywhere else, but Mongan had what it took to accomplish his task. In a relatively small art world, she knew lots of people and had total recall of whatever she had seen and heard. She also exercised care and know-how. Typical of the sort of letter of which she might send ten a day from the Fogg was one she wrote about Watteau to Parker on December 17, 1930:

> I seem to remember Richard Owen saying he sold one in San Francisco so I have written to the director of their Museum—a friend of mine who was here last year—asking him to send you a photograph of it and news of any other Watteau drawings on the West Coast, if there are any.

Besides Mongan's extensive circle of acquaintances, what made her so valuable at her task were her uncompromising standards. Consider a letter she wrote two years later to Robert Homans, a State Street lawyer. The issue was still Watteau—not only one of her specialties, but also a passion. With the same sort of tact that enabled her to get along with Paul Sachs when others could not, she addressed the issue of a positive attribution given to Mr. Homans's Watteau by Walter Gay. Gay was a consummate authority on the subject and owned a related piece. But he had seen Homans's drawing only in a photograph; Mongan had seen the actual object. "I regret that this time I cannot agree with the opinion of the keen and gifted connoisseur about your drawing," she wrote. She gave substantial reasons as to why she thought it was a copy by another eighteenth-century artist, not a second version by Watteau of the same subject—which is what Gay had called it. "Nothing would give me greater pleasure than to know that there was a drawing by Watteau in this vicinity, but my own doubts are too strong to let me believe that you have a work by the master himself."[9]

This sort of diplomatic practice of her expertise would be part of Mongan's daily routine for years to come. She became an information center in her field, not unlike Berenson in his, except that Mongan's reputation was never tinged by commercial motivations or any concern other than pure scholarship. From Mongan one could learn what was where. In 1932 she wrote a long essay for the Fogg Bulletin on Degas's portrait studies in American collections. It was no wonder that she could locate the objects under discussion; most of them belonged to Paul Sachs, John Nicholas Brown, or the Lewisohns. With her chosen artists Mongan not only knew every work that had been published or was in public collections, but she also personally knew most of the collectors.

Mongan wrote and published important magazine articles throughout the 1930s. Like Kirstein, Warburg, Soby, and Austin, she was on an independent bandwagon. Mongan was not just interested in naming the artist or researching the provenance. She, too, believed in something new, in an attitude that others had not had before, and her voice in its support could not have been clearer.

Her cause was the power of drawings. She championed the idea of collecting them, a practice for which there was little tradition. She first sermonized on behalf of this viewpoint in 1932 in an article in the widely read *American Magazine of Art,* for which she was one of the few female writers. The piece was technically an exhibition review—of the traveling show of the collection of Dan Fellows Platt of Englewood, New Jersey—but she used it to proselytize. Like many people with a new point of view, she was as quick to call attention to its general lack of favor as to its merits:

> We have no tradition of collecting drawings and no inherited treasure upon which to found our knowledge and develop our discernment. Hardly ten connoisseurs have ventured into the field, and where private collectors have been hesitant, museums have been scarcely more bold.[10]

To break new ground and to support a bold and surprising view was a big part of the adventure. Mongan was indeed Warburg's and Kirstein's soulmate; she too wanted to wake people up.

Like Warburg in his class oration or Soby in his Dali film show, she admired independence and courage. Mr. Platt "has found himself directing rather than following the trend of taste. . . . Mr. Platt has elected to explore not the great and directing currents of the stream of art history, but those eddying backwaters from which new currents sometimes stem."[11] For the majority of art viewers, drawings had traditionally been treated more as historical documents than as objects to be savored. The exceptions to that trend were deemed to be amateurs. But Agnes Mongan worshiped such amateurs; she considered them a class of rare distinction. The roster included the sixteenth-century Italian artist and biographer Vasari;

the seventeenth-century Cardinal Leopold de Medici; Pierre Crozat, who had been treasurer of France at the start of the eighteenth century; and Duke Albert Casimar of Saxony, for whom the Albertina Collection in Vienna had been named. Mongan considered them an elite whose discipleship should grow.

In her discussion of Dan Platt's drawing collection, Mongan evinced the eloquence and the power to observe and enjoy that would lead to decades of success as an advocate for drawings and as a curator, teacher, and author. Her language was clear and vivid, her ability to communicate pleasures vast; she was a stylist in the Berenson tradition, although with a voice distinctly her own. Of a drawing by the eighteenth-century Venetian Piazzetta, she wrote, "Black crayon touches the soft gray-brown paper so lightly that the misty light of Venice seems to hang about those gracious heads."[12] She described a Tiepolo drawing: "Brush and wash he handles with incredible surety and economy. In a few strokes his daringly foreshortened figures are projected into dazzling whiteness."[13] Commenting on the British pieces in the show, she remarked, "Gainsborough hangs a valley with English mist, but the very blue of his paper recalls Claude and clear air over the campagna."[14] Having refined the tone of her early El Greco paper, the young Bryn Mawr graduate already had a rare gift to relate artistic technique to its effect upon the viewer. And Mongan made drawings done centuries ago as immediately present, and brave, as experimental sketches created last week.

In the Platt essay, Mongan further demonstrated her uncanny ability to put people and places together. She could come up with sources for a pose or composition even if the source itself had long been destroyed and was known only through engravings. She identified two of Mr. Platt's drawings by the sixteenth-century artist Federigo Baroccio as studies for his *Crucifixion* in the Genoa Cathedral. This gave her occasion to analyze the effect of that startling crucifixion on Rubens when he visited Genoa in 1607 and on Van Dyck when he went there a decade later.

There is a provocative point to this information. Mongan's brief analysis of what Rubens and Van Dyck did with Baroccio's style was that "To Baroccio's suave and graceful manner of modeling, which has an almost feminine elegance, they added vigorous strength and, paradoxically, great subtlety."[15] These comments on gender came from a woman in a man's world. Her assumption seemed to be that vigorous strength is masculine, and inconsistent with great subtlety. That she made a feminine/masculine distinction of these traits is puzzling. What is certain is that, like her friends from the Harvard Society, Mongan herself combined elegance, vigor, and subtlety in happy congruity.

Mongan ended the Platt essay with a general plea for the patronage of drawings. Motivation was secondary—it hardly mattered whether people were "stirred to interest or to rivalry"[16]—so long as they followed Mr. Platt's lead. Earlier she had advised collectors to consider drawings in an article about the Platt collection in the *Boston Evening Transcript,* where she pointed out that prices were still low and one might still "happen upon hidden treasure."[17] Today art collecting is almost as common as golf among the rich; then it was still something people needed to be told to do. It was the needling of people like Mongan, Austin, and Soby—and their evocation of the luster art objects could give to one's life—that helped inspire thousands of prosperous Americans to accord art its current stature.

Two years after reviewing Mr. Platt's collection, Mongan had a chance to work directly on an exhibition of master drawings. Another former Sachs student, Gordon Washburn, had just become director of the Albright Art Gallery in Buffalo. He decided to make his first exhibition there a drawings show, and asked Mongan to help. An exhibition of this sort was a radical idea, and he knew he could count on her to bring it off. In her catalog introduction— which was quoted in its entirety in *The Art News*—Mongan articulated the qualities the medium held for her. The appeal of drawings, even from five centuries ago, was oddly similar to that of Calder's wire pieces and Picasso's brushwork. These disparate works share a relentless honesty. They reveal the artist's hand so palpably that the viewer feels as if the creator has been there only a moment ago. They are spontaneous. They show the stage before ideas of formal presentation have taken over. They precede fine-tuning and finishing touches. They reveal the artist's inner workings: personal fire more than outer display. She wrote that

It is in drawing that the real intention and essential character of a man or movement are most clearly revealed. . . . The world's greatest drawings have not been done either for display or as works of art. They have been by-products in the process of artistic creation drawn by artists to help in the clarification or formalization of their own problems. . . . They have the virtues of freshness, immediacy and utter honesty. In them banality, empty cleverness or mere trickery, can have no place. Like architects' plans they are usually the basis for erections in a more substantial material but they have a freedom and a vibrancy which ruled lines lack. Paradoxically drawing is both the very bones and foundation upon which great composition depends and the most subtle medium in which to capture the fleeting and the ephemeral.[18]

Collectors and curators should wake up. It would take decades before Agnes Mongan's views—and the sort of show mounted at the Albright—became a national trend, but within a few years their echoes would be felt in galleries and museums around the nation. Today they are everywhere.

The people who depended on Mongan as a living catalog and a voice of authority included some of the major figures of the American art world. She corresponded frequently with Erwin Panofsky, the great Northern Renaissance art authority who had fled Nazi Germany and relocated at the Institute for Advanced Study in Princeton. A consummate scholar of iconography, Panofsky had high regard for Mongan's ability to cite the various appearances of certain images and determine their significance. In 1936 he proposed that they combine forces for "a sweet little monograph" on "the piebald horse in art history." Between the two of them, they had come up with examples of this type of horse in thirteenth-century Persian faience, paintings by Brueghel, and other art objects; Panofsky thought it worth taking further. Mongan turned him down, but they remained in touch on various subjects.

Mongan periodically assisted Georgiana King and many other of her colleagues in their research. She also kept up communication with John Walker, who after his Harvard graduation spent several years as a beloved assistant to Berenson at I Tatti, and a bit later became director of the National Gallery in Washington. Mongan and Walker corresponded constantly. A typical letter was one in which she commented on Robetta's *Youth Captive and Free,* for which Walker was then researching the sources. She pointed out that the Pan figure was clearly based on a Pollaiuolo drawing that had been lost but was known because the artist copied it in his Venetian sketchbook. One of Robetta's angels resembled a figure in the Benozzo *Adoring Group* in the Riccardi Palace. Cain and Abel looked a lot like the central figures in the Pollaiuolo School engraving of *Battling Nudes*. In suggesting these sources, Mongan was contradicting Walker's own conclusions, but that was precisely the sort of challenge she enjoyed; as she wrote to Berenson, "It is most pleasant having John Walker nearby. We enjoy our arguments over attribution much more than the vehemence of our remarks would lead an outsider to believe."[19]

Pollaiuolo also figured in Mongan's voluminous correspondence with Alfred Barr. Barr's main concern was the art of his own time, but he also had a strong interest in earlier work, and remained in ways a traditional scholar. Sometimes his research was prompted by a personal penchant—as with Pollaiuolo, where Mongan could, off the top of her head, provide him with insights on the mythological themes, discussing, for example, the Manlius Torquatus legend of Roman warriors and Gaul as a source for the artist's *Fighting Nudes*. At other times Barr was helping friends of the Museum of Modern Art, trustees or key donors, research an old master drawing in their private collection. He counted on Mongan to help authenticate and date pieces by Ricci, Claude Lorrain, Tiepolo, and others. It was a luxury for him to be able to turn to someone so firmly rooted in traditional academia who was also sympathetic to his modernism.

For Mongan, Barr and his wife, Marga, were among the people who offered a bit of the sparkle and glamour she craved when the life of libraries and the Fogg seemed too confined. She mostly led the existence of a scholar, but there were times when she liked to don her fancy clothes and join her pals for one of their glittering evenings in Hartford or White Plains or Manhattan. In the midst of her quest for correct attributions and the precise provenance of each work in her Fogg catalog, it gave her a lift to get notes like the one from Marga Barr that said,

> Blessings, blessings my dear and get well and for Pete's sake die [*sic*] your hair. I will whisper to you that I had what is called a henna rinse and will continue to do so. If you like you can have your hair done in New York and I will hold your hand. I know the right place.[20]

Marga was forever writing to urge Mongan to spend more time with her—in New York or Vermont—and to arrange rendezvous in Europe.

With the Barrs, Mongan could also compare notes about Kirstein and Warburg. She opted for a more scholarly life than they, but they still offered her an essential amusement and friendship. Her role was as the stable, sensible one—intrigued but above the fray at the same time. So at the start of 1933 she wrote to Alfred Barr to describe a visit with Kirstein in New York when he had taken her to Jean Charlot's studio:

> to see his latest portrait—as Adam in what seemed to me a very horrible *Adam and Eve*. Perhaps you are such a Charlot enthusiast you would not mind his conception of Eve, but to me she was pretty repulsive. The latest *Creative Art* reports that Lincoln is about to depart for Tibet to study Buddhism. Haven't I heard that before?[21]

Barr's reply took a similar tone: "Lincoln seems more erratic than ever, but my devotion to him continues."[22]

Mongan kept up the dialogue:

> Lincoln has written me that nothing is further from his thoughts at the moment than Tibet or Buddhism. He is, he claims, deep in a life of Nijinsky, with little time for other thought.
>
> Eddie I have not yet seen. He is again holding forth at Bryn Mawr on Modern Art. I have only heard one comment but that was favorable: that he seems to have grown up considerably and that the effects of his tour have been all to the good.[23]

Mongan was deep in a sea of books and photographs, and hard at the meticulous work of artistic documentation, but she needed these dips into the old world of her Harvard Society for Contemporary Art chums. And she relished banter as much as scholarship. More than anyone else, it was the founders of the Harvard Society who offered her such pleasures. They had moved to distant points when she remained in Cambridge, but they stayed in close touch. If by chance they began to falter, she knew how to keep them in the fold. At the beginning of 1933, she wrote to John Walker,

I had a perfectly mad but entirely characteristic note from Lincoln this morning. And, for Christmas, a cable from Eddie from *Bethlehem*. Of that ancient and strange triumvirate, you alone remain to be heard from. You are not going to default, are you?

Warburg's cable from Bethlehem somehow amazed her; she reported on it in letters to the Barrs and to Kirstein as well. No one seemed to offer her more pleasure, and laughs, and friendship, than the fellow the newspapers had labeled as "the bad boy of Harvard Yard." Throughout the thirties, Mongan and Warburg visited one another frequently in Cambridge or New York or at his parents' house, and they corresponded regularly. Sometimes the tone was earnest and purposeful, such as a letter from July of 1934 that Warburg wrote from his office at the Museum of Modern Art to Mongan in hers at the Fogg in an attempt to give further assistance to Josef Albers. Warburg referred admiringly to the abstract woodcuts Albers had recently completed as his first American work. Having decided to circulate an exhibition of these pieces, Warburg wondered whether Mongan would like them for the Fogg. It was precisely the sort of thing he was doing all day long for struggling artists. At other moments, he wrote to his old Harvard friend with far more intimacy. Consider the letter addressed to "Ag Darling" in which he describes his first meeting with the woman he would eventually marry:

I met her at a cocktail party—decided she had class with a capital "K"—took her out to lunch the next day, . . . et, voila— l'amour. !!
     And that kiddies is the way I met your Grandma.

The majority of letters were a mixture of banter and serious discourse, and of their shared penchant for "gossip"—one of Mongan's favorite words at the time. Warburg was occasionally spending time with President Roosevelt, whose son James was a friend, and Mongan liked hearing about this sort of thing. FDR talked with Warburg about the latest archaeological discoveries. When the young art patron asked the president how he had time to read about such things, FDR asked him if he had ever read *The Congressional Record;* to Warburg's reply that he had only read a few pages once, the president explained that since he *had* to read it he depended on archaeological journals for kicks. It was precisely the sort of gossip that she enjoyed passing on to her friends. With Warburg, Mongan could jest about issues like Henry Russell Hitchcock's fears about going to New York; Hitchcock was terrified of further mention in Lucius Beebe's column, a distinction the Wesleyan administration frowned upon. Warburg could be counted on for a funny reply. The two would also discuss politics at the Fogg, the carryings-on of the Sachs museum course students, the problems of the ballet. Their tone was what Eddie's cousin Bettina, who had known Mongan ever since Bryn Mawr, called "so forthright as to be fifthright." Mongan signed her letters "Ag the Hag." Discussing a question of attribution of a Tiepolo drawing Warburg was considering for purchase, she signed off, "Draw your own conclusions. You will anyway."[24] When they were disputing the latest activities of Sachs's students out in the world— Warburg had found some museum course members out of line in their haphazard requests for loans from his father's collection for a show at the Fogg—Mongan summed up the way her attitude differed from his with "You have been prejudiced ever since the beginning of our acquaintance and so have I." But there was nothing they would not do for one another; the more flip the tone, the closer the link. At the beginning of 1936 Warburg wrote to Agnes to describe a jam he had gotten into because he had been mouthing off at a party at Vincent Astor's about the unique strength of American collections of the art of myriad cultures. He insisted that European scholars needed to visit America if they were to do thorough research in most areas of art history, and that American scholars would probably do better to stay at home than travel abroad. The result of this tirade was that he had been asked to do a piece on the subject, and document his viewpoint, for *TODAY* magazine. He wrote Agnes about what a burden this task was, and asked if she would give him some help in presenting the strong points of American collections. "At any rate, dear, loosen up the accumulated store of irrelevant facts that you have acquired through years of training at the Fogg,"[25] he implored.

She answered by return mail.

Whee! What a terrible order! Just a little something to occupy my idle moments and to keep me out of mischief, is that it? You describe it as a terrible thing that has happened to you. It seems to me that you are passing on the burden. Very easy, of course, and very wise, but your day will come if it hasn't already. . . .

Dear! Dear! I never thought I would see the day when you
would manifest such scholarly interest.

What followed in installments was perfectly in character: page upon
page of annotated listings of American collections, private and public, with everything from Japanese stoneware to New Mexican baskets to Renaissance drawings. It was as if Mongan even knew which
books each of a hundred thousand Americans had on his library
shelves. Both as a friend and as a bottomless source of information
she would gladly share, Mongan was without equal.

Agnes Mongan could lunch with Bernard Berenson and attend ballet
galas, but she could not go down the front steps of Widener Library
after 6 p.m. She had a study inside, and generally did her best to
abide by the rule that, although the library was open at night,
women were not permitted there after six. On one occasion when
she was so absorbed in her work that she stayed until six-thirty, she
was ushered into the basement and through tunnels so that she could
exit unseen by a side door—and avoid a scandal.

Nor could she join the Harvard Faculty Club, although women
were permitted as guests provided they entered by the side door.
Mongan's pragmatic solution was to have her father join, which as a
graduate of Harvard Medical School he was entitled to do. From
1930 on, she was able to sign on Dr. Mongan's account; at least she
could eat there, even if she could not enter by the same route as her
male colleagues. But when colleagues at the Fogg asked her to do
typing for them, her father's name was little help. Other than the
secretaries, Mongan was the only woman on the Fogg staff. Depression funding cuts had meant that she, as a woman, had been the first
to lose her secretary, and so was compelled to perform clerical work.
Those who saw her doing it assumed that she would type for them,
for which she had a solution as pragmatic as for the club issue. She
never learned how to do it; when professors asked her to type up
their notes, she generally replied that she would be happy to but did
not know how.[26] This deficiency served her well; in later life Mongan
came to feel that if she had allowed herself to be stuck behind a type-
writer, she would not have had a career.

On June 14, 1935, Agnes Mongan wrote to Lincoln Kirstein that she had been awarded a grant for the summer by the Institute of International Education to look things up at the Bibliothèque Nationale and the Cabinet des Dessins at the Louvre.[27] She would be sailing on the *Normandie* within a week and would be gone, she speculated, until the end of September. She was not telling her friend the whole story.

Earlier that spring, Paul Sachs had had a conference at Shady Hill with Gustav Mayer, a partner in Colnaghi and Company, one of the leading art galleries in London. Following their meeting, Sachs told Mongan that she should plan to go abroad that summer. Something was going to develop, but he was not free to say what it was. She must invent some pretext for the trip to tell her parents and others. Sachs had bought drawings from Mayer often enough in the past, and Mongan speculated that some important artworks might be coming on the market. She asked no questions. She went to Europe as instructed, and in August, when Sachs notified her that she should go to the village of Murren in the Swiss Alps, she headed there accordingly. At the appointed hotel, she soon received word that she was to get on the Orient Express in Zurich at 6 p.m. on September 6.

Mongan took the seat on the train specified by the ticket that had been sent to her. There she found Paul and Meta Sachs, along with Henry Rossiter, curator of prints at the Boston museum; W. G. Russell Allen, a collector and chairman of the museum's Print Department Visiting Committee; and Gus Mayer. She learned that they would all get off in Vienna.

The Austro-Hungarian Archduke Albrecht, allegedly owner of the Albertina collection of drawings—considered the finest holding of graphic art in the world—wished to sell the collection clandestinely. The Boston Museum and the Fogg would jointly be the purchasers. Gus Mayer had made the initial arrangements. As a woman, Mongan was told nothing about the business arrangements, but she was expected to help catalog and authenticate the collection, and prepare it for travel. High officials in the British Foreign Office and the U.S. State Department were aware of the secret plan, but under no circumstances were the Albertina's curators or others in Vienna to find out.

The Albertina collection was precisely the sort of thing about which Agnes Mongan already knew a great deal. It was one of the leading cultural attractions of Vienna. It had been formed in the eighteenth century by the Saxon Prince Albert, after he married the Archduchess Marie-Christine, daughter of Emperor Franz and Empress Maria Theresa. It had been housed since that time in a palace in the center of Vienna. It had remained in that location even after 1919, when the National Assembly had voted that the Republic of Austria now possessed the fortune of the House of Hapsburg—apparently including the Albertina—and the current leader of the family, Archduke Friedrich Hapsburg-Lorraine, had emigrated to Hungary. The International Treaty of St. Germain had designated Austria's artistic legacy as collateral for certain reparation payments that it imposed at the end of World War I, but France had prevailed over America in regard to the Albertina, and had maintained that this was an essential part of Austria's cultural heritage that could not be touched.

The collection consisted of over twenty-two thousand items. Those of the German School included a group of major Albrecht Dürer drawings, among them his *Praying Hands,* and important works by sixteenth-century masters like Albrecht Altdorfer, Hans Baldung Grien, Lucas Cranach, Hans Holbein, and Wolf Huber. The Netherlandish pieces included several major drawings each by Pieter Brueghel, Rembrandt Van Rijn, Peter Paul Rubens, and Anthony van Dyck. Of the Italians there were drawings by Lorenzo di Credi, Domenico Ghirlandaio, Michelangelo Buonarroti, Raphaello Santi, Paolo Veronese, Giovanni Battista Tiepolo, and Francesco Guardi. Among the French masters represented were Nicolas Poussin, Claude Lorrain, Jean-Antoine Watteau, and Jean-Honoré Fragonard. In chalk, sepia, pen, pencil, and wash, these were among the finest works on paper by each of these artists. In addition, there was a vast holding of prints; Henry Rossiter put the number at about a quarter of a million.

A few years earlier, a rumor had surfaced that the collection had changed hands. In 1922, there had been reports that Archduke Friedrich had sold the Albertina collection to an American consortium headed by Herbert Hoover, an expert on Austrian affairs, soon to become president of the United States. The quoted price was six million dollars. However, this story was quickly refuted. Austrian government officials made a public statement that the Albertina was no longer Friedrich's property; he had no right to dispose of its content, for it belonged to the Austrian nation. In response to the incident, Professor Hans Tietze, a prominent Dürer scholar who was senior civil servant to the secretary of education, declared that the collection was one of the major cultural properties of the German-speaking world, and should always be regarded as an inviolable national treasure. The Austrian government concurred.

Gustav Mayer's proposition made it clear, however, that in 1935 there were still those willing to consider the Albertina as marketable art. When Archduke Albrecht, Friedrich's son, approached Mayer to sell the collection for him, he claimed that the Austrian government had decreed that the Hapsburgs were entitled to all the imperial property it had previously confiscated. Hence the cache of drawings and prints were his private possession.

Albrecht needed money more than he needed portfolios of art. He hoped some day to become emperor of Hungary, and perhaps of Austria as well. In Budapest he ran a household that was like the Imperial Court. It required a constant influx of cash. So did the upkeep of his mistresses, of whom he had many in various lands; he maintained digs for girlfriends as far away as Brazil. Albrecht was a high-level, 1930s-style playboy. With his impressive physique and handsome face, he cut a fine figure at the gambling tables in Monte Carlo. He was always superbly turned out in English style for golf and hunting. As for things like art: this he would be happy to sell, in order to support his way of life.

So, acting on Albrecht's behalf, Mayer had headed to America, which in 1935 was the best place to find a buyer for an expensive art collection. He went to New York to approach officials at the Metropolitan Museum. But shortly after he arrived, Mayer ran into Henry Rossiter as they were crossing Fifty-seventh Street. Rossiter was surprised that Mayer had not let him know that he would be in America; having shared a trench during World War I, they had long been close friends. Mayer quickly explained the reason for the low profile on this particular journey. He was at that very moment on his way uptown to the Met.

Rossiter persuaded Mayer that he should give the Boston Museum the opportunity instead. They went to Boston together, where Rossiter immediately approached Harold Edgell, the museum director,

as well as the members of the committee that governed his department. Everyone was interested, and they all understood the need for
secrecy.

Paul Sachs was on that committee of the Boston Museum. He and
the other members all voted to make the purchase for an undisclosed
amount. The sum was sizable for the middle of the Depression,
but—in view of what was at stake—it seemed worth the struggle
and sacrifices to raise it. Sachs had spoken with the collector Robert
Woods Bliss, who agreed to put up a considerable percentage of the
money. The understanding was that the collection would go jointly
to the Boston Museum and to the Fogg; the various division heads
at both museums consented to give up all other acquisitions that year
in order to make the purchase. It was shortly after these decisions
were made that Sachs and Rossiter and Mayer agreed to go to Vienna
to consummate the deal, and that Sachs told Agnes Mongan to plan
her trip.

Once they arrived in Vienna, Mongan, the Sachses, Rossiter,
Mayer, W. G. Russell Allen, and W. A. Roseborough—the Americans' legal adviser for the deal—all took up residency at the Bristol
Hotel. Agnes Mongan began her work in the study room at the
Albertina. But neither in Vienna nor back in America did most
people know her task. The director of the Albertina, Dr. Anton Reichel, assumed that she was simply doing academic research. There
were a few people in Vienna, however, who knew precisely what she
was up to. The Austrian vice chancellor Starhemberg, and the minister for financial affairs, both close friends of Archduke Albrecht,
were doing everything they could to help the sale along. For a number of his countrymen, Starhemberg was a national hero. An aviator,
he personified the spirit of the new young, modern Austria. He was
also fiercely nationalistic and monarchistic. Starhemberg knew that
legally Albrecht had no right to the Albertina, that the collection
belonged to the republic, but he favored reinstatement of the Hapsburgs, and would do anything to help that cause. Starhemberg and
the archduke were very much people of the same class; they enjoyed
drinking together, and Starhemberg liked to accompany Albrecht
hunting in Hungary. So he rallied his forces to overcome obstacles
to the sale. Agnes Mongan had been warned that her telephone calls
would be recorded, her mail opened, and that she would be followed; all of this was done by Starhemberg's minions, who wanted
to make sure that she was not disclosing her work to the wrong
people.

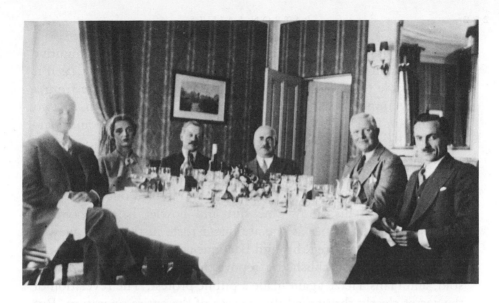

Victory lunch, Bristol Hotel, Vienna, Autumn 1935. From the left: Henry Rossiter, Agnes Mongan, Gustav Mayer, Paul Sachs, W. G. Russell Allen, and W. A. Roseborough.

The secret mission clearly had other proponents as well. Mongan, Sachs, and the rest spent a number of months in Vienna, during which they moved from the Bristol to the Imperial to the Sacher, three of Vienna's finest hotels. Someone was footing the bill. There are those who believe that in all likelihood it was covered by a special account bankrolled by the United States government.

Then, on December 30, Anton Reichel received an astonishing telegram. It was from Joseph Duveen, the New York art dealer. Duveen said he was representing people interested in purchasing the Albertina; they were prepared to pay at least 10 percent more than the amount currently being considered. No one knows for certain how Lord Duveen got wind of the intended sale, but this is how the Albertina's director found out about it.

Reichel immediately got in touch with the Austrian cultural minister, and together they brought up the matter to the chancellor, Kurt von Schuschnigg, who became adamant that the sale not take place. For one thing, if it did, it would put the Austrian government in bad grace with the Nazis; Schuschnigg and his cabinet had great fear of the Third Reich, and did not want to do anything that would make them susceptible to criticism from that side. But Albrecht and his cohorts still maintained that the archduke was in a position to sell the drawings, and the negotiations continued. The diminutive young woman from Somerville proceeded, at Sachs's behest, as if it were possible to take one of the jewels of European culture from a seemingly impenetrable bastion of Hapsburg imperialism to two museums in Massachusetts. After all, her friends Kirstein and Warburg had been able to import the heir to the Ballets Russes.

Mongan continued to walk every day between her elegant hotel rooms and the Albertina study room to proceed with her work, even if this meant being tailed by a character who looked out of a Hollywood movie in his shiny blue suit and bowler hat. She would glimpse him behind her as she ate linzer torte in the cafés, viewed the opera, and wandered through Baroque churches. In February the *Frankfurter Zeitung* published a report that the Albertina had been sold, and Hans Tietze again made a public protest. The revelation of the secret clearly threatened the success of the entire operation. But the would-be seller and purchasers persevered.

In April, Albrecht wrote to Gustav Mayer from Budapest to express his annoyance at the publicity about the sale. He blamed it on the indiscretion of the people at the Boston Museum and the Fogg, where the journalist from the *Frankfurter Zeitung* had apparently done some of his research. Albrecht neglected to mention that it was Duveen who had first spilled the beans, well before the newspapers had picked up the story, and that this was probably because Albrecht had approached the renowned dealer in hopes of getting the largest possible sum for the collection. Albrecht simply told Mayer that thanks to the press coverage he was now receiving other offers for the collection; the archduke acknowledged that he owed Mayer first refusal, but insisted that he had to consider the financial needs of his family.

Above all, Albrecht wanted to speed things up. Therefore he was forming an English company to negotiate with the Austrian government. What he hoped was that, if necessary, the final contract could be subject to international rather than Austrian jurisdiction. If it were challenged, it would be brought before The Hague Tribunal, where one of his personal lawyers was the Hungarian representative and had considerable power.

Mayer continued to believe that he could pull it all off. In May of 1936 he cabled Colnaghi's to send a conservator to remove the prints and drawings from their mats in order to take them to London en route to Boston; sixteen thousand works were ready to go. He scheduled "a Victory lunch" at the Bristol. A photograph of that event shows Agnes Mongan, the only woman—and a generation younger than everyone else there—sitting in Viennese splendor between Mayer and Rossiter, with Sachs, Allen, and Roseborough also at the table. She must have been excited, but wears a dubious expression. Perhaps she more than anyone else recognized the magnitude of the treasure that they hoped to secure; she also must have had more conscience about the appropriateness of its journey to America.

In any event, the victory was not real. In June, Gustav Mayer finally conceded defeat. The British ambassador and Austrian government officials had resolved that no one had the right to sell or buy the Albertina; Mayer informed the other interested parties accordingly.

Agnes Mongan, however, would enjoy one last lark out of the whole affair. Paul Sachs told her to pack up right away and take the next train to Paris, but she insisted that she must see the Danube one last time, and would leave the following day. Heading off that Sunday for this final bit of sight-seeing, she noticed that her usual shadow in his blue suit had been replaced. While the original tail was dark and large, his substitute was "a thin oily blond."[28] Mongan decided to give him some real work. First she journeyed to the outskirts of the city to cross its great river. Then, back in the center, she attended High Mass in a packed St. Stephen's Cathedral, where she stood through the entire service. Then she rushed to see the Lipizzaner stallions at the Winter Riding School, after which she doubled back to the Kunsthistorisches Museum for one final glimpse of the Brueghels. By the time she returned to the Bristol, she was running, and so was he. The last time she saw him—at the train station—the man was out of breath.

FORWARD MARCH

The American Ballet Company had ups and downs after its public premiere. Kay Swift saw her ballet firsthand two months after its opening in Hartford, in a benefit at Bryn Mawr College, where it was well received. Following that the American Ballet gave its first New York performances, at the Adelphi Theatre. They were there for a week, starting on March 1, 1935. They presented two programs. The first consisted of *Serenade, Alma Mater,* and a new work called *Errante,* for which the music was Charles Koechlin's arrangements of Schubert, and the costumes and lighting were by Pavel Tchelitchew. The second program revived *Dreams*—the ballet with music by George Antheil and costumes by Derain that had been performed at Woodlands—along with *Transcendence, Mozartiana,* and a new work called *Reminiscence,* with music by Benjamin Godard.

The press picked up on all of this enthusiastically, even if they dwelled as much on personalities as on the performances. First there was eager chitchat about the reception Eddie Warburg hosted on February 25 right at the Adelphi. Mrs. William K. Vanderbilt, who had become one of the angels to the new company, was there, as were Frank Crowninshield and Marie Harriman. Those same people added luster to the white-tie opening, an event with which Cholly Knickerbocker and other gossip columnists had a field day. By most accounts a milestone in dance history had taken place. The enthusiasm was such that the run at the Adelphi was extended a second week. Since the box-office take was about nine thousand dollars a week and Warburg was paying the dancers' salaries, this meant that the company could make up its deficit.

Not everyone approved, however. John Martin in *The New York Times* wrote that *Errante* was "cosmic nonsense . . . With all due respect to a platinum and diamond audience that cheered it to the echo, this is exactly the sort of thing the American Ballet must not do if it is to assume the place in the dance world to which it is entitled." *Alma Mater*'s rating was that it was "really a revue sketch rather than a ballet." *Serenade* was "a serviceable rather than an inspired piece of work." The only kudos were for *Reminiscence,* which Martin termed "the real delight of the evening." In general, Martin felt that the new company, contrary to its advance claims, was too much in the European tradition, and that it was "a colossal waste of time and energy to train dancers in the strict routine of the classic dance." A number of the pieces were "evidence of the decadence of the classic tradition as it is found in certain European environments, examples of what someone has aptly called 'Riviera esthetics.'" The conclusion was that the company needed to get rid of Balanchine and come up with an American director.[1]

Eddie Warburg countered Martin's points in statements quoted in the *Times* a week later:

> Just what one can call American in the arts is always debatable. I do not feel that we should consciously seek American forms, but rather should let them evolve. The most important thing is the quality of production and the fact that we are located here in America. . . . There seems no question that the ballet is wanted in this country. If it is good it will serve as a focal point for all the arts.[2]

This issue of the Americanness of the School of American Ballet had become pivotal, and it was up to Warburg to rally forces to the school's defense. Before he gave his interview to the *Times,* he had asked Alfred Barr to make written comment on this subject. He wanted something he could quote if necessary. Warburg appears never to have actually used Barr's letter, but it offered an essential voice of support. Barr wrote,

> I think that the School of American Ballet is a valuable and much needed project. While it is true that its methods and aesthetic ideals are imported this can also be said of every other artistic medium which has been developed and assimilated on this side of the Atlantic. To expect a full fledged native ballet overnight is absurd, and to condemn the School of the American Ballet because within a year it is not 100 per cent American is equally absurd.

Barr wanted to be as helpful as possible. "If this isn't the kind of statement you would like please let me know and I will hit some other tack,"[3] he offered.

As with the Harvard Society, Kirstein was the motivating force behind the idea, but Warburg was the one to win over supporters. From time to time, Warburg even had to accompany Lincoln to Lou Kirstein's offices at Filene's, especially when Lincoln was soliciting funds from his father. "Lincoln would splutter out some elaborate scheme, and then Lou, with his overhanging eyebrows and bearish growl, would turn and ask, 'Eddie, do you understand a word he says? Do you think I ought to do it?'" There was no end to how much Lou would taunt his son, who had considerably less humor than Warburg. More than once, Lou suggested to Warburg that the only reason he had such strong-willed offspring was that there was a firehouse not far from the family's home on Commonwealth Avenue, and that it was actually one of the young firemen who had sired Lincoln; Lincoln cringed while his father and Warburg roared. Then Warburg would ask Lou what he had against immortality, and suggest that in truth Lincoln's latest madness might make the family name famous. Lou would consent, crediting Warburg for his decision.[4] One way or another, the two young patrons of the arts forged ahead.

The American Ballet's next step after its New York run was to take off on a transcontinental tour organized by Alexander Merovitch, who was president of the Musical Arts Management Corporation and had lined up the Adelphi. When the company reached Scranton, Pennsylvania, disaster struck. Dancers, musicians, stagehands, and truck drivers all needed to be paid, and there wasn't a penny left in the till. Theater managers all over the country sued for expenses already incurred for performances that now would never take place. Eddie Warburg found himself to be "the nearest thing to an asset within miles."[5]

As Kirstein put it, "The matter of picking up pieces, restoring morale, paying bills offered little amusement to a generous, eager, and fun-loving young man."[6] But miserable as it made the grandson of one of the wealthiest men in America to find himself being attacked like a common criminal, pick up the pieces he did. His family's lawyers advised that he didn't have to answer to the theaters whose plans had been changed, but he took care of the ballet staff, and worked like crazy not to throw in the towel.

It was worth the fight. Warburg and Kirstein had managed to arrange for the American Ballet to link up with the Metropolitan Opera, housed in its grand headquarters at Thirty-ninth Street and Broadway. In the 1935–36 opera season, Balanchine provided dances for thirteen operas, including divertissements for *Carmen, La Traviata,* and *Die Fledermaus.* While Lincoln Kirstein was "in love with the whole dusty fabric of the Met,"[7] and Eddie Warburg felt that "our ballet, being fresh and modern, visually as well as musically oriented, definitely did not fit into the stodgy productions of the Met,"[8] they agreed that they would do what was needed to keep their company alive.

Being at the Met meant that, beyond music and theater critics, the popular press remained interested in them. Now Dorothy Kilgallen followed Lucius Beebe and Cholly Knickerbocker in setting her sights on the American Ballet. Her December 30, 1935, column in the *New York Evening Journal* was headed, "Maestro Assails Critics of Hi-di-Hi Ballet at 'Met.'"

> Mr. George Balanchine is the daring young man who lifted the Metropolitan Opera ballet out of its petticoats, gave it snake hips, a dash of hi-di-hi and achieved more terpsichorean authenticity than has been mentioned around the Met in many a year.
>
> He put a reptilian wiggle in the torsoes of the "Aida" chorus until the dowagers couldn't believe their lorgnettes. He staged an orgy in "Tannhauser" and was heard to remark:
>
> "This scene is in hell and in hell they don't dance a minuet." . . .
>
> Mr. Balanchine's ballet kicked the music critics in their aisle seats and sent them choking to their midnight typewriters with words formerly used only in reviewing Harlem floor shows. It was this which delighted, if also slightly disturbed, Mr. Balanchine today. . . .
>
> "This is why I say the critics know nothing."

II

The Wadsworth Atheneum, like the ballet, was also moving along as a vehicle of new ideas. The raised eyebrows of the insurance set in no way deterred Chick Austin and Jim Soby. On December 15, 1934, a week after the triumphant Balanchine performances, The

Friends and Enemies of Modern Music sponsored the premiere of part of the new opera *Hester Prynne,* written by Avery Claflin and directed by John Houseman. Virgil Thomson's Quartet Number Two was premiered the same evening, in a setting designed for the occasion by Pavel Tchelitchew. Tchelitchew had the quartet sit on a low black platform. The main element of their backdrop was a large arch made of rubber hose and draped in white tulle. Hanging from the ceiling by invisible wires, it was, according to Virgil Thomson, "like a stroke of penmanship."[9] The arch enclosed three panels on which Morris Grosser had painted the first three pages of Thomson's Quartet Number Two. Grosser did them in white on black, so that they looked like proof sheets or photo negatives; and he also painted some of Thomson's musical notations in black on twenty yards of the bright white tulle. Thomson was delighted with the effect: "As insubstantial as the sound of music, the set gave visual presence to the musicians and picked up the red brown of their instruments."[10]

Three days after that event, Salvador Dali showed the film *Un Chien Andalou* and gave a lecture. If Jim Soby's friends who had huddled in his West Hartford living room gazing at *L'Age d'Or* ever wanted to hear Dali's rationale for these films he had made with Luis Buñuel, now was their chance. Dali spoke of his wish to illustrate the world of dreams, and gave vast credence to all unconscious thought, however disarming it might seem. He showed the audience a postcard of Africans in front of a hut and then turned it ninety degrees to indicate that on its side it had many elements of a man's head as drawn by Picasso, and he demonstrated how a Leonardo da Vinci *Madonna and Child* contained a strong subconscious image of a vulture. He said that in his own work he wanted to cultivate these double meanings, whether they were the result of sheer accident or reflections of significant thought. This recognition of subconscious ideas was, Dali explained, a vehicle toward "liberty."[11]

The Hartford audience had all sorts of opportunities to be liberated. On January 18, 1935, Gertrude Stein spoke in the auditorium where her opera had opened less than a year earlier. The event was front-page news in the local paper. The headline in the *Hartford Courant* was "Miss Stein Speaks With Meaning Here," while the picture caption read, "Avery Audience Understands Most Of Her Address." She spoke in a slow, informal, conversational voice about her impressions of modern painting. Stein dealt out her usual surprises, but at least the gist could be followed. With statements like "The relationship between oil painting and the thing painted is nobody's

business" and "Familiarity does not breed contempt, it breeds familiarity," she kept the crowd with her.

Public response mattered deeply to Austin. From January 30 to
February 19 he put on a show of American painting and sculpture
from eighteenth-century portraits and allegories to Calder, Noguchi,
and Lachaise, and he issued a questionnaire encouraging everyone to
voice his or her view. There were questions like "Which picture in
the exhibition would you prefer to have in your home?" and "Which
picture or sculpture do you dislike most?" along with instructions to
put the completed form in a ballot box and the upper-case statement
"THE MUSEUM WOULD GREATLY APPRECIATE SERIOUS
ANSWERS TO THE ABOVE QUESTIONS." The results proved
to be mostly negative, however. One local citizen's answer was a
warning against forcing "this modern art jazz" on the public and the
claim that 90 percent of the local population detested it.[12] At the
trustees' annual meeting, Austin complained about low attendance
at both lectures and exhibitions.[13] The talk of New York was not
taking on the home front.

There was no stopping, however. From March 12 to April 14,
Austin mounted a solo exhibition of Tchelitchew's paintings. These
strange and startling works were diplomatically accompanied by an
exhibition of the nineteenth-century American realist George Caleb
Bingham—the artist whom the Museum of Modern Art had used as
counterpoint to the Gaston Lachaise show a month earlier—but this
concession to public taste was little more than a nod. From October
22 to November 17 he unveiled another truly pioneering exhibition:
"Abstract Art." In 1935 it didn't take three years' advance planning
to assemble such a show; Austin had gathered the work for it in
Europe that summer. Out of deference to the notion "that Abstractions cannot be taken in large doses,"[14] Austin confined the selection
to nineteen works by four artists all living in Paris at the time: the
Russian-born brothers Antoine Pevsner and Naum Gabo, and the
Dutch artists Piet Mondrian and César Domela. The sculptures, reliefs, and paintings were given an unusually simple and airy presentation in Avery Court, with lots of space around each work. The
exhibition demonstrated above all the notion that beauty lay in pure
shapes and forms without reference to subject matter. This was especially evident in the abstract Mondrian *Composition in Blue and
White* that Austin bought out of that exhibition for the Atheneum—
the first of the artist's work to enter the collection of a major American museum.

The simplicity and reductionism of the "Abstract Art" show may not seem startling today, but in 1935 it was all pretty radical for the public at large. The reaction of the cognoscenti, however, was encouraging. Although Austin might have been miffed that the immediate public didn't approve of what was going on in the museum, he must have been pleased with the words of the Swiss-born architect Le Corbusier, who on a visit from Paris lectured at the Atheneum on October 25. The result of Corbu's visit was his report back in France that Austin and his friends Soby and Hitchcock had made Hartford—"Petite ville au haut de Connecticut"—"un centre spirituel de l'Amérique, un lieu où la lampe d'esprit brûle." [15] Shortly after his visit Corbu proposed that his Paris friends Picasso, Léger, Braque, Laurens, Lipchitz, and Brancusi join him in building and decorating a villa in association with the Wadsworth Atheneum—an idea unfortunately never realized.

In Hartford, 1936 began with a Paul Klee exhibition. What everyone was awaiting, however, was the First Hartford Festival, devoted to all the arts. Dreamed up by Chick Austin, with James Thrall Soby as his unofficial assistant in organizing the various events, the festival was jointly sponsored by The Friends and Enemies of Modern Music and the Atheneum.

The festival opened on the afternoon of Sunday, February 9, with a concert called "Music of Today in Connecticut." A local entrepreneur—one of the developers of the self-service supermarket—and his wife gave a prize of two hundred dollars for the best work by a Connecticut Valley composer. The winning composition, by Ross Lee Finney, was entitled "Three Songs on Poems by Archibald MacLeish." It was performed by the Hartford Festival Orchestra, along with work by John Spencer Camp, Roger Sessions, Frederick Jacobi, Ruth White Smallens, and Werner Josten, in a concert conducted by Alexander Smallens and some of the composers themselves. Having by now conducted *Porgy and Bess* for the Theatre Guild in New York, Smallens's reputation had grown since he waved his baton for *Four Saints*.

The evening following the concert, four "Early Masterpieces of Cinematic Art" were shown. Iris Barry of the Museum of Modern Art had selected them and written program notes that dignified them with a level of scholarship then new to the study of films. The movies were *A Trip to the Moon,* made in 1902 by Georges Méliès; *The Whirl of Life,* made in 1914 and starring Irene and Vernon Castle; *A*

Fool There Was, made in 1914 with Theda Bara—of whom Jim Soby claimed "Everybody was Theda Bara's fool";[16] and *Entr'Acte,* a film on which René Clair and Francis Picabia collaborated in 1924. *Entr'Acte* had been set to music by Erik Satie and Darius Milhaud, and starred Picabia and Satie as well as Marcel Duchamp and Man Ray.

Satie's music was heard again on Friday the fourteenth, as part of the "Grand Concert Spectacle." As at the *Four Saints* premiere two years earlier, the winter weather was brutal—twelve hours of pelting snow, sleet, and high winds made it a major effort just to get to the Atheneum that night—but the Grand Concert went on regardless. People like Kirk Askew, Lincoln Kirstein, Mrs. Pierre Matisse, Henry McBride, Jere Abbott, Marga Barr, and Eddie Warburg wouldn't be put off by a little inclemency when another great modern entertainment was about to unfold.

The program for which they donned their wool mufflers and high boots opened with Igor Stravinsky's *Les Noces,* a Balanchine ballet called *Serenata,* and the American premiere of Satie's *Socrate,* a symphonic drama for tenor, soprano, and orchestra. It wasn't a bad program, but it represented a last-minute change of plans. What had originally been intended for that evening and a repeat later the following day were the American premieres of Kurt Weill's *Mahagonny,* with Lotte Lenya, and of Weill's operatic ballet spectacle *The Seven Deadly Sins,* choreographed by Balanchine and starring members of the School of American Ballet. According to one newspaper account, what went wrong was that "Someone forgot to consult the composers and when someone else thought of it, it was rather late and the authors proved troublesome." [17]

Once again, Alexander Smallens conducted. The Stravinsky, unfamiliar to most of the audience, got things off to a lively start. It was performed by four vocalists, a chorus, four pianos used as percussive instruments, and a percussive orchestra. The soloists and pianists were from the Art of Musical Russia, Inc. Serge Koussevitzky, conductor of the Boston Symphony Orchestra, had arranged this, and it gave the work rare authenticity. So did the rather severe sets, based on Natalia Goncharova's designs in the Lifar collection and executed by Chick Austin.

Balanchine's short ballet *Serenata,* which followed, was deemed an exquisite diversion. Chick Austin had commissioned it. It was subtitled *Magic,* since Balanchine had Chick Austin's performances as

"The Great Ozram" in mind for the action. Danced to a Mozart composition for eight instruments, it was both the first American appearance and the last public performance of Diaghilev's star ballerina Felia Dubrovska, and the debut of the great dancer Lew Christiansen. Tchelitchew designed the costumes and the set, a room enclosed by three walls of layers of white chiffon. Each wall had a black door hung on red and green ropes, and each door opened to reveal a rectangle of black velvet in front of which dancers stood while awaiting their entrance cues. The violet and mauve lighting came from behind.

But it was *Socrate* that made the biggest impression. Alexander Calder had designed his first mobile sets for it. As the soprano sang a text from the *Dialogues* of Plato, a bright scarlet disc suspended from invisible strings—it represented the sun—moved across the stage. When the tenor performed his aria, glittering chromium hoops revolved—in a couple of instances pushing him toward the side of the stage. Also suspended by invisible supports, they were like the outline of a glove. At the end of the piece, a tall white panel began to levitate. Then it descended to the floor, lay flat, turned over, and rose up—now a deep black. This was for the moment that Socrates drank the goblet of hemlock. The sun concurrently echoed the fatality by completing its diagonal descent across the sky and moving into shadow. Although Calder had provided motors to effect all of this motion, they had proved too weak for the task, so Abe Feder, the lighting engineer, and a stagehand had made it all happen by pulling ropes.

Calder's moving parts provided a lot to talk about, but what really attracted people to the Atheneum was the costume ball planned for Saturday evening. Another of the special Hartford trains out of Grand Central ferried people northward for the event. A performance of the Grand Concert was scheduled for 4 p.m. to accommodate them, but it was really just an hors d'oeuvre. Some New York visitors were already in Hartford, but most took the private train. Mrs. John D. Rockefeller, Jr. (this is how the society columnists referred to Abby Aldrich Rockefeller), was on board; she had reserved a box at the ball. The Viennese dancer Tilly Losch, Princess Natalie Paley (daughter of the Grand Duke Paul of Russia), Ziegfeld Follies composer Vernon Duke, Virgil Thomson, Roger Sessions, Fernand Léger, Margaret Lewisohn, and George Gershwin also made the Saturday trip. Journalists like Marya Mannes of *Vogue,* Gloria Braggioti of the *New York Post,* Wolfe Kaufman of *Variety,* "Mme. Flutterbye" of the *New York Journal,* and Henry McBride of the *New York Sun* were there to make sure that the rest of America was aware of the event. The party, known as the Paper Ball, began at 9:30 p.m. Those who attended would never forget it.

Tchelitchew created the setting. He covered the Avery courtyard with delicate decorations made of brightly painted newspapers. It had what Lincoln Kirstein called "the pathos and elegance of *le style pauvre.*"[18] Students at the Hartford Art School and other young Hartfordites had collected piles of newspaper throughout the city, and Tchelitchew cut, pasted, folded, and stitched it to craft two false tiers of elaborate theater boxes on the balconies that formed Avery Court. The normally flat expanses of white plaster were transformed into ornate balustrades, pillars, and elaborately swagged paper draperies with fanciful emblems or armorial shields. The pillars were striped in black-and-white newsprint and topped with curly plumes made from the comic sections, printed in color. The Baroque statue of a nymph and two satyrs in the middle of the court wore a paper mask and a headdress of colored papers.

In the midst of the balconies imaginary spectators appeared. Tchelitchew indicated these figures in gray, black, and white gouaches accented in shocking pink on sheets of newspapers he had mounted on frames. The impression was of "a fantastic audience looking down on the Ball" below.[19] Their faces were "expressions of nightmare grimace." But beyond that, the illusory assemblage had little in common. They represented

> every creed, color, race and station in life. Duchesses raised lorgnettes, Chinese stared over their long mustaches, hodcarriers sat with derby hats and feet on rail, be-monocled persons gaped, negroid features were arranged side by side with blonde Nordics, inebriates sat shoulder to shoulder with Puritans, on and on through these hundred or so boxes in the two tiers rising 60 feet high. They were the motley music hall audience at the fantastic circus.[20]

The materials reflected the realities of the Depression. The main ingredient was imagination. The choice of paper also said something about Tchelitchew's views on precious materials and on the power of art to bring about transformation. Like so many modern thinkers,

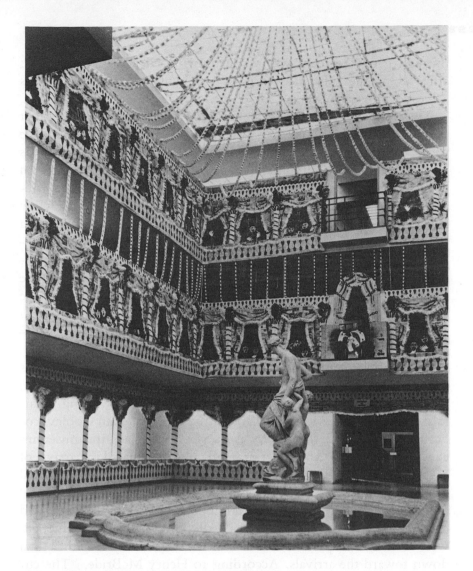

Avery Court decorated for the Paper Ball.

he was reconsidering traditional value judgments. The goal, according to the Russian artist, was "to show you how something elegant and beautiful can be made out of a scrap of paper, and bits of ribbon, and broken fragments of many kinds which you usually think are no good, and which you throw into the ashcan."[21] Newsprint could be brocade; tissue paper could be velvet.

In his ballet and theater designs Tchelitchew had worked with light and motion as much as anything else. To have wind blow through gauzy material was a consummate effect. Weightlessness, after all, is the substance of gaiety. And it was gaiety that was achieved above all else.

The Avery Court had become a stage setting, and the guests that evening performers more than observers. Their entrances did justice to the dreamlike environment. The theme of the grand pageant was "the Cirque des Chiffonniers"—or ragpickers' circus. Seventeen groups comprising 350 people paraded through the Morgan Memorial—decorated like a circus tent with light blue walls and a white gauze "big top"—and into Avery Court. Outside on Main Street, a celebrity-hungry crowd—the type that frequents Broadway premieres or Academy Awards ceremonies—looked on as the "ragpickers" arrived at the canvas marquee that had been erected between the street and the Morgan entrance. Once inside the Avery Court, those in paper costumes were awaited by an additional 450 guests more in the category of spectator than performer, and attired in ordinary evening clothes.

Each entrance into the court, directed by Tchelitchew—who was clad in overalls for the occasion—was made to a silent fanfare on paper trumpets held by two fully uniformed heralds wearing admirals' hats with paper feathers. One of the men was Paul Cooley, cochairman of the ball; the other was Robert Drew-Baer, the museum's executive secretary. Abe Feder dramatically illuminated the arrival of each group. To obtain his desired effects he had installed a special large switchboard for the evening and deployed forty powerful floodlights with a combined strength equal to one hundred thousand candlepower. These lights, periodically dimmed and brightened, were for the most part directed across the airy courtyard rather than down toward the arrivals. According to Henry McBride, "The cumulative effect of so much beauty was almost unbearable. Most of the dancers, though in paper, were copiously and imaginatively clad, though a few were beautifully unclad."[22]

Chick Austin led the procession in a scarlet, white, and black ringmaster's outfit designed by Tchelitchew. He drove a team of six ponies—women dressed in black paper lace ballet skirts and wearing black mitts that transformed their hands into hoofs. Mrs. Richard Bissell, a Hartford woman who had helped organize the ball, followed in her black riding habit, with another team of six horses. These were Hartford Art School students disguised as stallions, covered in white oilcloth spotted in black; they wore paper heads and long, flowing paper manes.

The denizens of Farmington and other local suburbs, for whom party attire was generally something that lasted a good ten seasons, donned getups a far cry from their usual pickings. Instead of the local emporia that put them in their usual, insurance-city-correct attire, tonight their couturiers included Tchelitchew, Calder, and Eugene Berman. In lieu of Liberty of London prints, the ladies now donned tissue paper cut to resemble fur, construction paper shredded into unruly fringes, crepe paper stretched to imitate silk or moiré, old-fashioned wallpaper pasted onto cheesecloth or tarlatan to simulate traditional evening gowns, and cellophane ruffles—all sprayed with fireproof liquid. Their puffed sleeves were made out of Chinese paper lanterns. Mrs. Sheffield Cowles, a snake charmer, had a paper boa constrictor wound round her. Mrs. Wilmarth Lewis—the former Annie Burr Auchincloss, and now wife of the Horace Walpole scholar who lived in Farmington—was draped in glistening silver metal paper fashioned after a gown in a Velázquez portrait. She was followed by half a dozen toreadors and a coal black bull.

Other large animals were meant to resemble unclassifiable creatures out of nightmares. Called "Nightmare Shadows" or "A Nightmare Side Show" (depending on which account of the event one reads), this group, appropriately, was led by Mrs. James Soby, who knew more about dream imagery than most of her friends did. It was Sandy Calder who made their costumes. Jim and Mimi Soby gave a dinner party before the ball at the house they had recently moved to in Farmington—one town west of West Hartford. Calder and his wife, Louisa, were to have been there at the same time as the other guests, in order to put everyone into costumes. However, the party itself became a bit of a nightmare when the Calders failed to show up as expected. Soby did his best to stay calm by reminding himself of the tale of the speed with which Calder had assembled the Harvard Society show in Eddie Warburg's room. Others grew edgy, however, and began to drink rather hard. When Calder did at last show up, it was pretty much a repeat of the Harvard performance. Everyone expected to see him appear with finished costumes; instead he arrived with nothing but "a large roll of brown wrapping paper as well as a stapler, scissors, needles and strong thread."[23] After dinner, he cut the brown paper into appropriate lengths and had the guests all lie down on the floor. He traced their bodies. Then he stapled and sewed. Winslow Ames—another former Paul Sachs student and at that time director of the Lyman Allyn Museum in New London, Connecticut—assisted. In a flash the Sobys and their friends became tigers, elephants, and other jungle creatures. They all wore gigantic masks of the brown wrapping paper, and were made to proceed on all-fours in large flaps of brown paper covered with brightly colored fragments. When they made their entrance downtown at the Atheneum, however, some of them had considerable trouble navigating and nearly fell into the shallow pool with its Baroque statue in the center of the Avery Court. Soby "had the most trouble with one of the elephants. The man inside this costume had a temporary problem with alcohol, and he kept bursting out of his costume at unlikely places to get another drink. . . . He had trouble keeping his trunk aloft and defiant as the night wore on." [24]

Fourteen members of the Hartford Art School formed the group of "Modern Artists." They simulated paintings. There were two Marie Laurencins, Léonide's *Fisherwoman with Net,* a Klee, a Pierre Roy, and Brancusi's *Blonde Negress.* Among the four de Chiricos was a Greek column made of corrugated cardboard and cheesecloth. Six of the students modeled themselves on Picassos, including *The Three Musicians* and Soby's *Seated Woman*—regularly on view at the Atheneum in those days.

Everything seemed possible with paper. Some local women were "A Calendar of Trees." Their torsos were swathed in brown to indicate trunks, while their upraised arms were covered with paper leaves and blossoms to suggest a lilac, a magnolia, a dogwood, an oak tree in autumn, and a holly tree. Fernand Léger, Mrs. Gerald Murphy (who was then living in New York), and Archibald MacLeish all went as gypsies. Mrs. Pierre Matisse was a giraffe. Oliver Jennings wore a paper smoking jacket. Lincoln Kirstein was part of a group led and designed by Eugene Berman and called "the ruins of Hartford in 3095." There was a paper Queen Nefertiti, and more than one paper Mae West, as well as South Sea islanders and peasant couples. Lauder Greenway was a paper stork, his sister a bird of paradise. George Balanchine led a group called "Beggards," costumed by Tchelitchew.

A man named Toby Freeman wore a paper leopard skin slung over a pink undershirt, and covered his wide-cut trousers with *New Yorker* covers. Propriety was definitely not the order of the day. Eddie Warburg observed that a big part of the pleasure that evening was "in taking away any modesty. Suddenly you found yourself parading into a conservative New England town looking like a ragamuffin. The more outrageous everything was, the more it was valued." [25] Indeed, halfway in the grand parade a group of young men appeared "almost as nature made them, and nature made them well"—this according to Henry McBride. On their shoulders they supported the actress Ruth Ford. She was the Muse of Poetry. Her costume, made by Tchelitchew, consisted of a basic black sleeveless gown covered in cellophane that was spangled with large alphabet letters cut out of newspapers. More letters adorned her wire headdress. These elegant creatures danced until dawn. To music written specially for the occasion by Nicholas Nabokov, George Antheil, and Vernon Duke, their paper costumes rustled away.

Even after most of the guests had returned to their proper Tudor or Georgian suburban homes or repaired to local hotel rooms, the party continued. Accounts vary as to the sequence of events as dawn broke, but, if they are all to be believed, first Toby Freeman and a young woman in voluminous eighteenth-century petticoats splashed into the shallow pool, and then Austin was thrown in twice. His initial plunge was the result of a push from Sandy Calder, and caused the marble floor to run scarlet from the dye in his paper costume. Later on, Charles Ford and Parker Tyler—another of the muse's porters—went skinny-dipping,[26] but they had not had much they needed to remove to begin with.

Parties were fine and good, but this was more than a New England city could take. The Paper Ball nearly cost Austin his job.[27] He was not one of the people with his clothes off, but these profligates were his invited guests. More and more, Hartford was growing uncomfortable with the color their local impresario was bringing to town. At a party back at the Sobys' house after the ball ended, two factions formed. One consisted of the Hartfordites who were adamant that this was all nonsense. The other group were the out-of-towners like Jere Abbott, Agnes Rindge, and John McAndrew from Vassar, Kirk and Constance Askew, Julien and Joella Levy, Pierre and Teeny Matisse, and Winslow Ames, all of whom thought this had been one of the highlights of their life. There were of course some locals who supported Austin. These were mainly people associated with the Atheneum like Paul Cooley, Austin's secretary Eleanor Howland, and Russell Hitchcock. But opposition was growing. When the March 15 *Vogue* described the Paper Ball as "the event that stood Hartford on its ear last month,"[28] they weren't kidding. And not everyone was comfortable standing on his ear. A lot of Atheneum trustees didn't approve of reading *Vogue,* let alone being mentioned in it.

There was no end to what Austin offered them, however. The

afternoon after the Paper Ball, for those who could pry open their eyelids, the Hartford Festival concluded with a "matinée musicale" directed by Virgil Thomson. Chamber music by Vivaldi, Scarlatti, Couperin, and Tartini was played on period instruments by the Renaissance Ensemble. Modern works were interspersed. These included three pieces for clarinet and bassoon by Jere Abbott, songs by Paul Bowles, and a septet paraphrase of "Swing Low, Sweet Chariot" by Henri Cliquet-Pleyel. They were played in front of a Eugene Berman setting, for which Jim Soby, who had in the previous few years acquired Berman's paintings en masse, had been Austin's liaison. It suggested a public square, full of colorful columns, behind which a painted backdrop made a vista of seventeenth-century Italian buildings against a night blue sky.

The Avery's auditorium was only half full for the Sunday concert, however. Nothing could have the draw of the Paper Ball, and many people who might have been at the concert were at home recuperating. But if it was a party that had garnered more attention than any other event in the Hartford Festival, this celebration had significance beyond mere frivolity. The Paper Ball challenged notions of reality and identity as surely as any Cubist picture or Surrealist tract might, and it provided a sense of theater that people craved.

III

James Thrall Soby had what Alfred Barr called "a taste bold enough to confront the formidable."[29] His collecting took its decisive direction in the course of the 1930s. It veered increasingly from what was pretty or traditionally tasteful to art that embraced emotional complexity. His Matisses may have seemed wild when Soby put them up in the place of the Connecticut Impressionists, but in little time the Frenchman's work had come to strike him as being "like lollypops."[30] Picasso's *Seated Woman* was a portent of Soby's growing passion for more unsettling art.

He acquired a number of smoothly painted, enigmatic works by the neo-Romantics Eugene Berman and Christian Bérard. Then, when Soby and Chick Austin mounted the Picasso retrospective, they both coveted two diminutive neoclassical paintings, one from 1921, the other from 1922. The artist had earmarked them for his family, but changed his mind because he was so pleased with the

American show. The Atheneum bought the statuesque 1922 *Nude Woman,* a weighty presence in spite of its size of 7½ × 5½ inches, while Soby acquired a tempera on wood that measured a mere 5⅞ × 3⅞ inches. The size of a postcard, Soby's *Nude Seated on a Rock* looms monumental and confident. Its ability to do so in spite of its small dimensions resulted in an unusual incident when Soby lent the painting to a midwestern museum several years after he bought it. The museum neglected to find out its actual measurements and sent a moving van to pick it up. Standing at the entrance of his West Hartford house, Soby couldn't get over the sight of three burly drivers lumbering toward the door to pick up a painting that he handed to them from one hand; carrying it off, they glared back at him over their shoulders as if he had played a wicked trick on them. But the confusion of the curators who had sent them was completely understandable, both because the work seemed so large in reproduction and because some of Picasso's neoclassical canvases were actually very big.

Then, in 1935, Soby purchased four major de Chiricos of the "metaphysical period"—1911 to 1917. To do so he sold Degas's *Woman Putting on Her Gloves* back to Wildenstein. At de Chirico's show at the Pierre Matisse Gallery, Soby had become "like a man gone crazy with lust."[31] Wanting more than he could afford, he had decided that selling the Degas was the solution. To exchange a Degas for de Chiricos is like giving up a Social Register wife who has gone to the right schools for a younger, wilder woman. Soby in fact kept to well-bred wives—although in that arena too he periodically made exchanges—but with paintings he was more and more interested in territory that other people scarcely understood at all.

The de Chiricos fit in perfectly with *After Picasso,* the book Soby published in 1935. He wrote it in the attic of his West Hartford house, where Russell Hitchcock would often visit to give editorial advice and Austin frequently proffered comments. Soby borrowed the idea for his title from Clive Bell's *Since Cézanne;* it didn't suggest that the painters under discussion replaced Picasso—rather that they were the natural followers for whom Picasso had paved the way. The first section focused on the neo-Romantics—primarily Bérard, Tchelitchew, and the Berman brothers; the second on Surrealism.

Giorgio de Chirico was the artist whom Soby credited above all. De Chirico "had provided the central starting point both for the reveries of the neo-romantics and for the affronts to logic of the surrealist painters."[32] The Italian's early credo—that he wanted to paint what he saw with his eyes closed—was central. The world that had nurtured Jim Soby stressed order and logic: the facts one could take in through wide-open eyes. Insurance executives and trust officers opt above all for rational explanations and systematic procedures—whether at their desks or on the fairways. This young gentleman, however, longed to legitimize the mysterious and inexplicable. No painting better glorified the puzzling, disconcerting side of existence than de Chirico's 1914 *The Enigma of a Day,* which was one of the pictures Soby bought from Pierre Matisse in that grand sweep of 1935. *Enigma* shows a late nineteenth-century statue of a properly dressed citizen, situated in a simplified piazza. The piazza, which is occupied by various ambiguous objects, recedes sharply toward two towers. In its surface appearance the composition is rather tame and literal, certainly not the same sort of affront as Picasso's *Seated Woman.* But, like most dream sequences, it resembled reality only to contradict it.

The large canvas (72⅜ × 55½ inches) had been a central monument of the Surrealist movement when it hung in André Breton's apartment. A number of the key Surrealists had been photographed together around it. They considered it pivotal to their immersion in dream life. They drew up a questionnaire concerning its contents, and filled it out to indicate what aspects of the subconscious the scene portrayed, and what each object meant. The statue, heroic and vulgar at the same time, evoked an inexplicable sort of nostalgia—and, to some viewers, contempt—for the values of a dramatically different era. For better or worse, it embodied the pose and propriety of their fathers' and grandfathers' generation. This painting enabled perceptive onlookers to assess such standards, and their own reactions to them, with the most modern and alert vision. James Thrall Soby shared the passionate wish of the Harvard Society founders not just to coast along following the patterns and tastes of an earlier generation. Their common goal was to understand previous values and to establish different truths for the present.

The new vision allowed unprecedented sensuousness in paintings like Crowninshield's Braque *Still Life* that the Harvard Society had shown in its second exhibition, and radical fantasy in work like de Chirico's. *Enigma* and three other paintings Soby bought—*The Great Metaphysical Still Life, The Duo,* and *The Faithful Survivor*—were an affront to the usual way of ordering things and to decorum.

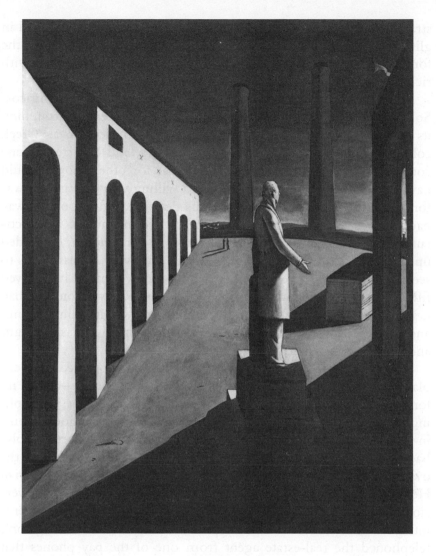

Giorgio de Chirico, The Enigma of the Day, *1914. Oil on canvas,*
6'1¼" × 55".

The Great Metaphysical Still Life was an odd juxtaposition of thick
boxy picture frames and skeletal easels, one frame containing a
painting of a lovely Renaissance villa with fountain and gardens, another supporting a panel on which two crusty breads—akin to both
bones and to human excrement—are mounted. *The Faithful Survivor*
is a complex assemblage of dismembered scaffolding and other

strange forms in which some tempting small biscuits—wrapped in glittering papers that are the essence of small luxury—dominate the foreground. It was a startling juxtaposition of deep anxiety with rich, if slight, everyday pleasures.

At about the same time that he was acquiring his de Chiricos, Soby bought his new house in Farmington. The events surrounding its purchase had many of the elements of a de Chirico canvas: Greek columns, unknown spaces, bizarre characters, and occurrences one could not have possibly anticipated. What for other people would have been a dream sequence they would willingly have forgotten was for Soby the occasion of a momentous decision. He was on his way back to West Hartford from a farm he owned in Canton, Connecticut, when, after going through the center of Farmington, he headed up a country road. In retrospect he wasn't sure why, unless it was to see the house of a prep school friend with whom he had stayed fifteen years earlier. Suddenly he saw a Greek Revival house he had never before noticed. Its grounds were overgrown, its paint peeling, and parts of the structure dilapidated. But it had a "for sale" sign, and Soby instantly fell "in love" with it.[33]

He knocked on the door. One of the owners appeared. She explained that she and her brother—the coproprietor—could no longer take care of the place. Soby walked in. Then, as he was looking up at the high ceilings and thinking that these were good rooms in which to hang paintings, he "fell over a soft, heavy object."[34] Soby had in fact tripped on a seated woman who was the niece of the owner of the house as well as the daughter of a man named Brian Hooker. Soby knew that Hooker was the translator of his favorite version of *Cyrano de Bergerac*. Everything about the place and these events intrigued him. He immediately proceeded to the local drugstore, telephoned the real-estate agent from one of the pay phones that had helped make his family their fortune, and offered the asking price for the place—even though he did not know the condition of the building or how much land was included. Within two hours of having first laid eyes on it, he had bought a new house—much as this annoyed his wife when he broke the news back at Westwood Road.

Soby realized that evening, however, that the four small square parlors would not accommodate his paintings and sculpture. So the next day he phoned Henry Russell Hitchcock to ask him to design a wing. When Hitchcock asked if the house was sided in clapboard or sheathing, the proud owner had no idea at all. But he quickly drove

by again and discovered it was flat sheathing, which is what Hitchcock had hoped for. Hitchcock came up with a plan, and Soby hired
a builder on a cost-plus basis so that he would not have to waste time
on estimates and contracts.

By January of 1936 he and Mimi had moved in. In no time at all
the place was in shape for them to give a housewarming that included a performance of The Friends and Enemies of Modern Music.
In the following month they hosted their parties both before and
after the Paper Ball.

All sorts of people converged at the Greek Revival structure. Le
Corbusier visited, and, standing on the flat roof of Hitchcock's
wing, proposed a roof garden. The Swiss architect also offered to
design a tree house in a large tulip tree nearby, and to link it with the
roof by a concrete ramp—although unfortunately this was another
Hartford-area project that failed to materialize. A few months after
moving in, Soby discovered a well behind Hitchcock's addition, and
commissioned Sandy Calder to do a standing mobile as a wellhead.
It was about twenty-five feet high. The main element was a long
horizontal metal pole on which a heavy circular form on one end
balanced a bucket on the other; here Calder had been influenced by
the elbow pieces of medieval suits of armor. Whenever the bucket
was lowered into the well, a series of smaller circular forms along
the pole gyrated up and down. The contractor for the piece—at the
Fuller Welding Company in downtown Hartford—thought both
Soby and Calder totally mad, but the artist and patron were delighted to see Calder's largest piece to date get erected, and to watch
its carefree motion in the breeze.

While Calder was assembling the wellhead and adjusting its balance outside the house, Eugene Berman was inside painting five panels in the dining room. Their work had little relationship, however.
The sculptor injected deliberate disarray into abstract forms; his
thinking could hardly have been more modern. Berman, on the
other hand, carefully organized representational imagery, in a style
in the mainstream tradition of European painting. Calder's only
comment on what was going on in the dining room was that it
needed fresh air. But Soby had space for both approaches.

Soby's relationship with Berman was similar to Eddie Warburg's
with Gaston Lachaise. For a time the collector supported the painter
in his Paris studio in exchange for artworks. He had discovered Berman at Julien Levy's, which, more than any other gallery, was his

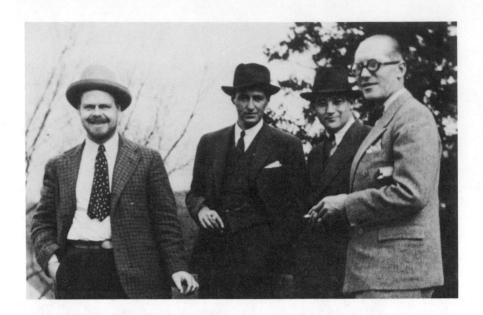

Above: From the left, Henry Russell Hitchcock, an unidentified person, James Thrall Soby, and Le Corbusier on the roof of the Sobys' house in Farmington, Connecticut, 1936. Below: Henry Russell Hitchcock and Chick Austin in front of Balthus's The Street, c. 1938, Soby House, Farmington.

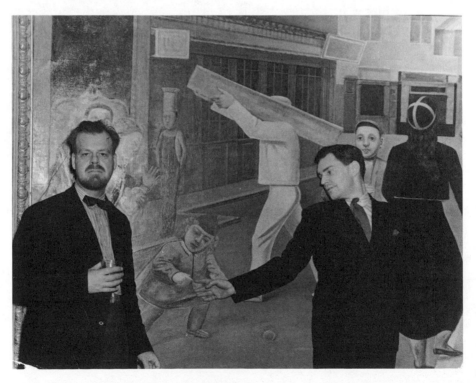

source for Surrealism and neo-Romanticism—although he regularly
frequented Pierre Matisse's and Kirk Askew's. At one point Soby
and Levy had been part of a group who had a contract with Berman
in which each member agreed to buy one painting annually, sight
unseen. Then, when the other members of the group dropped out,
Soby and Levy kept it going as a twosome, simply buying a larger
number of paintings. At that point he commissioned the dining
room murals.

In 1934 Soby had gone to the first solo exhibition of Balthasar
Klossowski de Rola—known as Balthus—at the Galerie Pierre in
Paris. Balthus, twenty-six years old, was two years Soby's junior.
Soby could hardly have latched onto the work of anyone more passionate or contemptuous of convention. The artist was both tremendously knowledgeable about the processes of painting and uniquely
imaginative. In a style nourished by traditional techniques, Balthus
captured a singular and extraordinary vision. Soby had admired one
painting in particular. It was the large—76¾ × 94½ inches—canvas
called *La Rue (The Street)* that Balthus had painted the preceding
year. Having brooded since then about not having purchased it, he
was greatly relieved when he returned to the gallery in 1937—almost
three years later—and to his astonishment found that the work was
still available. Now that he had space for this huge work in his new
house, Soby bought it. He was the first American to buy one of
Balthus's works and bring it back to American shores.

The Street depicts an assemblage of figures going about their
everyday life on the short Rue Bourbon-Le-Château in the sixth ar-
rondissement of Paris. What makes them arresting isn't just their
faces and costumes and poses, but above all Balthus's extraordinary
handling of paint and the bravura of the broad planes of the picture
composition. Balthus has depicted the stance and the angles of the
arms of each of the enigmatic nine figures with rare authority. At the
same time, he has given rich rhythm to the composition as a whole.
In his subtle paint surfaces and the richness of his color juxtapositions, Balthus puts painters like Léonide and the other neo-
Romantics to shame. Here was someone as mysterious and literarily
intriguing as the other painters who had captivated Soby, but with
aesthetic taste and skills that made him practically the equal of Watteau and Piero della Francesca. Balthus could animate a surface,
work paint, and establish forms as deftly as almost anyone.

Almost two decades after he bought it, Soby wrote about *The
Street,*

The figures have an hypnotic intensity, as though seen in a dream or viewed on a moving-picture film which abruptly and inexplicably has stopped on its sprockets. It seems likely that at this moment Balthus was especially intrigued by Seurat's ability to freeze contemporary life at a moment of poetic and ageless dignity; the figure of the chef in *The Street* is closely related to Seurat. The other figures are puppet-like in their sleepwalking irrationality, yet at the same time alive and majestically composed.[35]

It had many of the elements that most captivated him: a dreamlike trance, a defiance of easy explanations, and visual grandeur.

There were reasons why *The Street* had not been sold since the American collector had first seen it. For one thing, many collectors were put off by its size. But the main difficulty was a pair of figures on the left-hand side of the canvas. A young girl in a red cardigan is trying to escape a demonic young boy who has come upon her from behind. The boy not only grips her firmly by her left wrist with his left hand, and wedges his right calf between her legs to hold her in place, but—with the fingers of his right hand extended in an aggressively sexual way—reaches over the hem of her hiked-up skirt toward her genitals. The boy is, in Soby's words—"strangely Mongolian-looking . . . , his face taut with easily decipherable excitement."[36]

When he bought the painting, Soby had considered the position of the boy's hand a challenge. He knew that U.S. Customs might take it askance. But he also knew that the customs officials in Hartford, which was then a port of entry and where he had previously had numerous artworks inspected, already considered him an unusual character. When they opened the crate containing *The Street,* they simply confirmed that it was an original work of art and hence duty-free. One of them even commented that this was the first of Soby's imported paintings that he liked. Like Eddie Warburg, Soby often provided customs officials with plenty to talk about.

Soby hung the painting in his living room in Farmington. He enjoyed visitors' reactions to its licentiousness. One imagines him eager to point out the more provocative elements to his friends on whom other aspects of the painting would be lost. At first no one minded. But in time it grew awkward to have *The Street* on view. The year he acquired the canvas he divorced Mimi, with whom he had an adopted son, Peter. The next year Soby married Eleanor

Howland, known as Nellie. He had first met her when she was
Chick Austin's secretary, and had stayed in touch with her when she
became Alfred Barr's and then Julien Levy's secretary after she had
moved to New York to be near her aging mother. At first Peter was
living with Mimi, but in the late 1930s, when Peter was about five
years old, he moved to Farmington to live with Jim and Nellie. They
wanted to do everything they could to put his life on an even keel,
and it didn't help when Peter's friends began to titter wildly over the
Balthus. They carried home tales of the naughty painting at Peter's
house. Some of the parents challenged Soby. His defense that Giovanni Bellini's *The Feast of the Gods* at the National Gallery was
equally explicit carried little weight in a New England town. At first
Soby thought the solution might be to put a screen in front of the
work. He discussed that possibility with Russell Hitchcock—but
every time they considered its design they simply ended up having a
drink and laughing about it.[37] Finally Soby stored the picture in the
fireproof vault he had built adjacent to the garage.

Years later, Soby decided that he would bequeath *The Street* to the
Museum of Modern Art. But he feared that the museum would
never hang it. In 1956 he wrote to Balthus and explained the problem.[38] He dropped the hint that several restorers had offered to alter
the lurid passage, but that of course he would not let anyone but the
artist himself change it. In spite of the tact, he feared that this remark
would be the end of the valued friendship he and the notoriously
uncompromising Balthus had developed over the years. But, to Soby's astonishment, Balthus wrote back that if Soby would send him
the canvas, he would try to change the offensive passage. "When I
was young, I wanted to shock. Now it bores me,"[39] Balthus wrote.
After holding the painting for several months, the artist returned it
with the boy's hand moved upward and the extended fingers bent
inward, folded into a fist locked safely over the girl's dress.

When Soby had first brought *The Street* home to Farmington, it did
more than startle viewers with its naughtiness. The subtle mystery
of its frieze of characters riveted a handful of cognoscenti. There was
a lot to marvel at. The well-worked, frescolike impasto absorbs light
to an unusual degree. The posed cast of characters makes the picture
a commentary on daily rituals, enriched by the demonic trance of
many of the faces. Those heads forever turned away from us have
the allure of the unknown. The Atheneum set was suitably moved.

Paul Cooley visited Balthus that year in Paris where, to his surprise, the artist asked if he could do a painting of Cooley's wife, Jane. An extraordinary portrait of this tweedy West Hartford woman was the result. Several of Soby's friends and neighbors bought paintings at the otherwise rather unsuccessful exhibition that Balthus had at Pierre Matisse's gallery in New York in 1938. Soby himself bought Balthus's *Joan Miró and His Daughter Dolores* at that exhibition, but released it before even taking possession of it—because Alfred Barr wanted it for the Museum of Modern Art. Barr had managed the difficult feat of obtaining funds for it, and Soby felt that a public institution should always have priority over a private collector, even if the collector had gotten there first.

Chick Austin acquired for the Atheneum Balthus's richly loaded 1937 *Still Life*. Its earthy tones and textures liken it to Chardin's work, as do its lively rhythms and depiction of reflected and refracted light. This is a kitchen still life as they have existed for centuries—a firm wooden table, a basket heaped with bread, a lovely flask and handsome goblet filled with refreshing sustenance (presumably white wine). But in the center of the composition, lying head down on the table, there is a hammer. It has just struck. A second, thin-necked decanter lies shattered on its side, with broken glass fragments—they are an extraordinary feat of painting—surrounding it. The sharp knife that pierces the handsome half-loaf of crusty country bread looks equally destructive, like a weapon more than a kitchen implement. Even the fork that spears a potato at the other end of the table appears to attack and violate it.

Balthus had managed to lead the existence of a privileged European nobleman. To many he was the Count de Rola, able to paint in a fine Paris studio and in pleasant country châteaus. But he was not impervious to what was happening in the Europe around him. The treachery and tumult of his *Still Life* was akin to that of Miró's 1937 *Still Life with Old Shoe,* a painting that Jim Soby would buy in 1944. Balthus knew and admired Miró. Miró's studio was on the second floor of the Galerie Pierre; it was there that the Spaniard worked on *Still Life with Old Shoe* for about a month at nearly the same time that Balthus was having his exhibition below. The colors of the Miró are lurid and chemical-looking while Balthus's are restrained and earth-toned, but there too a chunk of a loaf of bread resembles a skull, and a fork stuck into an apple seems to impale it. These paintings depict destruction.

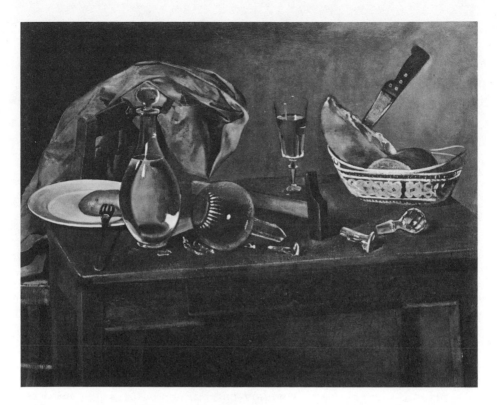

Balthus, Still Life, *1937. Oil on canvas, 31⅞ × 39⅜".*

In Miró's case the specific violence that he had in mind was the Spanish Civil War. What Balthus's *Still Life* reflects isn't one historical event so much as an attitude. And that attitude was, at the time that Chick Austin acquired the canvas for Hartford, beginning to take over the world. Broken glass wasn't just falling on people's kitchen tables. November 9, 1938, was Kristallnacht. One could still turn to the back of the newspaper to read the dance and art criticism or to check out Lucius Beebe's society accounts. But when the front-page headlines reported deliberate smashing, looting, and burning— and the information that in twenty-four hours a thousand German Jews had been killed, and thirty thousand arrested—it was impossible to pay attention to anything else.

For Eddie Warburg, the excitement of the ballet began to wear thin even before the rumblings of war overtook him. Toward the end of the 1930s, he was losing the drive to fight for new art forms. Like Chick Austin in Hartford, Warburg gradually wearied of opposition. For years they had both enjoyed defending unpopular points of view. But as time went on, Warburg and Austin were losing the patience to combat yet again the voices that said they were backing worthless causes. And they tired of struggling for the funds to do so.

Warburg had long been concerned about the audience he was serving. At Bryn Mawr he had come to feel that all that his students really cared about was the patina of sophistication. Nowhere in America had he seen real public enthusiasm of the type he had admired in the Soviet Union. With the ballet crowd, he began to lose faith completely. He questioned why he was working himself to the bone, and depleting his fortune, for people who seemed only interested in dressing up, seeing one another, and being written about by Lucius Beebe. He was providing entertainment for a few insiders who didn't really need it, not for the public at large. And given the realities that most of the population was confronting on a daily basis in that time period, this shortcoming seemed particularly heinous.

Warburg questioned his motives for everything. He could always manage an upbeat posture before the public, but in fact was full of self-doubt. He had written Agnes Mongan of his misgivings about museum work. He felt he had done 37 Beekman Place more to be part of the in crowd and gain the esteem of people like Johnson and Kirstein than out of real aesthetic commitment. Now the ballet was beginning to feel more like personal antics than that idealistic enterprise he and Kirstein had discussed at Harvard as the best possible combination of various art forms, bestowing benefits to the broadest group of creators.

But although he was losing his conviction, Warburg made a couple of all-out efforts before he entirely put on the brakes. For one thing, as everyone who had been at the Paper Ball knew, Tchelitchew was in America. In Europe Tchelitchew was well known for his set and costume designs. Shortly after arriving in America at the end of 1935, he had told Lincoln Kirstein that he would like to design a production for the American Ballet at the Metropolitan Opera House. Eddie Warburg agreed to foot the bill for the sets and costumes. They settled on the opera-ballet *Orpheus and Eurydice,* with music by Christoph Willibald Gluck, to be presented at the Metropolitan on May 22, 1936. Balanchine had complained that the Met used the ballet company as "a diner uses a napkin—to wipe his mouth before resuming his meal";[40] this would be an opportunity for ballet to be the main course.

Warburg had complained about the brocades and silks of the Met's productions. The scenery he funded was their antithesis. It was made of chicken wire, cheesecloth, and dead birch branches. The costumes revealed as much nudity as the times would allow: transparent T-shirts, translucent veils, and gauze netting, worn by characters who had wings mounted on their shoulders or lyres strapped across their backs. Tchelitchew had proved, after all, that torn paper was the stuff of fancy-dress balls. He liked to inspire a rethinking of standards. At the same time, he achieved stunning sights. For Lincoln Kirstein—whose faith in the ballet seemed to be ever ascending, even as Warburg's faded—the production of *Orpheus and Eurydice* became "the most beautiful visual spectacle I have seen on any stage."[41]

Tchelitchew's costume sketches suggested the atmosphere intended for the performance. The basic material was "artificial silk," a standard color "ox blood." The rough crosshatching indicated people with their arms stretched as far as possible. The idea was a look of longing, of reaching with all the intensity one could muster. There was nothing restrained or proper here; what Tchelitchew wanted in his characters, and Balanchine in his dancing, was raw emotion.

Lincoln Kirstein described the scenario:

The entire production was conceived without an element of paint. Rather, pigment was actually light. . . . Backgrounds were impalpable, chosen for their capacity to transmit, reflect, or change light. . . .

When the curtain rose, Orpheus, a big boy [danced by Lew Christiansen] in a transparent T-shirt and black trunks, impassive, frozen in grief, watches the construction of Eurydice's memorial monument. Friends and neighbors try to comfort him, bringing reminders of his lost happiness. On cross beams they drape rags, stack brooms, ladders, pots, ordinary objects of domestic ritual. This homely structure is capped by a cloth with Eurydice's wan portrait on a translucent veil. All except Orpheus himself were covered in gray body makeup, shades of sorrow. . . .

Hell, the second scene, was a Piranesian prison, crossbars of which were made of braided barbed wire. . . . Orpheus' crystal lyre seemed to draw blood from red-orange silk flames. Demon guards, masked in horse skulls with manes of serpents, brandishing snaky whips, lashed gangs of chained prisoners suggesting a Last Judgment or Doré's engravings for *Paradise Lost* or Dante's *Inferno*. This underworld was composed of stone and fire, chain and bone.

In the third scene, Orpheus' lyre led him through an airless Umbrian landscape in some tireless limbo. Birch trunks, stripped of leaves, hung in midair over a massive mound or burial barrow. A solemn procession of graybeards, vestals, and adolescent youths offered their meager homage of bone-dry laurel. In this anomalous ambience, dancers were swathed in doubled nettings of blue and violet which read as changeable taffeta, revealing naked bodies inside. . . .

In the final scene, spread across the wide sky, was a self-illuminated Milky Way, thousands of stars superimposed across the traditional diagrams of Lyre, Dipper, Cassiopeia's Chair, standing against a vibrating mosaic of tiny stars powdering the black velvet night.

The Warburgs had previously commissioned expensive jewelry constellations at Cartier's. There the medium was diamonds connected by thin platinum wires. Now the materials they funded were—by a combination of choice and necessity—as "valueless" as possible. Eurydice wore "mother-of-pearl chiffon which barely veiled her."[42] Amor had goose-feather pinions. The goal was that materials should be as light as possible, or disappear entirely. The vocalists and choristers sang, unseen, from the pit.

It was hardly the taste of the times. If Tchelitchew wanted to do a costume party for rich folk, that was one thing, but his ideas would win little approval in the opera circuit. Samuel Chotzinoff, in the *New York Evening Post,* wrote that the sets expressed, no doubt, something deep and cosmic, since they eluded identification. I thought that the Garden of the Temple of Love rather resembled a huge portion of sweetbreads. At the final curtain a backdrop with curious designs of lines and dots began to shimmer and glow, looking for all the world like an illuminated road map of Connecticut.[43]

Time, in an article entitled "Travesty on Gluck," called this "the most inept production that present-day opera-goers have witnessed on the Metropolitan stage." Hades was "a giant cage contraption which housed furies no more terrifying than Punch & Judy puppets." As for Balanchine's choreography, it suffered from "bogus conceptions."[44] The *New York Sun*'s take on the event was that "a more melancholy, ineffective and incongruous performance of Gluck's opera could hardly be accomplished."[45] *The New York Times* said,

So far as last night's production is concerned, it is regrettable to be obliged to say that it ranks as the most inept and unhappy spectacle this writer has ever seen in the celebrated lyric theatre. . . . It is ugly and futile, impudent and meddlesome, wholly ineffective in performance.

It was the choreography and position of the singers that took the worst lambasting, but Tchelitchew's sets were deemed

equally absurd. There is no good reason to discuss it in detail; but it is to be added that there is hardly any excuse, even in the name of original experiment, for this mannered, uninventive and incongruous fabrication being presented on the Metropolitan stage.

The people who would disagree with that viewpoint, and moreover were to blame for this travesty, were "certain sophisticates and dilettantes of the operatic stage." It was as if the writer—whose name was not given—was pointing his finger directly at Kirstein and Warburg.[46]

The "sophisticates and dilettantes" had their champions, however. Glenway Wescott followed up *Time*'s review of *Orpheus* with a letter of rebuttal. He claimed that *Orpheus,* "the only original undertaking of the opera association this season, gave as much pleasure to a certain public as offence to the critics." Wescott considered himself part of that public, "more deeply moved by the old myth than ever before." [47] He wrote that he and other people he knew longed for more such free and unconventional art.

Eddie Warburg was becoming discouraged, but voices like these, and his ongoing faith in Balanchine and Kirstein, were hard to resist. Balanchine deserved an even greater opportunity. It wasn't enough for him to choreograph opera ballets and curtain raisers for the Met. What was needed was an evening entirely of ballet.

In the winter of 1935–36, Igor Stravinsky was in America on a concert tour. That spring, Balanchine met with the Russian composer, whose work he adored. Balanchine, Kirstein, and Warburg decided that the all-ballet evening at the Metropolitan Opera House should be a Stravinsky festival. Balanchine would choreograph two extant Stravinsky works: *Apollon Musagète* and *Le Baiser de la Fée*—a tribute to Tchaikovsky based on a story by Hans Christian Andersen. In addition, Eddie Warburg commissioned the composer to create one entirely new work to be written for the American Ballet Company. He agreed to pick up the tab for the music, sets, costumes, and other expenses with the idea that the proceeds of the production would benefit the American Ballet School's scholarship fund.

For more than ten years Stravinsky had had the idea of a ballet in which dancers represented playing cards against a backdrop of a green baize card table in a gaming house. He had been intrigued by cards ever since he played *durachki* as a child. When he was young his family traveled to German spas, where he developed a fascination with casinos. Gambling suggested an interplay of numerical combinations that seemed a natural basis for a ballet score. He felt that "Playing cards are ideal material for a ballet if only because of the rich possibilities in combining and grouping the four suits." [48] M. Malaieff, [49] a friend of the composer's son Theodore, had suggested the specific theme of a poker game. Having already done some work on the idea, once he received the invitation of the American Ballet Company, Stravinsky completed the piece in the last few months of 1936. He called it *Jeu de Cartes: Ballet en Trois Donnes (The Card Game: Ballet in Three Deals)*.

For each of the three deals, the shufflings and handing out of the cards—or dancers—made a ceremonial introduction. Then, after the cards were played, they were cleared by the gigantic fingers of invisible croupiers. Throughout this action, the powerful joker reigned supreme. Omniscient because he could become any card in the pack, the joker was defeated only at the end, under the mightier force of a royal flush of hearts.

To put a poker game on the stage of the Metropolitan Opera House must have fulfilled some of Eddie Warburg's dearest dreams. Like Calder's wire figures, this redefined the nature of art. The rough-and-tumble was fine. As with *Alma Mater,* here was American subject matter—and of a type that touched a wider audience than did Ivy League high jinks. But at the same time that Stravinsky's ballet evoked a playful backroom diversion, it was a game of moral implications. The characters who at first appear to be omnipotent end up not so powerful after all. The demonic, self-possessed joker is defeated. Not only that, but the kings, queens, and jacks—seemingly the rulers—are eventually deposed by small cards that band together in an effective group. What the American Ballet Company was putting forward wasn't just new in sound and style. It was revolutionary in content.

This radical tale was told in a lighthearted voice. Stravinsky's music for the ballet is highly melodic, rhythmically complex yet carefree. In its twenty-three-minute-long nonstop course, it makes allusions to work by Beethoven, Rossini, Ravel, and Johann Strauss, as well as to Stravinsky's own earlier work and to jazz. Balanchine's choreography is similarly grounded in tradition, parody, and pure invention.

Jeu de Cartes was a close collaboration between composer and choreographer. Stravinsky went to New York to attend rehearsals. When Balanchine needed extra phrases of music to complete a sequence, the composer would provide them the next day. But generally Stravinsky had the upper hand. He knew the vocabulary of dancing almost as well as he understood music, and he often eliminated a pirouette or proposed other changes. When Balanchine's directives had the dancers in a fan shape like a hand of cards, the composer suggested the repetition of an earlier sequence. Lincoln Kirstein, in a newspaper interview of the time, described the manner in which Stravinsky made these points:

> He has about him the slightly disconcerting concentration of a research professor or a newspaper editor, the serious preoccupation of a man who has so many interrelated activities to keep

straight and in smooth running order that he finds it necessary to employ a laconic, if fatherly and final, politeness. The effect is all the more odd coming from a man who is at once so small in stature and who, at least from his photographs, appears not to have changed a bit in twenty-five years. When he speaks, it seems to be the paternal mouthpiece of a permanent organization or institution, rather than a creative individual.[50]

Kirstein and Warburg asked the designer Irene Sharaff to do the scenery and costumes for *Jeu de Cartes*. They urged her to study medieval playing cards and the tarot, so that by the time Stravinsky got to America, Sharaff had already done forty sketches giving the cards and backdrops a style that conjured a period five centuries earlier. Stravinsky thought this was all wrong. He called for Sharaff to drop the flourishes and make the dancers into ordinary, everyday playing cards that any viewer might recognize in an instant as old friends. Everything should be legible to the poker players in the audience.

The company rehearsed tirelessly for the Stravinsky Festival. These performances had to be the company's best. Kirstein asked Tchelitchew to design the set for either *Apollon* or *Le Baiser de la Fée,* but after the burning he had received for *Orpheus* he refused. So for *Baiser* Kirstein hired Alice Halicka, a decorator who was the wife of the painter Marcoussis. She came up with a set of tufted satin covered with glitter. For *Apollon* Stewart Chaney devised backdrops based on Poussin. It all had great promise.

Shortly before the actual event, Warburg decided that the musical accompaniment was inadequate. The Metropolitan Opera orchestra wasn't good enough. He arranged for the New York Philharmonic—of which his father was one of the major backers—to perform; Stravinsky agreed to conduct. April 27 and 28 of 1937 were to be the American Ballet Company's greatest moments so far.

Above all, everybody was eagerly anticipating the premiere of *Jeu de Cartes*. Publicity photographs whetted the public appetite. These shots showed the dancer William Dollar, George Balanchine, Stravinsky, and Eddie Warburg seated on cheap metal folding chairs at a folding card table. Dollar and Balanchine are in working clothes. The immaculately groomed Stravinsky wears a dark suit and white pocket handkerchief, and has a cigarette in a long holder hanging from his mouth. Warburg looks like the model of a well-brought-up

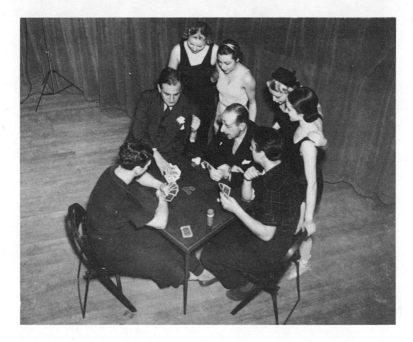

Publicity photograph for Jeu de Cartes: *poker game with Edward Warburg, Igor Stravinsky, William Dollar, and Georges Balanchine.*

young gentleman in his three-piece suit, with his father's signature boutonniere of a carnation. Four lovely young women, presumably ballerinas, look on. A crucial moment in the game has just occurred. A truly poker-faced Warburg, utterly cool, lays his cards on the table, faceup. Balanchine, Dollar, and Stravinsky, their cards still in their hands, look on. Stravinsky has a fantastic expression on his face, like a gambler who cannot believe his eyes, or at least doesn't want to believe what he sees. It seems that with this hand, anyway, the rich have just gotten richer.

The actual production opened with Irene Sharaff's rendition of the vast green baize gaming table, which she set against a crimson background. The table was flanked by two greatly oversized candelabra, near to which there were entrance doors that imitated decks of cards. The dancing cards entered and shuffled themselves. Then they took their positions according to the rules of Hoyle. Leda Anchutina danced around as the queen of spades, Lew Christiansen as the king of hearts. William Dollar—the joker—would periodically dance in

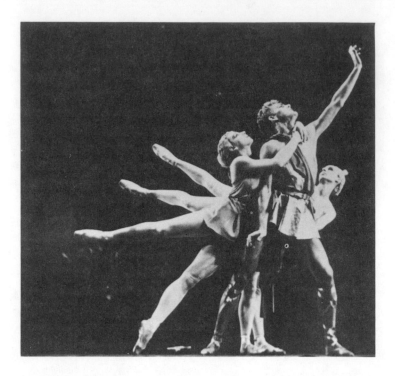

Above: Apollon—*Apollo and the three Muses. Below: Orpheus and Eurydice. Performance photograph by Richard Tucker.*

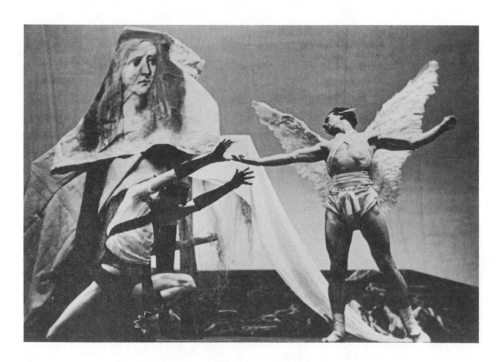

to make winning hands, until he suffered his ultimate defeat. The total effect was lively and original, and although *Apollon* and *Le Baiser de la Fée* were not as startling, both were romantic and enticing.

The relative success of the Stravinsky Festival was not enough, however. By the end of the next season, the American Ballet and the Metropolitan Opera went their separate ways. It was hard to tell who tired of whom first. According to Kirstein, the Met's director Edward Johnson "had hired the American Ballet on the promise of its youth and Warburg's backing, but he was not prepared to support us in ambitious aims for the renovation of dancing in opera, or to permit us a free hand in the development of a ballet repertory within his house." [51] The dancers were having a rough time on the opera stage. When Lew Christiansen was paired with Rosa Ponselle in *Carmen,* she refused to rehearse. In the actual performance the great soprano, after gulping a bit from a goblet of wine—in truth grapefruit juice— threw the remainder of the juice into Christiansen's eye before pulling down his head and kissing him passionately.

Meanwhile, Kirstein had formed a new organization called "The American Ballet Caravan," and Eddie Warburg was feeling more and more drained. The Stravinsky opening may have looked glamorous to some of his pals in the audience, but in truth it was no more relaxing for Warburg than his twenty-sixth birthday party at the moment that the clouds burst. Just before performance time on opening night, Warburg had asked Stravinsky to take his position in the orchestra pit. Suddenly Stravinsky "announced without warning, 'I am sorry—I am not conducting.'"[52] He was irked because the program said "*Apollon,* music by Igor Stravinsky" rather than "*Apollon,* ballet by Igor Stravinsky." Warburg worked things out, and Stravinsky conducted, but controversies like this were taking their toll. Above all, there was the recurring problem of who the audience was. Tickets were expensive that night at the Met, and Depression dollars were scarce. From Warburg's viewpoint, "this almost guaranteed a mindless audience, to whom the high spots of these evenings were the intermissions. . . . I asked myself: Why do I continue wanting to be involved in this strange form of torture? I decided that first night that I had had it."[53] He had lost the will to knock himself out for an overprivileged elite that didn't even appreciate what it was looking at. Warburg resigned from the American Ballet immediately following the Stravinsky Festival.

He had spent a fortune; his family's gibes about all the money he

was giving away had turned into real concern. He had also grown
fatigued by endless critical rebuke. What once seemed new and exciting had come to be a rugged routine. But more than any other
factor, the key reason for his change in priorities lay elsewhere. Warburg had come to realize that the essentials of existence had little to
do with what went on once the curtain went up or the museum
doors opened. In April of 1937 Igor Stravinsky's greatest problem
may have been a misattribution in program notes; little more than a
year later, there were graver issues to deal with. In May of 1938 Stravinsky's work—along with that of Schoenberg, Berg, Hindemith,
and Weill—was the subject of an exhibition in Germany called "En-
tartete Musik," or "Degenerate Music." The show in Dusseldorf displayed "decadent," "Jewish," and "cultural Bolshevist" music, and
blasted recordings of samples of this unacceptable material. A reproduction of a portrait of Stravinsky hung on the largest wall. Underneath it a placard gave the instruction, "Judge from this whether or
not Stravinsky is a Jew."[54] Without the freedom to live and work,
there could be no room for art.

THE WAR AND
ITS AFTERMATH

I

"The Second World War was the key experience of my time and it would have been impossible to avoid it. In fact, I loved it. I enjoyed the Army very much indeed." So stated Lincoln Kirstein when assessing the major achievements of his lifetime some forty-five years after he joined the U.S. Army.[1] As director of the School of American Ballet and Ballet Caravan, Kirstein had been fascinated with the processes of orderly physical training. What concerned him were "disciplines toward extremity: how do you manage extreme situations, whether they're spiritual situations or physical situations or psychological situations. This is what ritual is developed to handle."[2] He had long had a penchant for military organization and structures. The breed of modernism that relishes abandon and the absence of restraints had never held sway for him. He had always adhered to rules for his rule-breaking endeavors. And he had always had a sense of purpose. So enlistment was a natural sequitur to all that had preceded. Kirstein served both as a courier and interpreter, and in the "arts and monuments" section of the U.S. Army. He landed in Normandy three weeks after D day, after which one of his many tasks was to drive General Patton's jeep. Subsequently, in the Steinberg Salt Mine at Alt Aussee, he helped discover and recover a vast collection of art looted by the Nazis and intended for Hitler's proposed Führer Museum in Linz.

Eddie Warburg had landed on the Normandy beaches the day after D day. But even if he and Kirstein had arrived at precisely the same time, they would have by then had far less in common than at Harvard or in Balanchine's studio. When Kirstein had gone on the road with the Ballet Caravan, Warburg had not joined him. Six months after the Stravinsky Festival, Felix Warburg's death had left his youngest son multiple tasks to replace his ballet work. Once issues of culture took a backseat, Eddie's circle of acquaintances had changed as well.

F. M. Warburg's death was major news for New Yorkers. The headline announcing it on the front page of the *Times* was in the same large type as headlines about the mayor's budget battle, Third Reich aggression in Czechoslovakia, and fighting between China and

Japan. The public was informed that Felix's wife and five children
had all been at his bedside at 1109 Fifth, and that his sons would bear
his coffin at Temple Emanu-El. To be one of those sons was something to reckon with. That front-page piece identified their father as
"an indefatigable worker in the fields of charity and social wel-
fare. . . . Few worthy causes failed to win his support and his own
business affairs were at all times subordinated to his philanthropic
interests." He was a key figure in organizations that benefited immigrants, nurses, underprivileged children, and the victims of Nazism. He had served on the boards and often been an officer of
various hospitals, museums, and educational institutions. He had
also helped found the Hebrew University of Jerusalem, and
started—with Louis Marshall—the Jewish Agency to work with the
British government in the administration of Palestine. Most recently,
in the year of his death, he had actively opposed the British plan for
the partition of Palestine and taken "a stand for a bi-national state
with the recommendation that further efforts be made to reconcile
interests of Arabs and Jews within the same community." While he
wanted Palestine "developed as a refuge for the oppressed peoples of
Eastern Europe and as a great Jewish cultural center," he was noted
for having "consistently opposed the idea of a Jewish state."[3] Above
all he had run the Joint Distribution Committee and helped form the
Federation for the Support of Jewish Philanthropic Societies. Governor Herbert Lehman, Mayor F. H. La Guardia, former President
Herbert Hoover, Rabbi Stephen Wise, Chaim Weizmann, and scores
of other public figures in America, England, and Palestine all praised
him lavishly.

These were values to live up to, and Frieda was not about to let
her family tradition flag. Her husband had continued her father's
work; now it was up to her sons. A few days after Felix's death she
called a meeting of her children in which she designated successors
for each of their father's responsibilities. Eddie's assignment was the
American Jewish Joint Distribution Committee.

For years Eddie had been free to rebel against the family style, but
with his father no longer alive, it became his job to uphold it. He
didn't have much grounding in things like JDC work, but in 1934 he
had been Felix's representative at a board of governors meeting of
the Hebrew University of Jerusalem that Felix had deliberately
avoided so as not to have to take a side in a confrontation between
his two friends Chaim Weizmann and Judah Magnes, and Eddie had

proved his diplomatic skills. As an arts patron he had shown his ability in getting people to work together and in rousing audience interest and had demonstrated his eagerness to free people from any sort of oppression. Now he would put his abilities and passions to new purpose. Eddie soon became chairman of the organization devoted to the rescue, relief, and rehabilitation of Jews wherever they were oppressed. This became the new direction of his life.

The woman with "class with a capital K" about whom Eddie Warburg had written Agnes Mongan was the recently divorced Mary Whelan Prue Currier. Striking, elegant, and articulate, Mrs. Currier was assistant fashion editor for *Vogue*. On December 6, 1939—exactly five years after the curtain had risen on *Alma Mater* on the stage of the Wadsworth Atheneum—Eddie Warburg and Mary Currier were married in the apartment of Condé Nast, her employer and his brother's father-in-law. The bride wore a beige crepe afternoon gown trimmed with Manchurian ermine, and carried a Manchurian ermine muff decorated with yellow orchids. The night before, when everyone was in evening clothes, the family raised their glasses to the betrothed pair on the last great occasion in the tapestry-filled dining room of 1109 Fifth Avenue. Eddie Warburg had begun a new life, and he had also returned home.

Warburg's everyday companions switched from people like Stravinsky and Balanchine to diplomats, writers, and socialites. He continued to own his paintings and sculpture and to sit on museum boards, but the linoleum and chrome of 37 Beekman Place were quickly replaced by chintz and Chippendale in the East Sixties. When he and Mary moved into a town house decorated by George Stacey, the man who had watched Sandy Calder paint the bathroom and Lachaise craft his portrait stayed mum. "Look, I don't want to interfere with your decor—you and Mary are working that out— but tell me something: where do you visualize that you're going to put the various paintings?" "On the wall," Stacey replied. At least it beat the squash court.

Warburg had learned to seek new territory rather than take the predictable course. As the supporter of Calder and Lachaise, he had admired candor and bravery; he sought them in new forms. He had always liked entertainments grounded in ordinary people's everyday reality like football and poker games; in the late 1930s, he reconsidered what everyday reality was. The former arts aficionado was con-

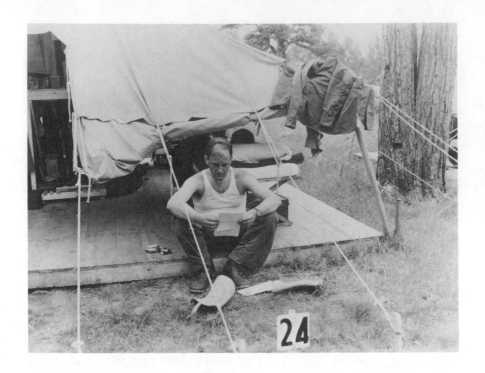

Edward Warburg at Citizens Military Training Camp in Plattsburg, New York, 1940.

tent to stump the country on a speaking tour for the JDC. He joined the New York Guard. He soon felt, however, that this was not enough for him. Because of what was happening in Germany, he decided to enlist. Not wanting to be part of the dreaded black-tie set or to use family position, and determined to be tested on his merits alone, he joined the army as a private. "Here at last was a chance for anonymity, a chance to get lost in the crowd, to demonstrate, at least to myself, just what if anything I had on the ball. I wanted to be free from the advantages and disadvantages of inheritance and publicity, and from the flattery of those who courted favor."[4]

From basic training on, Warburg proved himself. The way to do this was sometimes by providing entertainment. Early in his military career, he performed solo at a graduation ceremony from officers' candidate school; in a fireman's helmet from the local 5&10 and a greatly oversized overcoat covered with every discarded chevron and medal he could find, he parodied his instructors with an incomprehensible lecture on the use of obscure weapons. But by the time he had landed in Normandy as a captain in the First U.S. Army, life had become serious business. Six weeks after D day, when he checked up on the derelict headquarters of the JDC in Paris, he learned that ten thousand Jews were starving in Paris. The soup kitchens were desperate for supplies. Warburg arranged for food to be delivered immediately, and within a day he engineered an instant loan of sixty-five thousand dollars from the New York JDC office for relief for French refugees. Shortly after that, he took a role in Operation Lion—a complex mission to find the exiled King Leopold of Belgium—that earned him the Belgian Ordre de l'Officier de la Couronne.

II

In May of 1938 Hitler, Mussolini, Ribbentrop, and Ciano had a meeting of Axis partners in Florence, for which occasion the city's Fascist leaders put on a great military display. But for a while it seemed that the study of art history could go on unimpeded. To Agnes Mongan and Bernard Berenson, the politics of the Fogg mattered as much as the politics of Europe; the provenance of art objects still seemed more essential than the ramifications of the backgrounds of people.

As Berenson fine-tuned the plans for making I Tatti part of Harvard, he depended on Mongan to keep him entirely "au fait" about what was going on at the Fogg as people rose or fell from power. Mongan had a unique ability to remain objective about university politics, and to provide an accurate and unbiased account. Her explanation of Edward Forbes's resignation and planned retirement in the summer of 1938 was the only account of that event that made it comprehensible to him; she described the balance of power at the Fogg by remarking that Sachs always acceded to Forbes's wishes. Berenson thanked Mongan repeatedly for including him with the level of candor reserved for the inner circle. His letters to her were warm, beholden, and admiring. And once Mongan visited I Tatti itself that summer, she became as earnest and ardent as she would be to anyone in her life. She was overwhelmed by the experience of entering the baronial splendor of the great villa. There she felt respite from the midsummer Tuscan heat in the cool rooms with their sixteenth-century Bolognese furniture and masterpieces by Sassetta,

Bernardo Daddi, and others. She idled contentedly in the library that rivaled those of many universities. Before ascending to Settignano, Mongan had spent days looking at art for every minute that the Uffizi and other museums and churches were open. Not only did I Tatti offer more of the same intoxicating beauty, but her host had an intensity that matched her own. Berenson never tired of discussing this art, and making his own days as enchanted as the life depicted in Renaissance painting. "Dear San Bernardo da Settignano," Mongan wrote after her first series of calls to the villa,

> For the Fogg and above all to me, you have certainly assumed the rôle of a patron saint dispersing spiritual and temporal joys . . .
>
> My visit Sunday was a revelation (not only of weaknesses) but of beauty and astonishing richness. Why had no one told me you had such a vast quantity of really fabulous treasures? Why had I not heard of the enchanting Bonfigli, the magnificent Lorenzetti, the Daddi, and the wonderful Buddha's head to name the merest handful. I came away, after Nicky had completed my tour, in a real daze. When I came out of it I began to fear that, in my eagerness, I had kept you on your feet a long time in the middle of a hot day. I *hope* I did not exhaust you. . . .
>
> As for my visit of Friday night—I don't think I shall ever forget the sense of magic and the unearthly beauty which you lead [*sic*] me into when we emerged from the grove in darkness & there above us was I Tatti & the gardens in serene moonlight. Even now it seems scarsely [*sic*] possible that that peace & harmony & beauty was real enough to be touched & felt & lived in.
>
> Yes, your legend is wrong. The whole quality and flavor of it is wrong. But anyone who has created "I Tatti" merits a legend. Surely the right one, which is more exciting and wonderful than the wrong one, will begin to grow—must, if others have been moved as I have been, indeed continue to be, already growing. . . .
>
> > Devotedly,
> > Agnes[5]

Typically, Mongan was on a campaign. She would rectify Berenson's reputation. She had other wrongs to right as well. Eleven days later she wrote Berenson—whom by now she was addressing as "B.B."—from the Hotel des Alpes in Madonna di Campiglio, to voice her frustration at not seeing the drawings in the Pinacoteca in Bologna, where a new drawing and print cabinet were under construction:

It was absolutely impossible for me to see anything! I felt thwarted, tricked & enraged, until they let me go through the registrar's book and I saw there was nothing really worth seeing! However I'm going to start an agitation, when I have a moment, about restorations, repairs, and lendings. I don't think it's fair to concentrate all publicity efforts on what's to be seen. I think I'll suggest to the Editor of the Art news that next year when they make up their summer list of things to be seen, they should add an addenda of those which can't be! In the latter list this year would be the Bologna drawings, the San Vitale and Baptistry mosaics in Ravenna and the [frescoes in the] Vatican.

Do I sound horrid, cross & spiteful? I sincerely hope not, for I'd hate to have you think of me in those terms. I'm "letting out" to you because I know you can share my feelings & because I feel you may spare other pilgrims (who plan to tread the same paths I've just been over) some disappointment.

And yet every gallery and every museum in all Italy could have been locked and barred this year and my visit would still have been a successful one & not a failure—because there would have been all those wonderful & unforgettable hours with you at Settignano.

I don't know why you were so good to me, but I adored it all and I live in the hope and expectation of other equally joyous visits. Cosset yourself, turn away all bores, store up your tale and keep that wonderful glint in your eye until I come again. I promise it won't be long—for only the forces of nature doing unexpected turns can keep me away.[6]

Anyone who has ever tramped through hot Italian streets to find closed the cloister the guidebook said would be open will wish this self-anointed "pilgrim" from Somerville had succeeded in her mission of getting information about unavailable artworks disseminated.

What prompted Mongan's striking out at error was the depth of her enthusiasms. These she felt intensely, in Berenson the man and

in the visual experience about which she could commune with him.
After the problems in Bologna she wrote B.B. from Venice about a
happy reunion with "Daisy" (Marga) Barr. And what was

> in itself worth heat & mosquitoes & traveling Germans [was]
> San Rocco! Have you seen them recently? Of course, you have.
> I was so thrilled and stupefied and overwhelmed by their glory
> and beauty & magnificence that I could feel my bones turning
> to water and in that fluid state I knew I'd seen vast visions.
>
> I don't know whether I should regret your godly stature or
> not. Your demesne seemed to me so perfect of its kind that I
> would have neither it nor your powers altered. They are both
> considerable and wonderful as they are—& I should prefer
> them to remain so.[7]

From Venice Mongan was on her way to an Alp "to contemplate
the magnificence of nature rather than the handwork of man." Her
keen responsiveness had many sources. But little inspired such vehemence as Berenson himself. She often wrote him of her longing
for the next visit and for more frequent encounters, to which he
always responded in kind. After returning to Cambridge she let him
know that walking to and from the Fogg each day she would men-
tally compose letters to him. When too much time lapsed she would
open a note to him with statements that resembled the dialogue in a
Victorian novel. "How my conscience has tormented me because
I've been so long silent,"[8] one started; "Doubtless you have crossed
me off your list,"[9] commenced another. One letter began, "Dear
B.B., I can scarcely bear contemplating the breadth & darkness &
length of the shadow which must cover your thought of me"[10] because she had gone so long without writing.

But the dark shadow Mongan really had on her mind was the one
cast by what was happening in the world around them. In that same
letter where she voiced such guilt at not having written Berenson
sooner, she said of her work on the Fogg catalog, "in the face of
human need & anguish the importance of considering the beauties of
the past assumes a waiting role." Like other Americans who traveled
abroad, Mongan was more directly aware of the European situation
than were most of her countrymen. And after her own time in Italy
that summer, Agnes had heard from her sister Elizabeth, who visited
Berenson a couple of months later, about a train in Italy where the

passengers included the last group of people to get out of Austria before the borders closed, and about how on the voyage back to America the *Queen Mary* was packed with exiles. When she spent time in late 1938 doing research at the British Museum and Windsor Castle, she had used every available minute from opening to closing time because she felt that soon these collections would be shut down and their contents packed against damage from bombing. She wrote to the painter Rico Lebrun that she extended this trip "because when the international situation became both tense and grim, it seemed to me that I should see as many things as possible for no one seemed to know how long it would be before they would be blown to bits." [11] At Windsor she was looking through the 175th case of drawings, with sandbags piled up to the window ledge of the library, when word of the Munich Agreement came. The following morning, when Mongan arrived back at the castle library and a Church of England clergyman greeted her with a jaunty " 'It is to be peace,' " she replied, " 'I think it is a terrific price.' " [12] For this she was frowned upon and then avoided—a castigation she took with satisfaction.

Mongan ended her stay in London by helping Kenneth Clark wrap up paintings at the National Gallery so they could be moved from Trafalgar Square for safekeeping. Then, after she returned to America, she began helping with refugees. Through Eddie Warburg and Marga Barr and Eddie's cousin Ingrid Warburg, she met a flow of European exiles seeking work and housing in the Boston area, and she devoted herself to trying to assist them. To this she would have found Berenson less sympathetic than to her other activities. Berenson referred to such people as "refu-Jews." [13] He wrote to his wife that Jews were "neither a religion nor a nation nor a race any more, whatever they may have been at one time. . . . I wish one could define what they are, and why so attractive and repellent, re-pellent chiefly." [14] Berenson's primary disdain was for German and Austrian Jews, from whom he, as a Lithuanian, had suffered a degree of snobbery: "They may have Jewish noses and souls but their minds are super-German and that to me and not their Jewishness makes them a public danger." [15]

But Mongan and Berenson could continue to discuss drawings. After one of Mongan's visits to I Tatti, Berenson labeled her his saint, saying that no one's appreciation of his drawings meant more to him than did hers. From the Fogg she kept him abreast of her work completing the drawings catalog, for which she and Sachs always kept

Berenson's own book on Italian drawings at their side. Mongan reported on learning to use a slide rule to make proportional reduc-
tions of photos, and on doing freehand drawings of the watermarks.
At Paul Sachs's home in the Adirondacks, she made the index. And
finally she sent her "conscience," as she called Berenson, the three
hefty volumes. It was no easy task to get them to Italy late in 1940.
Together they weighed fifty pounds. The usual communications
channels were closed. But Mongan finally found a way, and to her
enormous satisfaction Berenson immediately applauded the catalog's
appearance, writing, tone, and informativeness as being without
equal. This was the first publication of its kind in America. There
was a comprehensive biography and bibliography for every artist
represented. Besides a full-size reproduction, each work had an entry
of its own that provided a full description, an analysis of the technique and subject matter, and a complete provenance and exhibition
history. For the portrait drawings, Mongan made comparisons to
every other portrait the given artist had done of the same sitter. In
keeping with the finest publications of the Louvre, the British Museum, and the Albertina, these volumes became the model for scholarly catalogs in America. As Sachs acknowledged in his
introduction, not only had Mongan joined him on all attributions,
but she had done most of the labor and research.

Mongan had taken risks. As she wrote to Berenson,

It is, I know, filled with glaring errors, many of which will leap
to nightmarish life before your eagle eye. And I am terrified lest
I might incur your wrath, for I have had the audacity to disagree with you here and there. (Poor Miss King is probably
turning in her grave, because any pupil of hers should be inca-
pable of disagreeing with you on any point.)[16]

Yet the catalog garnered only praise.

Mongan may have challenged Georgiana King's authority, but she
had dedicated the drawings catalog to her memory, and did a great
deal more to abet and honor her early mentor. For Mongan the most
direct effect of the Depression may have been that because of the
budget restrictions at the Fogg they had had to produce "horrid little
mimeographed affairs" rather than nice catalogs,[17] but in 1937, having learned that her former professor was retiring from Bryn Mawr
in poor financial circumstances, she had initiated communication

with the president of the college about how to raise funds clandestinely for King. Mongan also wrote King a glowing tribute, published in the *Bryn Mawr Alumnae Bulletin,* and sought similar testimony from others. Then, following King's death in 1939, at which point Mongan became her teacher's literary executrix, she undertook to have Harvard University Press bring out a hitherto unpublished book by King: *The Heart of Spain.* For this purpose she solicited funds from Berenson, recalling to him that it was G.G. who had first introduced her to him "in a small dark lecture room at Bryn Mawr. And long before I knew the dancing light in your eye, your swift, soft step and the movements of your hands, I knew the turn of your thought, the quality of your imagination & the vividness of your language."[18] The vividness of her own language succeeded, and B.B. assisted with the necessary subvention. Harvard published the book, with an introduction by Mongan. One of the people to whom she proudly sent it was Gertrude Stein.

Mongan liked to do right by people. After Felix Warburg's death, she finally realized her dream of making peace between Paul Sachs and Eddie Warburg in a way that greatly benefited her museum. Eddie was the family member most responsible for his father's art collection. With Mongan's coaxing, he pleased Sachs both by having key works go to the Fogg and by endowing a large exhibition hall named in his father's memory. In July of 1939 Eddie wrote "Ag" about what this meant as a reconciliation with his former adviser: "I feel it will do your heart good to know that there is a decent streak in me, and that I am burying the old hatchet. Frankly, it is awful how tolerant I am becoming."[19]

She replied in kind,

> I never thought I should see the day when you and uncle Paul would put your heads together for such calm discussion. I can't call it the lion lying down with the lamb because I don't think either of you could be termed lamb-like, but I do rejoice to see certain utopian tendencies evident in my own time.[20]

And loyal as she was to Bryn Mawr and the Fogg, the former champion of the Harvard Society for Contemporary Art had by no means dropped her support of what was new and pioneering. In 1944, shortly after Alfred Barr had been ousted from the directorship of the Museum of Modern Art, she heaped praise on him in *Art*

News. Through Paul Sachs she had been hearing about Barr and the Modern since before it opened its doors. Pointing to the "electric atmosphere" and educational role of the Modern in presenting the diverse strains of recent art—whatever one might think of it—she singled out Barr as the key factor behind the museum's success. She described Barr as "a man of deep learning, sound scholastic training, unshakable integrity, unflagging, wide-ranging interests, and true vision. . . . His curiosity is tireless, his prophetic sense ever alert." [21]

Bernard Berenson had little taste for Barr's sort of modernism. He regarded the enthusiasm for nonobjective art, particularly as it had taken hold in New York, as comparable to "the raptures with which even the people most greatly endowed with taste must have admired barbarian art objects when the last fires of Alexandrian art had gone out and these people were already satiated by the clumsy attempts produced out of the decadence of Rome." [22] But this did not prevent Agnes Mongan from doing everything within her power to make Berenson more aware of the Museum of Modern Art's director, whose wife B.B. had gotten to know.

> You have never met Alfred, have you? When you do many of
> the questions you asked me last year about Marga will be an-
> swered. I know of no pair more divergent in background, in
> emotional inheritance, or in outward manner—& more de-
> voted or more reliant upon the well-being of the other, and I
> like & admire them both immensely. Marga's Italo-Hibernian
> ebullience, quickness & force, Alfred's Scotch quiet, steadiness
> & tenacity, her gaiety & energy, his contemplative judgments &
> almost silent perceptions—& both for their extraordinary intel-
> ligence and taste and loyalty. [23]

While she was working for recognition for people like Georgiana King and Alfred Barr, Mongan continued to have her own battles to fight. She became a teaching assistant to Paul Sachs, but her name could not appear in the course catalog because she was a woman. In the mid-1930s, Sachs and Edward Forbes wanted her named "Curator of Drawings." The university administration responded that a curatorship was a corporate appointment; she could only be "Keeper of Drawings."

At the start of the 1940s Mongan continued to work tirelessly with scholars and museum people on issues of attribution, but the significance of the work was gone. "And so while the world goes on to its damnation, I skim across its frivolous surface,"[24] she wrote Bernard Berenson. She continued to read scholarly papers, but she also did her best to place refugees. "I doubt I am an ostrich & I try to do what I can to prove I'm not one. What more can one do? That & one's daily task."[25] If formerly she had been investigating the depiction of piebald horses in Renaissance drawings, in 1942 her research was for a handbook on what had happened to art objects and to contemporary German painters under the Nazi regime.

In the winter of 1942–43, the ninety-five-person staff of the Fogg was reduced to a skeleton crew of forty-two. Most of the men Mongan knew had entered military service. James Plaut joined the army, and Nathaniel Saltonstall the navy, so activities at the Institute for Contemporary Art slowed down considerably. Mongan wrote to Thomas Howe, who was enlisting in the navy, with news of Warburg and Kirstein in the army, reporting that Kirstein had lost twenty-five pounds in the first three weeks of basic training. Mongan had attended a party at Kirk and Constance Askews' after a concert sponsored by Virgil Thomson, but nothing was the same. "I was shocked and horrified at the faces of most, many of whom I had not seen since the war had started." Although she heard the next day that the party had lasted until 5:30 a.m., she left early. "My frame can no longer take it, even did my taste incline me to wish to."[26] Her energies went in other directions, like judging an exhibition called "Bandwagon on Parade," organized by the United Services Organization of the U.S. State Department, and featuring art by people in military service. Mongan had found her niche as a scholar and connoisseur at the Fogg, and was on as straight a course as the world would permit.

III

On January 6, 1938, another ballet had had its world premiere at the Avery Memorial in Hartford. Three years earlier the theme had been college football; now it was gas stations. Lincoln Kirstein had continued to look for American subject matter for the Ballet Caravan. He considered dances based on tales by Mark Twain, Hawthorne, and Melville, and he wrote the books for *Harlequin for President, Po-*

cahontas, Yankee Clipper, and *Billy the Kid.* What he wanted above all was to set the caravan's fifteen dancers in an ordinary, everyday situation. Like so many of the moderns, he eschewed the sort of refinement and elegance generally associated with high art. He spurned the usual subject matter and turned to the commonplace. The work that premiered in Hartford was called *Filling Station,* for which Virgil Thomson composed the music for the caravan's two pianos. Paul Cadmus designed the sets and costumes. A mural called *Shore Leave* that Cadmus had painted under the auspices of the Works Projects Administration had recently caused a scandal for its depiction of sailors in one of those moments the navy didn't like people to talk about; Kirstein knew Cadmus was the man for the job. The artist came up with a suitable set: a large window and rest room door to indicate the station, a neon sign that read in reverse, and a gas pump.

Mac, the station attendant, wore translucent nylon accented in red. To choreography by Lew Christiansen, he pumped gas, pointed the way to the telephone, and supplied a monkey wrench and road map. A family of tourists, some jerky truck drivers, a stylish pair of lovers, and several gangsters all stopped by. Thomson's music for all of this was "waltzes, tangos, a fugue, a Big Apple, a holdup, and a chase, all aimed to evoke roadside America as pop art." [27] In those days the "Big Apple" was the latest dance craze.

When *Filling Station* opened, the Avery auditorium had a different look to it. The neo-Romantic Kristians Tonny—admired by Jim Soby and Chick Austin—had graced its walls with murals of a dreamlike vision of flying horses. Things had slowed down since the Paper Ball, but the Atheneum was still advancing both art with literary themes and pure abstraction. At the end of 1936 Austin had mounted a show of paintings by the brothers Le Nain and of Georges de La Tour, who had been out of favor for centuries and whose reputation he and Soby helped revive. He also put together a show of abstract painting by Katherine Dreier, Werner Drewes, Paul Kelpe, and Josef Albers. Nineteen thirty-seven had been a quieter year for exhibitions, but Austin arranged concerts, film programs, and many more magic performances. He also managed to spend two and a half months in Europe, where he met up with Tchelitchew and with Jim Soby together with Nellie Howland. Throughout his travels he found paintings for "Modern Art from 1900 to 1937," which opened the February after the *Filling Station* performance. "Constructions in Space" by Naum Gabo followed.

But except for those individuals like Albers and Gabo to whom abstract art offered a necessary reprieve from worldly events, for many people it was becoming difficult to think of art in a vacuum. This wasn't true only for European painters like Miró and Balthus, but also for the individuals closely connected with those painters. Travelers to Europe were confronting the prospect of war before it became a crucial issue in America. Whether they were looking at Picasso's latest work, following the German Expressionists, or just heeding the latest news, they couldn't avoid reality the way that more isolated Americans could.

On October 9, 1938, an article appeared in the *Hartford Courant* with the headline "A.E. Austin Tells of War Ado Abroad."

A.E. Austin went abroad to talk about art and confesses that most of his time was spent with persons who simply would not discuss anything but the war which they believed was certain to come. France was within hours of mobilization, Austin reported, and there was a false report that Hitler was marching on Czechoslovakia, he said.

"The report was, of course, absolutely unfounded," he said, but the scars were so bad that no one wanted to sell or show pictures. The paintings in the Louvre had been removed. The French people who hadn't believed war possible suddenly decided that it might just be something they would have to go through. They didn't become excited but their faces were solemn. There was no laughter on the street.

With no laughter on the street in Paris, and no paintings to buy or borrow, it was getting harder to keep smiling in America as well. The mood of New York was changing too. Austin and Hitchcock began to cut down on their trips into the city; prospects for exhibitions and entertainments were rapidly shrinking.

Austin did, however, manage to divert Hartford for a while longer. But not only were the splashes slighter and fewer, they no longer avoided the dark realities of life. At the end of 1938 Austin borrowed from Julien Levy an enormous Tchelitchew canvas called *Phenomena*. This conglomeration of grotesques in a landscape of volcanic mountains and bizarre buildings put parodies of Gertrude Stein, Alice B. Toklas, Christian Bérard, Virgil Thomson, Edith Sitwell, and Tchelitchew himself alongside visages of Hitler and Mussolini. Depicting both the saviors as well as the despots of Western civilization, it made no one look good. Shortly after *Phenomena* was shown, Tchelitchew designed a backdrop for a performance of the Ballets Russes de Monte Carlo at Hartford's Bushnell Memorial Auditorium. It included six hands positioned to communicate with the twenty-five students from the American School for the Deaf in West Hartford who were at the back of the orchestra. Austin would do what he could to make the arts available for a larger public.

But in spite of the occasional high point, the pace was slackening at the Atheneum. There were no major shows in 1939. At the start of 1940 the museum showed "Some New Forms of Beauty, 1909 to 1936"—sixty-nine works from Katherine Dreier's Société Anonyme, among them paintings by Albers, de Chirico, Duchamp, Gorky, Gris, Kandinsky, Klee, Léger, Malevich, Miró, Nolde, Schwitters, and Villon—but this was no longer unusual material. For one thing, people in various parts of America had now caught on; the "new forms of beauty" had become standard fare for a greater audience. The Museum of Modern Art, already a decade old, had made its impact.

Early in 1942, Austin organized an exhibition of first-rate paintings all for sale at under a thousand dollars. The catalog voiced Austin's hope that Hartford's citizens, either individually or through their groups or clubs, would buy some of this art and give it to the Atheneum. There were some fine opportunities. Austin had arranged loans from eight art galleries—Durlacher, Julien Levy, and Pierre Matisse among them—that included two Kensetts for $150 each, a Cuyp for $850, a Utrillo for $750, three Salvator Rosas priced from $500 to $900, a Siqueiros for $500, Balthus's *Girl with a Cat* for $850, a Tchelitchew for $450, three Picassos, works by Miró and Matta, and drawings by Boucher, Delacroix, Matisse, and Goya. Yet even with such a fine idea, few of the paintings found their way into the Atheneum's collection. Austin next took another show from Julien Levy. Called "Painters of Fantasy," it had work by de Chirico and Ernst, as well as the perpetual court favorites: Léonide, Berman, and Bérard. But here, too, the public was no longer there. With America's entry into the war, most people had chosen to focus on reality. Mrs. Richard Bissell, who had had a leading role in both the Venetian fête and the Paper Ball, now turned her energies toward a benefit sale at the museum on behalf of the British War Relief Society.

In 1942 an Association of Arts for Defense was formed in the dance studio of Alwin Nikolais, not far from the museum. Nikolais was chairman, Austin vice chairman. But unlike Eddie Warburg, Austin was unable to change course entirely. Lincoln Kirstein had said he had his antennae up for what was happening; if that meant World War II, then Austin would make the theme of soldiery a drawing card to the Atheneum. At the start of 1943 he mounted an exhibition called "Men in Arms," its catalog a patriotic, star-studded red, white, and blue. The message of its paintings was the glamour and nobility of donning a uniform, even if that idea slightly took on the tone of a costume party. For Austin to borrow what he did for that 1943 exhibition was no small achievement. Drawing heavily on New York galleries, he put together a remarkable group of paintings including works by artists ranging from Lorenzo di Credi, Francesco Guardi, Rubens, El Greco, Giovanni Battista Tiepolo, and Paolo Veronese to Gilbert Stuart, Delacroix, Géricault, Derain, Marsden Hartley, Edward Hopper, and William Gropper. The show portrayed the laughing side of army life as well as the rigors of battle. The diversity of the pictures suggested the universality of taking up arms. It also ennobled that act. To glorify, and to find the light side of things, was what Chick Austin could be counted on to do.

Not that Austin saw war as only marching bands and shining armor. The tenor of the art he acquired for the Atheneum as battle raged in Europe reflected devastation above all. In 1942 Austin bought—with fourteen hundred dollars from the James Thrall Soby Allocation Fund—Max Ernst's *Europe After the Rains*. In 1943, again using funds from the Soby allocation, Austin bought Yves Tanguy's *5 Strangers*. Painted two years earlier, the canvas depicted an inexplicable ghost town. The tone could not have offered a more strident contrast to the qualities of the works that Austin had been purchasing only a few years earlier—the flippant optimism of the Mirós, the joy of the Lifar ballet art, and the positive assuredness of the Mondrian.

But what was increasingly interesting Austin more than art of any sort was theater. In 1941 he played Hamlet to the music Virgil Thomson had composed for Leslie Howard. In May of 1943 he starred in, and made the costumes for, the play *'Tis Pity,* by John Ford, set to music by Paul Bowles. Then, that July, he requested and was granted a one-year paid leave of absence from Hartford. The official story was that "he was tired and felt that he needed 'fresh ideas' to carry on his work. He said of his plans for the leave, 'I just want to wander.' "28

After this sabbatical, Austin returned to Hartford. He gave up his position as director, but, at the start of 1945, set about working on a catalog of the Sumner Collection. It was very much like Alfred Barr's role at the Museum of Modern Art at the same time. Barr had been removed from his position as director, but still had his hand in things. Functioning as deposed kings, these men could not quite give up the domain they had built to such a peak. But in May of 1945 Chick Austin left Hartford once and for all. He and Helen rented out their house on Scarborough Street, bought a place in Los Angeles, and—with Virgil Thomson in the car—headed for Hollywood.

By the time Austin had left Hartford, Jim Soby had also gone onto other things. In 1939 he had joined the Museum of Modern Art's Junior Advisory Committee. He was basing his activities more and more in New York. In 1940 he was appointed to both the Acquisitions and Photography committees at the Modern, and in 1942 he became a trustee—a position he would hold until his death thirty-seven years later. Alfred Barr replaced Austin as Soby's primary mentor. Barr became one of his closest friends, and he one of Barr's truest allies.

Soby moved to New York in February 1942 to direct the Modern's Armed Services Program—a project that further opened the museum to soldiers and sailors and helped provide art supplies to military training camps. When at the start of 1943 he was appointed the Modern's assistant director and director of the Department of Painting and Sculpture, he finally gave up his position as assistant secretary of the Atheneum. The Museum of Modern Art would be his workplace from then on. He ran the Armed Services Program until the end of the war, and although he was to keep his house in Farmington for quite some time, the Atheneum would never again be his base of operation.

IV

World War II marked the end of the period when American culture could be run from the seat of one's pants. Since 1945, it has been virtually impossible to do things with the impromptu style in which

Kirstein, Warburg, Mongan, Austin, and Soby had previously functioned. Nor could there be more covert operations to acquire collections like the Albertina; the arts have left the realm of the inner
sanctum and become very public.

Since the Second World War, art exhibitions, ballet performances,
and opera premieres have become part of a national, multimillion-
dollar industry. The costs have increased dramatically, and the
government and giant corporations have taken much of the responsibility. Even extremely wealthy patrons like Paul Mellon or J. Paul
Getty have made their decisions in carefully structured collaboration
with universities or federal agencies. If Lincoln Kirstein had previously engineered ballet performances in the Warburgs' backyard,
now he could arrange them in a large public theater with the support
of New York City and countless other donors. Calder and Picasso
and Surrealism have taken their places in every major museum
around the country. What was once relegated to two small rooms
over the Harvard Coop, or to the squash court, is given full honor
behind marble porticos and in grand climate-controlled halls.

What Kirstein, Warburg, Mongan, Austin, and Soby managed to
do before the start of World War II, and the way they lived then,
would never again be the same. Not only had priorities changed, but
the fun was gone. Everyone needed to readjust after 1945. The war
had made their world entirely different, both economically and socially. Moreover, these individuals had in their own lives moved on
from the years when everything seemed possible, and entertainment
rich, to middle age and the time when the value of earlier pleasures
and beliefs is less certain. Each would build on what he or she had
done before the war, but for none of them could there be a repetition
of what had occurred at a unique time in history and in their own
personal developments.

After the war, Edward Forbes was given a second opportunity to
find Chick Austin a job. On his sabbatical in Hollywood Austin had
helped found the Gates Theatre Studio and had designed the occasional set, but although he returned to Hollywood after his resignation from the Atheneum in January of 1945, in the long run it was
not the place for him. Later that year, his old mentor from the Fogg
was in Sarasota, Florida, when Florida's governor was looking for a
director to open the state-owned John and Mabel Ringling Museum
of Art. Forbes recommended Austin as the best person in the country to take the post. In April of 1946 he was appointed, and at the

end of the year the renovated galleries of the Ringling opened to the public.

That summer, Austin also opened a summer theater in the barn of the estate he had inherited from his mother in Windham, New Hampshire. He produced, designed sets and costumes, and performed there. He soon appeared on the stage in Sarasota as well, after joining a local drama group there. In 1948 he opened the Museum of the American Circus near the Ringling; the next year he mounted an exhibition called "Art, Carnival, and the Circus." Meanwhile, he kept up his usual Austin round of activities. He acquired Baroque paintings and showed modern ones. He arranged concerts, film programs, and readings by people like Dame Edith and Sir Osbert Sitwell. Then, in March of 1952 he installed, in Sarasota, a fine small eighteenth-century Italian playhouse from Asolo, where it had been torn apart by the Fascists. The gem of a theater opened with a performance of Pergolesi and Mozart with sets by himself and Eugene Berman. Austin brought to Sarasota everything from Desiderio and Rubens to Renoir, Tchelitchew, and Picasso.

In 1957, when he was fifty-six years old, Chick Austin died. Today his legacy can be felt above all in the extraordinary paintings ranging from Caravaggio, Luca Giordano, Tintoretto, Louis Le Nain, Goya, and Corot to Balthus, Dali, Ernst, Miró, and Mondrian—along with Lifar's collection of ballet art—at the Wadsworth Atheneum.

After the end of the war, Jim Soby's association with the Museum of Modern Art lasted for the rest of his productive life. With the Modern as his base, he was able to support the art he believed in—quite free of the sort of controversy he met up with in Hartford. An increasing number of people were now on the side of the art he wanted to buy, exhibit, and write about. In addition to chairing MoMA's Department of Painting and Sculpture intermittently until 1957, periodically chairing the Committee on Museum Collections, and remaining a trustee until the time of his death in 1979, Soby directed many major exhibitions in the 1940s and 1950s. He and Nellie took a floor-through apartment on East Seventy-ninth Street, and frequently entertained artists and museum people. Above all, Soby wrote prodigiously. His insightful and articulate texts include *After Picasso, Salvador Dali* (1941), *The Early Chirico* (1941), *Tchelitchew* (1942), *Romantic Painting in America* (written with Dorothy Miller in

1943), *Georges Rouault* (1945), *Ben Shahn* (1947), *The Prints of Paul Klee* (1947), *Contemporary Painters* (1948), *XXth Century Italian Art* (written with Alfred Barr in 1949), *Amedeo Modigliani* (1951), *Giorgio de Chirico* (1955), *Balthus* (1956), *Arp* (1958), *Juan Gris* (1958), and *Joan Miró* (1959); periodically he would bring out revised editions of these volumes. Soby's succinct prose easily led readers to an understanding of both the visual and literary sides of the art he discussed. This was true not only in the monographs, but also in the articles he wrote regularly for *The Saturday Review of Literature*. His pieces there, which were assembled in the 1957 book *Modern art and the new past,* were a model of clear perceptions and straightforward writing that opened the magazine's readership to the merits of both contemporary and older art of which they would otherwise have been unaware. No less an authority than Paul Sachs would say of Soby's writing in these essays, "Free of all pedantry he does what few closet scholars ever do—he conjures vision with words. He allows us to share his delight in details and he holds us entranced and exhilarated by revealing qualities in works of art that might escape our less practiced vision." [29]

Soby also continued to collect on a major scale. Sometimes this meant selling a picture. Although he swapped fewer works than in the early years, he did sell Derain's *Bagpiper.* Having paid fourteen thousand dollars for it in 1930, he received eighty-five hundred for it in 1949; Curt Valentin, who sold it for him, had received ten thousand from which he had deducted a 15 percent commission. But the loss did not bother Soby; profit and investment were not the goals of his art collecting. He bought paintings because he could not resist them, and sold them only when they lost their emotional hold on him. In the 1940s and 1950s he acquired, in addition to Miró's *Still Life with Old Shoe,* two other extremely important Mirós—the 1929 *Portrait of Mrs. Mills in 1750* and the 1937–38 *Self-Portrait;* a Morandi still life; several Yves Tanguys; major paintings by Francis Bacon; Joseph Cornell's *Taglioni's Jewel Casket;* an extraordinarily delicate painted bronze figure by Giacometti; some large canvases by Matta; Marini bronzes; a Peter Blume; and a Dubuffet. He was generally ahead of public taste, often buying work that the larger audience would only come around to years later; in 1958 he bought Jasper Johns's encaustic *White Target* when it was fresh from the easel—long before most collectors would have dreamed of considering it. Almost as soon as he acquired some of these paintings, Soby began to transfer them—along with his earlier purchases—to the Modern's permanent collection, a process completed by his will after his death.

Not that Soby's life always took a straight and easy course. At times the perfect New England gentleman was more than ever like a surreal character. Even when he was based in New York, Soby kept his house in Farmington, and in 1951 he created a scandal that was front-page news in Hartford. He had fallen madly for a woman who was married to one of his best Farmington friends and had two sons. The woman got a divorce in order to marry Soby. The ensuing custody battle, much publicized, dragged in everyone from child psychiatrists to an angry nanny, and made much of the new Mrs. Soby's heavy drinking.

By the time of the trial, greater Hartford had become too sticky a place to live, even on weekends. Jim Soby and his third wife, Melissa, switched their country address to New Canaan, again to a Greek Revival house with the large Calder outside—this time minus its well.

By the time Soby died in 1979, ambiguity and haze, whatever their horrors and drawbacks, had won out. But the presence of his art collection—above all the de Chiricos and Mirós, and Balthus's *Street*—today is one of the major glories of the Museum of Modern Art, and his books continue to elucidate some of the most obscure art of this century with insights and ease.

Lincoln Kirstein's achievements since the war until the time of this writing defy measure. He has worked in numerous capacities as a curator, impresario, and official adviser on the arts. In 1978 a bibliography was printed of his published writings ranging from fiction and poetry to stories for ballets and books and articles on dance, the visual arts, and other areas of culture. It has 473 entries. Above all else, Kirstein has made his mark as the general director of the New York City Ballet, which he and Balanchine started in 1948. The American Ballet had lasted from 1935 to 1938, and the Ballet Caravan from 1936 to 1940. The NYCB was, and is, the culmination of their efforts together.

Kirstein has remained relatively quiet and behind the scenes—in keeping with his understated listing on *The Hound & Horn* masthead and the anonymity of his essays for the Harvard Society for Contemporary Art flyers. But in both his positive and negative views, he has

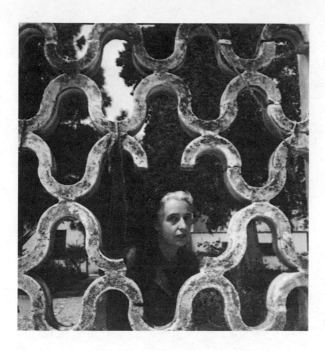

*Agnes Mongan,
Mexico, 1945.*

Portrait of James Thrall Soby with Jacob Epstein's Portrait of Oriel Ross.

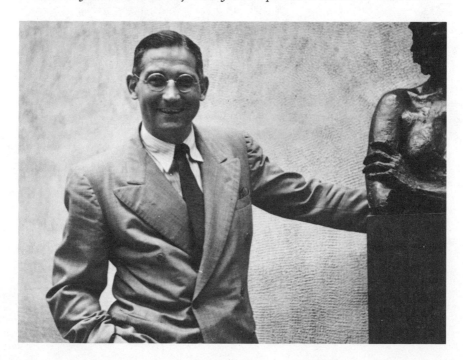

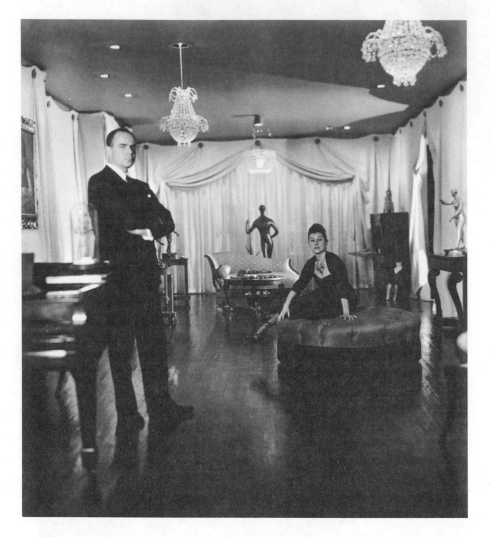

Lincoln and Fidelma Kirstein in the salon on East Nineteenth Street, photographed by Cecil Beaton, 1957.

vehemently opposed prevailing trends. He has publicly taken apart certain establishment institutions and tastes:

> The museums have been taken over by the dealers, and the appreciation of art is really the appreciation of negotiable value. . . . With the Manet show [held in 1983 at the Metro-

politan Museum] no one looks at the paintings or realizes what a lousy painter he was. They have just been in the precincts of status and they can rub some of this magic off on them- selves. . . . [Manet was] clumsy, easy to look at, unfinished, no interest in psychology whatsoever—a simple French bourgeois hedonist. . . .

One of the worst influences in cultural history is the Museum of Modern Art. It is a corrupt combination of dealer taste, mar- keting, and journalism, and it has nothing to do with the essen- tials of what made art whatever it was for the last two thousand years. . . .

Modern art, as I see it, is nothing but a terrible inflation of a kind of cancerous self-indulgence, the great availability of the media, the terrible effects of behaviorism and of the idea of pro- gressive education. . . .

There are very few people who look at anything, and if they do they're not equipped to look at it.[30]

In this lack of faith in the audience at large, Kirstein has grown even more cynical than Eddie Warburg was after Bryn Mawr and the Stra- vinsky Festival. Having once tried so energetically to educate the public and sway popular taste, on one level Kirstein lost his faith. Yet this has not prevented him from taking action where he can, primarily through his writing and the management of the ballet. Kirstein has done his best to see his taste take hold, by doing things like persuading Nelson Rockefeller to hire Philip Johnson to design the New York State Theater when Wallace Harrison was the architect for the rest of Lincoln Center. Unlike Warburg, Kirstein found the arts at their best to have sustaining power. Although contemptuous of trends, institutions, and the general public—and famous for the arrogance of his diatribes—he has still remained staunchly loyal to his personal notions of quality. He has written tirelessly in defense of his chosen painters and sculptors, and has championed dance with unique fervor and knowledge. The magic he felt as he watched those performances of Diaghilev's troupe at Covent Garden in 1929 has never worn off. And until 1989 Kirstein remained director of his and Balanchine's ballet company and president of their school—fulfilling that dream for which he, Eddie Warburg, Chick Austin, and Jim Soby had signed that affidavit fifty years before George Balanchine's death in 1983.

. . .

Agnes Mongan is another of the young stalwarts whose early passions have never waned. More than for any of the others, art continued to affirm her faith in life and to nourish her sense of purpose. And to some degree the world came around to esteeming Mongan and her discoveries. Having frequently claimed that for a woman to succeed she "merely had to be better than the men," she was just that. In 1947 Mongan was finally given the title of curator of drawings at the Fogg, and in 1954 her name appeared in the Harvard course catalog. But although her name became synonymous with the Fogg and she generally had the honor of escorting prestigious visitors through its collections, it was still many years before Mongan could take her rightful position as the museum's director. In the mid-1950s Alfred Barr went before the Harvard Corporation to urge that they appoint her to that post, but it was more than ten years later that the corporation did so. When she became the Fogg's director in 1969, she was the second woman in America—perhaps anywhere in the world—to direct a major museum, Adelyn Breeskin at the Baltimore Museum of Art being her sole predecessor.

Mongan continued to work in close cooperation with Bernard Berenson. As more people began to visit I Tatti in the 1950s, he wrote to her frequently about what he wanted the villa to be, and she kept him alert to the pertinent politics at Harvard and in other American institutions. Few people could offer more direct, trenchant assessments of others. Of John Walker—who Berenson had said was like a son to him, and who had become the second and longtime director of the National Gallery in Washington—Mongan wrote Berenson in 1948,

> John I'm afraid will never again do a serious, original, careful or inspired job. For one thing his social engagements would not permit him the time—such a job would need persistent reflection. For another he shares the National Gallery's suspicion of learning.

Mongan felt that her sister, who had become the curator of prints there, was the one true scholar at the National Gallery. And in this same letter in which she denigrated Walker, she added, "The only person I know who gets in deeper is Lincoln Kirstein. And he gets more done because he not only has more drive, he has more intellect." [31]

In 1961, two years after Berenson died at the age of ninety-four, I Tatti became the Harvard University Center for Renaissance Studies, since which time Agnes Mongan has helped raise money for its restoration and worked in myriad ways to help the villa perpetuate the finest sides of its owner's legacy.

At Harvard, Mongan taught a seminar from the 1950s to the 1970s in which she trained some of the most important curators in America. Since World War II she has edited numerous volumes; continued to write articles, reviews, catalogs, and books; and lectured all over the world. Her scholarship remains unique. She succeeded in identifying some key sixteenth-century portraits as being by François Clouet because she recognized the handwriting of Catherine de Médicis's secretary on one of them, which, since Clouet had worked for Catherine, enabled her to make the connection. Her research on the image of dogs in art led her to the discovery that seeing-eye dogs go back to the 1480s; the evidence is in a painting by Sassetta.

Like Kirstein, Mongan is relentless in her sense of standards. She crusades against the misuse of the word "exhibit," which she will point out is simply one object in an exhibition. She champions the cause of natural light in museums. The strong code and faith in her own beliefs that Mongan developed as a young girl have never failed her. But neither has her diplomacy. Mongan has devoted herself to the place where she once had to sneak out of the library, and she has thrived there. Time and again in the recent past she has been acknowledged as one of Harvard's treasures, and even if she has never again tried to make an acquisition that rivals the Albertina, she has expanded and improved the Fogg's collection and activities with fierce institutional loyalty.

Mongan appears to have had few regrets about not having led the usual life of women of her generation. She enjoys recalling that she had marriage proposals but turned them down in favor of her independence.[32] In the 1940s, at a time when she was trying to learn Spanish, she had written Bernard Berenson, "It would be a good deal easier if I had, like some other ladies, more leisure."[33] Her voice was clearly ironic. The reason she wanted to learn Spanish was that she had just been in Guatemala and had joined the Pan American Council, of far more interest to her than leisure time. Although she often had health problems and had the hectic pace of her life interrupted by illnesses, she also kept up a breathless schedule of travel, work, and socializing. Scholarly yet funny, warm yet prickly, she has a rare engagement in living.

Writing and scholarship were the best avenues open; Mongan took them gladly. By allying herself with as venerable an institution as Harvard, she endured certain obstacles as a Catholic and a woman, but she also gained access to the upper echelons of American and European life, and succeeded in making a mark. To do so Mongan was willing at first to assume the role of apprentice, to work for the establishment and be the young legs and eyes for Sachs and Berenson. She felt "always in the background, never in the foreground." [34] But it did not take her long to know her own strength and speak and write with an unhesitant clip and the authority of true knowledge. She maintained the tradition of real intellectual achievement and hard work in which she was raised. Mongan had never lost that craving and energy for knowledge she voiced to her father as a young girl, and which he did his best to encourage. Her only unfulfilled wish in life was to be an Orientalist, but she ultimately felt it would be foolish to take up the art of a culture of which one did not know the languages.

Agnes Mongan once wrote to Berenson, "How can one ever know enough or look enough? I try to keep my eyes open, but there are so many interruptions & so many little things to keep track of in our mad American life that looking & reading often come in sadly near the end of time." [35] But she has looked and read, and seen and conveyed, more than most people.

By the end of the war, Eddie Warburg had signed more affidavits than he could even remember to help refugees come to America. This was often at the request of Alfred Barr. After the fall of Paris in 1940, Barr had helped many artists escape to the United States, and the Museum of Modern Art had become a sort of life raft. Margaret Barr was often the person in charge of finding sponsors who would guarantee that the refugees would not be a burden to the U.S. government and that they were not Communists, and would provide about four hundred dollars for each person's passage. She worked on this with Varian Fry—another graduate of the Harvard class of 1930, and one of the founders and editors of *The Hound & Horn*—and with Ingrid Warburg. Curt Valentin, who had moved from Berlin to New York and opened an American gallery, also helped. They knew that Eddie could be counted on to assist—just as his cousin Bettina, through the American Psychoanalytic Association, enabled over two hundred people in her field to reach America—by finding jobs for them as high school teachers, or doing whatever else it took. In the 1950s when Eddie received a drawing from Marc Chagall inscribed "with thanks" and asked "thanks for what?" he learned that Chagall's were among the papers he had personally expedited.

Something Eddie Warburg had learned in the safe confines of his mother's sitting room may have given him his special compassion for European Jews. One day in the mid-1930s, when Frieda was upset because of news of Hitler's progress, she told Eddie that she had realized in the middle of the previous night that there was something important that she had neglected to tell him—that he was the only one of her children who had been "made in Germany." Whatever its source, Eddie's empathy and sense of obligation exceeded that of his brothers. When he returned to New York after the war, he worked as hard as national chairman of the Joint Distribution Committee— a position he held for a total of twenty-five years—as he had for the fledgling ballet company. He also served five terms as national chairman of the United Jewish Appeal.

With the issue of refugees, Warburg never had to ask himself why he was doing something. In the ballet years, the rushes of enthusiasm had been accompanied by his own flip, skeptical voice; now he could speak with conviction and intensity and feel that his audience really listened. One of his first listeners was John Hersey. Inspired by Warburg's account of the Warsaw ghetto, related at dinner one evening, Hersey began research for a short piece for *The New Yorker*. Warburg led him to various sources and invited him along as a guest on his next trip to Israel, the outcome of which was Hersey's *The Wall*. Results like that, and the money he could raise for Israel and for American Jewish causes, were worth fighting for.

Meanwhile, the family was moving more toward service and away from possessions. Frieda dispossessed herself of the house in the country and gave 1109 Fifth to the Jewish Theological Seminary to become the Jewish Museum. While his mother was ridding herself of real estate, Edward began to unload the paintings that had once occupied 1109's squash court. Over the years the high points of his collection had been at the Museum of Modern Art and in other public institutions almost as much as in his various residences. Gradually the paintings were becoming a burden; not only were there the loans to organize, but there were also insurance and security precautions, and the need for conservation-correct storage. Warburg sold *Blue Boy*—the painting the customs broker had insisted on reducing to one thousand dollars fetched a million dollars—as well as the Klees. Klee's *Departure of the Ships* now belongs to the National Gallery in Berlin—the city where its owner had first admired the artist's work in Curt Valentin's gallery. Warburg gave Lachaise's *Dynamo Mother*— as well as the Calder wire figures, other Lachaises, the large Siqui-eros, sculpture by Epstein, Barlach, and Noguchi, Mies van der Rohe's "Brno" chairs, and photographs by Abbott, Steichen, and Weston—to the Museum of Modern Art. He made similar gifts to the Smith College Art Museum, the Busch Reisinger Museum at Harvard, and the Fogg.

In addition to his work for Jewish charities, Eddie Warburg has served on almost as many boards as his father. He has also been a Regent of New York State. And even if visual arts were no longer the priority they had been in the Harvard and Bryn Mawr days, for years he remained on the board of the Museum of Modern Art. He also served as director of public relations at the Metropolitan Museum, under Thomas Hoving. While this was in fact a paying job— the only one Warburg has ever held—he always returned his earnings to the Metropolitan as part of his annual contribution.

In the past several decades Eddie Warburg has covered the United States and shuttled back and forth between America and Israel to meet with world leaders and raise funds. He has been the recipient of countless honors, and the subject of testimonials. But they haven't meant much more to him than his parents' coffered ceilings did when he was working for Calder or Balanchine, and he has always tried to go one step further.

AFTERWORD

In 1988, when the New York City Ballet celebrated its fortieth anniversary, Peter Martins asked Eddie Warburg, along with Lincoln Kirstein, to appear on the stage at intermission and to say a few words. As usual, Kirstein was the major force behind everything, but Warburg was the irresistible speaker. Warburg had his notes along, but didn't take long to look up from them and say what was really on his mind. He took the audience back to the days of NYCB's predecessor, the American Ballet. Reminiscing about the 1935 performances at the Adelphi Theatre, he said, "Only two rows were filled that night, and they were the freebies for the parents of the kids who were dancing."

Warburg pointed out just how different things were on this anniversary evening. When he and Mary had been walking across the Lincoln Center to the State Theater and a stranger had sidled up to them, they assumed he was trying to sell them dirty pictures. The stranger's question, however, was whether they had any extra tickets. Warburg told the capacity crowd, "And that's what happened in not so many years. Ballet is here to stay." It is just one of the many ways that the efforts of these patron saints have forever altered our contemporary cultural fabric.

At times there has been occasion to celebrate the changes *not* made, as well as the victories. Early in 1986, Walter Koschatsky, the current director of the Albertina, traveled from Vienna to give a lecture at the Fogg Museum. Koschatsky's subject was the art of drawing. The white-haired and visibly infirm Agnes Mongan attended. After the lecture, Mongan raised her hand, eager to make a point. The natural expectation from most of the audience was that Koschatsky was guilty of erroneous attribution, or at the very least had located an artwork in the wrong collection. Or perhaps he had neglected to see the origins of an iconographic detail.

But this was not at all the sort of statement that Agnes Mongan had on her mind. Even more intent on her point than usual, she said, with a tremor in her voice, that there was one issue in her life she needed to settle in order to sleep easily. It was a matter that had long troubled her. "I want to make peace with the Albertina," Miss Mongan asserted. At that moment, the Austrian scholar and the Somerville spinster moved toward one another, and threw their arms around each other in a long, and memorable, embrace.

Making peace, and living with change, have been important goals. This was apparent on quite a different level when in 1989 I had occasion to return to Woodlands with Eddie Warburg. After the war, his mother had given Woodlands to the town of Greenburgh, New York, so that the land could be used for a public high school, the house as nursery school space and classrooms for those who could not fit in at the regular high school, and the stables as administrative offices. Ostensibly we were there to see the exact terrain where George Balanchine's first American performance had occurred. Where the entrance gate had been, there was now a shopping center; where Kirstein and Warburg had walked through the woods, there was now a public high school. Nothing distressed Warburg at all— except that the house itself is now referred to as "the mansion," a word he found too grandiose.

We drove up the long driveway to the agglomeration of stone towers, balustrades, and half-timbered gables. "Be it ever so humble . . . ," Warburg remarked as he walked toward the double doors and glanced at the old family crest. Inside the place where he and his siblings had had their clothing laid out, there was a group of about forty teenage students who were there because they were unable to function in a regular high school. Frieda and Felix's bedroom—the room in which Eddie had been born over eighty years earlier—was packed with punk-cut, gum-chewing adolescents, many of whom were loaded with questions for this original resident of the house. He answered them easily, providing lots of information about the old days.

We walked into the dining room. Where Zorn's portrait of Frieda had once hung, there was a recruiting poster for the marines. In the space downstairs that was a swimming pool, there were now two nursery school classes, where most of the students were black or Hispanic. Warburg told me that when his mother gave the house to the town, it was at the same time that he was a Regent of New York State and there was considerable argument about busing. "But you see everyone is doing just fine," he remarked. He then helped one of the little girls button her jacket. Looking across the room at photos on a bulletin board, Warburg said, "There's Vernon Jordan. It's nice to see him here."

Walking through the former squash court, and into the old sitting room that overlooks the lawn where the rain broke on *Serenade,* we passed some of the high schoolers with whom Warburg had been chatting earlier. They asked him more questions, which he was only too happy to answer. The doorway to the old sleeping porch had been blocked off, and Fred's bedroom had been subdivided into offices. We walked out onto the veranda. Standing on the ballet lawn, we could hear the shouts of teenage boys shooting baskets on what had been the "second"—or all-weather—tennis court. Then the group of preschoolers walked by. A child waved. It was the little girl who, a few minutes earlier, had had her coat buttoned by the only living member of the original Woodlands family. "The house lives!" Eddie Warburg exclaimed.

ACKNOWLEDGMENTS

This book is about believers. It concerns people who gave support and cheered others on; in writing it I have been lucky enough to experience a parallel generosity. Not only have various individuals made this project possible, but they have also given vast pleasure to the work on it.

Of the individuals about whom I have written, all who are still alive have been supportive and informative. Their graciousness and pervading wit have done much to enhance the research process. I owe deepest thanks to Eddie Warburg, who is as kind a person as I have ever met. Agnes Mongan and Lincoln Kirstein have also been extremely forthcoming and consistently helpful. Philip Johnson has been generous with his time and insights as well as his keen diplomatic guidance. Ted Dreier and Anni Albers have willingly unveiled new facts while transmitting much delight in so doing. Kay Swift has done much to evoke the ambience and creativity I have tried to capture.

Rona Roob, the Museum Archivist at the Museum of Modern Art, has demonstrated the true significance of her profession by being not merely extraordinarily efficient and thorough, but also imaginative and unstinting. Besides being a superb friend as always, Samuel W. Childs—James Thrall Soby's stepson—has been wonderfully openhanded. Without help and guidance from these two sources, large parts of this book would not have been possible.

Vicky Wilson, the editor of this book, has functioned much in the tradition of a great and perceptive teacher. She has constantly inspired me to stretch my thinking and consider new possibilities. And she has applied her rigorous intelligence with unfailing kindness.

Gloria Loomis, my agent, has been *my* patron saint; I thank her for her warm understanding, alertness, and encouragement. Her guidance and acuity have become mainstays of my life.

Brenda Danilowitz has been unsparing in both her assistance and her advice on issues ranging from minute details to major issues of the text. Her diligence and meticulous attention to detail, all applied with profound intelligence and appreciation of the subject matter, have been essential to the completion of the text and to the assembling of the photographs and captions. Kelly Feeney has been gracious and efficient in her help with the preparation of the manuscript. Antoinette White has been perpetually supportive and helpful, attentive to myriad details with tremendous grace and efficiency. Louise Kennedy, ever marvelous, made numerous valuable comments on language and usage.

I am grateful to R. W. B. Lewis for his thoughtful suggestions on the structure of this book, for his help in getting me to the National Humanities Center to work on it, and for his marvelous encouragement in so many ways. To W. Robert Connor and Kent Mullican at the Center itself go my thanks for providing idyllic working conditions at an essential stage of my work.

My great thanks also go to William Koshland, Eleanor Bunce, Joan Lewisohn Kroll, and Andrea Warburg Kaufman for giving me their time and recollections. John Hollander aided considerably with his observations of the difference between the patronage that is my topic and the more current styles of backing art. Morris Dickstein contributed with some of his thoughts on the 1930s in general. And, many years ago, Jill Silverman, who was working on an oral history of the Wadsworth Atheneum, introduced me to much of the subject matter in this text with her enthusiastic and informative accounts of her interviews.

Certain institutions have been invaluable resources for work on this project. These include the Museum of Modern Art Archives and its library, the Dance Collection at the New York Public Library for the Performing Arts, various branches of the Yale University Library system, and the Harvard University Archives. Janis Ekdahl at MoMA has been especially helpful. And even if I do not know their names, I want to express appreciation to the many other efficient and helpful people at these places. Special thanks go also to Priscilla England, David Sinkler, and Fiorella Superbi for both their diligence and the generosity of their approach. For their help with photographs I thank Mikki Carpenter, Everett C. Wilkie, Jr., Judith Ellen Johnson, Raymond Petke, Graham Southern, Kendall L. Crilly, Norman Kleeblatt, Anita Friedman, Athena Tacha Spear, Marc George Gershwin, A. Hassberger, Geraldine Auerbach, David Burnhauser, Marie-Luise Sternath, Eugene Gaddis, Jerry Thompson, and Ashley Ringshaw. For their aid in various ways I thank Clare Edwards, Phoebe Peebles, Maria Morris Hambourg, Mark Simon, Jane Schoelkopf, Ponjab Dashi, John B. Pierce, Jr., and Rita Waldron.

I am especially grateful to Lee Eastman, Sanford Schwartz, Nicholas Ohly, George Gibson, Julie Agoos, John Ryden, Barbara Ryden, Nancy Lewis, Stuart Van Dyke, Kendra Taylor, Julia McConnell, Rachel Wild, Phyllis Fitzgerald, and Phyllis Rose. I thank my father, Saul Weber, for that initial steer toward Santayana and all he represents, and my sister, Nancy Weber, for her unwavering good humor and support. I am grateful to my late mother, Caroline Fox Weber, in myriad ways. She helped nourish this book with her particular sense of Hartford, and with her insistent distinction between art patronage in its true function and in its guise as a vehicle for social hobnobbing.

One is especially lucky to have knowing counsel and good cheer close at home. Lucy Swift Weber and Charlotte Fox Weber may have been only eight and seven years old at the time of most of my work on this text, but that did not prevent them from raising the important issues at pivotal moments, and from providing constant refreshment and inspiration. And by dedicating this book to my wife, Katharine, I hope I give some glimmer of just how much all of her patience and help and insights have meant.

N. F. W.
Bethany, Connecticut
October 1991

NOTES

THE HARVARDITES

1. George Santayana, *The Last Puritan, A Memoir in the Form of a Novel* (New York: Charles Scribner's Sons, 1936), pp. 424–25.

2. "Boston Revolt," *The Art Digest,* September 1928.

3. Quoted in Albert Franz Cochrane, "Approaching Dawn of Boston's Important Art Season," *Boston Evening Transcript,* September 15, 1928.

4. Albert Franz Cochrane, "Boston Arts Club Opens Season in Newly Decorated Galleries," *Boston Evening Transcript,* October 20, 1928.

5. Edward Waldo Forbes, "The Relation of the Art Museum to a University," *Proceedings of the American Association of Museums 5* (1911): 52.

6. Brochure for the Harvard Society for Contemporary Art. All of the original documents from the Harvard Society for Contemporary Art are in scrapbooks prepared and given by Lincoln Kirstein to the library at the Museum of Modern Art.

7. Quoted in "American Taste," *The Art Digest,* October 1, 1927.

8. In his memoir *Self Portrait with Donors* (Boston and Toronto: Little, Brown, 1974), John Walker lists Frank Crowninshield and Mrs. John D. Rockefeller, Jr., as also having been on the board. Although these two people were aware of the Harvard Society for Contemporary Art, this claim that they were trustees is erroneous. In *Alfred H. Barr Jr. Missionary for the Modern* (Chicago: Contemporary Books, 1989), Alice Goldfarb Marquis repeats the mistake.

9. Julien Levy, *Memoir of an Art Gallery* (New York: G. P. Putnam's Sons, 1977), p. 113.

10. Conversation between Philip Johnson and NFW in New York City on March 30, 1989.

11. Walker, *Self Portrait with Donors.*

12. I am grateful to Philip Johnson for his observations along these lines. Johnson also characterized Walker as "the goy you have around for your reputation."

13. Walker, *Self Portrait with Donors.*

14. Letter from Felix Warburg to E. M. M. Warburg on the occasion of his twenty-first birthday, June 1929.

15. E. M. M. Warburg in telephone conversation with NFW, January 9, 1989.

16. Conversation between Lincoln Kirstein and NFW in New York City on March 30, 1989.

17. Walker, *Self Portrait with Donors,* p. 24.

18. Conversation between Agnes Mongan and NFW, Cambridge, February 1, 1990.

19. Faculty meeting minutes at Bryn Mawr College, June 21, 1916, p. 1, quoted in Susanna Terrell Saunders, "Georgiana Goddard King (1871–

1939): Educator and Pioneer in Medieval Spanish Art," in *Women as Interpreters of the Visual Arts, 1870–1979*, ed. Claire Richter Sherman (Westport, Conn.: Greenwood Press, 1981).

20. Agnes Mongan, "Georgiana Goddard King: A Tribute," *Bryn Mawr Alumnae Bulletin*, July 1937.

21. Ibid.

22. Unpublished school paper from 1927, courtesy Agnes Mongan.

23. *Museum News*, September/October 1975, p. 31.

24. Conversation with Agnes Mongan, February 1, 1990.

25. "The Jew and Modernism," *The Art Digest*, November 1, 1927.

26. Lincoln Kirstein, "Loomis: a Memoir," *Raritan*, Summer 1982, pp. 16–17.

27. All quotations from "Brancusi," an essay that originally appeared in *The Little Review*, viii, I (Autumn 1921), reprinted in *Literary Essays of Ezra Pound* (Norfolk, Conn.: New Directions [undated]).

28. "Revolutions and Reactions in Painting," *International Studio*, LI (December 1913), pp. cxxiii, cxxvi.

29. Joan Simon, *Portrait of a Father* (New York: Atheneum, 1960), pp. 217–18.

30. Quoted in Cleveland Amory's introduction to *Vanity Fair* (New York: Viking Press, 1960), p. 9.

31. Conversation with Philip Johnson, March 30, 1989.

32. Lincoln Kirstein, *Flesh is Heir. An Historical Romance* (New York: Brewer, Warren & Putnam, 1932), p. 193.

33. Ibid., p. 192.

34. Ibid., p. 188.

35. Ibid., p. 195.

36. Ibid., p. 198.

37. *The Times* (of London), July 7, 1929, quoted in Nesta MacDonald, *Diaghilev Observed* (New York: Dance Horizons, 1975).

38. Nicholas Nabokov, *Old Friends and New Music* (Hamish Hamilton), p. 83, quoted in MacDonald, *Diaghilev Observed*, p. 355.

39. Kirstein, *Flesh is Heir*, p. 195.

40. Unpublished school paper from 1927; courtesy Agnes Mongan.

41. Serge Lifar, *Serge Diaghilev* (New York: De Capo Press, 1976), p. 372.

42. Ibid., p. 360.

43. *Misia and the Muses, the Memoir of Misia Sert* (New York: John Day, 1953), p. 157.

44. Edmonde Charles-Roux, *Chanel and Her World* (London: The Vendome Press, 1979), p. 234.

45. Conversation with Agnes Mongan, February 1, 1990.

46. Edward M. M. Warburg, *As I Recall* (privately published, 1978), p. 33. All unidentified quotations from E. M. M. Warburg come from the many conversations—in person and on the telephone—held between him and the author in the course of 1988 and 1989.

47. Frieda Schiff Warburg, *Reminiscences of a Long Life* (published privately in New York in 1956), p. 176. In the introduction to this book, Mrs. Warburg credits her son Edward for its concept. In conversation, Eddie has called it "one of the best things I've ever written."

48. Ibid.

49. Undated notes of interview with E. M. M. Warburg conducted on behalf of Jewish Theological Seminary.

50. Schiff Warburg, *Reminiscences*.

51. Lincoln Kirstein, *Quarry* (Pasadena: Twelve Trees Press, 1986), p. 68.

52. Louis E. Kirstein, *Better Retail Advertising,* New York: National Better Business Bureau, 1925.

53. Walker, *Self Portrait with Donors,* p. 17.

54. This is how Edward Warburg and Lincoln Kirstein recall the event. John Walker, in *Self Portrait with Donors,* tells it differently: "I remember that Eddie Warburg and I got a truck and went to meet Calder's train. I headed for the express office to pick up the boxes containing the exhibition, and Eddie went to the platform to greet our artist. To my horror no boxes had arrived. I joined Eddie and Sandy, and there was the sculptor with a coil of wire over his arm. He said he intended to make the exhibition in the gallery; forty-eight hours, he stated, was plenty of time" (p. 27). Walker, however, seems less reliable than Warburg and Kirstein; he gets the list of trustees all wrong, and also makes the erroneous claim that the society was the first place where Calder's Circus was ever exhibited; it's true that it was the first *public* exhibition, but it had previously been performed on a number of private occasions. That mistake is repeated, with further errors, in *Modern Art at Harvard* by Caroline A. Jones (New York: Abbeville Press, 1985), where it is stated (p. 45), "Alexander Calder rode up on the train from New York with a reel of bailing wire and some clippers to create his first 'circus.'" The false claim is also made by Alice Goldfarb Marquis in her *Alfred H. Barr Jr. Missionary for the Modern,* when she quotes Walker about the pickup at the train and his assembling his show at Harvard, and then goes on to say (p. 45), "The work that resulted is *Circus,* the object of reverent gazes from the multitudes who daily mill around the lobby of New York's Whitney Museum." Despite these assertions, Calder unquestionably did not create the Circus at Harvard.

Russell Lynes, in *Good Old Modern* (New York: Atheneum, 1973), makes it sound as if Warburg's memory of the Calder event was erroneous, but Lynes somewhat contradicts Calder's account in support of that claim. Lynes says, "Legend (which Calder now denies) says that he arrived in Cambridge with nothing but a suitcase containing a few pieces of clothing, a coil of copper wire, and a pair of pliers" (pp. 24–25). What Calder actually says in his autobiography is "I repeated my bundle of Berlin days, but Eddie protested that I arrived with nothing but a roll of wire on my shoulders and pliers in my pocket. I admit there was some truth to this, for I always traveled with a roll of wire and a pair of pliers. I took the circus along too, and showed it to the Harvard boys. I stayed on a cot in Eddie's quarters in the Yard" (p. 108 in Alexander Calder, *An Autobiography with Pictures* [London: Allen Lane, The Penguin Press, 1967]). What seems most plausible is that Calder did take along, as he says, his Berlin bundle—which was the Circus and which he assembled a few days later for its presentation in the Fogg courtyard—but that he made all the wire sculptures, which were the substance of his exhibition at the Harvard Society for Contemporary Art, on the spot.

55. Conversation with Philip Johnson, March 30, 1989.

56. Richard S. Kennedy, *The Window of Memory* (Chapel Hill: The University of North Carolina Press, 1962).

57. Calder, *Autobiography with Pictures,* p. 107.

58. Thomas Wolfe, *You Can't Go Home Again* (New York: Harper & Row, 1934), p. 231 and pp. 278–80.

59. So the documents indicate; Kirstein and Warburg, in conversations with NFW, were both incredulous on being told this.

60. *Isamu Noguchi* (New York: Harper & Row, 1968), p. 19.

61. April 3, 1929.

62. *An Account of the Committee of the Museum of Modern Art, 1931–1938,* MoMA Archives. My special thanks go to Rona Roob, the museum's archivist, for steering me to this document.

63. May 9, 1938.

64. Note by Margaret Scolari Barr attached to photocopy of Barr article "Contemporary Art at Harvard," *The Arts,* April 1929. MoMA Archives: Alfred H. Barr, Jr., Papers; RR/AHB Bibliography # 199.

65. A. Conger Goodyear, *The Museum of Modern Art: The First Ten Years,* copyrighted 1943 by A. Conger Goodyear, New York; produced under the direction of Vrest Orton, p. 47.

66. *New York Herald Tribune,* March 15, 1931.

67. *The Nation* 131, no. 3391 (July 2, 1930), pp. 6–7.

68. E. M. M. Warburg, *As I Recall,* p. 37.

69. Ibid.

70. Undated clipping from *Harvard Crimson* in Harvard Society Scrapbooks.

71. Henry McBride, "The Inimitable Picasso at Large," *New York Sun,* December 5, 1931.

72. May 11, 1932.

73. May 8, 1932, *The New York Times.*

HARTFORD, CONNECTICUT

1. "Masquerade Ball Planned by the Atheneum," *Hartford Courant,* March 19, 1928.

2. Quoted in " 'The New Athens': Moments from an Era" by Eugene R. Gaddis, in *Avery Memorial* (Hartford: The Wadsworth Atheneum, 1984), p. 42.

3. "Prof. H. R. Hitchcock Discusses Modern French Artists," *Hartford Times,* December 7, 1929.

4. These and other Soby quotations are all from the unpublished memoirs of James Thrall Soby. They were provided to me by Soby's stepson Samuel W. Childs, to whom I am exceptionally grateful.

5. Ibid.

6. Soby, unpublished memoirs, p. 7 of the section called "1924–28."

7. Henry Russell Hitchcock, Jr., "Soby Collection Placed on View," *Hartford Times,* November 17, 1930.

8. "French Paintings Praised by Austin," *Hartford Times,* November 19, 1930.

9. *A. Everett Austin, Jr.* (Hartford, Conn.: The Wadsworth Atheneum, 1958), p. 18.

10. Wadsworth Atheneum Annual Report, 1931, p. 4.

11. *A.E.A., Jr.*, p. 33.

12. Julien Levy, *Memoir of an Art Gallery* (New York: G. P. Putnam's Sons, 1977).

13. "Atheneum Plans Major Exhibits," *Hartford Times,* November 7, 1931.

14. Ibid.

15. Levy, *Memoir of an Art Gallery*, p. 80.

16. This is what Henry Russell Hitchcock suggested to the Atheneum Bulletin, October 1931, p. 30.

17. *A.E.A., Jr.,* p. 33.

18. Soby, unpublished memoirs, p. 10 in chapter 1. (Each chapter has its own page numbers.)

19. Fleur Cowles, *The Case of Salvador Dali* (London: Heinemann, 1959), p. 212.

20. On pp. 150 and 151 of *Memoirs of an Art Gallery,* Julien Levy discusses at some length his attempts to import and show this film. There seems to be no connection with the screening at Soby's, for which the main source of information is Soby's unpublished autobiography. Eleanor Bunce, who was Mrs. James Thrall Soby from 1938 to 1952, attended the screening on Westwood Road—although it was years before she married Soby. (Conversation with NFW, July 18, 1989.)

21. Conversation with Eleanor Bunce, July 18, 1989.

22. Cowles, *Salvador Dali*, p. 213.

23. Soby, unpublished memoirs, chapter called "Chick Austin," p. 3.

24. Alfred H. Barr, Jr., *Picasso: Fifty Years of His Art* (New York: The Museum of Modern Art, 1946), p. 148. (This is in part a later edition of the 1939 book.)

25. Soby, unpublished memoirs, chapter called "Collecting: The Early Years," p. 6.

26. Ibid.

27. "A. Everett Austin, Jr.," catalog for the Brummer Gallery, Inc., February 9–29, 1932.

28. Soby, unpublished memoirs. Unnumbered manuscript page.

29. AEA address to WA trustees, AEA Archives, quoted and footnoted in "From the Fogg to the Bauhaus: A Museum for the Machine Age" by Helen Searing in *Avery Memorial.*

A BALLET SCHOOL

1. Copy of letter in Dance Collection of the New York Public Library at Lincoln Center.

2. Conversation with Philip Johnson, March 30, 1989.

3. *A. Everett Austin, Jr.* (Hartford, Conn.: The Wadsworth Atheneum, 1958), p. 64.

4. Interview with Paul Cooley, quoted on p. 67 of *Avery Memorial* (Hartford: the Wadsworth Atheneum, 1984).

5. Lincoln Kirstein, *The New York City Ballet* (New York: Alfred A. Knopf, 1973).

6. Copy of telegram in Dance Collection of the New York Public Library at Lincoln Center.

7. Kirstein, *New York City Ballet,* p. 20.

8. Eddie Warburg's and Lincoln Kirstein's versions of this early period of the ballet differ considerably. The primary source for Kirstein's account of that time is *The New York City Ballet*—for which he wrote the text—published by Alfred A. Knopf, New York, 1973. Warburg touched on the ballet history in *As I Recall* (privately published, 1978), but the primary source for his reminiscences of the period is the author's extensive interviews with him in late 1988 and early 1989, and tapes he dictated in response to the author's questions and that were kindly transcribed by his secretary, David Sinkler. Kirstein makes it sound as if a lot of the decisions about support were Felix's; Eddie says his parents were not involved in the least. When Eddie remembers that walk in the woods at Woodlands, all that he recalls is agreeing to pay the round-trip steamship fare for either Balanchine or Dimitriev, with the understanding that Kirstein would pay for the other. Kirstein says that Warburg had in fact already agreed to cover both fares, in a letter he had written to Kirstein in Paris a few weeks earlier. If Warburg thought he had agreed to nothing more than travel costs, what Kirstein felt he gained during the walk in the woods and subsequent conversations, some with Felix sitting in, was "Eddie Warburg's guarantee of at least two years' help of solid financial support for the new institution." Eddie may not have spelled it out as such, but it was Eddie's response that "made it easier to think of approaching George Balanchine with a bit of conviction . . . His later large support permitted us to make promises that led to the first steps without which nothing could have followed" (p. 18, *New York City Ballet*). Eddie's comment is "I signed the necessary checks rather than giving any time guarantee for the maintenance" (January 11, 1989).

9. Marian Murray, "Dancers Leap Hurdle at Port," *Hartford Times,* October 18, 1933.

10. Soby, unpublished memoirs, section 4, p. 16.

11. "Divergent Views on Ballet Here," *Hartford Courant,* October 19, 1933.

12. "Ballet School Here Cancelled by Austin," *Hartford Times,* October 28, 1933.

13. Advertisement for the School of the American Ballet, *The New York Times,* December 3, 1933.

14. Letter from Edward Warburg to Alfred Barr, August 31, 1933; MoMA Archives; AHB Papers.

15. Quoted in Hans M. Wingler, *The Bauhaus,* trans. Wolfgang Jabs and Basil Gilbert, ed. Joseph Stein (Cambridge, Mass.: MIT Press, 1969), p. 188.

16. Soby, unpublished memoirs, p. 9–9 in "Collecting: the Early Years."

17. Telephone conversation between Ted Dreier and NFW, June 4, 1989.

18. Martin Duberman, *Black Mountain: An Exploration in Community* (New York: E. P. Dutton, 1972), p. 19.

19. Ibid. p. 29.

20. Telephone conversation with Ted Dreier, June 4, 1989.

21. Conversation with Philip Johnson, March 30, 1989.

22. Undated letter from Philip Johnson to Alfred Barr, MoMA Archives; AHB Papers.

23. Letter to NFW of March 6, 1989.

24. Letter of April 4, 1933, Beinecke Library, Yale University.

25. Gerald Nordland, *Gaston Lachaise* (New York: George Braziller, 1974), note II-19.

26. Letter of March 3, 1933, NFW translation, Beinecke Library.

27. Conversation with E. M. M. Warburg, January 13, 1989.

28. Museum of Modern Art press release of July 10, 1934, Beinecke Library.

29. Letter of September 28, 1933, to his stepson Edward Nagle, Beinecke Library.

30. Transcript of E. M. M. Warburg's answers to interview of Steven Watson, November 24, 1987.

31. A.H.B. to E.M.M.W., February 1935, MoMA Archives; AHB Papers.

32. *New York Sun,* October 26, 1935.

33. Letter of September 1, 1939, Beinecke Library.

1934

1. Letter in the Dance Collection of the New York Public Library at Lincoln Center.

2. *A. Everett Austin, Jr.* (Hartford, Conn.: The Wadsworth Atheneum, 1958), pp. 66–67.

3. T. H. Parker, "Negroes Mastering Stein Opera," *Hartford Courant,* December 25, 1933.

4. Virgil Thomson, *Virgil Thomson* (New York: Alfred A. Knopf, 1966), p. 105.

5. From Carl Van Vechten's introduction to *Four Saints in Three Acts* (New York: Random House, The Modern Library, 1934), p. 6.

6. Thomson, *Virgil Thomson,* p. 219.

7. Ibid., p. 236.

8. John Houseman, *Run Through* (New York: Simon and Schuster, 1972), p. 101.

9. *Four Saints,* p. 47.

10. T. H. Parker, "Negroes Mastering Stein Opera."

11. December 16, 1933, quoted in James Mellow, *Charmed Circle* (New York: Avon Books, 1974), p. 440.

12. Program, February 13, 1934.

13. Thomson, *Virgil Thomson,* p. 239.

14. Joseph W. Alsop, Jr., "Gertrude Stein Opera Amazes First Audience," *New York Herald Tribune,* February 8, 1934.

15. Houseman, *Run Through,* p. 115.

16. Julien Levy, *Memoir of an Art Gallery* (New York: G. P. Putnam's Sons, 1977), p. 141.

17. Houseman, *Run Through,* p. 116.

18. *New York Herald Tribune,* Sunday, February 11, 1934.
19. Houseman, *Run Through,* p. 118.
20. Levy, *Memoir of an Art Gallery,* p. 142.
21. Mellow, *Charmed Circle,* p. 442.
22. Interview with Gertrude Stein conducted by NBC reporter William Lundell on November 12, 1934, on WJZ and NET radio; published in *The Paris Review,* Fall 1990, pp. 89 and 95.
23. Agnes Mongan, "Stein on Picasso," a review of *Picasso* by Gertrude Stein, *The Saturday Review of Literature,* March 18, 1939, p. 11.
24. Agnes Mongan to A. Everett Austin, March 7, 1934, by permission of the Harvard University Archives.
25. This is how Mongan frequently referred to Warburg and the others in her letters of the period.
26. Agnes Mongan to Georgiana Goddard King, February 15, 1934, by permission of the Harvard University Archives.
27. Alfred H. Barr, Jr., *Picasso: Fifty Years of His Art* (New York: The Museum of Modern Art, 1946), p. 106.
28. Ibid., p. 122.
29. Laurie Eglinton, "Picasso Exhibit a Notable Event in Avery Opening," *The Art News,* February 10, 1934.
30. Conversation between Agnes Mongan and NFW held at Harvard Faculty Club, April 7, 1989.
31. "Some People Think It's Awful, Others Say It's Marvelous: An Explanation of the Picasso Exhibition at Avery Museum," *Hartford Courant,* February 25, 1934.
32. Thomas Craven, *Modern Art* (New York: Simon and Schuster, 1934), pp. 177–93.
33. Lincoln Kirstein, letter to Agnes Mongan, undated, by permission of the Harvard University Archives.
34. Dino Ferrari, "A Challenging View of Modern Art," *The New York Times Book Review,* May 20, 1934.
35. Frank Jewett Mather, "Real and False Among Modern Artists," *New York Herald Tribune Books,* May 13, 1934.
36. George Brooks Armstead, "Notes on Belated Defense of Modern Movement in Art. Current Deflation of Picasso Stein and Vacuous Bohemia," *Hartford Courant,* May 29, 1934.
37. "Revolution on Beekman Place," *House & Garden,* August 1986.
38. Ibid.
39. Stephen Birmingham, *Our Crowd* (New York: Harper & Row, 1967), p. 189.
40. Lincoln Kirstein, *The New York City Ballet* (New York: Alfred A. Knopf, 1973), p. 24.
41. Richard Buckle, *George Balanchine* (New York: Random House, 1988), p. 88.
42. James Paul Warburg, *The Long Road Home* (New York: Doubleday, 1964).
43. *Washington Post,* December 9, 1934.
44. *Providence Rhode Island Journal,* December 3, 1934.
45. Lucius Beebe's column, *New York Herald Tribune,* November 1934.

46. T. H. Parker, "Ballet Wins Ovation in Avery Debut," *Hartford Courant,* December 7, 1934.

47. R.E.R., "Ballet Appears in a Burlesque of Our Foibles," *Washington Post,* December 9, 1934.

48. Beebe is wrong on this point. He reports that people gathered around her, but I know from Kay Swift herself, as well as from others of her family members, that she was in Reno at the time.

49. *Hartford Times,* December 8, 1934.

50. T. H. Parker, "Ballet Wins Ovation."

51. *Washington Post,* December 9, 1934.

52. Kirstein, *New York City Ballet,* p. 42. From Kirstein's point of view—fairly nasty here—part of the significance of *Alma Mater* is that it took Eddie Warburg out of his frustrated rich boy role. "Warburg could feel that his contribution, for once, was more on the side of art than cash . . . *Alma Mater* had some importance economically and even politically, because it temporarily proved to Eddie that he had use past signing checks" (pp. 41, 42).

THE LOVER OF DRAWINGS

1. Mary Berenson's diary, November 18, 1903, quoted in Ernest Samuels, *Bernard Berenson: The Making of a Connoisseur* (Cambridge, Mass.: Harvard University Press, 1979).

2. E. H. Gombrich, *Aby Warburg* (Chicago: University of Chicago Press, 1986), pp. 142–43.

3. F. M. Warburg to B.B., September 17, 1926. I Tatti.

4. F.M.W. to B.B., January 5, 1928. I Tatti.

5. A.M. to B.B., September 9, 1929. I Tatti.

6. P.J.S. to A.M., June 1, 1933, by permission of the Harvard University Archives.

7. A.M. to B.B., July 25, 1934. I Tatti.

8. August 21, 1930.

9. Letters by permission of the Harvard University Archives.

10. Agnes Mongan, "Drawings in the Platt Collection," *American Magazine of Art,* July 1932, p. 49.

11. Ibid.

12. Ibid., p. 53.

13. Ibid., p. 54.

14. Ibid.

15. Ibid., p. 53.

16. Ibid., p. 54.

17. Agnes Mongan, "Collector of Old Master Drawings," *Boston Evening Transcript,* December 21, 1931.

18. Agnes Mongan, "Rare Drawings in Fine Art Exhibit Held in Buffalo," *The Art News,* December 29, 1934.

19. A.M. to B.B., July 25, 1934. I Tatti.

20. Letter from M.B. to A.M., September 23, 1935, by permission of the Harvard University Archives.

21. A.M. to A.H.B., January 20, 1933, by permission of the Harvard University Archives.

22. A.H.B. to A.M., February 19, 1933, by permission of the Harvard University Archives.

23. A.M. to A.H.B., March 2, 1933, by permission of the Harvard University Archives.

24. June 4, 1936.

25. January 15, 1936, E.W. to A.M., by permission of the Harvard University Archives.

26. Conversation with Agnes Mongan, February 1, 1990.

27. Letter by permission of the Harvard University Archives.

28. Conversation with Agnes Mongan, February 1, 1990.

FORWARD MARCH

1. John Martin, "The Dance: The Ballet," *The New York Times,* March 10, 1935.

2. "E. M. Warburg Sees Future for Ballet," *The New York Times,* March 17, 1935.

3. Letter from Alfred H. Barr, Jr., to E. M. M. Warburg, January 17, 1935. MoMA Archives, AHB Papers.

4. Conversation of January 11, 1989.

5. E. M. M. Warburg, *As I Recall* (privately published, 1978), p. 55.

6. Lincoln Kirstein, *The New York City Ballet* (New York: Alfred A. Knopf, 1973), p. 43.

7. Ibid.

8. E. M. M. Warburg, *As I Recall,* p. 55.

9. Virgil Thomson, *Virgil Thomson* (New York: Alfred A. Knopf, 1966), p. 250.

10. Ibid., p. 251.

11. "Dali Gives His Theories on Painting," *Hartford Courant,* December 19, 1934.

12. *Avery Memorial* (Hartford: The Wadsworth Atheneum, 1984), p. 52.

13. "Austin Raises Question over Art Interest," *Hartford Times,* January 20, 1935.

14. T. H. Parker, "Avery Opens Exhibition of Abstract Art," *Hartford Courant,* October 25, 1935.

15. Le Corbusier, *Quand les cathédrales étaient blanches: Voyage au pays des timides* (Paris, 1937); quoted in *Avery Memorial,* footnote 79.

16. Soby, unpublished memoirs, p. 7–2.

17. Wolfe Kaufman, "Hartford Arty Festival Flivs," *Variety,* February 19, 1936.

18. *A. Everett Austin, Jr.* (Hartford, Conn.: The Wadsworth Atheneum, 1958), p. 71.

19. "Ballet Event Tonight on Avery Stage," *Hartford Courant,* February 14, 1936.

20. T. H. Parker, "Society Attends Gay and Exotic Paper Ball Here," *Hartford Courant,* February 16, 1936.

21. Ibid.

22. Henry McBride, "All Arts United in Hartford," *New York Sun,* February 22, 1936.

23. Soby, unpublished memoirs, 7–5, and conversation with Eleanor Bunce, July 18, 1989.

24. Ibid., 7–5, 7–6.

25. Telephone conversation, June 10, 1989.

26. The issue of who went into the water has about as many versions as there were people at the Paper Ball. Eleanor Bunce says only one person went in, but also admits that although she didn't leave the party until dawn, there were still a few people there.

27. Julien Levy, *Memoirs of an Art Gallery* (New York: G. P. Putnam's Sons, 1977) p. 145.

28. "Paper Ball," *Vogue,* March 15, 1936.

29. "James Thrall Soby and His Collection," in *The James Thrall Soby Collection* (New York: Museum of Modern Art, 1961), p. 19.

30. Conversation with Samuel Childs, March 4, 1990.

31. Soby, unpublished memoirs, pp. 9–20.

32. Ibid., 9–19.

33. Ibid., 6–1.

34. Ibid., 6–2.

35. Exhibition catalog for the Balthus exhibition he mounted at the Museum of Modern Art in 1956.

36. Soby, unpublished memoirs, 26–3.

37. Conversation with Eleanor Bunce, July 18, 1989.

38. My account of these events is based largely on Soby's unpublished memoirs, and therefore differs slightly from the account given by Sabine Rewald in her book *Balthus.*

39. Soby, unpublished memoirs, 26–8.

40. Bernard Taper, *Balanchine* (London: Collins, 1974), p. 154.

41. Kirstein, *New York City Ballet,* p. 44.

42. Ibid.

43. "Orpheus and Eurydice Given at Metropolitan," *New York Evening Post,* May 23, 1936.

44. *Time,* June 1, 1936.

45. "'Orfeo' Presented at Metropolitan," *New York Sun,* May 23, 1936.

46. "The Opera 'Orfeo' Done in Pantomime," *The New York Times,* May 23, 1936.

47. "Pleasure from *Orpheus,*" *Time,* June 15, 1936.

48. Igor Stravinsky and Robert Craft, *Themes and Episodes* (New York: Alfred A. Knopf, 1966), pp. 36–37.

49. None of the sources provide a first name for this man.

50. Lawrence Gilman, "Stravinsky's Card Party," *New York Herald Tribune,* 1937 (clipping undated).

51. Kirstein, *New York City Ballet,* p. 48.

52. E. M. M. Warburg, *As I Recall,* p. 56.

53. Ibid.

54. Stravinsky and Craft, *Themes and Episodes,* p. 36.

THE WAR AND ITS AFTERMATH

1. W. McNeil Lowry, "Conversations with Kirstein—1," *The New Yorker,* December 15, 1986, p. 52.

2. Ibid., p. 53.

3. *The New York Times,* October 21, 1937.

4. E. M. M. Warburg, *As I Recall* (privately published, 1978), p. 82.

5. A.M. to B.B., July 12, 1938. I Tatti.

6. A.M. to B.B., July 23, 1938. I Tatti.

7. A.M. to B.B., August 4, 1938. I Tatti.

8. A.M. to B.B., October 29, 1940. I Tatti.

9. A.M. to B.B., August 10, 1939. I Tatti.

10. A.M. to B.B., December 15, 1938. I Tatti.

11. A.M. to Rico Lebrun, December 2, 1938, by permission of the Harvard University Archives.

12. A.M. to B.B., December 15, 1938. I Tatti.

13. B.B. to William Ivins, February 19, 1938, quoted in Ernest Samuels, *Bernard Berenson: The Making of a Legend* (Cambridge, Mass.: Harvard University Press, 1987).

14. B.B. to Mary Berenson, January 24, 1937, quoted in Samuels, *Bernard Berenson.*

15. B.B. to Ivins, ibid.

16. A.M. to B.B., October 29, 1940. I Tatti.

17. A.M. to B.B., July 25, 1934. I Tatti.

18. A.M. to B.B., January 21, 1941. I Tatti.

19. Letter of July 8, 1939, by permission of the Harvard University Archives.

20. Letter of July 11, 1939, by permission of the Harvard University Archives.

21. Agnes Mongan, "What Makes a Museum Modern?," *Art News,* August 1–31, 1944.

22. B.B. to Mary Berenson, July 10, 1937, quoted in Samuels, *Bernard Berenson.*

23. A.M. to B.B., January 2, 1939. I Tatti.

24. A.M. to B.B., November 29, 1940. I Tatti.

25. Ibid.

26. A.M. to Thomas Howe, June 25, 1943, by permission of the Harvard University Archives.

27. Virgil Thomson, *Virgil Thomson* (New York: Alfred A. Knopf, 1966), p. 275.

28. "Austin Will Request Sabbatical Leave," *Hartford Times,* June 11, 1943.

29. Paul J. Sachs, Introduction, *Modern Art and the New Past* (Norman: University of Oklahoma Press, 1957), p. viii.

30. Lowry, "Conversations with Kirstein—1."

31. A.M. to B.B., January 9, 1948. I Tatti.

32. Telephone conversation between A.M. and NFW, June 14, 1990.

33. A.M. to B.B., January 21, 1941. I Tatti.

34. Telephone conversation between A.M. and NFW, June 14, 1990.

35. A.M. to B.B., January 11, 1947. I Tatti.

INDEX

Note: Page numbers in *italics* refer to illustrations.

PERMISSIONS ACKNOWLEDGMENTS

*Grateful acknowledgment is made to the following for permission to
reprint previously published and unpublished material:*

Victoria Barr: Excerpts from letters written by Alfred H. Barr, Jr., to Agnes Mongan
and to Edward M. M. Warburg, and from a letter written by Margaret Scolari Barr
to Agnes Mongan.

The Berenson Archives, Villa I Tatti, The Harvard University Center for Italian Renaissance Studies, Florence, Italy: Excerpts from letters written by Bernard Berenson.

Bryn Mawr Alumni Bulletin: Excerpts from Agnes Mongan's "Georgiana Goddard
King: A Tribute," *Bryn Mawr Alumni Bulletin,* July 1937.

Samuel W. Childs: Excerpts from James Thrall Soby's unpublished memoirs.

Theodore Dreier: Excerpt from the letter written by Theodore Dreier to Nicholas
Fox Weber.

Harvard University Archives: Access to letters from the collections of Alfred H. Barr,
Lincoln Kirstein, Agnes Mongan, Irwin Panofsky, Paul Sachs, and Edward M. M.
Warburg.

Philip Johnson: Excerpts from letters written by Philip Johnson.

Elizabeth S. Jones: Excerpt from the letter written by Paul Sachs to Agnes Mongan.

Lincoln Kirstein: Excerpts from letters written by Lincoln Kirstein.

The Lachaise Foundation and The Beinecke Rare Book and Manuscript Library, Yale University: Excerpt from a letter written by Isabel Lachaise to Edward M. M. Warburg,
and excerpts from letters written by Gaston Lachaise.

Agnes Mongan: Excerpts from Agnes Mongan's unpublished paper on El Greco and
from letters written by Agnes Mongan.

The Museum of Modern Art Archives: Excerpts from *An Account of the Advisory Committee for The Museum of Modern Art, 1931–1938,* and from the minutes of the Museum of Modern Art Board of Trustees meeting, April 18, 1930 (confirmed by Rona
Roob, Museum Archivist).

The Museum of Modern Art Archives, The Alfred H. Barr, Jr., Papers: Excerpts from a
note written by Margaret Scolari Barr attached to a photocopy of Alfred H. Barr,
Jr.'s, article "Contemporary Art at Harvard," *The Arts,* April 1929 (RR/AHB Bibliography #199); excerpts from letters written by Alfred H. Barr, Jr., to Edward
M. M. Warburg; by Edward M. M. Warburg to Alfred H. Barr, Jr.; and by Philip
Johnson to Alfred H. Barr, Jr.

New York Herald Tribune: Excerpt from Joseph Alsop's article "Gertrude Stein Opera
Amazes," February 8, 1934. Copyright 1934 New York Herald Tribune Inc. All
rights reserved.

Edward M. M. Warburg: Excerpts from letters written by Felix Warburg and from letters written by Edward M. M. Warburg.

The Yale Collection of American Literature, The Beinecke Rare Book and Manuscript Library, Yale University: Access to letters written by Gaston Lachaise and by Isabel Lachaise; to Carl Van Vechten's *Introduction to Four Saints in Three Acts* (New York: Modern Library, 1934); and to a Museum of Modern Art press release of 1934.

PHOTOGRAPHIC CREDITS

Grateful acknowledgment is made to the following for permission to reproduce the photographs on the pages indicated:

SELECTED BIBLIOGRAPHY

ARCHIVAL AND UNPUBLISHED MATERIALS

Beinecke Rare Book and Manuscript Library, Yale University, New Haven. The Yale Collection of American Literature. Gaston Lachaise correspondence; Museum of Modern Art press release; Carl Van Vechten's introduction to *Four Saints in Three Acts*.

Berenson Archive, Villa I Tatti, The Harvard University Center for Italian Renaissance Studies, Florence. Bernard Berenson Correspondence.

Harvard University Archives, Cambridge, Mass. Letters from collections of Alfred H. Barr, Jr., Lincoln Kirstein, Agnes Mongan, Erwin Panofsky, Paul Sachs, and Edward M. M. Warburg.

Museum of Modern Art Archives, New York. Alfred H. Barr, Jr., Papers; James Thrall Soby Papers; Museum Advisory Committee documents; minutes of Board of Trustees meetings.

Museum of Modern Art Library, New York. Harvard Society for Contemporary Art. Scrapbooks: three volumes of original catalogues, publicity material, reviews, installation photos, and other materials compiled by Lincoln Kirstein.

New York Public Library for the Performing Arts. Dance Collection. Microfilm of New York City Ballet Scrapbooks.

BOOKS AND ARTICLES

Amory, Cleveland, and Frederick Bradlee, eds. *Vanity Fair: A Cavalcade of the 1920s and 1930s*. New York: Viking Press, 1960.

Barr, Alfred H., Jr. "James Thrall Soby and His Collection." *The James Thrall Soby Collection*. New York: The Museum of Modern Art, 1961.

———. *Picasso: Fifty Years of His Art*. New York: The Museum of Modern Art, 1946.

Birmingham, Stephen. *Our Crowd*. New York: Harper & Row, 1967.

Brown, Milton. *American Painting from the Armory Show to the Depression*. Princeton, N. J.: Princeton University Press, 1955.

Buckle, Richard. *George Balanchine*. New York: Random House, 1988.

Calder, Alexander. *An Autobiography with Pictures*. London: Allen Lane, The Penguin Press, 1967.

Charles-Roux, Edmond. *Chanel and Her World*. London: The Vendome Press, 1979.

Cowles, Fleur. *The Case of Salvador Dali*. London: Heinemann, 1959.

Craven, Thomas. *Modern Art*. New York: Simon and Schuster, 1934.

Duberman, Martin. *Black Mountain: An Exploration in Community*. New York: E. P. Dutton, 1972.

Forbes, Edward W. A. *Everett Austin, Jr.* Hartford, Conn.: The Wadsworth Atheneum, 1958.

Gold, Arthur, and Robert Fizdale. *Misia: The Life of Misia Sert.* New York: Alfred A. Knopf, 1980.

Gombrich, E. H. *Aby Warburg.* Chicago: University of Chicago Press, 1986.

Goodyear, A. Conger. *The Museum of Modern Art: The First Ten Years.* New York: Vrest Orton, 1943.

Houseman, John. *Run Through.* New York: Simon and Schuster, 1972.

Jones, Caroline A. *Modern Art at Harvard.* New York: Abbeville Press, 1985.

Kennedy, Richard S. *The Window of Memory.* Chapel Hill: The University of North Carolina Press, 1962.

Kirstein, Lincoln. *Flesh Is Heir: An Historical Romance.* New York: Brewer, Warren & Putnam, 1932.

————. *The New York City Ballet.* New York: Alfred A. Knopf, 1973.

————. *Quarry.* Pasadena, Calif.: Twelve Trees Press, 1986.

Kirstein, Louis E. *Better Retail Advertising.* New York: National Better Business Bureau, 1925.

Levy, Julian. *Memoir of an Art Gallery.* New York: G. P. Putnam's Sons, 1977.

Lifar, Serge. *Serge Diaghilev.* New York: De Capo Press, 1976.

Lynes, Russell. *Good Old Modern.* New York: Atheneum, 1973.

MacDonald, Nesta. *Diaghilev Observed.* New York: Dance Horizons, 1975.

Marquis, Alice Goldfarb. *Alfred H. Barr Jr.: Missionary for the Modern.* Chicago: Contemporary Books, 1989.

Mellow, James. *Charmed Circle.* New York: Avon Books, 1974.

Mongan, Agnes. "Drawings in the Platt Collection." *American Magazine of Art,* July 1932: 49.

————. "Stein on Picasso." *The Saturday Review of Literature,* March 18, 1939: 11.

Noguchi, Isamu. *Isamu Noguchi.* New York: Harper & Row, 1968.

Nordland, Gerald. *Gaston Lachaise.* New York: George Braziller, 1974.

Russell, John. "Lincoln Kirstein: In the American Grain." In *Reading Russell.* New York: Harry N. Abrams, 1989.

Saarinen, Aline B. *The Proud Possessors.* New York: Random House, 1958.

Sachs, Paul J. *Introduction to Modern Art and the New Past.* Norman, Okla.: University of Oklahoma Press, 1957.

Samuels, Ernest. *Bernard Berenson: The Making of a Connoisseur.* Cambridge, Mass.: Harvard University Press, 1979.

————. *Bernard Berenson: The Making of a Legend.* Cambridge, Mass.: Harvard University Press, 1987.

Santayana, George. *The Last Puritan: A Memoir in the Form of a Novel.* New York: Charles Scribner's Sons, 1936.

Schwartz, Sanford. "An Aristocrat of Life and Culture: Lincoln Kirstein's *Elie Nadelman.*" In *The Art Presence.* New York: Horizon Press, 1982.

Sert, Misia. *Misia and the Muses: The Memoir of Misia Sert.* New York: John Dix, 1953.

Sherman, Claire Richter, ed. *Women as Interpreters of the Visual Arts, 1870–1979.* Westport, Conn.: Greenwood Press, 1981.

Simon, Joan. *Portrait of a Father.* New York: Atheneum, 1960.

Soby, James Thrall. *Modern Art and the New Past.* Norman, Okla.: University of Oklahoma Press, 1957.

Stein, Gertrude. *Four Saints in Three Acts*. New York: Random House, The Modern Library, 1934.

Stravinsky, Igor, and Robert Craft. *Themes and Episodes*. New York: Alfred A. Knopf, 1966.

Taper, Bernard. *Balanchine*. London: Collins, 1974.

Thomson, Virgil. *Virgil Thomson*. New York: Alfred A. Knopf, 1966.

Wadsworth Atheneum. *Avery Memorial*. Hartford, Conn.: The Wadsworth Atheneum, 1984.

Walker, John. *Self Portrait with Donors*. Boston and Toronto: Little, Brown, 1974.

Warburg, Edward M. M. *As I Recall*. Westport, Conn.: 1978.

Warburg, Frieda Schiff. *Reminiscences of a Long Life*. New York: 1956.

Warburg, James Paul. *The Long Road Home*. New York: Doubleday, 1964.

Weber, Nicholas Fox. "Philip Johnson: Revolution on Beekman Place." *House and Garden,* August 1986: 56–60.

————. *The Woven and Graphic Art of Anni Albers*. Washington, D.C.: Smithsonian Institution, 1985.

Wingler, Hans M. *The Bauhaus*. Trans. Wolfgang Jabs and Basil Gilbert, ed. Joseph Stein. Cambridge, Mass.: MIT Press, 1969.

Wolfe, Thomas. *You Can't Go Home Again*. New York: Harper & Row, 1934.

ADDENDUM TO PHOTOGRAPHIC CREDITS

Grateful acknowledgment is made to The Museum of Modern Art
for permission to reproduce the illustrations on the pages indicated:

(front cover) The Harvard Society for Contemporary Art, Inc. Cover of the exhibition brochure from *An Exhibition of Painting and Sculpture by The School of New York. October 17 to November 1* (detail). Cambridge, The Harvard Society for Contemporary Art, Inc., 1930. Offset, brown ink printed on tan, 11 x 8 1/2" (27.9 x 21.6 cm). The Museum of Modern Art Library, New York. Gift of Lincoln Kirstein. Photograph © 1995 The Museum of Modern Art, New York.

(back cover, p. 93) Alexander Calder, *The Hostess,* 1928. Wire construction, 11 1/2 x 4 1/2 x 11 7/8" (29.2 x 11.5 x 30.2 cm). The Museum of Modern Art, New York. Gift of Edward M. M. Warburg. Photograph © 1995 The Museum of Modern Art, New York.

(p. 6) The Harvard Society for Contemporary Art, Inc. Statement of Purpose and Membership Form. Cambridge, The Harvard Society for Contemporary Art, Inc. (c. 1928). Offset, black ink printed on white, 11 1/4 x 8 1/2" (28.6 x 21.6 cm). The Museum of Modern Art Library, New York. Gift of Lincoln Kirstein. Photograph © 1995 The Museum of Modern Art, New York.

(p. 42) The Harvard Society for Contemporary Art, Inc. Cover of the exhibition brochure from *An Exhibition of the School of Paris 1910–1928. March 20 to April 12, 1929.* Cambridge, The Harvard Society for Contemporary Art, Inc., 1929. Offset, black ink printed on white, 9 1/8 x 6" (23.2 x 15.2 cm). The Museum of Modern Art Library, New York. Gift of Lincoln Kirstein. Photograph © 1995 The Museum of Modern Art, New York.

(p. 87) The Harvard Society for Contemporary Art, Inc. Cover of the exhibition brochure from *An Exhibition of Painting and Sculpture by The School of New York. October 17 to November 1.* Cambridge, The Harvard Society for Contemporary Art, Inc., 1930. Offset, brown ink printed on tan, 11 x 8 1/2" (27.9 x 21.6 cm). The Museum of Modern Art Library, New York. Gift of Lincoln Kirstein. Photograph © 1995 The Museum of Modern Art, New York.

(p. 109) Installation view of the exhibition "Cézanne, Gauguin, Seurat, van Gogh." The Museum of Modern Art, New York. November 7 through December 7, 1929. Photograph © 1995 The Museum of Modern Art, New York.

(p. 109) Townhouse at 11 West 53rd Street, home of The Museum of Modern Art, New York. 1936. Photograph © 1995 The Museum of Modern Art, New York.

(p. 119) The Harvard Society for Contemporary Art, Inc. Cover of the exhibition brochure *Bauhaus 1919–1923, 1924. Weimar Dessau. December 1930 1931 January.*

Cambridge, The Harvard Society for Contemporary Art, Inc., 1930. Offset, black and red ink printed on white, 9 3/16 x 5 15/16" (23.3 x 15.1 cm). The Museum of Modern Art Library, New York. Gift of Lincoln Kirstein. Photograph © 1995 The Museum of Modern Art, New York.

(p. 171) Pablo Picasso, *Seated Woman,* Paris, 1927. Oil on wood, 51 1/8 x 38 1/4" (129.9 x 96.8 cm). The Museum of Modern Art, New York. Gift of James Thrall Soby. Photograph © 1995 The Museum of Modern Art, New York.

(p. 206) Gaston Lachaise, *Torso,* 1934. Plaster, 45 x 41 1/4 x 21 1/4" (114.3 x 104.7 x 54 cm), including base. The Museum of Modern Art, New York. Gift of Edward M. M. Warburg. Photograph © 1995 The Museum of Modern Art, New York.

(p. 233) Pablo Picasso, *Sleeping Peasants,* Paris, 1919. Tempera, watercolor and pencil, 12 1/4 x 19 1/4" (31.1 x 48.9 cm). The Museum of Modern Art, New York. Abby Aldrich Rockefeller Fund. Photograph © 1995 The Museum of Modern Art, New York.

(p. 305) Giorgio de Chirico, *The Enigma of a Day,* 1914. Oil on canvas, 6' 1 1/4" x 55" (185.5 x 139.7 cm). The Museum of Modern Art, New York. James Thrall Soby Bequest. Photograph © 1995 The Museum of Modern Art, New York.

(p. 349) James Thrall Soby, photographed with Epstein: *Portrait of Oriel Ross.* n.d. Photograph Courtesy The Museum of Modern Art, New York.